"My wife. . . . She's on the beach. She's dead."

Justin Barber pulled the 4Runner off the road at Guana Preserve. The headlights stabbed into the darkness to show that the parking-lot gate was closed and locked. He parked the 4Runner on the sand, and they walked hand in hand across the highway, down the boardwalk and waded in the surf.

They hadn't gone far when a man headed toward them in the darkness, pointing a handgun. He came close and stopped, shouting at Justin, who couldn't understand what he was saying. When April spoke, the assailant turned the gun on her and fired.

Justin grabbed for the gun. Then he was grabbing for the man's arms, hands, shirt, anything he could get his hands on. Justin heard another gunshot and that was all he remembered until he "came to" on the beach, facedown, with the surf washing over him. April was nowhere to be seen.

Dazed, Justin got to his feet and started shouting her name. He stumbled up and down the surf looking for her. He found her floating facedown beyond the breakers. Justin ran to his wife and turned her over. He saw no blood but there was a hole just below her left eye. . . .

TO LOVE, HONOR, AND KILL

LEE BUTCHER

PINNACLE BOOKS
Kensington Publishing Corp.
http://www.kensingtonbooks.com

Some names have been changed to protect the privacy of individuals connected to this story.

PINNACLE BOOKS are published by

Kensington Publishing Corp.
850 Third Avenue
New York, NY 10022

All Kensington Titles, Imprints, and Distributed Lines are available at special quantity discounts for bulk purchases for sales promotions, premiums, fund-raising, and educational or institutional use. Special book excerpts or customized printings can also be created to fit specific needs. For details, write or phone the office of the Kensington special sales manager: Kensington Publishing Corp., 850 Third Avenue, New York, NY 10022, attn: Special Sales Department, Phone: 1-800-221-2647.

Pinnacle and the P logo Reg. U.S. Pat. & TM Off.

ISBN-13: 978-0-7860-1908-3
ISBN-10: 0-7860-1908-5

First Printing: April 2008

10 9 8 7 6 5 4 3 2 1

Printed in the United States of America

Acknowledgments

There were a number of people who offered their help and expertise so that I could write this book. My thanks to the St. Johns County Sheriff's Office, the St. Augustine Clerk of Court, and the St. Augustine State Attorney's Office. Detective Howard "Skip" Cole, the intrepid detective who was instrumental in solving this case, helped guide me through a maze of information and gave me invaluable insights into the investigation. I thank the lead prosecutor, Assistant State Attorney Chris France, for taking time to talk about the case and to explain points of law. Thank you as well to Robert S. Willis and Lee Hutton, Justin Barber's defense attorneys, for their invaluable help. Bonnie Fruchey again helped with copy reading and was She-Ra in digging me out of a computer-generated cave-in. As always, thanks to my encouraging and patient editors at Kensington Books, Michaela Hamilton, editor in chief, and Richard Ember, senior editor. All of these people and others helped make this a better book. Any errors are my sole responsibility.

Chapter 1

Wesley Pryor saw an SUV with its hazard lights flashing and coming up fast behind him in the darkness. The car swerved all over the two-lane highway at about eighty-five miles an hour. It was about midnight on August 17, 2002, as Pryor approached the first traffic he had seen in a ten-mile stretch along Highway A1A on the isolated stretch of beach between St. Augustine and Jacksonville Beach, Florida.

The first thing that went through Pryor's mind was that a reckless drunk was behind the wheel and that the guy had better slow down before he killed someone. The SUV swerved past Pryor on a right-turn-only lane, careened off the road, plowed into thick shrubbery and screeched to a halt. Pryor braked to a stop moments later when a man ran in front of his headlights, waved his hands and pounded on the window.

"That guy over there says he's been shot," the man said, pointing to the Toyota 4Runner SUV, which was partially concealed in the shrubbery. "He thinks his wife was shot somewhere on the beach. He thinks she might be dead. Do you have a cell phone?"

A man about thirty, with reddish brown hair, gripped

the steering wheel and rocked back and forth, wailing. Kimberly Gamble (Pryor's ex-wife and now engaged to him again) opened the door on the passenger side of the 4Runner to see what was happening. As the door opened, the SUV was flooded with light and she had a clear view of the driver. He looked pale, shaken, and was hyperventilating.

Pryor was trained in CPR and knew that it was important to keep an injured person calm so he wouldn't go into shock.

"My wife . . . my wife . . . ," the driver said.

"Okay, where is your wife?"

"She's on the beach. She's dead. . . . She's dead."

"Okay, where's she at?"

Kimberly climbed inside to see if she could help. At first she couldn't tell whether or not the man had been shot. Then she saw holes in both shoulders and on the lower right side of his shirt. The man's shirt and pants were stained with blood. The victim seemed to be in anguish that was more emotional than physical. She put her arms around his shoulders and tried to comfort him.

Pryor, who had seen gunshot wounds before, didn't think the wounds were life-threatening, but one never knew. The wounds weren't bleeding much, which was a good sign. He saw what appeared to be a gunshot wound through the man's left hand. A bullet wound to the man's lower right chest worried him because he feared there could be internal bleeding. The bullet wound to the hand was crusted with dried blood, but Pryor saw no fresh bleeding. The man continued to wail, rock and babble incoherently.

Pryor found the man's wallet and saw that his name was Justin Barber, age thirty, from Jacksonville. "My wife," Barber said again. "She's on the beach. I think she's been shot. I think she might be dead."

"Where on the beach?"

"On the beach . . . on the beach . . ." He looked at Pryor and slumped forward. Pryor thought he had passed out.

"C'mon, man," he said. "Stay with me. Hang on, hang on. You've made it this far. Help is on the way."

Several other vehicles had stopped and the drivers and passengers gathered around to see what was happening. A man who had a cell phone talked to the 911 emergency dispatcher.

"Tell them that a first responder is here and confirms that the man's been shot," Pryor said. Instead, the caller handed the phone to Pryor, who told the dispatcher that the victim had been shot in both shoulders, left hand and lower right chest, and that the victim said his wife had been shot dead and was somewhere on the beach.

The dispatcher asked Pryor where they were, but Pryor and Gamble, on vacation from Tennessee, were visiting the St. Augustine area for the first time and didn't know the landmarks. Pryor told the dispatcher that he was on Highway A1A, somewhere between Jacksonville Beach and St. Augustine. He told this to the dispatcher and described his present surroundings as the first of several police cars and emergency vehicles arrived.

Emergency dispatchers from St. Johns County, Jacksonville Beach and Jacksonville were somewhat confused by the rapidity and inconsistencies in the calls coming to them. At one point, the Jacksonville Beach 911 dispatcher called the 911 dispatcher in St. Johns County.

"There's been a shooting," the Jacksonville Beach dispatcher said.

"Okay, we were just talking to the guy. . . . You're 10-97 (at the scene)?"

"Right."

"Do we need to be there? Is it in our county or your county?" the St. Johns dispatcher asked.

"Yeah, you got two people shot."

"I have two shot?"

"Two shot, yeah. We got rescue en route and they're gonna be calling on . . . Want a 'copter also."

"Are you-all working it, or are we working it?"

"We're there for now," said the Jacksonville dispatcher, "but it's in St. Johns County."

Officer J. S. Neace, of the Jacksonville Police Department (JPD), was the first officer to arrive. Neace's log showed that he arrived at the scene at 11:10 P.M. He checked the victim's driver's license to verify that his name was Barber. Barber told Neace that his wife's name was April. The police officer wrote that the victim had four gunshot wounds to the chest area and left hand.

"The victim appeared to be in shock, but said that his wife, April, had also been shot," Neace stated. "[He] said that he and April were on the beach when what appeared to be a white male approached them and asked for money. The white male shot them both."

Barber had tried to carry April to his car afterward, Neace stated, but had been unable to do so. Barber told the officer that he got into his car to go look for help.

Neace helped Deputy K. Dorough, one of four other Jacksonville police officers who had arrived, administer first aid and secure the crime area until police and emergency medical technicians (EMTs) sped in. Rescue workers from the Jacksonville Fire Department (JFD) and deputies from the St. Johns County Sheriff's Office (SJSO) arrived just minutes later. Four deputies from the SJSO hurried to the victim's car. He was barely coherent, but managed to tell them that he thought his wife had been shot and he had left her on the beach while he looked for help.

He seemed to be in a daze and repeatedly said that he thought his wife was dead, but he wasn't able to give them an exact location where she might be.

Brent T. Marshall, an EMT from St. Johns, cut Barber's shirt off with trauma shears and examined the wounds, while the police questioned the victim. "The patient had four entrance wounds," Marshall said later. "No exit wounds were found. The wounds were bandaged using dressing, gauze and tape. Patient stated that he had tried to carry her (April), but couldn't."

Another Jacksonville Beach rescue unit arrived at A1A to find other EMTs already tending to the victim. EMT Suzi Brown saw a white male with "multiple small-caliber wounds." She noted a "lateral wound" at the base of the neck, one at the left shoulder, another on the right chest, just below the nipple, and a wound through the left hand.

"All wounds appeared to be entry type," Brown said. "Minimal hemorrhage was noted. He was asking about April. 'Has she been found yet? Is she okay?'"

The EMTs told Barber that a St. Johns emergency medical services (EMS) worker had found April and that she was being treated.

Brown noticed that Barber's shirt was open so the wounds could be examined. His pants were damp and sandy. EMTs cut the sleeves off Barber's shirt to remove it, put adhesive bandages on his wounds and prepared to transport him by helicopter to the Shands trauma unit. In the air rescue unit, he continued to ask about his wife.

EMT John W. Morgan arrived while Barber was being helped at the intersection. He heard him say, "I couldn't carry her any farther, so I left her on the beach."

"Where?" a deputy asked.

"I don't know."

Pryor told the deputies that he had seen Barber's car parked by a boardwalk a few miles south. Both Pryor and

Kimberly said they had seen a dark K-car (a series of Chrysler cars that use essentially the same frame) parked near the SUV on the opposite side of the highway. The deputies knew of only one area where there was a boardwalk from the highway to the ocean—Guana Wildlife Preserve, located about nine miles south of where they were. The patrol cars took off with lights flashing as an emergency medical helicopter arrived. Barber was placed on a gurney and lifted into the rescue helicopter and flown to Shands Hospital in Jacksonville, where a trauma team was standing by. The flight took about fifteen minutes.

Before the helicopter was in the air, Detective Sergeant Mary Fagan, of the SJSO criminal investigation division (CID), directed several deputies to go to the boardwalk area at North Guana Beach and start looking for the second victim and for the shooter. They were advised that the assailant should be considered armed and extremely dangerous. Deputy Dorough, of the SJSO, who had helped secure a landing site for the helicopter, was told to head for the beach and help with the search.

Several patrol cars left the scene at A1A and headed south toward the boardwalk area to look for the second victim. Pryor and Kimberly wondered if they could help the police find the scene faster, since they had already driven past it.

"Do you think we should help them?" Pryor asked Gamble as they started to drive toward Jacksonville. "They might never find the place."

"You're the driver," Kimberly said. "Do what you think we should do."

Gamble knew Pryor would help, because he always did when people were in trouble. She called him "Mr. Rescue." Wesley made a U-turn and followed the sheriff's patrol cars, which were already so far ahead that he could see only the faint glow of blinking lights.

Sergeant Raye Tanner and Deputy Jamie Zell, of the SJSO, were headed toward the emergency on A1A when the dispatcher told them there was another shooting victim on the beach at an unknown walkway on A1A. Tanner mentally shifted gears and drove to the North Guana parking lot. The police officers cautiously made their way through the darkness with their flashlights, keenly aware that an armed shooter might still be in the area. As they walked down the boardwalk and neared the beach, the scene that they came upon was not one they wanted to see.

"I located a white female lying on the walkway right at the beach," Tanner said. "I checked for any signs of life, but there were none. I then secured the scene and notified the dispatcher that we had found the victim."

It was 11:20 P.M.

Zell reported in her affidavit: *Almost at the end we saw a white female laying on the boardwalk at the edge of the beach. Sergeant Tanner scanned the area [to make certain it was safe].* Zell then checked for vital signs on the victim and found none. *She was cool to the touch,* he wrote, *and there was no brachial or radial pulse. Her lips were blue. Some ants were crawling on her feet and legs. I saw a very small red smudge on her left arm.*

Tanner told the dispatcher that they had found the victim and secured the crime scene and started a log while they waited for EMTs, Florida Department of Law Enforcement (FDLE) agents, the medical examiner (ME) and other CID technicians to check the crime scene. Both of the deputies had noticed a coagulated stream of blood from the victim's left nostril that smeared the left side of her face.

The patrol cars that left the intersection of A1A and Ponte Vedra Lakes Boulevard arrived at the boardwalk and pulled over onto the sandy shoulder. Moments later,

Pryor and Gamble arrived and noticed that the K-car they had seen before was no longer there. Three deputies headed toward the parking area, and a woman in uniform stepped into the glare of Pryor's headlights.

"What do you want?" the deputy asked. "Who are you?"

Pryor told her he was the man who had talked with the 911 dispatcher. At the same time, he noticed the three deputies were moving to the parking lot on the west side of A1A.

"They're looking in the wrong place," Pryor said. "The Blazer was parked on this side. The K-car was over there."

The deputies started toward the boardwalks that began at the highway shoulder and split into two stairways that led to different parts of the beach, which was about fifty yards away.

"Do you want me to come?" Pryor said. "Maybe I can help." He explained that he had experience as a first responder.

The deputy told him to come along. Kimberly waited in the car. The deputies swept the darkness with their flashlights and had their guns drawn as they cautiously made their way down the boardwalk, which led about one hundred yards to the beach. It was dark and desolate and the ocean made a soft growling sound as sea foam swirled at the shoreline. The deputies saw nothing suspicious among the sea oats, saw grass, palmettos and other harsh vegetation on both sides of the boardwalk. They didn't expect to find the shooter close to the scene after so much time had passed, but this was still an operation that required caution.

They met Deputies Tanner and Zell at the end of the boardwalk and saw the body of a woman lying with her head on the boardwalk's bottom step, tilted to her left, and her petite body sprawled on the sand. There was a small hole in her face just below the left eye, and the skin on her upper arms was abraded. Even though the body was wet and awkward in death, it was clear that she had been a beautiful young blonde woman.

Pryor borrowed a flashlight from one of the deputies and checked to see if her eyes reacted to light, but the pupils didn't dilate or shrink. The eyes had the glassy stare of death. Pryor checked her wrist for a pulse and listened for a heartbeat with his ear against her chest. There was nothing. Pryor wasn't certified to make an official pronouncement, but it was clear to him and the deputies that the woman was dead. He looked at her face, but didn't see blood from the wound on her cheek. Police later surmised that he had not seen the blood because April's face was turned to the left and away from him.

A small army of police, rescue vehicles and EMTs arrived on the scene just after midnight on Sunday morning. Brian Erb, a fire/rescue technician, with St. Johns County, was sent to help the SJSO at North Guana Beach. After he walked over to the beach, he and his partner, Mike Carter, found the body.

I observed a female patient that was unconscious and not breathing, Erb wrote in his report. *I checked for a pulse and found none. I looked for breathing and found none. I attached a cardiac monitor. No rhythm.*

Erb removed the monitor cables and turned the victim over to SJSO and left.

Mike Carter, a St. Johns County Fire Department firefighter and paramedic, was on Engine 1 when it was dispatched to a possible shooting of a second victim at North Guana Beach. Carter was taken to April's body at the bottom of the boardwalk by an SJSO deputy. Carter was the first EMT to check April's body.

"The patient was supine, with legs pulled back under her body," Carter said. "I checked the patient's airways, breathing and carotid pulse." Carter found no heart activity when he attached a cardiac monitor. He wrote how he saw *obvious lividity and asystole confirmed in two leads with a cardiac monitor. Adhesive pads left on patient's body to preserve crime scene. Patient and crime scene left in charge of SJSO Sgt. Tanner.*

Carter confirmed that April was dead on arrival (DOA). He also noticed the blood stream from April's left nostril that encrusted the left side of her face.

Police and CSI technicians from two counties responded to the bulletin about a double shooting at Guana Beach. Yellow crime scene tapes were stretched out over a wide area of the beach to prevent contamination of possible evidence. Deputies with metal detectors and K-9 unit handlers with their dogs slogged through the dense growth and almost impenetrable darkness along both sides of the beach, battling a heavy infestation of poisonous snakes, which included rattlesnakes, coral snakes, copperheads and cottonmouth water moccasins. A bite from any of these snakes is enough to kill a man or a dog.

Sometimes crawling on their hands and knees through muck and patches of thorns, police officers searched all night for a killer on the loose and for evidence that may have been left behind. A helicopter flew low along the beach with a bright searchlight that raked both sides of the highway while technicians from the sheriff's crime scene investigation (CSI) unit bagged evidence and taped off drag marks from the beach to the boardwalk. They found three .22-caliber bullet casings. The bullets could have been fired from a rifle or a handgun. They photographed footprints and drag marks made when April was pulled from the surf to the boardwalk, and bagged DNA and fiber samples. They tested for gunpowder residue. They searched both sides of the beach, gathering evidence, taking pictures and looking for anything that might be tied to the murder.

An intense search of the crime scene that would last weeks had started.

Half an hour after Wesley Pryor looked at April's body, a rescue unit from the Jacksonville Fire Department arrived. James Ado, an EMT with five years' experience, checked the body of the beautiful young woman. As an EMT, he was trained in the use of lifesaving techniques and medical equipment that was on the rescue ambulance. Like Pryor, Ado saw no blood on the woman's face.

The body wasn't moved for several hours because the ME was expected to arrive. Two hours into the investigation, police on the scene learned that the ME couldn't look at the victim until Monday. Police photographs of April's face showed streams of coagulated blood from the left side of her mouth and left nostril that had run down the left side of her face and pooled on her cheek. One small drop had coagulated at the tip of the right nostril. Although the technicians worked gently, copious amounts of blood came from the cheek wound when April's body was moved. After being placed in a body bag, the victim was taken to the morgue, where it would remain over the weekend.

Chapter 2

While Barber was rushed by a rescue helicopter to the trauma unit at Shands Hospital in Jacksonville, the intense police investigation continued with the Central Communications at the SJSO keeping Sergeant Mary Fagan up to date on latest developments. Fagan, playing the chess master, dispatched detectives and technicians to the beach and to the crime scene at A1A and Ponte Vedra Lakes Boulevard as needed.

The trauma team at Shands Hospital had been notified and was prepared to treat Barber immediately. They discovered that Barber had been shot four times with small-caliber bullets. He was lucky. None of the bullets caused much damage. Barber had been shot in the right shoulder, just above the left clavicle, the left upper arm, in the lower right chest about six inches below the nipple, and through the left palm.

None of the bullets damaged vital nerves or major blood vessels, at least partly due to the relatively low power of a .22-caliber bullet. Had the assailant used a more powerful weapon, such as a nine-millimeter gun, the damage from all of the wounds would have been extensive. The most serious wound Barber suffered was a fracture of the right shoulder bone. Except for the wound in his hand, which passed cleanly through, the other bullets were still in Barber's body. These posed no danger to him and weren't removed. The wounds were so minor that they were treated with antibiotic ointment and covered with small bandages. The trauma surgeon on duty said that Barber's wounds required no more than "conservative" medical care.

At 11:40 P.M., Detective Howard "Skip" Cole was jarred awake by a telephone call from Sergeant Doreen Taylor from the Communications Center. Taylor told Cole about a victim at A1A "with multiple gunshot wounds," who said his wife had been shot also and was still on the beach.

Cole dressed quickly and telephoned Sergeant Fagan, who told him to report to Shands Hospital and interview the male victim. Cole had been promoted to homicide detective with the SJSO less than a year ago after three years on the force. Although he was a rookie detective, he realized how important it was to interview eyewitnesses while the event was still fresh in their minds. Barber had been the only eyewitness to the shootings except for the assailant.

This guy is going to be my best witness or a suspect, he thought. Cole wasn't making a judgment about Barber's involvement, but he knew that violent crimes are usually committed by a friend or a member of the victim's family. Of course, most assailants were not shot four times.

"Let's face it, you have a husband right there at the scene. If he's a suspect, you've got to follow every lead to eliminate him and move on," Cole said. "We were trying to eliminate him."

As he pulled into the Shands parking area, Cole learned that April had been pronounced dead. The detective entered the hospital's trauma unit at 12:30 A.M., Sunday, and found Justin Barber in a bed behind a privacy curtain. Cole saw a pale man, with reddish blond hair, propped up in bed with three bandages on his body and one on his left hand. Barber's blue eyes peered from beneath eyebrows the same color as his hair. To Cole, Barber seemed too relaxed, too unemotional, and apparently not very concerned about his wife. Barber's demeanor struck Cole as being inappropriate. "He wasn't drunk and he wasn't grieving," Cole said. "He was very matter-of-fact about everything. He didn't act like a husband who was worried about his wife."

Cole introduced himself and asked Barber to let him tape-record an interview about what had happened. Barber agreed and started to tell a story of a romantic walk on a moonlit beach that turned into terror. Barber said he and his wife were celebrating their third wedding anniversary two weeks late. Barber, a business analyst on a fast track to top management at Rayonier, a Fortune 500 company, had recently been transferred to corporate headquarters in Jacksonville. Barber and his wife had purchased a condominium in Jacksonville, and April visited almost every weekend from her apartment in Tifton, Georgia, and later, her house in Thomasville. Barber said they planned to live together in a few months after April finished a two-year apprenticeship at a cancer treatment center.

According to Barber, he earned more than $125,000 a year and said his prospects were bright. He said April earned $75,000 a year as a radiation therapist at an oncology clinic, plus $2,000 a month for working a second night job as a private-duty therapist. April had expected a dramatic increase in her income when she finished a two-year internship in three weeks and became a certified dosimetrist (a specialist who determines the amount of radiation needed to treat individual patients). Barber said the couple had no money problems and were happily married. There were no affairs by either husband or wife. They had the usual tiffs that married couples experience, Barber said, but nothing serious.

April was a beautiful, petite twenty-six-year-old blonde with sparkling eyes and a huge, friendly smile. She grew up in Hennessey, Oklahoma, a rural town of two thousand, and was as comfortable with a rowdy blue-collar crowd as she was at a five-star restaurant. April was one of those rare people who made others want to be better than they were. Friends were drawn into her orbit by her magnetic personality.

According to Barber, the couple had spent a lazy day and had several drinks during an intimate afternoon at their condominium. They had decided not to buy presents to celebrate their third anniversary, Barber said, but they drove to Jacksonville Beach, just before sunset, to have dinner at Carrabba's Italian Grill. Carrabba's is one of the most popular chain restaurants in the Jacksonville area and people often wait half an hour or so for a table. No one seems to mind the wait because they can have drinks inside or on a tropical outdoor patio while waiting for a dining table.

April and Justin chose to sit on the outdoor patio in the fading daylight and watch the sky change into rich kaleidoscopic colors as the sun melted below the western horizon. Long shadows fell at twilight while they chatted and enjoyed a drink.

Barber didn't remember them talking about anything in particular, but said they were having a good time. They were laughing a lot, he said, and he had two more drinks, even though April didn't. Once a dining table was free, April and Justin ate their meal among the casual camaraderie of a Florida beach restaurant.

Barber, who said he had a buzz on, drank wine with his meal, but April abstained.

It was dark when they emerged from the air-conditioned coolness of Carrabba's into the August humidity that stifles Florida during the scorching summer weather. Neon lights gave the streets a carnival-like flair as men and women in shorts, T-shirts and flip-flops strolled along—beachside hustlers, tourists, dope addicts and respectable citizens mixed up in one crazy cocktail. One of Barber's friends had recommended a pool emporium called the Ritz, which was only a few blocks away, and he said he took April there to shoot a few games.

Barber said he had another drink, and at around 10:00 P.M., April wanted to go for a romantic moonlit walk along the beach at Guana Wildlife Preserve, about ten miles south on Highway A1A. They had been there on other special occasions, Barber said, and had made love under the star-swept sky on a remote boardwalk that led to the isolated beach along the Atlantic Ocean.

A1A is a flat, almost straight highway that knifes along the length of Florida's Atlantic Coast. The two-lane highway between Jacksonville Beach and Guana Preserve is dark and lonely at night, especially in the hot summer months. Few tourists come to Florida in the off-season and the locals stay inside in refrigerated air that is free of mosquitoes. Near Jacksonville Beach, large, gated homes that cost millions of dollars stand aloof on the east side of A1A and overlook the Atlantic Ocean. The less expensive houses, costing only one or two million dollars, are on the west side of the highway along the Intracoastal Waterway. There are no houses or streetlights along a six-mile stretch that cuts through the Guana Preserve. It is dark and desolate. The rugged beach is composed largely of crushed, foot-gouging coquina shells, instead of soft sand. The west side of the park is a morass of thick, primitive shrubbery that provides a habitat for every type of poisonous snake to be found in the United States. It was a setting that could be frightening as well as romantic.

Barber pulled the 4Runner off the road at Guana Preserve. The headlights stabbed into the darkness to show that the parking-lot gate on the west side of A1A was closed and locked. He parked the 4Runner on the sand, facing south. There were no other cars. Barber said he and April walked hand in hand across the highway, down the boardwalk, kicked off their sandals and waded in the surf. They hadn't gone far when Barber said he felt April tense. A man ran toward them in the darkness, shouting incomprehensibly, pointing a handgun, and closing fast. The man wore a dark T-shirt with an image imprinted on it and a black baseball cap with a white logo.

The man was "loud and angry," Barber said. He came close and stopped, waving the gun, shouting at Barber, who couldn't understand what the assailant was saying. Barber noted that the man was about six feet tall and weighed around 220 pounds. April stood slightly behind Barber, he said, and started to talk. "I didn't know if she was talking to him or to me," Barber said.

When April spoke, the assailant turned the gun on her. Barber tried to move between them. The gun fired. Barber grabbed for the gun and thought he hit it. Then he was grabbing for the man's arms, hands, shirt, anything he could get his hands on.

"We started fighting," Barber said. "I felt like he was hitting me . . ."

"Right," Cole said.

". . . and I don't know what happened after that."

Barber heard another gunshot and that was all he remembered until he "came to" on the beach, facedown, with the surf washing over him. He was wet and covered with sand. Barber had no idea how long he had been unconscious, but believed it was for only a short period of time.

April was nowhere to be seen.

"And then what happened?" Cole asked.

"I didn't know where he had gone," Barber said. "I didn't know where April had gone."

Dazed, Barber got to his feet and ran up and down the beach, shouting April's name. He stumbled up and down the surf, looking for her. "I found her in the water," he said. "It wasn't deep. She was floating there."

"Okay, do you remember what position she was in or anything like that?" Cole asked.

"She . . ."

"I hate to do this to you, but I just need to try and get all the details."

Barber said he found her floating facedown beyond the breakers.

Barber said he ran to his wife and turned her over. He saw that April was bleeding from a hole just below her left eye.

"Was she breathing?" Cole asked.

Barber didn't answer.

"Could you tell whether . . . ?"

"I pulled her out and I couldn't tell," Barber said. "She wasn't responding."

"Then what happened?"

"I tried to pick her up, but I couldn't get her over my shoulder. I couldn't get . . . my arm to work, and I couldn't carry her, so I pulled her . . . and I kept getting dizzy, and I pulled her. . . ."

Barber said he alternately carried and dragged April to the edge of the water and had to stop frequently because April was too heavy and he was dizzy. April was five feet three inches tall and weighed 112 pounds. Barber said he held April under the arms and knees in a "cradle carry," but didn't get far before he had to stop. After he caught his breath, Barber said, he draped April over his back and tried a fireman's carry, but he couldn't stay on his feet for more than a few yards. Barber said he was so focused on getting help for his wife that he didn't notice he had been shot.

In desperation, Barber struggled to his feet again, grabbed the waistband on April's capri pants, gripped her under the arms and dragged her backward. He made it to the boardwalk before he collapsed again, an agonizing trip of about one hundred yards.

"I felt confused and nauseous," Barber said. "I had no control over my body. At some point, I saw blood on myself and knew something was wrong with me. My body wasn't responding."

Barber gathered his strength to try and carry April up the boardwalk to their vehicle. He wanted to raise her up from the waist and prop her against a post on the boardwalk, but he couldn't lift her. He managed to raise her body just inches off the ground before she slipped from his arms. April's head made a sickening thump on the boardwalk while the rest of her body lay on the beach.

Afraid that April was dead or dying, and afraid that he was unable to drag her any farther, Barber said he went to A1A and tried to flag down a passing car. "So I ran out to the road, but nobody would stop," Barber said.

"How many cars would you say passed by you?" Cole asked.

"At least three."

"Really? Were they headed south or north?"

"Both . . . but nobody would stop."

"Did they see you?"

"I was in the middle of the road. They had to swerve to avoid hitting me."

Barber said one car slowed, but kept going. Another, he said, almost ran him off the road. Barber didn't have his cell phone and he didn't know where April's phone was. Discouraged, he decided to leave April on the beach and drive to find help. Barber said he sped toward Jacksonville Beach, bypassing darkened houses with gated driveways, thinking they wouldn't open up for a stranger at night. In his confusion, Barber said, he believed he shouldn't disturb old people who were asleep. Nine miles from Guana Beach, Barber swerved off the road at a traffic signal where he saw other vehicles, and came to a screeching stop in shrubbery on the median. This was when he found people to help him.

"Think back," Cole said. "Try to picture or remember anything you can about this guy (the attacker). Just think back."

"He was white . . . but I think he was dark . . . ," Barber said. "He was taller than me, stronger than me. He was heavier than me. I don't know what his face looks like. He . . . had a hat . . . a ball cap. It had something on it, but I don't know what it was. Uh . . . a dark T-shirt."

"What did he say to you?" Cole asked. "Try to remember exactly what he said."

"I was trying to understand. . . . I heard 'cash.'"

"Did he get anything from you at all?"

"I don't know."

"Did you have anything with you?"

"I had my keys."

"What about your wallet?"

"I don't think I had it."

"Okay, so you didn't have any cash in your pockets or anything like that?" Cole asked.

"I normally carry cash in my pockets."

"But you didn't this time?"

"I don't know."

"Do you remember him rifling through your pockets or anything like that?"

"I don't."

"Did April have any cash on her?"

"I don't know."

"Okay," Cole asked, "what was the extent of your and April's activities on the beach? Did you basically just walk?"

"We walked . . ."

"You know what I'm saying?"

"We were going to have sex," Barber said. "That's why we went there."

"I've been down there, so I know."

"But that's it. We walked . . ."

"You never . . ."

"We held hands."

"You never . . . ?"

"No . . . we were going back to the deck. That's where we were going to have sex."

"I'm just trying to think of anything I can, you know?" Cole said. "It's the simplest little thing. . . . During the struggle, did you recall hearing the gun fire?"

"I heard it once."

"That was it?"

Barber said it was.

"Were you able to get any hits in on him? I mean, if we find him, would he have any injuries on him or anything like that?"

"I didn't get to hit him. I was grabbing for the gun. I wasn't swinging at him."

"Did you ever get ahold of the gun then?"

"I had ahold of his arms."

"Okay. So, do you think that you were shot first, or do you think April was shot first?"

"I don't know."

"Is there anything else?" Cole asked. "When you pulled up (arrived), did you see any other cars?"

"No, I looked, because I didn't want any other cars to be out there."

"Do you think if you heard this guy's voice again, [is it] possible you could recognize it?"

"I don't know. It was just so fast."

"Do you think if you saw his face again, would you recognize it?"

"I don't know. I mean it's . . . I . . ."

"It's hard to say?"

". . . It's dark," Barber said.

"You never got a good look at his face?"

". . . so fast."

"When you were carrying the . . . This is difficult, I realize that," Cole said. "What was her condition?"

"She was limp."

"Could you tell where she had been shot?"

"Her face was bleeding."

Cole ended the interview, thinking that he had not learned anything that would help him find the shooter. Barber's general description of the assailant could apply to half of the people in the Jacksonville Beach–St. Augustine area. Cole believed it was going to be a tough case.

"Most homicides are solved in a matter of hours," Cole said. "Somebody shoots someone, someone else sees it, the shooter drops the gun. Everything usually falls into place quickly."

The gun used to shoot April and Justin Barber might never be found. If it had been disposed of in Guana Park, the gun would be anywhere in a 2,400-acre wilderness that included ponds, lakes, a river, the Atlantic Ocean and acres upon acres so thick with primordial vegetation that few humans had set foot on it. Under such circumstances, the gun would be found only by a great stroke of luck.

Barber, the eyewitness, would have been considered a strong suspect except that he had been shot four times. Who in his right mind would risk serious injury or death by shooting himself four times to cover up a murder? Added to this was the complication that Barber could only describe the shooter in vague terms.

After finishing the interview, Cole telephoned Sergeant Fagan to make his initial report. She told him to take photographs of Barber's wounds and check the victim for gunpowder residue. Cole described "what appeared to be four small-caliber gunshot wounds. One entry wound to the upper portion of the right shoulder, one entry wound to the upper portion of the left shoulder, one entry wound to the right side (mid-torso area), one entry wound to the center of the palm of the left hand, and an exit wound to the backside of the left hand.

All of these wounds were described to be non–life-threatening injuries. It should be noted that J. Barber did not have any other visible injuries, Cole initially wrote.

Barber had asked Cole what had happened to April. Cole told him that she had died of her injuries. *J. Barber put his head down for a moment and then continued on with conversation,* Cole wrote.

Fagan had asked Cole to get the telephone numbers for April's next of kin so they could be notified of her death.

Barber told Cole that he had all of the numbers programmed into his cell phone. Usually he carried it all the time, Barber said, but had left it on the charger because April was "hurrying me out the door." Barber said he relied so much on his cell phone that he didn't even have a landline in his Jacksonville condominium.

April's closest relative was Patti Parrish, April's aunt,

Barber said. April's mother was deceased and her father was in prison. Parrish was a lawyer in Oklahoma City who had prospects of becoming an Oklahoma district judge. Parrish, Barber told Cole, was in charge of family affairs.

At 1:45 A.M., Sunday, Barber signed a Permission to Search form so the police could search his home in the San Marco area of Jacksonville for his cell phone and any other items the police thought might have evidentiary value. Cole obtained permission from Barber to swab his hands for the presence of gunshot residue. Cole took two samples from each hand and bagged them for laboratory examination by the FDLE.

Chapter 3

While Cole was at Shands Hospital, Detective Robert Shaw, a veteran with the SJSO, helped check the 4Runner for evidence. There was a blood-soaked Hawaiian shirt inside the car, several buttons and what appeared to be blood smears on the inside driver's door and steering wheel. The keys were still in the ignition. Shaw looked inside the passenger side and saw a black purse propped against the center console. Shaw looked inside Barber's wallet and found a receipt from Carrabba's restaurant with the waiter's code. Shaw thought he should talk with the waiter to see if anything unusual had occurred. After making sure other detectives had the crime scene well in hand, Shaw drove to the restaurant. Joshua Queitsch, the waiter who had tended to April and Justin Barber, had gone home, but he returned about ten minutes after midnight when summoned by the manager.

Queitsch told the detective that sometime around 7:40 and 7:45 P.M. he noticed a strikingly beautiful blonde, wearing a pink T-shirt and capri pants, with a blue-and-white floral design, sitting at one of his tables at the south end of the patio. The waiter hurried to meet her within the maximum thirty-seconds standard the restaurant uses for customers to be greeted from the time they enter.

Queitsch asked the woman if she would be eating outside or was she waiting for an inside table? "She was very pleasant," he said. "She indicated that she was waiting for her husband and then they would be dining inside." Queitsch gave her a menu and resumed tending his seven assigned tables. When a man arrived and sat at the blonde's table, Queitsch hurried over.

"I went over to them and greeted the gentleman," Queitsch said. "He was quiet, but cordial. I took their drink order at that time and rang their drinks in at exactly seven fifty-three P.M. and delivered them." After seating them inside a short time later, and serving their meals, Queitsch didn't observe much.

Each had the same drink they carried in from the patio. They didn't order other drinks. This was a contradiction to what Barber had told Detective Cole. According to that statement, Barber said he had another drink and ordered a bottle of wine, which April ignored. Barber had told Cole he didn't remember specific conversations, but that he and April were talking, laughing and having a good time.

Not so, according to Queitsch. He said the couple hardly spoke to one another. "They were very low-maintenance," he said. "They never asked me for anything. Not a carryout box, not a refill, or anything. They were very introverted."

Barber paid the bill at 8:45 P.M. with a credit card, and by 9:02 P.M., Queitsch said, they were gone.

Shaw reported Queitsch's statement to Sergeant Fagan. Afterward, he visited EMTs at five different stations who had responded to the 911 call. One EMT at Jacksonville Fire/Rescue Station 50 reported seeing Barber's wounds. He said Barber continually asked about April. At St. Johns County Fire/Rescue Station, EMT

John Morgan said he had heard Barber say, "I couldn't carry her any farther, so I left her on the beach."

Sergeant Fagan moved back and forth between the crime scenes at Guana Beach and A1A and Ponte Vedra Lakes Boulevard as she guided the investigation. A great deal of information had been gathered by 5:00 A.M., Sunday, approximately six hours after the attack at Guana Beach. Detective Joan Belcher reported that, in addition to the gunshot wound to the cheek, "there was . . . foam that had been expelled from (April's) mouth." This proved to be crucial evidence.

Chief R. K. Porter and crime scene technician (CST) John Holmquist, of the FDLE, followed drag marks and footprints from April's body to the beach. The markings didn't coincide with Barber's story of what had happened. Holmquist made videotapes and photographs of the crime scene. The diamond ring was loose on her finger and could easily be turned. The ring would not have been left by a robber, since it was so easy to remove. Holmquist bagged several swabs to be analyzed in the lab and secured a sample of the foam around April's mouth. Several hours of searching had revealed no traces of blood on the boardwalk.

The investigation, so far, left the detectives with more questions than answers. The only thing they knew for certain was that both Justin and April Barber had been shot and that April was dead. But why would an armed robber use a .22-caliber pistol? Armed robbers rely on intimidation and generally use the largest-caliber gun they can find. Why would an assailant shoot the woman once and kill her, while shooting the man four times, and inflicting only superficial wounds? April was small and Barber represented the greatest threat. An assailant would shoot the most dangerous adversary first.

Why were the drag marks on the beach inconsistent with Barber's version of what happened? Where was the K-car Pryor and Gamble reported seeing near Barber's car? How reliable was Pryor as a witness when he saw no blood on April's face and continued to refer to Barber's Toyota 4Runner as a Chevrolet Blazer? If Barber and April were having such a good time, as Barber asserted, why did they appear so glum to the waiter at Carrabba's?

If the shootings were by an armed robber, why didn't he take anything? Even April's jewelry was left behind. There was another thing that bothered the police. Why in the world would Barber leave his wife, who had been shot and was unconscious, on the beach? At night. Alone.

"There is no way in hell I would have done that," Wesley Pryor said. "I would have flagged a car down. Sooner or later, somebody would have stopped or simply called 911 to report me. Help would have arrived before long."

Sergeant Fagan left the beach at 3:00 A.M. and Cole left the hospital at 5:00 A.M. They planned to meet Detective Shaw at 6:15 A.M. to search Barber's apartment. It had been a long day and no one could have guessed that it was just the beginning of a case that would take four years to solve. Police would match wits with an ingenious killer who left obvious clues that were almost impossible to use against him.

Even though the police were convinced they knew who the killer was in a matter of days, proving it would stretch their ingenuity to the limit. And the killer had not counted on a determined detective who simply refused to quit.

Chapter 4

At 6:20 A.M., Sunday, the eastern sky turned pink and pale blue as the sun began to rise out of the Atlantic Ocean. Detectives Fagan, Cole and Shaw had driven to Jacksonville from St. Augustine to get an early start. By land mass, Jacksonville is the biggest city in the United States, and driving at peak-traffic hours is similar to running with snails. On this early Sunday morning, the freeways were wide and clear.

The downtown area has a beautiful skyline, with elegant high-rise buildings and bridges that are artfully designed and pass over the broad expanse of the St. Johns River, which skirts the downtown and San Marco areas. Along the river are popular entertainment areas, such as Jacksonville Landing, with indoor and outdoor restaurants, and where music from modern rock to Dixieland can be heard day and night. There is a feeling of high energy that electrifies Jacksonville, an intense exuding of power that one can only find in urban areas that constantly throb with the beat of life. It bills itself as the city *Where Florida Begins.*

The city has more homicides per capita each year than

any other city in Florida, which has earned it the unofficial, and despised, nickname "Murder Capital of Florida."

San Marco is an older part of Jacksonville that is both arty and gentrified. The wide St. Johns River flows for miles past beautiful old homes that have been remodeled, but retain the flavor of the Old South. Among these are homes that are designed with modern elegance in mind, and both new and older remodeled condominiums.

Detectives Fagan, Cole and Shaw entered Barber's condominium on LaSalle Street at 6:20 A.M. They had taken catnaps and wolfed down a hasty breakfast, but they were still tired. Luckily, St. Augustine was only about a twenty-mile drive from Jacksonville.

The condominium was in a four-story complex, with Barber's one-bedroom unit taking up part of the top two floors. The front-door entrance to the condo was on the third floor of the building, over another unit. Barber's unit was not very large, having only one bedroom on the top floor. It was also where he worked at his desktop computer. The front door to the condo opened into a kitchen/living room. There was a tiled center island in the kitchen holding an empty Villa Marie wine bottle.

There was a fireplace and built-in bookshelves on a wall adjacent to the kitchen. The shelves were filled with framed family photographs, as was the fireplace mantel. There were more family pictures on the walls in the bathroom and living room. There was a television, black leather sofa, matching love seat and coffee table in the living room, but no furnishings in the dining area. An open wooden staircase led from the living room to the bedroom upstairs. All of the clothing in the closets and drawers belonged to Barber. There was a duffel bag on a chest at the end of the bed that contained a few of April's clothing and personal items.

Shortly after the detectives entered the condo, Fagan received a message to telephone Officer Rick Amos, of the Wetumka Police Department (WPD), in Oklahoma. Amos told Fagan that Joey Beth Smith, Justin Barber's aunt, had been in touch, and Amos asked Fagan if she would call and answer some of the woman's questions.

Fagan made the call and Smith answered the phone. She wanted to know what had happened.

Justin was walking on the beach with April, Fagan said, when someone tried to rob them and shot them both. "Mr. Barber left April on the beach while he drove to find someone to help them," Fagan said.

The detective asked Smith if she wanted to tell her something. Smith said that "April and [Justin] Barber loved each other very much." Linda Jean Barber, Justin Barber's mother, and his grandparents Mr. and Mrs. Charles Masengale were in Jacksonville a few weeks ago, Smith said, and everything "was fine." Barber had rented a condo for them on St. Augustine Beach, she said, because the San Marco condominium wasn't big enough to house everyone.

Barber didn't get to see his relatives very much on that visit, Smith said, because he had to work long hours, but he tried to visit them every evening after he left the office. Fagan asked Smith if she had telephone numbers for any of April's relatives and Smith did not. It wouldn't be long, however, before the deputies were swamped with news from April's family and friends.

The three detectives began a methodical search, as they had been trained. Cole said they didn't specifically know what they were looking for, but would be interested in anything unusual. Strewn on the floor around the desk, Fagan found mail, financial documents and a photograph of a silver-colored sports car. A yellow pad on the desk contained information on the couple's 2001 income: Barber made $96,121 and April earned about $59,000. The detectives thought it was a lot of money for a thirty-year-old man and twenty-seven-year-old woman.

The real shocker was yet to come. When Cole looked in the bedroom closet, he found a filing cabinet filled with Barber's financial documents. Among these was an insurance policy on April's life for $2 million, which had been purchased a little more than ten months earlier. There was another policy on April's life for $125,000, which was purchased two years ago.

The three detectives looked at the two-million-dollar insurance policy. Cole was stunned. "This is a young couple," he said. "It was staggering to see so much life insurance. I thought this was a possible motive."

Another surprise was that Justin Barber had been previously married while in college and was divorced in Norman, Oklahoma, in 1997. Cole found a burglary report from the Norman Police Department and Shaw found a gun-cleaning kit for a .357-caliber Magnum in the master-bathroom closet.

After they finished the search and bagged and marked evidence, the three detectives left the apartment and headed back to St. Augustine.

At the sheriff's office, Detective Fagan looked through Barber's daily planner and found the telephone number and address for Patti Parrish, April's aunt. Fagan called Parrish in Oklahoma City, identified herself and began to tell April's aunt what had happened. But Parrish already knew. Barber's mother, Linda, had stopped by Parrish's house after talking with her son and told Parrish the news. Linda was on her way to the airport to catch a flight to Jacksonville.

Parrish asked Fagan to tell her the details. Fagan said that a man had tried to rob April and Justin while they were walking on the beach and shot them. Parrish asked if it was true that none of Barber's injuries were life-threatening.

"That's my understanding," Fagan said.

There was a brief pause. Parrish asked Fagan if she could tell the officer something in confidence. "I told her I couldn't promise her that, but if she felt she needed to share something with me, then she needed to let me know."

Parrish said that about a year ago, April told her she and Justin were getting life insurance policies on one another for $2,500,000. Justin didn't want anyone in April's family to know about it, Parrish said, and had made April swear not to tell anyone. Furthermore, Parrish said, things were not good between April and Justin Barber. April had visited Oklahoma City the previous Friday through Wednesday, Parrish said, and April and Justin were fighting. April wasn't sure she would stay in the marriage. The couple was also having money problems. Both had "incredible" student loans and were making mortgage payments on a house and the condominium. In addition, April paid her rent in Georgia and both were responsible for their own living expenses.

The three detectives were thunderstruck at the magnitude of Barber's lies. Barber had looked Cole straight in the eye and said that the marriage was good and that they had no monetary problems.

"The harder we tried to eliminate him as a suspect, the more everything turned around and pointed back to him," Cole said.

There was no physical evidence to show that Barber had killed his wife, but circumstantial evidence pointed to him. The investigation was less than twelve hours old. There was a mountain of forensic evidence to examine, more questions to be asked and a huge amount of information to be gathered. The investigation had just scratched the surface.

Even so, Cole thought, *This is our guy. This is the guy who did it.* The hair on the back of his neck prickled.

Barber spent the night at Shands Hospital in case there were unexpected complications with his wounds. Shortly after 10:00 A.M., Sunday, his telephone rang. Barber answered and Patti Parrish was on the line. She was calling from her car as she drove from Stillwater, Oklahoma, to Hennessey with April's sister, Julie. The drive is almost a straight shot from east to west through some fifty miles of rich Great Plains farmland.

When Parrish identified herself, Barber started to cry.

"I'm so sorry," he said. "I tried to save her. I tried to save her." He continued to repeat it between sobs.

Barber said he had been shot five times, but didn't know whether April had been shot or not. "I can't even remember what beach we were at," he said. "I can't remember anything."

Parrish told him that his mother should be there soon.

"I know," he said. "I told her not to come."

Parrish asked if she could bring April back to Hennessey for burial.

"Okay," he said.

The search continued at Guana Beach for the gun that was used to shoot April and Justin Barber. The beach area was divided into quadrants that were precisely marked by Global Positioning System (GPS). Every inch of the broad search area could be located by a satellite orbiting the earth. The GPS was used in case searchers wanted to return for a follow-up on something they had previously found: the GPS would lead them to the exact spot. Scores of technicians, including the Naval Criminal Investigative Service (NCIS) from the Mayport Naval Station, stood shoulder to shoulder as they looked at every inch they could access. Days would pass before the entire area could be searched.

"The brush and thorns were so thick that people just couldn't get through them," Cole said. "They were on their hands and knees and crawling on their stomachs. Even the canines couldn't get through."

The morning sun was hot and the white sand almost blinding. The pale sky contrasted with the darker blue ocean and the thick, emerald shrubbery. A soft rumbling came from the Atlantic as swells rolled onto the sand and receded in a swirl of sea foam. Already the air was thick with humidity and the searchers' bare skin turned fuzzy gray with swarms of bloodthirsty mosquitoes.

Beer cans, shoes, sunglasses and loads of other junk were found, including the spent casings of several bullets, none of which were .22-caliber. A small makeshift shrine with a picture frame, shoe, necklace and an old photograph were discovered. Who knew what kind of strange ceremony occurred at this shrine? Several live .45-caliber rounds were found in the sand. Nothing turned up that seemed remotely connected to the shooting of Justin and April Barber.

Cole telephoned Patti Parrish at 5:00 P.M. Parrish reiterated the information she had given Detective Fagan about April's troubled marriage. Furthermore, Parrish said, April had talked to several friends on her most recent trip to Oklahoma about her difficulties with Justin. Parrish gave Cole the names and telephone numbers of several friends and family members. She told him that April worked at the Archbold Medical Center in

Thomasville, Georgia. April's supervisor was Ramish Nair, who was also a close friend. All of them could have important information for Cole.

Cole learned that April lived in Thomasville in a house that she rented from the medical center. She commuted to Jacksonville on weekends to be with her husband.

The SJSO established its initial search area by standing on various parts of the boardwalk and throwing a .22-caliber pistol as far as they could. This covered a large area of the beach, but there were 2,400 acres in the preserve, plus miles along Highway A1A where a gun could have been thrown from a car.

"I thought the only way we're ever going to find the gun is to burn the whole preserve," Cole said. "The gun could have been anywhere. It could have been in the Atlantic Ocean. I was wondering if we could ever find it."

Following the search, Cole telephoned Amber Mitchell, April's best friend, in Oklahoma City. Patti Parrish told Cole earlier that Mitchell could probably shed light on his investigation. April and Mitchell had been sorority pledge sisters at Oklahoma University and had remained close. Mitchell was one of the friends April visited on her most recent trip to Oklahoma a few weeks ago.

Mitchell added explosive information to a case that seemed ready to blow up in Justin Barber's face. April thought Justin had a mistress, and she was angry about it, Mitchell said. April said Justin regularly played tennis with a woman in Jacksonville, even though he had never played tennis. Justin became angry when April asked him about it.

According to Cole's report, Mitchell said, "He (Barber) became defensive and refused to discuss the subject. April believed Barber was cheating on her and she did not want to be in that type of relationship."

Mitchell said April told her she confronted Justin Barber on August 3, 2002, which was the day before their third wedding anniversary. April told him that she would leave him if things didn't improve. According to April, Justin wasn't impressed. He didn't offer to discuss things or to work on making the marriage better. He refused marriage counseling. Once she finished her internship at the end of the year, April told Mitchell, she did not plan to go back to Justin Barber.

"Is there anything you know about the case and the Barbers' marital problems that seemed suspicious?" Cole asked.

"You're going to have to prove to me that Justin didn't do it," Mitchell said.

Cole told Mitchell he would be in touch. He considered what they knew so far. Barber lied about not having money problems. He lied about the good time he and April had at Carrabba's restaurant. April had already told Justin she was leaving him. Under such circumstances, would April suggest making love at the beach? Barber also lied to police and EMTs when he said he knew April was "on the beach," but not exactly where. Yet, he knew they were going to Guana Beach and that they had been there before.

Now a possible mistress had been thrown into the mix. Along with more than $2 million of insurance on April's life—a policy that wasn't even a year old. And April had recently told Barber she would leave him if things didn't improve. There would be no insurance payoff without April's death. Now there was a possible affair that could be an added incentive for murder.

At 10:30 P.M. Cole talked with Barber, who was being moved to room 821 at Shands Hospital. Barber gave

Cole his new telephone number and asked, "Do you have a suspect yet?"

"Not yet," Cole said. "It's very important for you to remember anything you can about the assailant."

"I'm trying, but it was very dark and I didn't see his face very well," Barber said. "I was very drunk and passed out during the struggle."

"How are you feeling?"

"Fine," Barber said. "I'll probably be released sometime tomorrow."

Cole gave Barber the medical examiner's telephone number and told him he might want to start making arrangements for his wife's burial, Cole said. Barber said the funeral services would be in Oklahoma so that April would be near her family.

When he went to bed that night, Cole pictured how April's friends described her. It was obvious that she was pretty. From all accounts, almost everyone loved her and she loved them back. She was conscientious and had survived personal tragedies without dimming the light of her spirit. Then he thought of her lifeless body, wet and sandy, sprawled at the end of the boardwalk.

Tomorrow morning, Cole would attend one of the most important aspects of the investigation: the autopsy.

Chapter 5

On Monday at 9:00 A.M., there was a conclave of acronyms at the medical examiner's office, like a huge bowl of alphabet soup. Detectives Fagan, Shaw, Cole and Captain West, of the SJSO, CSTs John Holmquist and Steve Platt, of the FDLE, Kenney Moore and Don Hardy, CSIs for the ME, attended April's autopsy, which was performed by Dr. Terrence Steiner, the ME.

An autopsy is one of the most important procedures in a homicide investigation. Only the ME can determine the cause of death and whether or not it was homicide. An autopsy can show the caliber of bullet used in a shooting, damage to organs and nerves, what kind of knife was used in a stabbing or the type of blunt instrument that bludgeoned someone to death. There may be traces of the assailant's DNA under the victim's fingernails or elsewhere on the body. A fiber may show what the assailant wore and allow investigators to trace it back to the store that sold the item and the person who bought it.

The ME took X-ray pictures of April's head, examined her clothes, fingernail clippings and scrapings, then bagged them for further study. He also saved a spent

.22-caliber bullet and blood samples. There was no evidence of alcohol in April's blood and a complete drug screen proved she had not taken drugs.

Dr. Steiner reported that April was a healthy young woman. He noted that her clothing was "moderately" damp and there was sand on her body, particularly on the back. There was a large amount of blood on the back of the head and scalp.

Sand and smeared blood was found on her left hand. April's diamond ring was still on her finger and a watch still adorned her wrist. Dr. Steiner removed the ring "easily." He found blood smears on the left hand, and blood had dripped down the right arm from the shoulder onto the forearm. Both hands and arms were sandy.

The ME found no blood spatter on the body, but extensive liquid blood coming from the left cheek, left nostril, as well as the left angle of the mouth and onto the left side of the face. There was no blood spatter or smearing on the back. Hoop earrings were removed and bagged. There were no injuries on the scalp and no damage to the inner or outer ears.

Two small pointed abrasions were found below the left ear. They were about one-eighth of an inch in diameter. A gunshot entry wound was found on the left cheek. There was an irregular linear abrasion over the left clavicle, about three-eighths by one-eighth inch in size, but there were no traumatic injuries.

On the right front chest was an orange circular abrasion. The same red-orange abrasions were found on the upper and lower arms. There was another such abrasion on the elbow. The ME found multiple sharp abrasions on the neck, shoulder, scapula and right shoulder blade.

Dr. Steiner found a "moderate" amount of frothy red fluid in the bronchial tubes. The bullet that killed April entered her left cheek at a ten-degree angle, punctured the left sinus and stopped after shattering the first cervical vertebra. Bullets are made with metal jackets, which are meant to keep them from fragmenting or flattening, or without a jacket, which allows it to distort, thereby causing maximum damage. The bullet recovered from April did not have a metal jacket and was intended to cause the most damage possible.

Dr. Steiner found that April died from this single gunshot wound to the head. This wasn't surprising, considering the blood flow from the wound in her cheek. Another shocking fact that made the murder more heinous was that April had suffered a "near drowning" in salt water before she was shot. The ME called it "perimortem submersion in salt water." In layman's terms, this meant that April was unconscious and almost dead from drowning and might not have recovered—even with advanced medical care. But April *was alive* when the bullet was fired into her face.

This stunning discovery added more confusion to evidence the detectives were gathering. Why would a robber try to drown April and then give up when he had all but accomplished the job? Why stop the drowning, drag her one hundred yards to the boardwalk, and shoot her? Why didn't the assailant drown April? The near-drowning scenario cast grave doubt on Justin Barber's story about April and himself being shot before he dragged his wife from the surf. The ME said April was shot and killed where she lay and that she was not moved after death. If Justin Barber had shot both himself and April, why go through the near-drowning episode and drag her to the boardwalk before the shootings? None of it made any sense.

The ME ruled that the death was an official homicide. The SJSO had already treated April's death as a homicide. The investigation was ratcheted up another notch.

* * *

Justin Barber talked with Patti Parrish in Oklahoma by telephone. Barber told her that he had spoken with a counselor and that, physically, he was okay. He expected to be released from the hospital and would be in Oklahoma on Tuesday or Wednesday after he took care of some business in Jacksonville. Barber said police had listed him as "John Doe" for security reasons. The police feared "the guy who shot me may come back," Barber said.

Parrish asked him again to tell what had happened at the beach.

Barber said he would tell her in person when he arrived in Oklahoma. He said he would tell the story one time—and one time only. Parrish could tell the rest of the family. Parrish asked if he had heard any new information from the detectives. Barber told her a witness had seen a Dodge Aries (K-car) and the police were trying to find it.

Barber said Sergeant Fagan told him there had been several break-ins at houses near the beach and these were being investigated to see if there was a connection.

Parrish asked, "Is it true that you just left April lying on the beach and drove ten miles?"

"Yes," he said. "To find help."

"Was April alive when you left?"

Barber said he didn't think so "because she would not talk."

"Did you try to find a pulse?"

"No."

"Did you try mouth-to-mouth resuscitation?"

"No," Barber answered.

"Did you even know for sure she was shot?"

"No."

* * *

Following the autopsy, the police intensified their investigation. Crime scene technicians Holmquist and Steve Platt, of the FDLE, went to the sheriff's evidence bay to check Barber's 4Runner. They were accompanied by Detectives Fagan and Shaw. Almost immediately, they found April's purse, which contained a charged cell phone, in plain view on the center console, where she always left it. Barber had told the police that he had left April on the beach because he couldn't find her phone to call for help on the night they were shot.

There was little else in April's purse: a package of chewing gum, checkbook, two credit cards, Delta Sky Miles card and a pen. Justin's wallet contained his Social Security card, seven credit cards, phone card, two association cards and his Rayonier health benefits card. All evidence found in the 4Runner was bagged and marked.

Sergeant Fagan and the CSTs stopped to pick up metal detectors and went to Guana Beach. They joined dozens of other searchers and looked for a gun, casings and any other possible evidence. Holmquist boarded *Air 1,* the SJSO's helicopter, and searched the preserve from the air and took several aerial photographs. After more than six hours of looking, the searchers once again found nothing. Fagan also boarded *Air 1* and shot aerial videotapes of the path Barber drove from Guana Park to Ponte Vedra Lakes Boulevard and A1A.

In the meantime, Detective Shaw contacted the police department in Normal, Oklahoma, then faxed them a request for a copy of the burglary report at Barber's house on July 8, 1997, when he was married to his first wife. Shaw also asked the Thomasville Police Department (TPD) in Georgia to send him copies of the burglaries of April's home and car in late July 2002.

Although the police didn't take the report of a K-car being at Guana Beach on the night of the shooting seriously, the SJSO issued a bulletin for all units to be on the lookout for a dark-colored Dodge Aries. Agents for the FDLE made plaster castings of tire tracks where Wesley Pryor had reported seeing the Aries. SJSO deputies also found the names and addresses of all K-car buyers in St. Johns County for the past two years and asked where they were on the night of the shootings.

A local newspaper published this statement from the SJSO: *We are keenly interested in finding the murder weapon and are on the lookout for anyone who may have seen an older model series K type Plymouth or Dodge near the North Beach walkover at Guana on Saturday night.* The spokesman gave a telephone number and asked the public for help.

The SJSO didn't want too much of the information they gathered to be leaked. Those who were interviewed by the SJSO were asked to keep their own counsel. A deputy said, "We have talked to a number of people about a woman who made a difference in so many lives."

The murder caused a media sensation. St. Augustine, the oldest city in the United States, is known mostly for the old churches, forts and other buildings built by the Spanish conquistadores for God, gold and glory. In modern times, conquistadores in the form of real estate developers still come to Florida for gold, but leave God and glory to fend for themselves.

St. Augustine is a quaint little town with huge live oaks that stretch up to form a cathedral-like ceiling over many of the streets. Gaily decorated horses and their drivers carry tourists around the small historical area to the rhythm of hooves beating on centuries-old cobblestones.

A miniature train carries other sightseers among places of interest.

St. Augustine is better known for seafood tourist attractions than for a shooting and murder during a romantic midnight walk on the beach. Reporters from far and wide sniffed out parts of the Barber story, and within hours St. Johns County was invaded by media hawks from newspapers and television. Firemen, EMTs, deputy sheriffs and others tried to go about their usual business amid the constant ringing of telephones and answered questions almost nonstop from a seemingly insatiable press.

Justin Barber, shot four times, found no safe haven from the inquisitive media. Barber talked with Cole to tell him that his mother, Linda, and one of his aunts had arrived. The media were hounding him, Barber said, and he was moving into the Omni Hotel to avoid reporters. Barber gave Cole his cell phone number.

Cole had other calls to make. He called Oklahoma City and talked with Amber Mitchell, who told him about more problems in the Barber marriage. April had recently learned that Justin was hanging out with a lot of new friends, some of them single women. According to Mitchell, Barber didn't seem to care that it upset his wife.

"He blamed her . . . because they lost all of their old friends because April was always too tired on the weekends to go out," Mitchell told Cole.

Why wouldn't she be tired after working two jobs all week and commuting to Jacksonville from Georgia? Cole wondered.

While detectives searched and questioned, the FDLE forensic investigators delved into the more arcane processes of criminal investigation. Technicians investigated hundreds of items that ranged from the Bar-

bers' sandals from Guana Beach to strands of April
Barber's hair.

The gunshot residue test that Detective Cole had
made of Barber's hands at Shands Hospital turned out
to be meaningless. Gunshot residue is relatively easy to
remove and an analysis is considered invalid if the test is
taken more than eight hours after a gun is fired. Residue
can also be eliminated by wearing gloves or by carefully
washing parts of the body that were exposed when the
gun was fired. The samples Cole took from Barber at
Shands were well within the eight-hour limit.

The FDLE reported that *analysis cannot distinguish between discharging a firearm and being in close proximity to a
weapon when it is discharged. For this reason, gunshot residue
found in samples collected from Justin Barber is being returned
to you un-worked.*

"There wouldn't necessarily have to be gunshot residue," Cole said. "They were at the ocean and it would be
easy to wash the residue off."

FDLE guidelines instruct field investigators: *Do not
sample subjects known to have washed/rinsed their hands or
bathed since the alleged shooting incident. Washing or rinsing
the hands can be expected to remove essentially all gunshot
residue present.*

In cases such as this, the test is part of investigative
protocol. Gunpowder residue on Justin Barber might
prove nothing, but lack of it could help eliminate him as
a suspect. Getting shot exposed him to gunshot residue;
it wouldn't be possible to determine whether or not he
had fired a gun within the past eight hours.

Technicians at the FDLE examined the casts made of
the tire tracks from the crime scene, swabs of the discol-
orations on April's right wrist and upper left arm and the
foam from her lips. They studied her fingernail clippings,

a strand of April's hair and her clothing and made tests to establish her blood standard.

Tests showed that the bullet removed from April was fired from a .22-caliber weapon. This caliber bullet is made in two sizes: long and short. The "long" bullet has a larger casing, holds more powder and has a higher velocity than the "short" version. A .22-caliber bullet can be fired either from a rifle or a handgun. Technicians couldn't tell whether the bullet that killed April was a long or a short version, or whether it was fired from a rifle or a handgun.

Tests were made on various items found in the 4Runner Barber had driven in his race to find help. There were buttons from his shirt, which the EMTs had cut off to remove, the shirt itself, with bullet holes and bloodstains, and swabs taken from the vehicle's interior. Technicians studied swabs to determine Barber's blood standard and examined the clothing he wore when the assault occurred.

The scrapings taken from the asphalt and the stain on the parking-lot gate at the crime scene tested negative for blood. The bullets removed from April and Justin were so deformed that it was impossible to tell if they had been fired from the same gun. This was also true of a .22-caliber slug found on the beach.

The blood found on April's pants, shirts, underwear and bra belonged to her, according to the FDLE. In this initial report, the FDLE found *no profiles foreign to April Barber* on the clothing. If Barber had dragged and carried April, as he had said, his blood should have been on her shirt and pants. Some DNA on the clothing couldn't be interpreted under the technology available. All pertinent DNA samples were immediately preserved and sent for further testing.

The tire track castings, April's fingerprints and a roll

of film taken of the sandals found at the beach were assigned to the Latent Print Section for further examination. Various swabs from April's body, nail clippings and
other evidence related to DNA were forwarded to the
Serology Section. Barber's shirt and swabs from the
4Runner were also sent for further study. The bullet
from April's body was sent to the Firearms Section.
Barber's shirt, already marked to be examined by the
Serology Section, was also scheduled to be tested by the
Firearms Section, as was April's clothing.

Besides all of the other tests scheduled for April's
clothing, it was determined that it should be examined
by the Microanalysis Section. So was Barber's shirt.

One item that received special attention was Justin
Barber's home computer. The police received permission from Barber to remove the computer a day before
they picked it up at his condo and turned it over to the
FDLE for analysis in the computer forensic laboratory.
Barber said that he used the Internet often to search for
information. The SJSO detectives wanted to see if there
was anything stored on the computer's hard drive that
was relevant to the investigation.

On Monday, August 19, 2002, Sergeant Fagan received a call from Justin Barber, who wanted to pick up
his 4Runner. Fagan gave him directions to the SJSO, and
when Barber arrived, his mother and an aunt accompanied him.

Barber said he was sorry he hadn't been able to do more
to help the investigation. He asked if there was anything
else he could do. Fagan said if he even vaguely saw the suspect's face, an artist might be able to do a composite.

"It all happened so fast and it was so dark out," Barber
said. "I can't remember seeing his face."

Fagan chatted with Justin and told him that when he was in Oklahoma, he should take his time and think about the suspect. Maybe something would come to him and he would remember.

Barber repeated what he had said before: "I'll try, but it was so dark out and it happened so fast. If you find the suspect, though, I might be able to identify him."

Fagan accompanied Barber to the evidence bay and Lieutenant Gribble turned the 4Runner over to Justin. Linda got behind the steering wheel and her son sat on the passenger side. *They sat there for a couple of minutes and Barber got my attention,* Fagan wrote in her report. *He had a helpless and confused look on his face and said he never saw the silver colored watch before that was laying on the back seat.*

Fagan put the watch into evidence after Barber left. Justin called a short time later and said his driver's license was missing and suggested that the suspect might have taken it. Fagan said it was more likely that a deputy or paramedic had taken it to identify him, and then put it into evidence.

"Was your vehicle broken into?" Fagan asked.

"I don't know."

"Do you remember whether or not you had to unlock the vehicle when you returned to it, or whether it was unlocked and the door open?"

"The doors were closed, but I don't remember if I had to unlock it or not."

"Is there anything else missing?"

Barber said, "I don't think so."

The Omni Hotel in downtown Jacksonville, where Barber was staying to avoid media attention, was bustling with a business crowd at 8:20 A.M. on August 20, 2002. Detectives Cole and Shaw were on their way to

Thomasville, Georgia. They met Justin in the lobby. He told them he would be moving back into the condo the next day and asked if they had made any progress with the case.

Shaw said they would keep Barber informed. What they needed now was for Barber to sign a Permission to Search form so they could legally search April's house in Thomasville, Georgia, for evidence. Barber signed the form and gave Cole a questioning look.

"Aren't you going to ask me about the incident?" he asked.

"We need to focus on the suspect's identity," Cole said. "Anything you can remember would be very useful."

Barber said it was dark and he couldn't see very well during the attack, but he added that he thought he could work with a sketch artist and come up with a composite of the assailant once he got back from April's funeral in Oklahoma. Even though he had been very drunk, Barber believed he would recognize the assailant if he saw him again.

"Have you found a gun?" Barber asked.

"We're looking," Cole said.

"I'm sure I grabbed ahold of it," Barber said. "I think I grabbed it several times."

The detectives said they had to leave because they had appointments in Thomasville, which was about 160 miles away. Shaw asked Barber when he was coming back from April's funeral.

"I'm scheduled to come back August twenty-seventh," he said. "I could come back earlier to assist in the investigation."

Cole and Shaw stepped out of the refrigerated air of the Omni and into the already hot and humid subtropical air blanketing Jacksonville.

"Did you notice anything unusual?" Cole asked.

"He was eager to be helpful," Shaw said.

"Too helpful, maybe?"

Shaw nodded. "Could be."

The drive took the detectives a little less than three hours, giving them some time to discuss the case and see if they were overlooking anything. They had followed proper investigative procedures, but the harder they tried to eliminate Justin Barber as a suspect, the more the evidence pointed to him.

Cole and Shaw received the keys to the small brick house that April rented from the Archbold Medical Center in Thomasville. There were leafy trees and shrubbery around the grounds, unlike the palm trees and tough vegetation that survives in Florida. Although it is located in a rural area, the Thomasville complex serves as flagship for an organization that includes five hospitals and four nursing homes with eight hundred beds. The center employs more than 2,500 people. John F. Archbold intended to build the hospital on the banks of the Hudson River in New York City. Friends convinced him to build it instead at his summer home in Thomasville, and on June 30, 1925, it was completed and given to the city in memory of John's father, John D. (Dustin) Archbold.

April's house was a single-story brick home with white trim. It was located about one hundred feet from the intersection of Mimosa Drive and Pasttime Drive. Feathery mimosa trees dotted the yards. The two detectives took photographs of the house and its contents and then made a videotape before starting the search. The house had been burglarized a few weeks ago and the break-in had terrified April. Justin, living at the condo in Jacksonville, ignored April's concern and offered her no advice on how to improve security.

The detectives found the usual things in the house. In spite of the problems with her marriage, April still had high hopes that love would conquer all. There was a double metal frame that contained a wedding portrait of April and Justin. In the frame next to that was cursive text shaped like a valentine. The text read: *Love is Patient. Love is kind & is not jealous, love does not brag & is not arrogant, does not act unbecomingly; it does not seek its own, is not provoked, does not take into account a wrong suffered, does not rejoice in unrighteousness but rejoices with the truth, bears all things, believes all things, hopes all things, endures all things. But now abide faith, hope, love, these three; the greatest of these is Love.—First Corinthians.* Below that in boldface type was **Justin and April Barber.**

April also appeared ready to protect herself. Between the mattress and box spring on her bed, the detectives found a large bowie-style hunting knife in a leather sheath. They also found three Oklahoma real estate magazines with several listings circled in ink. April apparently was serious about leaving her husband. And she was afraid of something that made her think she needed a knife for protection.

The detectives went to the oncology center, where April had worked, and returned the keys to April's house. Kevin Guidry, who was one of April's coworkers, talked with Shaw, while Cole met with Ramish Nair, who had been April's friend and supervisor. Both detectives heard similar stories.

Guidry had known April for two years when they worked together at the cancer center. Both worked as dosimetrists. Guidry was certified and April was studying toward certification. "We shared the same office and spent the majority of our days together," Guidry said. "My wife and I occasionally socialized outside the office with April." Guidry said he learned on the morning of August 19 that April had been killed the previous weekend. He had been in an "emotional stupor" ever since.

Shaw asked Guidry if he had noticed any change in April's behavior over the recent days. Guidry replied that he found April to be "somewhat moody," but the moodiness changed into something darker.

"In the last couple of weeks, I did notice something wasn't quite right," Guidry said. "I guess that suspicion was somewhat concerned [*sic*] when I received a call from April the day she left Oklahoma on her last visit with her family.

"She telephoned the office that morning and we somehow got on the subject of her thinking of moving back to Oklahoma," Guidry said. "She had never made it a secret that after her two years of on-the-job training for her certification in dosimetry, she would eventually move back to Jacksonville to be with Barber.

"But this was the first time about the move back to her home. She said that she had been trying to make things good for four years now and that she was tired of trying. I had some indication of what she was talking about," Guidry said. "I knew that things have been running hot and cold between her and Justin ever since I knew April. I assumed that was what she meant.

"'The best thing you can do is to come on back and give yourself some time to think about it,' I told her. She agreed."

Since that conversation, Guidry said, he had thought of several things that seemed strange about April's relationship with Barber. He told her frequently how odd he thought their marriage was.

"Although I believe there was nothing more she wanted out of life than a loving relationship with her husband, I don't think it was ever to be between them," Guidry said. "I guess a larger part of the problem was financial. I know for a fact that they kept their finances totally separate and that she hardly knew anything about Justin's private finances. It's almost as though she was too afraid to ask him about things if they were too personal. I found that extremely odd, considering the fact that they were married for several years.

"I guess one of the things that sticks out the most in my mind ever since this happened was something that occurred a few months ago. Justin had persuaded April that they needed additional life insurance, which is not uncommon, except for the fact that he was talking a couple of million dollars' worth."

Guidry mentioned that there was an opening for a dosimetrist in Jacksonville that April could fill, but April replied that she wanted to move back to Oklahoma. April asked Guidry to let her know if he heard of openings in that state. She had several weeks to complete her apprenticeship and then she wanted to move back to Oklahoma. Guidry told Shaw that April didn't seem happy about Barber shopping for such large life insurance policies.

"If anything happens to me," April told Guidry, "Justin should be investigated."

April also told Ramish Nair, her supervisor and a close friend at the oncology center, that she was anxious about the two-million-dollar insurance policy on her life. Nair had known April since 1999 and had worked closely with her since January 2001.

April told Nair that in June 2001 Justin Barber was shopping for life insurance.

"We're having a difficult time because some companies are rejecting me, based on my high cholesterol and the family's general disposition to cancer," April said. "Justin tried several different companies and I was finally accepted."

Nair was stunned when April told him that the policies were for either $2 million or $2,500,000 for each of them.

"Why such a large amount for a twenty-six-year-old?"

"Justin thought it was the best thing," April replied.

Barber found the insurance he wanted through Jay Jervey, a Jacksonville agent who represented First Colony Life Insurance (now Genworth) and others. First Colony agreed to insure the Barbers for $2 million each. Barber told April not to tell anyone about the new insurance or the amount of the policies. April thought this was odd because her uncle, Patti Parrish's husband, also sold policies through First Colony. Why didn't her husband want to keep the business in the family?

"If anything happens to me, make sure you suspect foul play," April told Nair. "Promise me two things. Make sure I'm buried next to my mother in Hennessey and make sure my two diamond rings and diamond pendant go to my aunt Patti."

Nair discovered that April didn't know anything about her husband's finances, and Nair thought that was strange.

"They had a common account that they used for groceries, but separate checking accounts," Nair said.

"He fancies himself a financial genius," April said, "so I let him make all financial decisions and file the taxes."

In early July 2002, Nair said he began to realize that April was in an abusive relationship. April told Nair that during their frequent fights, Barber mimicked her voice and mannerisms to belittle her. "I came to know this to be a form of verbal/emotional abuse," Nair said.

Chapter 6

Sergeant Fagan directed a massive search, fielded calls and conducted investigations and interviews, while Detectives Cole and Shaw headed for Georgia. As the third full day after the murder on Guana Beach began, newspapers, radios and television stations had told the story to people around the world. The northeast coast of Florida buzzed with fear and excitement as thousands of people waited anxiously for the assailant to be taken into custody. Eagle-eyed citizens called the police to report suspicious-looking characters. People were careful to lock their houses at night, and since it was Florida, where gun laws are lenient, they kept their guns within easy reach.

Mary McCrone called to say that on the morning of the murder she saw a man walking to a house on Ponte Vedra Lakes Boulevard. She described him as a "white male, plaid shirt, long pants, brownish blond long hair, beard and dirty-looking."

Protecting sea turtles, which come to the beach to lay their eggs, is a major avocation for hundreds of conservationists along Florida's coasts. They are trying hard to protect an endangered species. Janet Koehler was on turtle patrol at Ponte Vedra Beach early on August 17 when something caught her attention.

Koehler saw a white man, with blond hair, "wearing camouflage fatigues, with long sleeves and pants, walking in and out of the dunes." Koehler said she was alarmed because she thought he was a much despised poacher looking for turtle eggs. Perhaps a turtle poacher would not be above murder.

Barbara Thompson called the SJSO because she saw a "suspicious character" coming from Guana Beach on Saturday, August 17, between 12:15 and 12:45 P.M. Thompson said the man looked like a bum.

"The transient was a white male, very tan, dirty, strawberry blond, shaggy hair, about five feet ten inches tall and slender," Thompson said. "He was wearing dark green pants and a dark green plaid shirt."

It turned out to be another wild-goose chase. None of the hundreds of calls about suspicious persons did anything but slow progress. But Fagan received a telephone call at about 9:30 A.M. that made her ears perk up. The call was from Tracey Bolling, who worked for State Farm Insurance.

Bolling told Fagan that she was uneasy. The State Farm branch where she worked sold $125,000 life insurance policies to both April and Barber about two years ago. Bolling had met Justin Barber, but had never seen April.

"Is there any chance of seeing a picture of April?" Bolling asked. "I have some concerns."

"What are your concerns?" Fagan asked.

Bolling explained that during the past month, she had seen Justin Barber having lunch with a woman at the deli at the corner of Forsyth and Julia. She considered introducing herself, Bolling said, because she thought the woman with Barber must be April. She didn't approach them, Bolling said, "because I remembered April was supposed to be in Georgia during the weekdays." She described the woman with Barber as having a medium build and long, dark hair.

"This whole thing is weird," Bolling said. In fact, she thought it was so weird that she had reported it to State Farm Life Insurance Company that very morning. The Barbers were apparently good customers: both Justin and April had life insurance policies for $125,000, which were purchased two years ago. Their condominium had been insured with the company since February 2001 and their cars since March 2001. Bolling said Barber had filed a claim against his stolen Audi, but had not yet filed for April's life insurance.

Before leaving Thomasville, Shaw met Detective Bob Sise, of the TPD. Sise delivered reports on the burglary of April's house that the two detectives had discussed earlier by telephone. They talked more about the break-in.

"Was there anything that seemed out of the ordinary about it?" Shaw asked.

"I felt that the way the burglary was conducted and the things taken, that it was done by someone who was familiar with the interior of the house," Sise said. "I told her she needed to be more cautious because this might be more than a random break-in."

One of the things taken was a stun gun that April kept on a bedside table.

Following the burglary, April thought it would be a good idea to have a roommate. She made arrangements for a woman going through a divorce to share the house in Thomasville. April told Shasta Meeks, "It will help me out by helping pay the bills and because I'm scared to stay there by myself anymore."

* * *

"I don't want to know the breakdown of the funeral bill," Barber said. Both April and Justin Barber were back in Oklahoma. Barber stood in the summer light of the Great Plains, where April had grown up as a cute, bubbly towhead whom everyone loved. The vivacious girl, who had become a beautiful, caring woman, came home in a casket. April grew up in Hennessey and this would be where her remains returned to the earth.

Parrish told Justin she would keep track of the paperwork and they would talk about it later. It was the morning of Wednesday, August 21, 2002, and they were at Cordry-Gritz Funeral Home in Hennessey to make April's funeral arrangements. Although Barber asked Parrish to pay for the funeral until he collected on April's State Farm life insurance policy, he approved decisions as next of kin.

Not that he wanted to—Barber seemed content to let Parrish do everything. Ben Gritz asked how much they wanted to pay the preacher and for music. He suggested $100 for the preacher and $50 for music. Barber said that wasn't enough.

They were all close to April, Parrish reminded him, and probably wouldn't want anything. Nevertheless, they decided to pay $250 for the preacher and $100 for the music. Barber said it was all right for April to be buried directly behind her mother, Nancy. Then he asked Parrish to buy the two plots behind April's mother, two more behind Parrish's first husband and the two plots behind Parrish's sister-in-law, Valerie.

The price for the six lots totaled $1,200. Parrish said she had intended to buy the plots and just hadn't done it yet. Parrish said it wasn't necessary for Justin to pay for them.

"It's something I want to do for the family," Barber said

They drove to Garden's Edge, a florist, parked and sat in the car for a while. Parrish told Justin she would buy the funeral spray for the casket if he wished. Barber asked her to do it because he knew nothing about flowers. Parrish asked if he knew what April's favorite flowers were. No, he did not. Parrish thought it would be sunflowers. Barber told her that would be fine.

"Be sure to keep track of all you spend," Barber said. "If you pay for the funeral, plots and flowers now, I will pay you back."

Barber told Parrish that he and April used to have insurance policies on each other, but he had let them lapse a month and a half ago. They still had a policy with State Farm, which would cover the funeral expenses and provide for the education of April's siblings, Julie and Kendon. Barber said April had a small policy through her job, but he didn't know what it was worth or who the beneficiary was.

"Call me when April is ready to be viewed, and my mom and I will come back to Hennessey this evening," Barber said. He asked Parrish, a lawyer, what to do about April's checking account and credit cards. Barber told Parrish that she could have the diamond rings and necklace that Parrish had given to April.

The next day, they met in Hennessey to see April. Justin's brother, Charles, a naval officer, had come from Japan to be there, and Parrish brought Rameson Kamesh, a family friend, to view April's body and to see Kendon and Julie. After paying their respects, Parrish asked Justin if they would have an opportunity to talk before he returned to Jacksonville.

"I need to hear all the details," she said.

"Sure."

Parrish told him that if he had time, she was ready then and there.

"Okay," Justin said. "This is so hard." He started to cry, and then told Parrish that he and April were celebrating their anniversary late. They hadn't celebrated before because his family, plus Kendon and Julie, were in town. After dining and playing pool, Barber said, April wanted to go for a drive and walk on the beach. Barber told Parrish they went to the beach on their previous anniversary and also on April's birthday.

(The night of the murder, Barber told detectives and paramedics that he didn't know where they had been on the beach. He did not mention having been there before.)

Barber told Parrish the story about the assailant, of finding April in the water, dragging her to the boardwalk and leaving for help.

Parrish asked if he had seen the car that had been reported there and was gone when he left. Barber said no. He said it might have been because the gate was locked, and Barber parked on the side of the highway and that he and April had walked about fifty yards to the boardwalk. Barber explained that he didn't have his telephone with him. Although he knew April's phone was in her purse, Barber said, he couldn't find the purse. (It was later found on the center console, where she always kept it.)

Parrish asked if anyone had broken into his car. Barber said he didn't know.

"Well, were the windows broken?" she asked. "Could you tell if they tried to force open the doors?"

Because his mother drove when Barber retrieved the car from the SJSO, Barber said, he hadn't noticed any attempt to break in. But none of the windows had been broken.

"I would have given him anything," Barber said. "It's all my fault. I should have gotten the gun. I almost had the gun."

"Did the guy have an accent?" Parrish asked. "Was he from another country? Was he mumbling? Why couldn't you understand him?"

"I just couldn't. The guy was not acting right."

The lawyer side of Patti Parrish seemed to come to the fore as she questioned Barber. He might have felt like he was on the witness stand. Apparently, Barber was intimidated by strong women; one of April's friends said his greatest fear was that April would become Patti Parrish.

Parrish was relentless. Did the man come up from behind? No, he was coming toward them. Barber said he was looking at the water and April saw the assailant first. Parrish wanted to know if Justin thought the man took April off and raped her. Barber said he didn't think so, because she was clothed. What about the gun? A doctor or nurse told him it was probably a .22-caliber gun. It had to be small, Barber said. It did not look like a gun.

How could it be possible that he was shot five times with non–life-threatening results while April was killed with one bullet? Parrish persisted.

Barber said he didn't know. He didn't see what happened to April. Barber said that he was drunk and that April had been drinking.

The murder had happened just when things were finally starting to go their way, Parrish said. They were getting out of debt. The house in Covington was sold; insurance had fully reimbursed them on the stolen Audi; April had sold her Isuzu and was about to finish her training to be a dosimetrist. Barber agreed that was true and told Parrish that April was already looking for a job in Jacksonville. (She was actually looking for a job in Oklahoma, but Barber didn't know that.) It had been awfully hard living apart for so long, he added.

They discussed payment for April's funeral for a while

and Parrish acknowledged that she would pay. Barber said he would reimburse her when he cashed April's State Farm life insurance policy. Parrish said that might take some time because the death was a homicide; she assured him there was no hurry.

Parrish had something else to say. "I told him that April's killer would be found. Her death would not be unavenged." She reminded him there were friends and family who had the resources to pay for whatever it took. "I told him, if necessary, I would hire a private detective and that I would never let this case go unsolved. It may be a long time before this is solved and maybe never, but I will never quit trying."

Barber was silent; then they said good-bye.

On August 23, 2002, April's funeral was held. More than three hundred people—more than the church's entire congregation—attended to say farewell. The town officials honored April by naming her Hennessey's "Woman of the Year." A high-school friend remembered, "She was very popular, pretty, smart and funny. A cheerleader, a scholar, an honest person. I thought it was wonderful that she would talk to everyone—even the 'undesirables.' She was a genuine lady. She made me become a better person."

After the funeral, Justin told Parrish that he was leaving the next morning for Jacksonville because he wanted to help police with the investigation. Barber said he had been thinking about what Parrish had said yesterday and her angry determination to do whatever it took to find April's killer. He had been unemotional before, Justin said, because he was so stricken with grief. Now, he said, the anger was setting in. He, too, was determined to do everything he could to find the killer.

With a determined lawyer devoted to catching her niece's killer, and the police investigating him, Justin Barber may have also felt the stirrings of anxiety.

* * *

Justin Barber had not seen Amber Mitchell since April died. His first words to April's best friend at the funeral were bizarre and didn't seem to be those of a grieving husband. He said, "Thank you for introducing April to Brian. I always knew I had a chance compared to him."

Mitchell had introduced April to Brian Stedman in the autumn of 1998 and they had gone on a date. By socializing with mutual friends, Justin and April had met. After that, there were no boyfriends but Justin. "There was no one in the picture after that," Mitchell said.

Mitchell was perplexed and uneasy. She had already expressed her conviction to Detective Cole that Barber had killed April. Now Barber was thanking her for introducing April to one of her previous suitors.

Mitchell said they didn't talk much because she was "very uncomfortable" and felt that Barber was, too. What little conversation there was centered on Barber's complaints that April's family had squeezed him out of helping to make April's funeral arrangements.

"I feel really bad that the family was making all the arrangements and taking care of everything," Barber said.

Mitchell said she was "kind of surprised" by this complaint. "When we were sitting in a circle with the minister talking about the service, the family repeatedly asked for his opinion on stuff and he never had one," Mitchell said. "And he was given several opportunities to voice his opinion and didn't exercise them."

Mitchell said she thought Barber was about to offer an explanation for this. They had stood together without saying a word. Then Barber said, "It's just been so hard . . . so hard. . . ."

Mitchell wasn't about to listen to self-pitying comments from the man she thought murdered her best friend. There will be plenty of time to talk later, Mitchell said, but that, for now, they should just concentrate on getting through the funeral. Mitchell didn't talk to him after the funeral.

Just a week or two before her death, April had told Mitchell that she was feeling lost. April said she didn't feel like she knew what was going on in her husband's life. Living apart was hard, and after commuting to see Barber after finishing work on Friday, April was often too tired to socialize.

Justin had made new friends and he rarely took April out, even on Saturday or Sunday. During this same period, he wanted her to meet different people. He blamed April for not wanting to socialize more. But the times they did go out, April said, she felt like an outsider. April felt increasingly alienated from her husband.

Talking about it always led to arguments.

Why didn't he share things with her from his life? she would ask.

"Because you wouldn't understand my fucking problems anyway," he said.

Mitchell remembered that in almost all of the conversations she had with April over the years, Barber was always talking about getting ahead at Rayonier. But in the past few months, April had told her things that made Mitchell suspect that Justin was getting frustrated and bored with his job. This didn't mean much to Amber, because she had often changed jobs to advance her career, but it was a change in Barber's way of thinking. April told Mitchell that Barber was offered a transfer/promotion with Rayonier, but he was thinking of refusing it so he could remain in Jacksonville. April said Barber liked the social life he had developed in Jacksonville and didn't want to leave.

Barber was increasingly critical of April, according to

Mitchell. He warned her not to gain weight, even though she retained her petite 112-pound figure. Justin was so obsessed with his own body image that every month he tried on a pair of jeans he had worn in high school. If the waist was tight, he dieted until the pants fit.

April told Mitchell that their high-school anniversaries were coming up before long. April joked that she wouldn't attend unless she was really skinny or pregnant, because she didn't want to be overweight. Justin said he wouldn't go unless he was a vice president at Rayonier. On further reflection, that wasn't enough to lure him: he said he would also have to be the commencement speaker.

April would not attend that anniversary or any others. Everything she had was taken away from her. Tragedy had been an enduring part of her life, but it had never destroyed her optimism and sunny disposition, or the happiness she brought into the lives of others, or the comfort she gave to patients with cancer. A sudden violent death destroyed that forever.

Chapter 7

Hennessey is in Kingfisher County near Stillwater. It is a rural town of about two thousand people, but April would have stood out anywhere. April's mother, Nancy Shaw Lott, entered the beautiful little girl in beauty pageants, where April glowed as the brightest star. She was a country girl with a Hollywood sparkle. April possessed a strong sense of family and loyalty, and was unmovable when it came to everyone getting a fair break.

"It didn't matter who you were, April would stick up for you if you were the underdog," one old friend said. "I didn't want to be like April, I wanted *to be* April. Everybody loved her."

April was a high achiever in everything she did. She was one of the best students in her class and was popular. She was comfortable in situations ranging from a science lab to eating in a fancy restaurant. April's radiant good looks and sunny personality belied a young life that had been filled with tragedy. April was a senior in high school when her mother was diagnosed with lung cancer and died after six months of excruciating pain. April was not just big sister and best friend to her brother, Kendon, age one, and sister, Julie, nine, she assumed the role of surrogate mother to them and caregiver to her mother before she died. April's father worked in the oil fields, but he fell apart when his wife became ill. He got mixed up with drugs and was sent to prison. April wasn't bitter about shouldering such a heavy load; she didn't get angry with her father, never abandoned him, and she telephoned, wrote and visited him regularly until she died. She visited him a week before she was murdered.

Other relatives took the children in, but April was the focal point of their lives while they were still at home with their dying mother.

"She was my best friend, my sister and my mother," Julie remembered. "She took care of us. She would get me up for school, get me off to school. She'd cook us dinner. She just took the place of our mother."

Nancy Lott died when April was seventeen. In spite of all the extra work, April was an All-State Scholar and salutatorian of her graduating class. She was also voted "Most Likely to Succeed."

"Everything I am, or hope to be, I owe to my angel mother," April said as she accepted her diploma and exited the stage with a spring in her step.

The family wasn't wealthy, but with a combination of scholarships, family help, part-time jobs and student loans, April attended premed at Oklahoma State University (OSU). April remembered her mother's suffering and decided she wanted to help people with cancer. She transferred to the University of Oklahoma (OU), where she earned a degree in radiology.

"She was very giving. She was full of life, fun to be around and very supportive if we ever needed anything," a high-school classmate of April's said. "April always had a smile."

April was popular in college, too. She was invited into the Kappa Delta Sorority during rush week. It was at OU that April met Amber Mitchell, a pledge sorority sister who became her best friend. Mitchell knew a handsome blond named Justin Barber, who was smart, religious, had a strong sense of family and was going places in the world. Barber was enrolled in an elite MBA program at OU and was selected to enroll in a program to put him on a fast track to top management at Rayonier, one of the world's largest corporations. Rayonier's 2003 Form SEC 10-K, a document that publicly owned corporations must file with the federal government, showed sales that year of more than $1.1 billion. The company reported thirty-seven subsidiaries in seven different countries.

April and Barber seemed to be made for one another. They were both blond, smart (Barber was valedictorian of his high-school class, as was his older brother, Charles), and placed high values on church and family. Barber grew up in Wetumka, a town of 1,500 people, even smaller than April's hometown. The two towns were four hundred miles apart and the two had never met.

Justin grew up on a 120-acre ranch owned by his parents, and he lived a typically rural life. He herded cattle, fed livestock, rode horses, was studious and became an accomplished high-school athlete. Even as a boy, Justin took his intellectual development seriously, and he took his Church of Christ upbringing to heart. An adult who knew Barber as a boy said, "I always thought of him as the all-American boy." Barber enrolled in OSU and met a girl named Dana Renae Montgomery and they were married on December 23, 1992.

Little information is available about the marriage. Dana said he wasn't very good with money and couldn't hold a job. Barber earned his bachelor's degree from OU and bounced from one menial job to another, until Dana divorced him on June 10, 1997. The divorce caused a major upheaval in Barber's family and he felt that he had embarrassed all of his relatives. Barber was so distressed that he made a halfhearted attempt to commit suicide with a butter knife.

After the divorce, Barber enrolled in the OU MBA program, where he attended classes with Mitchell. "He was the best and brightest of us," Mitchell said. Mitchell thought April and Barber would make a good match. April liked the fact that Barber was so intelligent and single-minded in his desire to make something of himself. The two met at a social occasion and lightning struck. April thought Justin Barber was not only dynamite handsome, but the most intelligent man she had ever met. Hopeful young men swarmed around April like hyperkinetic bees, but she wanted only one man in her life: Justin Barber.

Barber seemed smitten by the same qualities April saw in him. She was intelligent, ambitious, religious, funny and committed to God and family. "There was a deep sadness in her that was somewhat obvious," Barber observed. "But she hid it. And when she smiled, she lit up the room."

Barber told April about his previous marriage and the recent divorce. She had mixed feelings about it. To her, the divorce showed a lack of commitment, but the anguish and embarrassment it caused Barber and his family made her believe that he would try all the harder to prevent being divorced again.

About the same time Barber was being divorced from his first wife, April's mother died, and April moved into her aunt Patti Parrish's house in Oklahoma City, where Parrish lived with her son, Johnny.

When they began to date, April and Barber started to talk about getting married. They had plans to bring Kendon and Julie into their home and become a family. At the time, April's brother and sister were living in Hennessy between their uncle Jim's and uncle Mike's houses. All three of the kids missed one another.

Justin told April he wanted to raise Kendon and Julie as their family. Barber seemed excited about it and wanted April's brother and sister to move in with them right after the marriage. April was cautioned by friends and relatives that this would be a huge strain on a new marriage. They advised her to wait until she and Barber adjusted to living as husband and wife.

"One of the things I like about Justin is that he accepts the fact I want to raise the kids," April told Parrish. She added that Justin would work hard to make the marriage work because of his previous divorce.

I did not know a lot about Justin's [former] wife, Parrish wrote later. *But I knew it (the divorce) was a big source of contention between Barber and his family. April said they took the divorce very badly and Barber felt he had embarrassed and let his family down. Once April mentioned that [Dana's] picture was in the local newspaper along with her husband's and Justin was angry because it again brought attention to the fact he had failed at a previous marriage and that his ex-wife's new husband was black.*

Parrish told April she had concerns about the kids moving so soon. *I told her being a sister was much different than being a mother figure,* Parrish wrote, *and that it would be hard to go from being a sister to a disciplinarian. April had tremendous guilt issues because she said she promised her mom on her deathbed that she would raise the kids. This, coupled with the fact that her father was unable to care for the kids, made her desire to raise them even stronger.*

April also planned to have a large wedding in Oklahoma so friends and family could attend. It was more work than she had expected. Halfway through the planning, April and Justin agreed to have a small wedding in

The Bahamas, with just a few family members and friends present.

In late July 1999, April and Barber packed their things and boarded a flight bound for Nassau, The Bahamas. The weather was glorious and the islands were like small emeralds set in a sea the color of clear turquoise. The sand was as fine and white as powdered sugar. April and Barber were perfectly satisfied with their accommodations at the Breezes, a luxury beachfront hotel.

Back in Oklahoma, Patti Parrish had asked her friend, Judge Vicki Shawson, to go to The Bahamas with her so she could attend the wedding. She packed April's white wedding dress into a suitcase and flew to The Bahamas with Shawson. They were booked into another beachside resort called Atlantis. Barber later complained to April that the Breezes, where they were booked, wasn't nearly as nice as Atlantis.

On August 4, 1999, the red sun seemed to coalesce and rise from the still blue waters of the Caribbean Sea. Parrish was busy trying to steam the wrinkles out of April's beautiful white wedding gown. An area on the beach was set aside for the marriage ceremony. April looked as if she had stepped out of a fairy tale, with her beautiful gown, petite figure and glowing blond tresses. In formal black tie, Justin Barber could have rivaled any Prince Charming with his chiseled good looks and wavy golden hair.

There, on a beach, their life together began. Three years later, on a much different kind of beach, their life together ended in a blaze of gunfire.

The investigation in St. Augustine remained in high gear during April's funeral arrangements and burial in Hennessey. The SJSO subpoenaed telephone records and credit Chapter 8 reports, checked gun purchases and continued the thorny search at Guana Park for evidence. It was hot, muggy and miserable in the thickets.

From Oklahoma, Justin telephoned Sergeant Fagan to check on the progress of the investigation and asked what he could do to help. Once again, Fagan told Barber the best thing he could do was try to remember everything he could about the assailant.

"It was so dark, I couldn't see him," Barber said. "I would never be able to identify him. It was dark and I was very drunk. We were both drunk."

"Even if it was dark, if you looked at the guy, our composite artist might be able to pull the description from your memory," Fagan said. "When you have some time to think, maybe the guy's face will come to you in a dream or you may remember more. Anything you remember will give us something to work with, since we use composite drawings to eliminate people."

Barber did remember more about the shooting. "I jumped in between them and was fighting with him for the gun," he told Fagan. "I didn't want him pointing the gun at April." Barber said he would be back soon and wanted to help.

The detectives met regularly to discuss the case; most important, the sixteen inconsistencies and outright lies they had found:

(1) When Barber asked for help at A1A and Ponte Vedra Lakes Boulevard, he said he didn't know where April was. The truth is, he knew that Guana Beach was where they were going for a walk. Or perhaps make love.

(2) Barber said he forgot his cell phone. But everyone said he *always* carried his cell phone and didn't even have a landline phone in his condominium.

(3) Barber said he couldn't find April's purse to use her cell phone to call for help, but the purse was on the

center console, where April always kept it, with the telephone inside.

(4) The aerial photos of the beach did not show a third set of footprints where the struggle allegedly took place.

(5) The drag marks weren't consistent with the marks that would have been made if Barber had carried April in the ways he had described.

(6) Barber said both he and April were drunk. The waiter at Carrabba's said they only had one drink. The autopsy showed no alcohol or drugs in April's body.

(7) Barber said the couple had no problems and were economically sound. April's friends and family said they argued constantly, and they were heavily in debt. Their finances were kept separate and April didn't even know how much her husband earned. Until weeks before April was killed, they owed mortgages on two houses, plus rent on a house, and had living expenses at both houses. Barber had high payments on an expensive Audi, which had been conveniently stolen and dumped in the river only weeks before. Insurance paid him more than he owed for the Audi. Justin Barber had accumulated $59,000 in credit card debt *alone* in the past twelve months.

(8) The blood flow pattern on April's face wound couldn't have occurred if she had been dead in the surf. Furthermore, there would have been blood smears and spatters everywhere as Barber moved April's body into different positions. Instead, there was only blood flowing from April's left nostril, left side of her mouth and down her cheek. The coroner said April died from a single bullet wound fired from where her body was found.

(9) April suffered from partial drowning. Why didn't the assailant finish the drowning instead of dragging her back to the boardwalk to shoot her? April would not have

survived the partial drowning without help from medical technology.

(10) Why would an assailant shoot a man four times and leave him with superficial wounds, while killing a woman with a single well-placed shot to the face?

(11) Why would a robber shoot his victims and leave without taking anything from them?

(12) The officer who investigated the burglary at April's house in Thomasville thought it was done by someone familiar with the interior. He urged April to be cautious. Had that been a failed attempt to kill April?

(13) Why had Barber shopped so hard for two-million-dollar life insurance policies on himself and April less than a year before the murder? Why did he want it kept secret from her family and friends?

(14) If Barber was the killer, why didn't he finish drowning April instead of taking her back to the board-walk to shoot her? Would that have upset his carefully developed plan?

(15) Would a man deliberately risk death by shooting himself four times to take suspicion off himself?

(16) It was understandable that a husband would lie about having an affair, but the police now had the name of the woman: Shannon Kennedy. Were there others?

The police had a great deal of circumstantial evidence that pointed to Justin Barber as the killer, but nothing solid. Most of what they learned during their interviews was inadmissible in court because it would be hearsay. They had no murder weapon and no eyewitnesses. The forensic evidence—such as DNA, blood spatter, ballistics and blood flow—was still being processed. There was no telling how long it would take to get those results, and Chris Hendry was still working on Barber's home computer hard drive at the FDLE's laboratory in Tallahassee.

The state attorney didn't have enough evidence

against Justin Barber to show probable cause and win a conviction in court. So far, there was no case against Barber and little chance of putting one together. He was either the luckiest victim or the smartest, most cold-blooded killer the St. Johns County police and prosecutors had ever encountered.

Detective Cole spoke with Patti Parrish by telephone and she told him she had talked with Barber at the funeral home. Among other things, Parrish said Barber told her that he and April had life insurance policies on one another, but he had allowed them to lapse about a month ago. At the time, Barber didn't realize that Parrish and the SJSO knew about the two-million-dollar life insurance policy on April.

Later, Sergeant Fagan received a call from John Hoschgraefe. Hoschgraefe was in the insurance business and called a company in Plant City, Florida, to find out if the two-million-dollar life insurance policy on April had expired. Barber told the police that the policy had lapsed. Barber lied. The premium for April's policy was paid in June and the policy was in full force, Hoschgraefe told Fagan, and the company had already marked it as payable on the Monday morning after April was murdered. The two-million-dollar policy was sold by J. Jervey Agency in Jacksonville.

Barber had received April's pertinent information and shopped for the insurance by himself. He decided the amounts of the policies and how they should be set up. Barber decided on the two-million-dollar policies based on how much each of them earned. Jervey later told the police there was nothing unusual about how Barber went about getting the policies. Each would pay the premiums on their separate insurance policies. But in June, Barber stopped making payments to his policy and let it lapse. April paid the premium on her policy and kept the insurance in force. Justin Barber was the beneficiary.

The police saw this as a clever way for Barber to give himself "plausible deniability" if his own policy lapsed and April's didn't. It was more evidence that pointed toward Barber implementing a cold-blooded plan to murder his wife and get away with it.

On August 22, 2002, Detective Cole talked with Barber by telephone and learned that Barber was returning to Jacksonville on August 24, instead of August 27, because he was anxious to help with the investigation. He told Cole, "Let me know if you find anything, and call me if there is anything I can do."

Patti Parrish told Cole on August 23 that Barber intended to return early. She thought it was perplexing because his older brother, Charles, a career U.S. Navy officer stationed in Japan, was flying in specifically to be with him.

Dana Vinson, Barber's former wife, returned a telephone call to Cole just after noon the next day. Cole asked if she knew anything from her previous marriage to Barber that might be important to the case. Vinson said they were both young when they got married, and he wasn't good at handling money, nor could he hold a job. At one point, Barber borrowed money from her family to start a business, but it failed after a few months.

"He always wanted something for nothing," Vinson said.

One other thing that Vinson found interesting was how often Barber seemed to be burglarized. Vinson said she believed Barber received insurance money to replace the stolen items with new ones. There was one incidence of behavior that Dana had found odd. Once, she came into the apartment and couldn't see Barber, but there was a large, man-shaped object covered with a blanket on a living-room chair. Dana thought it was Barber, playing a trick on her, and she ignored the lump. After about fifteen minutes, the lump stirred and Barber's head emerged from the blanket.

"Oh," he said. "I didn't know you were here."

Dana said he never explained what he was doing, and she never asked.

Chapter 8

Cole and Shaw had picked up e-mail correspondence between April and Justin Barber in Thomasville. On May 29, 2002, April had e-mailed Justin at his Rayonier company computer to ask how much they paid for life insurance. She wanted to know if the rates went up every year. April said a friend wanted insurance and had asked her.

Barber replied: We pay one thousand seventy two dollars a year each for two million dollars coverage each. It's a twenty-year term fixed rate policy, which means the premium is fixed for twenty years; after twenty years, the premium will be reset annually at a much higher rate. Keep in mind that we were in the sub-thirty year-old bracket (some of us still are) when we signed up! Isn't Ramish (Nair) self-ensured by now?

April replied: What is self-insured? How do you know our rates off the top of your head? He wants to know where to look for a hit man.

On September 4, about 3:30 P.M., Justin Barber arrived at the SJSO to talk with Fagan. She escorted Barber to the CID and offered him a soft drink, which he declined.

"How are you doing?" Fagan asked.

"Okay, because I'm blocking everything out," Barber said.

"That's not good, you're just repressing everything," Fagan told him. "There's a lot of help available and you really ought to get some."

Barber said a counselor at the hospital had talked with him and given him information on other help he could receive. "So far I'm staying on top of it."

Fagan told Barber that because of the life insurance on April and his affair with Kennedy, it made people ask questions as to whether or not he had something to do with his wife's murder. She informed him that she needed to advise him of his constitutional rights before she asked any further questions. Barber said he understood (he had denied the affair until he learned that Shannon Kennedy was in the next room and admitted to it).

Fagan read from a rights form, Barber acknowledged that he understood and signed the form.

"Our goal at this moment is to eliminate you as a suspect," Fagan said.

"I understand."

Fagan told him the SJSO had a support group for family members of victims of violent crimes, and he could probably get assistance through his insurance at work. Barber said he didn't know what he was going to do. Barber complained that he couldn't sleep. The doctor at the hospital had given him nothing for sleep. Barber said he didn't have a sleep pattern yet, but he was going back to work in a day or two.

"I didn't do anything last week. I just curled up in a ball."

Barber told her that he had been to Thomasville to pick up April's furniture and things, but the house was empty when he got there. He said that Patti and John probably took everything.

"Did you give them permission to do that?"

"Patti said she wanted a few things and I said okay, but I didn't know they were going to take everything."

"Maybe she thought she was doing you a favor by cleaning the house out so you wouldn't have to worry about it."

"Maybe. I collected all of April's mail and made arrangements for it to be forwarded to my address."

In Thomasville, Barber returned the house keys and filled out forms for April's company life insurance and retirement fund. April also had life insurance on Barber.

Fagan made small talk for a while and then got down to business. "Did you and April use your computer a lot?" she asked.

"I do," Barber said. "I use the Internet, check newspapers, and surf. I use e-mail a lot."

Fagan asked Barber to describe his job at Rayonier. He told her that he was the vice president's assistant and answered directly to him. Barber said he was the liaison between the field and corporate headquarters when there was a capital project.

"Is your job important?" Fagan asked.

"I'd like to think so."

Barber explained that he was in a "fast-track management program," where Rayonier placed one new MBA each year. He was the last person selected before the corporation stopped the practice. Barber said his starting salary was $63,000 a year and that his first position was as an analyst.

"I add strength to the management team," he said. "One of our premier companies is in New Zealand. I travel there three times a year. I just missed a trip to Chile."

Barber had been employed with Rayonier for three and a half years. He told Fagan that top management seemed "pleased" with him. A workday, he said, varied from banker's hours to sixteen hours. "Whatever it takes," Barber said. April decided to pursue her career in Thomasville, he said, when he was promoted to Jacksonville headquarters.

"April tested solid," he said. "She could handle any difficulty."

In addition to being in the Rayonier program at OU, Barber was working as an analyst for Dow Jones Market when he met April and she was a waitress at Lone Star Steakhouse. April was also a college student. "We fell in love pretty quick," Barber said. He proposed to her on Valentine's Day, 1998. Rayonier hired him almost immediately and sent him to Connecticut. Barber said he and April had a "long-distance relationship" for the six months he was in Connecticut.

Sergeant Fagan asked about his and April's financial situation. Barber was almost blasé about it. "We both made a lot of money and we both spent a lot of money," he said. Their expenses were high because, Barber said, they still paid the mortgage on their Georgia house, as well as the Jacksonville condominium and April's rent, until June, when the house in Georgia finally sold.

"Even with the second house payment, we were not struggling," he said. "We had a combined annual income of one hundred fifty thousand dollars, with seventy percent of that going to bills." Barber varied their income, depending on what he thought were his best interests.

He added that they were paying on three cars until his expensive Audi was stolen, less than two months ago.

"Why did you get two-million-dollar life insurance policies?" Fagan asked.

Barber laughed and poked fun at himself. "That was my 'turning-thirty crisis,'" he said. "That was when I got the Audi and when I thought I needed to get a two-million-dollar life insurance policy." He explained that his father died young and he wanted enough to provide for April, Julie, Kendon and his mother.

"I researched life insurance and found that it was so affordable," he said.

But a month or so ago, he and April had another discussion about life insurance. "I was over my 'turning-thirty crisis' and we decided we didn't really need the insurance." Barber said it was important to keep *his* life insurance for the reasons he previously stated. He said he paid the last $250 premium on his insurance and thought "that was the end of it." April also had life insurance through State Farm. He believed that "the big policy" had lapsed "because that is what we decided to do, and I didn't pay the premium on it."

Although Barber earned more than April, he said, she made the mortgage payments on the house in Covington "because she had extra income." He didn't mention that April worked a second job for that income, or her tearful telephone calls to Patti Parrish because she was being crushed by such a heavy financial burden. When Barber's Audi was stolen in June 2002 and dumped in the St. Johns River, he said his "turning-thirty crisis" was over and that he bought a less expensive Toyota 4Runner. Barber paid for the Toyota with one of his credit cards. Barber didn't mention his anger at having to buy a less expensive car because it would appear that he couldn't afford anything better.

Barber paid for the 4Runner with a credit card, even though he had a $700 monthly mortgage payment, and owed $50,000 in credit card debt. A week before April was killed, Barber told Fagan, he refinanced the condo from a thirty-year mortgage to fifteen years. This increased the payments by $200 a month. Strangely enough, April cosigned on the remortgaging on August 15, just two days before she was murdered. She telephoned Nair and said, "I feel like I've signed my life away." Barber didn't mention that when he was transferred to Jacksonville, April made the entire mortgage payment on their house in Covington, even though she had to pay rent for a house nearer to work in Thomasville.

Fagan asked about the handgun in the Audi that was missing when the stolen car was hauled from the river. Barber said he bought the gun in late 1999 or early 2000 from a sporting-goods store in Folkston, Georgia, near the Okefenokee Swamp. Having a gun in the house seemed natural to him, Barber said, because his father had a .22-caliber pistol and a .30-30 Winchester rifle. Shooting had become a new hobby, Barber said, and he shot at the Gun Gallery range on Beach Boulevard in Jacksonville on many occasions.

"Did you ever buy any other gun besides the nine-millimeter?" Fagan asked.

Barber hung his head and looked down for several seconds, then said, "No."

Fagan was interested to learn that Barber had formal training with guns. The American Legion sent him to a training program one summer with the state patrol when he was growing up. He was taught self-defense and high-speed driving, as well as marksmanship. Barber told Fagan he bought the 9mm handgun to keep in the car as a "protection thing" on his trips to Oklahoma.

Barber continued to insist that everything had been fine with the marriage.

"We had our ups and downs, but no real problems," he said.

He denied having abused April physically or mentally and insisted that the only affair he had was with Shannon Kennedy.

They took a short break and met again later. "Is there any problem with letting us look through any paperwork at your condo?" Fagan asked. Barber said it was fine.

"Would you have a problem if we had someone, possibly with the FDLE, look through your computer?"

"I don't have a problem with that."

"Could we meet you at the condo later this evening?"

"That's fine," Barber said. "Are you investigating anyone else besides me?"

"We're still looking for the K-car," Fagan said. "We haven't received any other information."

Barber told Fagan he had considered some things the police should check out. A newspaper had reported that a man whose car was stopped by police pointed a gun at one of the officers. This happened three days after he and April were shot. The newspaper reported that the man had three guns in his car. Barber suggested that they also check out a man who had been arrested for attacking a police officer with a knife.

In Florida, incidences involving guns being pointed at people are as common as seagulls. "We get numerous reports every day about people pointing guns at other people," Fagan told him. "Besides, Willard, Georgia, is a long way from Guana Park. You and your wife were shot, not stabbed." She paused a moment. "We'll see you at the condo in a little while."

Cooperative as always, Justin Barber met Fagan and Shaw at his condo door with the office computer wrapped and ready for transport. Shaw told him that before they could do anything, he had to read a Permission to Search form, and he needed sign it.

"Do you need to go through everything in the condo?" he asked.

"No, just the paperwork upstairs," Fagan said.

"Fine."

Upstairs in the bedroom, Fagan saw a check ledger

beside Barber's computer. Barber picked it up immediately and said it belonged to April. He opened it to show Fagan that April had paid her life insurance premium to First Colony in June. Fagan saw another check ledger by Barber's computer, which he said was his "old" one. It was fine with him if the detectives took the ledgers with them. Barber showed them a filing cabinet containing what he said was all of his paperwork.

"Can we look through it?" Fagan asked.

"Okay."

Shaw put the files in three plastic bags and put them in the police car. Barber later complained that he didn't give the detectives permission to search his files. The only thing he authorized them to take, he would say, was his computer hard drive.

Fagan noticed that the closets seemed to have been cleaned up since they last visited the condo. Fagan noticed that April's duffel bag was missing. She asked Barber what had happened to it.

"I cleaned out all of April's belongings and got rid of them," he said. "I have a bag of her clothes downstairs to give to the Salvation Army."

Chapter 9

Fagan had picked up Barber's desktop computer at home on their first visit to the condominium. Computers use similar technology so that a computer in Jacksonville can communicate with another one anywhere in the world. A computer stores this information on a hard drive.

Hard drives can store millions of documents, photographs, music and assorted information. A user can look at this information anytime. When the data aren't wanted anymore, they can be put in a delete basket. The information can be restored to operating status. Entering a command to empty the delete basket removes all traces of the information from the computer's operating system. But the information doesn't vanish into thin air. It is transferred into arcane nooks and crannies that can only be discovered by experts and special software. Even then, it isn't always possible to retrieve the deleted data.

Barber's home computer and the laptop he used at Rayonier were dissected by Chris Hendry, a forensic specialist in the FDLE's computer technology laboratory. Hendry, a veteran of almost twenty years in the FDLE's forensic department, used sophisticated software to make duplicate copies of the information on both hard drives and the originals were returned to the evidence locker.

All Internet downloads, e-mails, documents and financial records that had ever been put into the computers could be accessed. Barber had downloaded hundreds of songs from the Internet as well. The information found on his home computer showed that Barber's financial situation was far more precarious than he had said. He was in debt up to his ears.

Barber had engaged in day-trading in the stock market. Day traders buy and sell fast-moving stocks minute by minute in the hope of making fast money. Unfortunately, it doesn't usually work that way. Day-trading is so risky that the U.S. Securities and Exchange Commission (SEC) publishes a free document titled *Day Trading: Your Dollars at Risk*.

It is a warning: *Be prepared to suffer severe financial losses; day traders do not "invest"; day-trading is an extremely stressful and expensive full-time job*. To make it even more fiscally suicidal, day traders often buy stock with money borrowed from their brokers and can lose more money than they invested and have to repay the brokers.

During the past year, Barber's stocks went south. He bought on margin and paid margin calls in one of the worst possible ways—with credit card cash advances from companies that charge the highest interest rates in the nation.

In less than a year of trading, Barber accumulated credit card debt of almost sixty thousand dollars to pay his losses. Besides that debt, Barber had a car payment, two home mortgages, student loans and his personal living expenses. He and his wife kept their finances separate, except for vacations. April paid her own expenses from her personal checking account.

"The debt could be a motive for murder, since Barber was the beneficiary of April's two-million-dollar life insurance policy," Detective Cole reasoned.

Barber often used Google to conduct Internet research. He had entered more than twenty thousand key words for Google to search. The words that popped out to the SJSO detectives were: trauma cases gunshot right chest and medical trauma gunshot chest.

Those searches could have a direct link to the case. Did Barber shoot himself to look like a victim instead of a killer?

Barber's involvement in day-trading showed that he wasn't afraid of taking chances. In debt, with his wife threatening to divorce him, would Barber risk his life to hit a two-million-dollar jackpot? He would not get money in a divorce. But what if April died first? Why would he be boning up on gunshot wounds to the right chest?

Barber researched how much blood someone would have to lose to be considered dead, providing there was no body. He asked how to go about immigrating to Brazil. He also researched the key words Florida divorce and Life Insurance Homicide.

As rich as this computer treasure seemed, there was no way to know when the searches were initiated and deleted. Without a time that made the research relevant to the murder, it wasn't evidence. The information was somewhere on the hard drive, but the technology to find it didn't exist. It became even more frustrating for the detectives that Barber had downloaded and deleted a song on his home computer on the night of April's death. It was downloaded just hours before April was killed: "Used to Love Her" by the rock group Guns N' Roses. The lyrics are about a man who loved a woman, but he had to kill and bury her because of her complaining.

Had Barber played this song to psych himself up for what he planned to do? Unfortunately, for the song to be entered into evidence, it had to be played from the original hard drive. That wasn't possible without restoring it, which could amount to evidence tampering.

Some of the detectives wanted the state attorney (SA) to issue an arrest warrant charging Barber with murder, but the SA saw no case. The detectives were frustrated, especially Cole, who was the new kid on the block. "I was a rookie detective and I wanted everything to end up in court," he said.

"They (the SA office) wanted everything beyond a reasonable doubt. They wanted finances to be definitive and the computer evidence to be definitive. I was frustrated, but they were absolutely right."

The frustration would last more than three years.

April wasn't sure she wanted to marry Justin Barber, even after she had accepted his proposal and planned the wedding. Detectives Cole and Shaw learned this during interviews with April's friends and relatives in Oklahoma in early September 2002. Something nagged at her not to go through with it. She expressed this in vague terms to friends a few weeks before the wedding was to take place.

It appeared that April knew the marriage would take a lot of work on her part. Barber made it clear to her that his career was of foremost importance. Rayonier's executive path called for them to move often, and she was expected to quit whatever job she had and go with him. She had to be petite and not gain an ounce. Barber rarely complimented her and often criticized her grammar, demeanor, cleaning and even her personal hygiene.

April was initially struck by how much more mature

Barber seemed than other young men she knew. He was intelligent and focused on his career. He knew where he was going. Most of April's boyfriends didn't have a clue. April even considered Barber's previous divorce as a plus. The divorce had upset him so much that she thought he would try hard to make their marriage work.

April had no doubts, however, about Barber's family. She adored them. "She got a big dose of us," said Linda, Barber's mother. "She was so gracious. We loved her like a daughter."

April had a tight schedule that spring. She planned an August wedding to be followed by a short honeymoon. After the honeymoon, Barber was to work for Rayonier in Douglas, Georgia. Barber wanted to buy a house midway between where he and April worked, so neither would have to commute too far. Julie and Kendon would follow and they would become one happy family.

The newlyweds bought a house in Douglas, Georgia, following the honeymoon. Things turned sour within days after they returned from The Bahamas. Barber complained of a rash on his penis. A stunned April listened as he blamed it on her.

"You're dirty," Justin told her. "You gave me herpes."

"You have to see a doctor to find out if it's herpes," April said.

"Well, you've given it to me because you don't keep yourself clean."

April was shocked and mortified. She told friends later that she was terribly hurt by her husband's outburst. Although she was positive she didn't have herpes, April made an appointment with a gynecologist as quickly as possible.

The gynecologist told April that she had nothing

more than a mild yeast infection, which wasn't unusual for any woman. April probably developed the infection, the doctor said, because of the heat and humidity in The Bahamas, and any number of things. It was nothing serious and certainly wasn't herpes or any other sexually transmitted disease.

April told Barber, "The doctor said I have a yeast infection, not herpes." She explained, as best she could, what the doctor had told her.

Barber didn't care what the doctor told April. He told her again that she had given him herpes and that she was "dirty."

It is an understatement to say that their financial arrangements were unusual for a married couple. Barber insisted that April was responsible for all of her personal expenses. Should she need a dress, April would buy it with her own money. She cosigned on the mortgage, even though Barber wouldn't tell her how much the house cost. April was responsible for paying half the mortgage, taxes, electricity, water, food and anything else associated with them as a couple.

April, however, was not allowed to pay for any of these expenses directly. She had to put money into a joint checking account that Barber managed. Barber knew every detail of April's finances, but April didn't even know how much her husband earned. That was none of her business, he said.

Problems plagued the couple before they had been married a month. Nevertheless, Justin pushed ahead with plans to bring April's siblings to live with them. April wanted to have Julie and Kendon, but she wasn't certain how her husband would treat them. The marriage was already strained. They continued to talk about it, and April also talked with Patti Parrish, who had doubts about the arrangement. April wanted to keep the deathbed promise to her mother, and this affected her resolve to wait until she and Barber had adjusted to married life.

"At the time of the marriage, Julie and Kendon were living in Hennessey between their uncle Jim's and uncle Mike's house," Patti Parrish said. "After April and Justin married, Julie and Kendon wanted to move to Georgia. Julie and Kendon were talking to April almost on a continuous basis and they were all very sad and missed one another."

Everyone eventually agreed that Kendon and Julie could live with the Barbers.

"I finally decided that if they did not try it, they would forever regret the fact that they did not have a chance to be together," Parrish said. "I agreed, and in September 1999, the kids were off to Georgia."

Uncle Mike drove Kendon and Julie to Memphis, Tennessee, so that April and Barber could pick them up for the remainder of the trip to Douglas.

Trouble found them before they got home. April and Justin towed Julie's used car, and when they arrived in Douglas, they discovered that the transmission had been damaged too badly to be repaired. Barber's solution increased tension and humiliated April.

April's old Isuzu Rodeo shimmied, knocked and rattled. She needed a more reliable car in order to go to and from work, but she hadn't been able to get enough money together. A newer car didn't seem to be in the cards, because they were so strapped for cash. In Justin's hands, money seemed to vanish.

"Douglas was a real wealthy, ritzy town," Julie said. "Justin had wanted to live in one of the country clubs, where all the rich kids lived. Everybody knew you had money if you lived in the country clubs. The house they bought was a step down, but wealthy people still lived there."

Barber didn't want it to look as if he couldn't afford

the best, according to Julie. "I could have had any car I wanted, like a BMW, but I picked a Firebird," Julie said. "He wanted me to be equal to everyone else at my new school."

Barber bought a Firebird for Julie. It was a flashy model that was much nicer and newer than April's old Isuzu. April told friends that they were broke and having trouble meeting expenses. How did her husband think they could afford a Firebird for her teenage sister while April drove an old Isuzu?

"April did not say much about the Firebird, but I knew she did not like it because she was driving an older car than I was," Julie said.

Barber stayed out late, sometimes until the wee hours of the morning. He didn't tell April where he was. When she asked, Barber said he was hanging out with pals. April knew some of his "pals" were women, but he told her they were married and it shouldn't make her jealous. April felt the sting of her husband's criticism for almost everything she did. He never told her she was pretty. Her grammar was terrible. She wasn't smart enough to understand him. April would try a new hairstyle and ask Barber how he liked it. Barber never had an opinion. Most hurtful was his continuing criticism about her being dirty and warning her not to get fat.

April was tiny, but she took diet pills—against her doctor's advice. She was afraid to gain an ounce. A doctor warned her that it was dangerous, but April was more afraid of giving her husband something to complain about.

About two months after they bought the house in Douglas, Barber rented an apartment for himself in Milledgeville. The town was a two-hour drive to their house in Douglas, but only twenty miles from Barber's office. April was stuck with paying the mortgage and all of the expenses on the home in Douglas. Barber said it was fair because he paid his expenses in Milledgeville. When April asked about sharing the mortgage, Barber said she used more space because of Kendon and Julie.

"April went to see him every weekend," Julie said. "Justin hardly ever came back home. Kendon would go with her. He would throw a fit because it was so boring."

Once Barber rented the apartment, April had difficulty reaching him after office hours. Barber's cell phone was attached to him, almost like an appendage. He never went anywhere without it and always answered when it rang. He was so attached to the cell phone that he didn't have a landline in his apartment. The times that April reached him to ask where he was, Barber would give a vague answer or tell her he was out with friends.

The only piece of furniture in the Milledgeville apartment was an air mattress in the living room. That was where April and Barber slept on the weekends she visited. Those visits became fewer as time passed. April found herself with a full-time job as a radiation therapist, taking care of a house and caring for Kendon and Julie without help from her husband. She was exhausted most of the time.

The transition from sister to surrogate mother and disciplinarian proved to be difficult, as Patti Parrish had warned her. Kendon got into trouble at school for using a calculator, and he and a friend allegedly took Poké-mon cards from another friend. These were small offenses that weren't unusual for children.

Nothing came of it but a scolding, until days later when they were all together at the dinner table. Julie remembered it. "I started to tease Kendon about using a calculator. He got upset and threw a fit and knocked food off the table. Justin got upset and jerked him up by his arm and took him back to his bedroom and spanked him.

April and I were both shocked and just looked at each other like, 'Oh, my God.'"

Barber's outburst had a weird twist. Barber gave Kendon one smack on the behind for every Pokémon card he had taken. But it seemed to turn into a game. After the spanking, Barber allowed Kendon to spank him, one slap for each one that Kendon had received.

Like most teenagers, Julie tested the limits of what she could or couldn't do. Sometimes it got her in trouble. In March 2000, Julie went to a party at a neighbor's house. The party was noisy and someone called the police. Everyone was arrested because they were all underage and drinking beer.

"I had to call April," Julie said. "She and Justin came and picked me up. When we got in the car, Justin was very angry and was just yelling."

"You can say good-bye to the Firebird!" he said angrily.

Julie continued: "When we got to the house, Justin unlocked the door and punched it with his fist. It came flying open. Justin was still yelling. I walked away and went to my room and went to bed. Nothing else was really ever said by Justin about that."

"It was rather rocky once the kids moved in," Patti Parrish said. "April was not happy that Julie ended up with such a nice car (the Firebird) at a time when they were financially struggling. April also did not like the fact that Julie had a nicer car than she was driving. April would call and talk to me about issues with the kids—such as the night Julie called from the police station, Julie's boyfriend, Jason, who didn't live up to expectations, Kendon's using the calculator at school when he wasn't supposed to and the Pokémon cards.

"April also indicated Justin was upset because he thought Julie had a black boyfriend," Parrish continued. "It was a struggle for April and she indicated she felt like she was always caught between the kids and Justin."

It seemed clear to April that she should have followed Aunt Patti's advice about getting used to marriage before moving the kids in. She had not had a moment's peace with Justin since the wedding. He belittled her, mocked her and grossly exaggerated her mannerisms while repeating in a mincing, high-pitched voice things that April said.

April told no one at the time, but she had not wanted to stay married to Justin. She wanted to get an annulment as soon as they returned from the honeymoon. When she realized how eagerly Julie and Kendon anticipated living with her, she decided to try and make the marriage work.

Justin worked at the Rayonier office in Eatonton when he had his Milledgeville apartment and April lived in the Douglas house. April was offered a new job as a radiation therapist in Conyers. Barber wanted to buy a house in Covington, Georgia, which was twelve miles away from April's new job. Barber would give up the Milledgeville apartment and commute to his Rayonier job in Eatonton a little more than forty miles from Covington.

Julie was upset about moving. "I just got settled in and I had made friends that made me feel at home and I did not want to go out and make new ones," Julie said. "April knew I did not want to move and was kind of upset about it, but we never got into knock-down-drag-outs about it."

That summer, Julie and Kendon went back to Oklahoma to visit relatives during school vacation. April told her aunt Patti that she had a new job in Conyers and that they were moving to Covington. Justin wanted to buy a house, but April didn't think it was a good idea.

"April was concerned about buying a house, because she thought they may not be there very long, as Justin would probably be transferred again," Parrish said. "She said Justin wouldn't listen to her and told her it was financially a good deal because if he was transferred, Rayonier would have to buy it if it did not sell within a certain amount of time. April said Justin thought it was a no-lose situation."

April and Barber returned to Douglas and prepared for the move to Covington. April had been concerned about buying the house in Douglas as well, because she thought Barber would be transferred quickly. Her fears came true. They lived in Douglas just seven months and had barely settled in.

They had just moved into the house in Covington when the kids returned in August from their summer vacation. There was trouble waiting. One of Julie's friends telephoned to tell her that they had to split a telephone bill that was around $800. The charges were racked up on a calling card Julie's friend had taken from another girl. Julie said her friend claimed that the telephone card belonged to her. The two girls proceeded to make telephone calls that reached a total of about $800 before Julie said she discovered the card didn't belong to her friend. They had to pay the actual card owner the full amount.

April was angry when she heard about it, but Justin didn't say much. April was stressed about money, because they were financially struggling. They had the mortgage on the house in Douglas, on top of the mortgage for their house in Covington. April couldn't easily accept such a waste of money already in short supply.

The issue of Julie's telephone bill never got off the back burner, and as it continued to stew, Justin bought a Great Dane for the kids. They named the dog Harley. April's friend Amber Mitchell said, "Justin picked out the dog and April didn't care for it much, because it was big and tracked in mud. They started getting complaints from the neighbors because the dog ran loose."

They began to tie Harley up in the yard when they were gone and were cited for animal cruelty. "It was going to cost them money to fence in the dog to avoid more complaints," Mitchell said. It was money they didn't have. Not long after the animal cruelty citation, Barber told April that he had taken care of the dog. "I asked what that meant," Mitchell said. "She said, 'I think he killed it, but we aren't going to tell the kids that.'"

April's story about Harley, as related by Shasta Meeks in an interview with Detective Robert Shaw on September 12, 2002, was equally inconclusive concerning the dog's fate. Meeks told Shaw she was visiting April in Covington and asked, "What happened to the dog?"

"Don't ask," April said.

"I took care of the dog," Justin told Meeks.

"Okay, what does that mean and where is he?" Meeks asked.

Meeks said Barber told her that Kendon and Julie thought the dog ran away, but that it was actually dead.

Meeks said April interrupted: "I don't want to talk about this anymore."

"Yeah," Meeks quoted Barber. "Dead."

According to Meeks, Barber didn't make it clear whether or not Harley had been euthanized by the veterinarian, but she told the detective that Barber used his index fingers to emphasize the word "dead."

"It freaked me out," Meeks told Shaw.

This additional trauma concerning Harley placed more pressure on the family. One evening the family was in the living room when the subsurface anger erupted. No one was relaxed. Julie was lying on a couch and April sat near her.

"April accused me of stealing the phone card and I said that I didn't," Julie said. "She kept on saying I stole it and I kept on saying that I didn't."

Suddenly Barber exploded. "Stop being a smart-ass!"

he said, jumping from his chair. In an instant, he was in front of Julie and slapped her face.

Julie said that she screamed and yelled at him.

"Go upstairs to your room!" Barber said angrily.

Julie obeyed, but she continued to scream at him. "You're not my father!" she said. "You should not have hit me."

When Julie got to her room, she continued to scream and yell at Barber. Then Barber stepped into her room, flushed with anger.

"Did it hurt?" he yelled at her.

"Yes."

"I didn't even hit you that hard."

"Yes, you did."

"I'll show you pain!" Barber said.

He ripped the footboard off its hinges on the bed and broke it over his head. Then he broke two bed slats the same way. Barber looked at her.

"Now that's pain!" he said.

Little Kendon joined in the fray, trying to protect his sister.

"Don't you slap my sister," he yelled.

"Go pack your stuff," Barber told Julie.

Kendon protested. "Go start packing your things, too." Barber tossed the boy a trash bag.

"You better find someone in Oklahoma you can stay with," Barber said to Julie.

April was hysterical and couldn't stop crying as she telephoned Parrish to tell her that Barber had kicked Julie out. She told Parrish that the decision was Barber's, not hers. Sobbing, April asked if Parrish would please pick up Julie at the airport because Justin was sending her home.

When it was decided it would be best for Julie to live with family in Oklahoma, Barber wanted Kendon to remain with them. April wanted him to go with Julie because he had never been separated from her.

Mitchell stated Justin was very attached to Kendon and did not agree with the decision to send Kendon back home, Cole wrote in his log. *Mitchell stated that April told her Barber would never forgive her . . . and believed she had given up on her family. . . . This was why Justin would not have children with her.*

Barber told April that he would never choose her over his own family.

As Detective Cole learned more about the relationship, the clearer it became to him that Justin Barber was the most likely suspect. He looked at what he knew: a bad marriage, an affair, debt, arguments over children, living apart, separate expenses. A two-million-dollar insurance policy on April's life, to which Barber had sworn her to secrecy. All the evidence was circumstantial and nothing could be proved. But Cole believed Barber murdered his wife. There was no doubt in the detective's mind: Justin Barber had motive and opportunity.

But it couldn't be proved.

Chapter 10

"Justin thinks Julie is disrespectful and an embarrassment," April said.

Although Justin had intended to kick Kendon out of the house, too, he changed his mind and wanted Kendon to stay. Parrish discussed Kendon's situation with April and other relatives at great length. Parrish thought Kendon should come home because Julie had been the only constant in his short life. Kendon's father didn't see him, his mother had died and April went to college. Julie was always there. Parrish thought this stability was important for the little boy.

April said that Justin would be "very angry" with her if she sent Kendon to Oklahoma. Justin Barber was almost obsessive about outward appearances and he wanted a favorable corporate image as a good husband and father. Often Barber told coworkers how important it was to be married and have a family if you wanted to get ahead in a corporation.

"He doesn't want to appear a failure at raising children," April said.

Although Kendon's situation was still uncertain, Barber had decided that Julie was out. Still angry, Barber made arrangements for Julie to be on a plane to Oklahoma City. "Justin would not let April take me to the airport because he knew she would not make me get on the plane," Julie said. "Justin made the reservations at work and two days later I was to leave."

Barber drove Julie to the airport in October 2000 and didn't leave until she was on the plane. "When I was fixing to get on the plane, he said he was sorry it did not work out," Julie said. "And if I was going to be mad at someone, be mad at him, and not my sister, because it was his decision." Julie moved in with her uncle Mike and in November he became Julie's guardian.

April and Parrish continued their emotional discussions about where Kendon should live. Barber was adamant about Kendon staying.

"I tried to explain to April they were not failures and she should talk to Justin—or I would be happy to talk to Justin," Parrish said. "I told her raising a baby was much easier than taking on two older kids who were pretty much set in their ways."

Parrish asked April, "Should I talk with Justin?"

"It won't do any good," April said.

April told Parrish that Barber thought they could still have a positive influence on Kendon's life. Barber told April that if Kendon went back to Oklahoma, "he would never go to college or amount to anything."

During the discussions about Kendon, Barber was notified about being transferred to Rayonier's corporate headquarters in Jacksonville, Florida. April was offered a job as a radiation therapist in Thomasville, Georgia, which would put even more distance between her household and Justin's apartment. Parrish was not about to give up on doing the best she could for her niece and nephew.

"If (you) and Justin are not going to be in the same

town, I definitely think Kendon should move back," Parrish said she told April. "I tried to reason with her and tell her she needed to get her life and career in order and there would be plenty of time to help Kendon later."

Parrish arranged for Kendon and Julie to talk with a doctor about their living arrangements. "He advised that it did not matter where Julie and Kendon were, but they needed to be together—whether in Florida or Oklahoma," Parrish said. "April was still resistant."

Once, April said, "I just did not realize how big of a deal this was with Justin."

Parrish reflected that "it was like he considered the two of us in a competition and it was a battle to see who got their way."

Parrish told April to telephone and talk with the doctor who had seen Julie and Kendon. April made the call. Afterward, she telephoned Parrish.

"I realize Kendon needs to be with Julie," April said. "But I'm stuck in the middle between the family and Justin."

Parrish had enough of the family being torn apart. She was a lawyer and knew how to deal with difficult family situations.

"Tell Justin he has no choice," Parrish told April. "Tell him Kendon is coming back, even if I have to take you to court. If Justin feels this strongly, you can hire an attorney and we would let Judge Susie Pritchett make the decision."

This was too much for Justin Barber to handle. He could push a teenage girl and little boy around, and intimidate his wife, but he was not about to cross swords with Patti Parrish. Justin did an about-face, and in December 2000, Kendon moved back with his uncle Mike, who was later made Kendon's guardian.

"[Justin] was always looking down on April because

she gave Kendon back to my aunt and uncle," Julie said. "Justin really wanted Kendon to live with them. I think he was worried about how it would look."

"April was a wonderful young woman," said Detective Cole later. "She was a shining spirit and everybody loved her. People we talked to about her describe her as being almost a saint. And yet her husband beat her down, called her dirty and emotionally abused her."

Things had been hard for April. In seven months, she had planned a large wedding, dropped it for a small wedding in The Bahamas and married Barber, even though her instincts warned her against doing so. They bought a house in Douglas and brought Kendon and Julie to live with them. Barber accused her of giving him herpes and called her dirty. Barber belittled her by buying her teenage sister a better car than April drove. Barber mocked April. There were problems with the kids, resulting in both Julie and Kendon being sent back to Oklahoma.

The time had not been easy for Justin Barber, either. Besides being newly married, he had a new job and a new family. Marriage, changing jobs, moving and having children are among life's major stressors. Barber experienced all of them, too. When Barber was transferred again, April found a new job and they bought a house in Covington, even though they were deep in debt.

April was so fearful of doing anything to displease Barber that she didn't tell him she was sick early in 2002. Really sick. April's abdomen hurt so much she went to see a doctor. A pap smear was taken, and it showed abnormalities. The doctor told April that she needed surgery.

April eventually drove to the hospital alone to have the surgery performed. She was in such pain that she could hardly walk and had to telephone a friend from work to drive her home, where she recuperated alone.

Aimee Williams couldn't believe Barber's indifference. "I was just amazed that Justin couldn't take one day off to be with her," she said.

April wanted children and Barber didn't. He continued mocking her as being an unfit mother. Detective Cole wrote in a report on an interview that *Mitchell stated . . . April was crying because she wanted to have a baby and Barber didn't. Amber . . . stated that whenever April and Justin talked about having children, Justin would say, "Every time I look at you, it reminds me that I can't have children." Mitchell said this accusation really hurt April.*

Chapter 11

Justin Barber cheated on April just two months after they were married. Brian Stedman, who was dating April when she met Barber, told Detectives Cole and Shaw that Barber liked to brag about his conquests. Family and friends of April's flooded the two detectives with information.

"April had returned to Oklahoma City in July of 2002," Detective Cole said. "She was really unhappy with her marriage. She talked with all of her friends about how bad it was. Unfortunately, no one knew the full story. She told about different events to different people."

Stedman was a friend of Justin Barber's in graduate school, but they had not remained close, although they talked occasionally. Stedman, who lived in Edmond, Oklahoma, filed an affidavit to that effect on September 11, 2002. He said that in October 1999, Barber told Stedman that he had an affair with a woman in New Zealand. "I think she was an associate or something," Stedman said. "They would see each other when he went down there on business. He still saw her after she found out he was married."

Before they were married, Stedman, his girlfriend and Barber picked April up to take her to the OSU/OU football game. "He had been dating April for a few months at the time, but I don't think he slept with her," Stedman said. "They did a lot of hugging and kissing. . . ."

Sometimes Barber exhibited strange behavior, Stedman told Cole. Around Thanksgiving in 1998, Barber and Stedman were at a bar with Brad Carter, another friend, when Barber told them he was tired. "(He) went out to my truck," Stedman said. "When Brad and I came out to the truck, Justin asked me where I hid my pistol. I asked him why and he said if he had found it, he would have killed himself. This was over the grief about his father."

Barber's father had died earlier that year, not long after Barber's divorce from Dana, and he had been devastated by the loss. Before Justin and April were married, she lived with him for a few months at his house in Stillwater. The fact that April was moving in, and that they were engaged, didn't stop Barber's sexual activity.

"Justin told me about sleeping with one or two girls prior to April moving out there," Stedman said. "Justin and I would speak candidly about our lives. He told me that he would never have children with April, and about his affairs. In the past six months or so, when I would ask Justin how things were, he would give me the same pat answer. 'I'm happy with how things are.'"

Stedman told Detectives Cole and Shaw that he knew nothing about Justin's affairs with women in 2002.

April moved to Thomasville not long after Kendon was sent back to Oklahoma. Justin's assignment in Georgia ended in just seven months. April had predicted that it would be a short-term assignment and thought it was foolhardy to buy the house in Covington. Barber was transferred to Rayonier's World Headquarters in Jacksonville, Florida. They would have to move yet again.

Near the end of 2000, April telephoned Parrish to say

they were looking for a place to buy in Jacksonville. April was already worried about their debt. She thought it was foolish to buy a house before selling the one in Covington. In spite of Barber's assurances that it was a "win-win" situation, April worried that it would not sell quickly. What if Rayonier didn't buy it back from them? Barber told her not to worry, he would make the payments.

April and Barber looked at several places in Jacksonville. April wanted a house with a yard that wasn't too expensive. Barber fell in love with a condominium on the St. Johns River in the San Marco area. The condominium was small and had only one bedroom. April thought it was too small and too expensive, but Barber wouldn't consider anything else.

"He loved the location and particularly the fact that it was on the river about ten minutes from his office," Parrish said. Later, when Parrish visited Jacksonville, April took her for a drive and showed her the houses she had liked.

In Thomasville, April rented a small brick house on the campus of Archbold Medical Center, where she worked. Justin moved into the Jacksonville condominium and began to live like a single man. Although they lived apart, and April commuted on weekends to see him, they argued constantly. Barber frequently didn't wear his wedding ring, joined a singles club in Jacksonville and continued to tell April she wasn't a fit mother, she was dirty and she would give their kids away.

The house in Covington didn't sell as quickly as Barber had said it would. The house stayed on the market for months and they had to make the mortgage payments. To try and make ends meet, April took a night job as a private-duty radiation therapist. In the meantime, Barber was in Jacksonville, finding female jogging partners and sexual encounters. April suspected, but didn't know for certain, that he was having an affair with a woman with whom he played tennis. Her name was Shannon Kennedy.

April told Parrish, "He has no business trying to make people think he is single."

Parrish said, "Justin told her it was 'the club' to be a member [of] and he was not going to quit."

April called Parrish on occasion and told her about the money problems they had because the house in Covington hadn't sold. "One time she called crying because she did not know what to do," Parrish said.

April was worried about finances and worked two jobs to get them out of the hole they were in. Barber, who had a master's degree in finance, continued to play the big spender to impress his friends. Money burned a hole in his pockets. Even as they struggled to get by, Barber's jealousy of his friend Eric Maxwell's Porsche got the best of him.

Barber and April were arguing over finances and his clandestine late-night activities. Kendon's return to Oklahoma was still a raw sore that Barber wouldn't allow to heal. In mid-June, Barber decided to get a car that would rival Eric's Porsche. He telephoned April and told her he didn't want her to drive to Jacksonville that weekend. He didn't want to see her.

April remained in Georgia as ordered. The following week, Barber telephoned to tell April that he had bought an Audi TT, an expensive sports sedan. He told her to come to Jacksonville the following weekend and cosign the payment forms.

"April was mad about the car," Mitchell said. "He didn't talk to her before buying it. She told me she was tempted to not go back and sign the papers, so he would have to return the car. I told her that my marriage would have serious problems if one of us bought a large purchase without consulting the other."

So much for Barber's claim to the police that the Audi was his "turning-thirty" car and that "April was fine with it."

April told Mitchell that Barber didn't include her in financial decisions. He referred to the Audi as his "baby" to April and e-mailed her a photograph of the car.

In an affidavit, Mitchell said that April had been concerned about finances throughout her marriage. Mitchell didn't realize "the magnitude" of their problems. She knew they had credit card debt, school loans, the house payment and car payments. April told Mitchell in 2002 that they still had credit card debt.

"Why didn't you pay that off?" Mitchell asked.

April said she couldn't discuss it with Barber because he would blame the debt on extra expenses incurred when Kendon and Julie lived with them. On holidays, vacations and extended weekends, April would make the long drive from Thomasville to Oklahoma for family gatherings because she couldn't afford airline tickets.

"April said she just hated the Audi because there wasn't enough room for all of them," Julie said. "April had a hard time driving it because she couldn't see out of the windshield. She just hated the stupid thing."

Payments for the Audi, added to all their other bills, caused distress for April. She wanted her life to be normal, not mired in conflict, being demeaned, criticized and financially strangled. She often confided in Parrish, who seemed to be a rock for the family. April was so stressed that she confessed to a friend, "I just want to be loved again."

"One time she (April) called crying because she did not know what to do. . . . They were so broke," Parrish said. "They had payments on the Covington house, April's Isuzu, Justin's GMC and Audi, the school loans and credit cards."

Parrish offered to help them by making the mortgage

payments on the Covington house. April and Justin could repay her when the house was sold.

April cried even harder. "They are over one thousand dollars a month," she said. "I can't always come to you to fix things."

April told Parrish several times that Barber was still "furious" because Kendon had moved back to Oklahoma. That was several months ago, Parrish said. Why was Barber still so angry?

"Justin can hold a grudge for a long time," April said.

Barber continued to blame April for the fact that Kendon had to move. April told Parrish again what Barber repeated so often: "I could not believe you chose him [Kendon] over our family. I would never do that. I'll never have kids with you because you would give them away, too."

Parrish wrote in her affidavit about a conversation with April when she came for a visit in either March or April 2001. April told Parrish that she was unhappy and *the marriage is no good.*

Justin was unrelenting in criticizing her, April said. She said she would never be able to please him. Barber constantly criticized her appearance, April said, and told her she was too fat. Parrish asked if counseling would help. April said she would ask Barber to see if he would go.

April asked and Barber refused. Any problems they had, he told April, were her fault. "If you want to go to counseling, that's just too bad," Barber said. April told Parrish that she didn't know what to do.

When Barber had bought the Audi, April called Parrish. "She was again very angry," Parrish said. Barber had bought the car without discussing it with her. April complained that the Audi was impractical, too expensive, and that they still owed money on the GMC and Isuzu. April said she complained, but Barber wouldn't budge.

Barber said, "You need to go downtown and sign the papers."

Barber told April to start driving the GMC, which was what he drove before buying the Audi. She was to take over the payments on the GMC. The Isuzu, which was April's car, would be sold or leased to Justin's friend Eric Maxwell, who owned the Porsche that had made Barber so jealous. Barber said he would make all payments on the Audi.

"Don't [sign the papers] if you don't want to," Parrish said.

"If I don't, my life will be miserable," April told her.

When April visited Oklahoma in May 2002, she told Parrish not to tell Barber's mother, Linda, about the Audi. Barber was proud of the Audi as a symbol of his success, but he didn't want his family to know about the car.

"Why?" Parrish asked.

"Who knows?" April replied.

About two months later, Parrish and her son visited April in Jacksonville at the same time Kendon and Julie were visiting. Parrish knew that the marriage was rocky and had gotten worse.

Things were very bad at this point between April and Justin, Parrish wrote in an affidavit. *April told me she found out Justin had a girl spend the night in the house. Justin and Eric went out drinking and met up with two girls. They were all extremely drunk and Justin and Eric did not want the girls to drive home drunk, so they stayed at April's [condominium].*

April found the earring of one of the girls on the couch. They had a huge fight and Justin told April that there was nothing wrong with it and that she was over reacting, Parrish wrote. *Later, April told me she found out the girls actually left their cars at the bar and rode with Justin and Eric. She was again furious and they had a big fight.*

Again, Barber insisted that there was simply nothing wrong with what he had done.

Parrish and Julie both remembered that Barber had taken April to dinner that week at a restaurant on the Jacksonville Landing. This is a colorful area on the St. Johns River with restaurants, stores and bars. Music is played by live bands inside the establishments and also outside on the boarded platform on the water. It is a casual, interesting place to relax and have fun. But it wasn't fun for April.

Instead of having a good time with her husband, April found herself with a group of his friends that she didn't know. Some gave her inquisitive looks, but none gravitated toward April, the beautiful, effervescent blonde who had always attracted friends and admirers just by her presence. April found herself isolated. Barber and Eric continued to roam around and talk with others, while April was left with strangers. Everyone appeared to be giving her suspicious glances.

Detective Cole explained this later. "Everyone was used to seeing Justin with a lot of different women," Cole said. "Then they became accustomed to seeing him with Shannon Kennedy. Justin didn't talk about April. They thought the woman they saw him with most of the time was his steady girlfriend. They looked at April as if *she* was the intruder."

Parrish had taken her son and Kendon and Julie out to dinner that same evening. They went home early and Julie was at the condominium when April came home alone, looking as if she had been crying. Julie asked what was wrong and April told her about being left with strangers for most of the night.

April then told Julie about Barber joining a singles

club. "She was mad because he was a married man and should not be going out with single women," Julie said. April also told Julie that Barber usually didn't wear his wedding ring.

"She confronted him about it," Julie said. "Justin said the reason he joined it (the singles club) was because it was a way for him to meet friends."

April said she knew about a girl who had spent the night with Justin at their condominium. "Eric had another girl," Julie said. Justin simply restated that the girl slept on the couch and "it was no big deal."

April told Parrish about the night at the Landing, too.

"Once, she went looking for Justin and found him and Eric talking to some girls," Parrish said. "April was so angry that she left early and went home. April told me she did not know how much longer she could put up with Justin."

Wylie Davis was one of April's boyfriends before she met Barber. The two had remained friends over the years, and April saw him in Oklahoma the week before she was killed.

April told Davis that she was leaving Justin, but she was scared because Barber had told her he would not get another divorce. But April had made up her mind and intended to move back to Oklahoma when her apprenticeship ended in December. She told Davis that she had already been looking at real estate advertisements.

"I just want to be loved again," April told Davis.

April told Davis that she and Barber didn't exchange gifts, flowers or cards on their third wedding anniversary. Davis told Cole that April said Justin was cheating on her with a woman with whom he played tennis. When April left, it was the last time Davis saw her alive.

Chapter 12

Detectives Cole and Shaw heard almost every witness they interviewed in Oklahoma City say that Barber treated April more like a chambermaid than a wife. Aimee Williams, another of April's aunts, said she was surprised that April had married him.

"April and I had a closer relationship than just niece and aunt," Williams said. "She was more like a little sister to me. I lived with her growing up part of the time and she lived with me during most of my high-school years."

Williams remembered April's bridal shower in July 1999. She was standing outside Alicia's Tea Room with April and Linda Barber. April told them how Justin's job would cause him to be transferred often.

"I was surprised that April would want to move that much," Williams said.

"Justin's job is very important to him," Linda told them. "His job will always come first."

Williams said that April telephoned her every two to three weeks. The calls usually came on Friday evening when April left work and drove three hours from Thomasville to Jacksonville. Money was a recurrent theme.

"April would comment often about how broke they

were due to the fact that they had two house payments, her rent payment and two car payments," Williams said. "She was very upset about Justin buying the Audi. She said he was always jealous of his friend Eric, who had an expensive Porsche."

The conflicts in the marriage never seemed to end. Justin continually belittled April and blamed her for everything. April's sister, Julie, said, "He looked down on her, as if she wasn't good enough for him."

Don Lott, April's father, was serving a prison sentence after being convicted on drug-related charges. No one tried to hide this from Barber, who had heard about it from April before they were even engaged. Although Barber was obsessive about maintaining a pristine image of wealth and propriety, this didn't change his mind about the marriage. But it was something he wanted to be kept secret. In the spring of 2001, April was in Oklahoma and the family, including Barber's mother, went out for dinner. Before Linda arrived for the outing, April told them that Linda didn't know about her father.

"She said Justin would be very embarrassed if his family knew Don was in prison," Williams said. "They haven't told any of them [about Don]. This was the first time I felt that Justin was very secretive."

Sometimes Amber Mitchell would ask April if they were going to have children. "It would upset her because she wanted some," Mitchell said, "but she didn't even know if she liked Justin or not."

Around Thanksgiving in 2001, April asked Williams if she would buy some things for her in Oklahoma. April mailed a check and Williams noticed that the account was in April's name only. The next time Williams talked with April, she asked in a joking way, "Do you not share your money with Justin?" April said they had always had separate finances.

"I would be in big trouble if Gary and I functioned like that," Williams said.

"I don't even know how much money Justin makes," April replied.

In December 2001, Williams had a birthday party for Patti Parrish. April, Barber, and his mother, Linda, were celebrating with other members of the Williams family. Williams had prepared a lasagna dinner for the special occasion. Barber commented that the Williams children were cute.

"So when are you having one?" Williams asked.

"Justin doesn't want one," April replied.

"I do," Barber replied. "Just not right now."

"I guess you have your baby in your garage," Williams said, joking about the Audi.

April shot her a look of alarm. There was dead silence. No one spoke for a while.

"Later I found out that Justin didn't want his mom to find out he had bought such an expensive car," Williams said.

That same holiday season, April fretted over the Rayonier Christmas party and what she could wear, which would meet her husband's approval. "I don't want to embarrass him by wearing the wrong thing," April told her aunt Patti by telephone. Parrish said that she might have something for her to wear.

"I told her I had this cute top I had bought that would be perfect for her," Parrish said. "I told her it was a little wild, but it was very cute."

Parrish sent the top to April by Federal Express. April was delighted. She telephoned Parrish and said she loved it. "Justin was leery at first, but then approved it," Parrish said. "April said she was so nervous about going to the party."

After the party, Justin told April, who had tried so hard to please him, "Thanks for not embarrassing me."

Chapter 13

Detective Shaw recorded a statement from Pamela Davis, one of April's close friends, in Oklahoma City. Patti Parrish had provided the detectives with an office for their interviews and a secretary to record and transcribe. In that office, Davis remembered how April's marriage was far from the idyllic relationship Justin Barber had described.

Davis and April telephoned each other every month, because they were very close. "She lost her mother to cancer and she always told me I was her other mother," Pamela said. "I felt she was my daughter."

During a telephone call in January or February 2002, April told Davis, "My marriage isn't what I thought it would be."

"What do you mean, April?"

"It's just not going as I thought a marriage should."

April telephoned again in March to tell Davis that she was going to be in Oklahoma April 6 for a Kappa Delta sorority sister's wedding. April said the wedding was at 4:00 P.M. and she wanted to come over for a visit afterward. The two women greeted each other with hugs when they met at Davis's house around 6:00 P.M., and April stayed for about three hours. They didn't talk about personal things, because Davis's husband was taking part in the conversation.

At about 9:00 P.M., Davis walked April to the car. Although nothing had been said about it that night, Davis noticed that April didn't sparkle as much as usual and seemed somewhat stressed. Davis surmised that things had gotten worse between April and her husband. They sat together in April's car and Davis asked, "How is your life going?"

"Terrible," April replied.

"Is it work?"

"No, I love my work. My marriage is not doing well."

"What do you mean by 'not doing well'?"

"I think Justin is having an affair."

"What do you base that on?" Davis frequently talked to April like a mother and didn't feel that she was being overly intrusive.

"Well, he's gone a lot," April said. "I can't find him a lot of the time. He goes out late at night, and when I call his residence, he isn't there."

They sat in silence for a moment and Davis remembered some things April had said during a telephone conversation in March when her friend seemed to leave some questions unanswered. Davis felt that she needed the answers if she was to help her friend.

She asked, "April, is Justin abusive of you?" Davis knew that "abuse" could be interpreted in different ways and asked a more specific question: "Let me rephrase that. Is he emotionally abusive to you?"

"Yes, he is emotionally abusive," April said after a few moments.

It was the answer Davis expected because she had seen her own daughter go through seven years of emotional and physical abuse in her marriage. April had stood by her during that time. Davis reminded April of everything her daughter had suffered and talked to her for several minutes about different forms of abuse. Davis felt sure that April was starting to recognize the signs in her own marriage.

"Is he physically abusive to you?" Davis asked.

April lowered her gaze for a few moments, then looked at Davis. There were tears in her eyes. Davis knew immediately that the answer was yes, but April didn't say so right away. Davis tried again.

"April, are you afraid of him? Has he been physically abusive?"

"Yes."

"Sometimes people think they're being abused when they're really not," Davis said.

"There have been a few times when he's grabbed me and thrown me against the wall, or shoved me. He threw me against the wall."

"Were there any bruises?" Davis asked. "Did you talk to a counselor?"

April replied that she had asked Justin on two separate occasions to see a counselor with her and he had refused both times. From the experiences of her own daughter, Davis felt that April was in danger.

"This isn't a safe situation," said Davis. "Whatever you do, please keep yourself safe."

"I promise I will," April said.

Those were the last words April ever spoke to Davis.

Shaw wanted to know whether or not April went into details about Justin's emotional abuse or if she had mentioned specific incidences.

"He was always putting her down, critical of her," Davis said. "She never looked nice enough. She never did anything right. April had so much on the ball in her work and her life's goals, that all she ever wanted was to be loved for herself.

"I told her, 'When you finally love yourself, then any relationship you're going to have will be so much better because you know who you are as a woman.' She said he was very critical of her and that it had been going on for about two years. The first year and a half, I don't think there were too many problems, other than normal. But . . . I think he was putting her down constantly."

Davis looked at Detective Shaw. "I have some things . . . I can't say that, can I?"

Shaw told Davis that she could say anything that April might have told her during that conversation, which the witness had forgotten to mention. That was enough to get Davis started again.

"She told me she was miserable in her life because of her marriage and that Justin wouldn't go to counseling. I asked, 'Have you ever thought of leaving him?'

"She said, yes, she had."

Davis asked if she had made it clear to Justin that there was a problem in the marriage, and if he wanted to stay married to her, things had to change. He had to do something.

Justin simply wouldn't go to counseling, April told her.

Davis knew that April would complete her internship in December.

"I'm just miserable and I want to come back to Oklahoma," April told Davis.

They called one another off and on, and exchanged greeting cards, and April told Davis that things weren't any better. Davis told Shaw that April told her that Justin would go out at night and not come home for hours and didn't think that he had to answer to her.

"I know what I had gone through with my daughter in a very abusive relationship," Davis told the detective.

"Over seven years. I was there in that situation and I saw the same signs with April and that's why I told her to keep herself safe and get out. I told her she deserved better, any woman does. They don't deserve that kind of treatment.

"I didn't see her again," Davis continued. "She did say she was afraid of him."

Back in Florida, Sergeant Fagan rubbed perspiration out of her eyes and squinted against the blinding sand of Guana Beach. A small army of searchers, including divers and K-9 dogs, moved with precision over carefully marked areas of the beach. The search for evidence had been under way without a break since the murder and shooting three and a half days earlier. Men and women with trowels, shovels, axes, saws and various other hardware stooped and crawled, shoulder to shoulder, through the thickets of thorns, saw grass, sand spurs and other hostile vegetation.

Sergeant Gary Meares led the sheriff's dive team as they searched for a gun on the surf or in deeper water. They searched for hours and found nothing. Sergeant Teresa Meares supervised a K-9 search of the rough brush on the beach, plus in and around the parking lot across A1A. Two of the dogs were trained to detect gunpowder and caused some excitement when they began whimpering and digging in the ground near the parking lot. Excited searchers cleared brush in the area and conducted a thorough search. After several hours of searching the area, nothing of evidentiary value was found. Disappointed, but determined, the searchers continued. Members of the NCIS, which has a detachment of experts at nearby Naval Station Mayport, sent experts to help. Hundreds of man-hours had already been expended in an investigation that was just more than two days old.

Fagan found two stained areas on the parking-lot gate that she thought might be blood. CST deputy David Tarbert photographed these and took samples for laboratory analysis. Tarbert also photographed and bagged a sample of what appeared to be a bloodstain on the asphalt. These samples would turn out to be useless. The searchers at the preserve kept hitting dry holes.

April had been emotionally battered during the first two years of her marriage. Tragically, the storm she was caught in would intensify and end with dreadful consequences. Try as she might, April could do nothing to please her husband. The harder she tried, the less regard he seemed to have for her.

Patti Parrish was married in April 2002 and April traveled to the wedding alone. Barber didn't come, she said, because they were too broke to afford two plane tickets. Both she and her husband would be there for Julie's high-school graduation on May 1, April told Aimee Williams.

Barber accompanied April to Julie's graduation, as promised. Williams and April met at Panera Bread (part of a chain of soup, sandwich, dessert, bread and salad restaurants) to have lunch on Tuesday and then spend the day together. Williams was enjoying a rare relief from responsibilities, because her children were taking part in "Mother's Day Out," where children are at play under adult supervision to give moms a respite.

Williams arrived at Panera's late because she had been talking with the Internal Revenue Service (IRS) about her family's taxes.

"It's a mess," she told April.

"Justin's been handling our taxes and is upset with me," April said. Barber said she should have had more money withheld from both of her jobs. "He filed for an extension because we're going to owe more money."

Problems with money continued to dominate the conversation. April was terribly disappointed that the house in Covington had not sold. "We're so broke, and I took the second job to help [pay] for things," she said. "Justin's car is so expensive and I have to drive the Jimmy (GMC) and it's breaking down. The car was broken into and I can't afford to replace the radio that was stolen. If we don't sell the Covington house, we won't be able to go to the beach this summer." As usual, April tried to sound optimistic about the future. "We'll do it for sure next summer," she said.

At the end of their day together, April found a hummingbird feeder she wanted to buy for Barber's grandmother.

"It's very expensive," Williams said. "I can probably find one cheaper."

"I'll only pay half," April said. "Justin will pay me for the other half."

Williams thought it was odd that they even split the cost of birthday gifts for Barber's family.

Chapter 14

In spite of all the dissension and Julie having been thrown out of the house by Barber two years prior, April's siblings and other relatives continued to visit the Jacksonville condominium when April was there. Occasionally they would be at the condo with Barber for a day or so while April was at work in Thomasville.

April called Aimee Williams in June and was happy because the house in Covington had sold. They could have a summer vacation in late July, after all, and the Williamses could join them in July so all the kids could be together. Williams said they couldn't make it that year.

Although April was happy about selling the house in Covington, she was upset because Justin had arranged for his mother and grandparents, Mr. and Mrs. Charles Masengale, to visit at the same time so they could see the kids, too. April had taken a week off from both of her jobs to be with her siblings. She had planned to stay in the Jacksonville condo.

April told Justin there was no way they could have so many people in the small condo, and she wasn't about to make the children conform to the elderly people's expectations. She asked, "How do you expect me to entertain three generations?"

When April first heard that Justin had invited his relatives, she had mixed feelings. She would be glad to see everyone, but angry that her husband refused to take time off from work to help her entertain everyone. She sent an e-mail to Parrish on July 18, 2002, and told her aunt she was looking forward to seeing them, even though she was upset that Barber's mother and grandparents were to arrive on Saturday or Sunday.

April was dismayed that Barber's relatives chose that week to visit because she would have her hands full taking care of the kids. Barber planned to work, she complained, and he had no intention of taking time off to spend with the family. Barber made arrangements to rent a condo on the beach in St. Augustine that was about thirty minutes away from the Jacksonville condo but April was stuck with paying the rent. April told Parrish that Barber thought everyone would stay in St. Augustine except for him and that he planned to spend the time by himself in the Jacksonville condominium.

"He has another think coming b/c I am not making those kids behave for the older people," April wrote. She said that Barber's mother Linda still believed they were all staying with them in Jacksonville. April wondered where Linda thought she would put everybody.

April told Parrish that the sale on their house in Covington fell through but the complicated financial arrangement they had with Rayonier and Prudential Insurance left her and Barber free and clear of any fiscal liability.

In spite of April's reservations, Kendon and his cousin Nathan arrived in Jacksonville on Friday, July 19, 2002, and Julie arrived five days later. Justin had rented the condo from July 20 to Saturday, July 27. April and the children stayed at her condo in Jacksonville, while Justin's mother and grandparents stayed at St. Augustine.

April worked hard to make sure everyone had a good time. They met at the beach almost every day and April found something to keep everyone entertained. She wasn't happy about having to do most of it alone. Justin, who had created the generational and crowding crises, appeared only two times during the week, claiming he had to work late. Part of the time, he was with Shannon Kennedy. The good-looking young brunette, with hair flowing to her shoulders, had first gone out with Barber on July 9, just a few weeks earlier. They went to Juliette's, a bar in the Omni Hotel, for drinks after work and then drove to San Marco to play pool at Sherwood's. The two slept together for the first time a week or so later.

On Friday, July 26, Barber didn't meet with the family until about 9:00 P.M., several hours after he said he would arrive. It was his last chance to spend time with them, because they were leaving the next morning. Barber's lack of interest in visiting with the family aggravated April. "He has an office job," she said to Julie. "He doesn't have to work that long. I'm sure he could have had some time off to visit his family if he had asked. He's just trying to make them think he's so important that he has to be there. But really, he's just an asshole."

April was also upset with Barber because he had booked the condo in St. Augustine without consulting her. According to Julie, both April and Barber's mother fumed at the arrangement. April was angry for another reason: even though the extra space was necessary because Barber's relatives had visited, April had to pay the rent for the St. Augustine condo. It cost her $800 for the week.

The stressful holiday ended on Saturday, July 27. Barber's mother and grandparents left for home, and April, the kids and Justin returned to the Jacksonville condominium. That evening, Barber and the two boys went out to do something together, while April took Julie to have dinner at a restaurant named La Napolera. Julie and April chatted over dinner and started to talk about Justin. Suddenly April burst into tears.

"I wish I had never married him!" April said. "I was going to back out two weeks before the wedding, but just went through with it."

Julie listened as April continued: "After I got home, I wanted to get a divorce. Justin doesn't believe in divorce and I don't want to be the 'divorced one.'"

April poured her heart out. "He always makes comments on my weight," she said. "Sometimes I say things that are goofy or silly, and Justin says, 'Why did you say that? It was stupid.' He looks down on how I talk, like I'm not sophisticated enough for him."

"If you're not happy, you need to leave him," Julie said. "You need to do what's best for you." Julie asked if they had planned to do anything to celebrate their third wedding anniversary, in just a few days.

"Probably not," April said.

The next day, April, Justin and the three kids went to St. Augustine and spent most of that Sunday on the beach. Late that evening, April drove with Nathan and Kendon to Thomasville. Julie stayed in Jacksonville with Justin. When April arrived at her house, she found that someone had broken in.

April had always been frightened of being alone at home and the burglary scared her. She called her husband for advice and reassurance. Julie was in the room when Barber took the call.

"He wasn't even concerned at all about what had happened," she said. "He wasn't scared for her or anything. April was the type of person who was scared by little bitty things."

Julie heard April ask: "What should I do? Should I get a hotel?"

"I guess so" was all Barber said.

The next morning, Julie drove Barber to work. He seemed tired and sleepy. She asked if anything was wrong.

"Your sister kept me up all night," Barber said. "She was scared because the detectives told her it looked like whoever broke into her house spent a lot of time in her bedroom and they might come back and rape her."

Julie thought that Barber acted as if he wasn't bothered by the incident.

"Do you have any cash?" Barber asked Julie.

"A little."

Barber pulled out a hundred-dollar bill and handed it to her. "Don't spend it all in one place," he said.

Afterward, Julie and her friend Tiasha drove to Daytona Beach. On Tuesday, Julie took Barber to work and he told her he would pick up a rental car after work, because he had to drive to Rayonier's mill in the morning. April telephoned Julie later that morning and warned her that Barber might be in a bad mood, because she had sent him an e-mail saying she wished he would share more of his activities with her.

"Later on that evening," Julie said, "I called Justin to see what he was doing. He said he was at the Omni with some friends. I could hear people in the background. I said we might go to the movies. Tiasha and I got home about twelve and Justin was still not home. He finally came home between two and three A.M. I could smell alcohol on him."

Barber asked what Julie and Tiasha would do the following day. Julie said they were going to see April in Georgia. Barber said fine, then went to bed.

The next morning, April made her usual Wednesday

telephone call to her sister before Julie left for Georgia. Julie told April about Justin giving her $100. "He took it from a jar full of money," Julie said.

"That was my money," April said, sounding surprised. "Has Justin said anything about an e-mail I sent, telling him I wanted to know what he was doing?"

"No."

April mentioned that she always told Barber what she was doing, even if she just went to the grocery store.

"I found out about a girl named Shannon that he plays tennis with," April said, sounding upset. "Where was he last night?"

"At the Omni. He didn't get home until between two and three in the morning."

"Do me a favor," April said. "Go upstairs and find the clothes he was wearing."

"Okay," Julie said. She went to the bedroom upstairs and found the clothes. "What do you want me to do?"

"Smell them," April said.

"Smell them?"

"Yes."

Julie smelled the clothes. "I was, like, she was thinking maybe they smell like perfume or something, because she had found out about this girl."

Julie told her sister, "They just smell like smoke."

April said Barber told her that he was only Shannon's friend and that Shannon had a boyfriend. "He said she's an all-state player and that it wasn't a big deal."

April added that Barber had not telephoned her since she e-mailed him to ask about his social activities.

Julie put Barber's clothing back and said, "I'll see you later today."

Julie met April in Tifton on Wednesday evening and they left for Thomasville. By Friday, Barber still had not telephoned about the e-mail. April was anxious, but not surprised.

"She knew that when Justin was mad, he wouldn't talk to her until he got over it," Julie said. "She knew he wouldn't talk to her until he calmed down."

Chapter 15

April was nearing high noon concerning the show-down with Justin over his responsibilities as a husband. Driving from Thomasville to Jacksonville on August 2, two days before their third wedding anniversary, April spent the three-hour drive talking with Amber Mitchell.

Julie was following in her car with Kendon for a last visit to the beach before school vacation ended.

"The conversation started out kind of lighthearted because we were talking about Julie going through rush and our plans to get together in Oklahoma," Mitchell told Detective Cole. "But when I started asking other questions about her life, she started crying."

April told Amber about the horrible week she had just experienced, having to entertain three generations for a week in St. Augustine. She mentioned continuing problems with Justin and told Amber she had just discovered that he was playing tennis with a woman and had not told her about it.

"She was really upset about this and was afraid that he was having an affair," Mitchell said. "She had asked him something about it that past week."

According to Amber Mitchell, Barber said the woman

worked at a car rental business and that was where he met her.

"They had had fights that week about why he kept it a secret," Mitchell said. "April said that she had never known him to play tennis, before meeting this girl. Justin was really hateful to her about it and basically told her that she was being paranoid and that it was really none of her business who he spent time with during the week anyway."

April started to cry, then asked, "Amber, do you think I'm being ridiculous for wanting to know about this woman playing tennis?"

Mitchell replied, "I don't know any married women in America who would find that acceptable, especially if her husband was hiding [it] from her."

Mitchell told Cole that April was struggling with this, "and the fact that he was trying to make her feel like she was just being a jealous, overreactive wife." Mitchell said that Barber told April he and Shannon were just good friends.

"Why do you want to meet a woman?" April asked him.

Barber told April that he had lost all his friends when he moved to Jacksonville and had to make new ones, Mitchell said. Barber blamed the need to find new friends on April.

"Justin said they had lost their other friends because of April," Mitchell said. "He was invited out by them, but had to turn them down because he didn't want to go alone and had to make new friends. April told me she didn't feel like that was a legitimate reason, because she was always willing to do things on Saturdays. But she would ask him to turn down things on Friday because she worked a full day in Thomasville and then had to drive to Jacksonville. She was usually tired and not in the mood to turn around and go out with friends of Justin's that she didn't know."

April told Amber she knew her husband jogged with

a married woman, but that didn't bother her. The reason it didn't was because Barber didn't try to hide it.

"She said the reason she felt so strongly that he was having an affair [was] because Justin was not just secretive about Shannon," Mitchell said. "He was defensive about it."

The two women had known one another for several years and were fast friends. They were pledge sisters at college and April was maid of honor at Mitchell's wedding. This wasn't the first time they had talked about the difficulties in April's marriage. It seemed to her that April was finally fed up.

"She told me that night that she didn't want to be in a marriage like that anymore," Mitchell said. "She was ready to give him an ultimatum about leaving him. This [was] the first time she'd ever said that, even though she had previously talked about her frustrations and her concerns. I know we talked on many occasions about marriage counseling, which Justin would always refuse. But this was the first time that it was clear in her mind, and she was actually saying that she had given up . . . that she was ready to leave him."

April was nearing the end of her training to become a dosimetrist. Mitchell asked what she intended to do afterward. April said that was something she had to figure out, but she definitely wouldn't be moving to Jacksonville. April had been telling Mitchell that for quite some time.

"She never really had a problem with the fact that they were living apart," Mitchell said, "even when the arrangement was originally set up. It was something she was comfortable with. A year and a half ago, when they were first starting to do this, she said that she didn't see him a lot during the week anyway, and she knew his job kept him moving. She knew there was a chance that he would move again and uproot her, and she felt like . . . they would make it work."

Mitchell said issues between April and Barber were rarely solved. Barber's response, Mitchell said, was to "get really mad at her and then refuse to talk . . . about things . . . and wouldn't talk to her until he was ready." Mitchell mentioned the same e-mail that April told Nair she had sent to Barber, asking, "Would you tell me when you're doing stuff with other women?"

That her husband might be having an affair "was the final straw for her, because they'd had so many problems before," Mitchell said. April told her that she was trying to disentangle her finances with Barber. "I don't want any more of his debt," April told Mitchell.

Just a week or so before, Barber had come home late from a party and told Julie that he had been at the Omni. April told Amber that Barber informed Julie because he knew Julie would pass it on to April.

"She was really dreading to go see him," Mitchell said, and she wasn't going to talk about leaving until Julie and Kendon went back to Oklahoma from their short vacation. "Their anniversary was that weekend and she wasn't going to buy him anything," Mitchell said. "She even told Justin, 'I hope you're not planning to celebrate, because I'm not buying you anything.'"

Shasta Meeks was one of April's closest friends in Oklahoma. The week before her death, April visited Meeks and they drove to Lake Hefner for a quiet conversation. They parked at the lake and April turned to Shasta.

"I think I'm going to leave my husband," April said.

This wasn't a shock to Meeks. She had heard all about April's problems with her marriage and how she wanted desperately to get away from Justin. However, April had told Shasta that "Justin will never give me a divorce."

"What's going on? What's happened to bring you to where you've made this decision?"

April told her that nothing had gotten better between them. Their relationship wasn't going anywhere and she wasn't happy. April said that on their third anniversary, August 4, 2002, she intended to give Barber an ultimatum: change or she was leaving. April told Meeks that Barber made no effort to work on the marriage and that things had not improved.

There were lots of little things going on that weren't normal, April said, but among the most serious problems was that her husband was playing tennis with a single woman named Shannon. April had never met Shannon and didn't know anything about her. Barber mentioned Shannon to her when he suggested they have a Christmas party and invited Shannon and friends from work.

"April sat back and didn't say anything for a while," Meeks said. "She knew it was already too late. She couldn't wait until their anniversary to talk with him. She had to get it off her chest."

"You're worrying about nothing," Barber said when April brought it up. "You need to stop being silly."

"I think it's odd that you took up tennis when you never played before."

"I've played tennis before. You don't know everything about me."

April told Meeks that she tried to drop the subject, but other things came up. She told Meeks that she and her husband did nothing to celebrate their anniversary.

"Things are going to have to change or there would be repercussions," April said. "You're not happy and I'm not happy. We're both miserable and it's not worth it to live like this anymore."

Barber refused to talk about it, according to Meeks. She continued to recount April's narrative:

"It's not just that," April said. "It's little things. It's you hanging out with people I don't know anymore, and you going out all the time and hanging out with Shannon, who I don't even know, and other females. If I was hanging out with other guys, you wouldn't like that."

"I don't care," he said.

April thought her husband said it just to hurt her feelings. "If I lived in Jacksonville, would I always wonder where you were and who you were with?"

"No. If you were in Jacksonville, you would have a right to know."

They continued to have a heated argument for a long time, April told Meeks, then stopped without settling anything. After a while, April tried to bring it up again.

"We're not having this conversation again," he snapped. He looked at her and said angrily, "April, I'm not getting a divorce. I'm not going through that again."

Meeks said April told her that they both went to bed angry in separate rooms. The next morning, April got up before dawn and started driving to Thomasville. It was very much against her nature to do such a thing, because she was afraid to be alone in the dark.

"Well, I'm graduating from the dosimetry program in December and can live wherever I want to," April told Meeks.

"Aren't you looking for a job in Jacksonville?"

"No, not really. I know there are openings, but I'm not really interested in them," April said. "Thing aren't going to get better. I might look here, as much as I don't want to move back to Oklahoma."

Meeks said that April felt that she had failed and would

be coming back to Oklahoma as a defeated woman. Meeks tried to persuade her otherwise.

"'You're choosing to come back,'" Meeks told April. "'You're not coming back because you have to.' That seemed to make her feel better about thinking she was a failure."

Meeks asked April if she really intended to come back, or if she would talk to Barber again. April replied that she had been talking to him and it didn't accomplish anything. She said she would try again, and if he didn't pay attention, it was all over. April said that her husband usually became angry when he was confronted and wouldn't discuss things with her.

"I want to talk and get things settled and he just gets mad and leaves until he decides he isn't mad anymore," April said. "There is never a discussion. Justin is only concerned about things that are important to him or affect him in a direct way. He really has no feelings about anything that happens to anyone else."

April told Shasta that she had told Justin a short time ago that she wasn't happy. He didn't reply.

"I don't know why I try to talk to him when he probably doesn't care anymore," she said. "I don't know if Justin loves me anymore, but I don't think he likes anything about me."

April decided to have it out with Barber two days later, on their third wedding anniversary. The argument was unresolved, and when April had left the Jacksonville condo for Thomasville, they were both still angry.

In spite of the disastrous state of the marriage, April accepted a call from her husband during the final week of her mini vacation from him.

She told Ramish Nair about it when she was back in Thomasville.

"How are things between you and Justin?" Nair asked.

"He never called me in Oklahoma and didn't call me Wednesday," April said. "He called today and was being so sweet that he must want something. The only other time he was nice and sweet was when he wanted me to cosign a loan, like the Audi TT coup."

"The car he loved more than you," Nair said.

April agreed.

April mentioned "the other woman" to Nair just two weeks before April's murder. She told him that Barber was seeing a woman named Shannon Kennedy, who had played tennis in college. Kennedy worked at Enterprise Rent-A-Car, located in the Omni Hotel, which Barber often visited.

"April wanted to ask him about it, but [she] was very scared to do so," Nair said. "Finally she decided to e-mail him at work, taking . . . the chance of getting him angry."

That would be easier said than done, Nair thought, because Barber didn't like to receive telephone calls or e-mails from her at his office. Barber behaved as if he wanted to keep his married life a secret, although he often talked to fellow employees about how important a good marriage and children were for a man's career.

"I don't think she had ever been to his office unannounced, because he did not like that," Nair said.

April sat down at her computer and fired off an e-mail to Barber and waited for what she expected to be a scathing response. Barber didn't disappoint. He sent a long e-mail answer back in a little more than fifteen minutes. It was scathing, but it didn't satisfy April.

"He didn't answer anything that I asked about," April said. "I'm going to talk to him about it after my brother and sister go back to Oklahoma."

Julie and Kendon had been visiting April in Thomasville following the multigenerational-vacation disaster in Jacksonville.

Chapter 16

April went to Jacksonville on Friday, August 2, for the weekend, including her anniversary on Sunday, August 4. Instead of a celebration, April essentially told him to mend his ways—or she was history. Barber wasn't impressed. Instead of being contrite about his affair, he flaunted it. He told April that his social life was none of her business because they didn't live together.

April asked why he had brought Julie into the mess by telling her he had been at the Omni lounge the week before. Barber said he told Julie because he wanted to be certain that April heard about it, and he was sure Julie would tell her.

Nair asked April on the following Monday how the confrontation had gone.

"If things don't improve, I'm leaving," she told him. "Justin told me he doesn't tell me a lot of things because there is no way I can help him."

Nair said that April didn't elaborate, "because I don't think she knew what that meant."

* * *

April left for Oklahoma after work on Wednesday, August 7. She had not planned on being present for Julie's bid day, Patti Parrish said, "but she and Justin were fighting so bad she decided she needed some time away. She said they were even fighting on their anniversary and did not celebrate—as if there were anything to celebrate."

They were arguing about "Justin's girlfriends," April said. She complained that Justin had two girlfriends that he always hung out with. One was a running partner and one was teaching him tennis.

"She was mad because he had no guy friends and did not care if she was upset about the girls," Parrish said.

April told her that the running partner was married and she wasn't worried about her. But she worried about the woman with whom he played tennis because she was single.

"April said they 'constantly fought about this and Justin is never going to change his ways,'" Parrish said.

April told Parrish that Barber wanted to refinance the Jacksonville condo, even though he most likely would be transferred to Georgia or California within a year. Parrish supported April's opposition to the plan.

"It doesn't make any sense if you're going to sell it," Parrish told her.

April agreed. "Justin is now saying he'll never sell that condo."

Barber was supposed to transfer to Baxley, Georgia, and that's what she wanted him to do.

"We won't need the condo," she told him.

"Even if I have to go to Baxley, I'm keeping the condo," he said.

April told Parrish: "There is no way I'm living in Jacksonville. This is never going to work out and I have known that for some time."

April told Parrish how angry Barber was when she told

Amber Mitchell that they bought a used 4Runner to replace the Audi. "Justin got really mad that Amber thought
we were downsizing and could not afford the Audi," she
said. "I'm sick of trying to please him. He was so jealous of
everyone and particularly Amber. He thinks Amber did
well because she was a woman and ability had nothing to
do with it."

April told Parrish that she wasn't going to tell Linda,
her mother-in-law, that she was in town. April asked Justin
to do the same, but he told anyhow. Linda had called several times and left messages on April's phone. April said
she didn't want to see Barber's family on this trip.

"They think he can do no wrong and I'm tired of putting on a front for them," she said.

April mentioned that she had called one of her pro-
fessors to ask about job openings for dosimetrists in Oklahoma. "She told me she was probably going to move
back to Oklahoma at the end of the year, but they were
getting a Gamma Knife at work and she might stay until
she was trained to use it," the professor said.

"I have no plans to stay in Jacksonville," April said.

April's mini vacation away from her husband opened
the floodgates to feelings she had kept bottled up. It
seemed cathartic for her to talk to her friends and family
about her intention to end the marriage.

Randas Hawke was not only April's cousin but a good
friend, who was just a few years younger. Hawke didn't
have a sister, and April was the person she shared "girl
talk" with when they were growing up.

But their conversation was more serious when the two
got together on August 12, the day before Julie's bid day.
Hawke took a day off from work because she had not seen

April for a while. April took Hawke and her roommate to lunch, and afterward, the two cousins went shopping. They went to an antique store on the outskirts of Oklahoma City. April and Hawke had fun looking at antique jewelry, which they both loved, but the mood changed.

"Then we got to all the old baby cribs and . . . they were really cute," Hawke said. "I asked her when she and Justin were going to have kids. She said Justin would not have kids with her. That he didn't want them. She was just basically saying that he really didn't want to commit to that, and he was just kind of selfish, and he didn't want the kids."

After listening to this, Hawke said jokingly, "You just need to leave him."

"Yeah, I'm going to."

Hawke was surprised.

"Yes, as soon as my training's done at work, I'm leaving him." April told Hawke that her training was done in January and she had testing in June. "Then I'm going to be done and I'm moving back to Oklahoma City."

Hawke was shocked. "You're not, either!"

"Yes, I am," April said. "It's over. There's nothing to keep us together."

Hawke said April told her that she was "sick of trying."

Hawke joked that she would leave her boyfriend and they could be single together.

"They're going to be sad without us," she said.

April disagreed. "Justin probably has another girl lined up."

Hawke was shocked again. "God."

Hawke changed the subject as they continued sightseeing in the huge antique store. They came upon another group of baby cribs. Hawke thought they were so cute, she mentioned having babies again.

"I'm leaving him," April said once more.

Although April spoke firmly of leaving Barber, she may have harbored hope that the marriage could still be saved. They came across some Oklahoma University memorabilia and April wanted to telephone Barber to see if he wanted it.

"You're a traitor," Hawke joked, knowing that April was an Oklahoma State University fan.

April laughed and dialed Barber's number. It rang several times and Barber didn't pick up.

"April was mad, because he always had his cell phone on him," Hawke said. "She said it seemed like he never answered when she called. It really made her mad."

On their way home, April telephoned a friend at OU Health Alliances and left a message. April said she wanted to know about the job market in Oklahoma City or around Oklahoma, because she was returning and wanted to start a new life there. They continued driving home and saw a house they both liked.

"I'm going buy it," Hawke said.

"Good, because I know I couldn't afford it."

April continued to tell Hawke that she was leaving Barber and coming back to start over again.

"Are you really going to do it?" Hawke asked.

"Yes."

Hawke was impressed with April's resolve, because she didn't consider herself a strong person. If Hawke got into a fight, she would apologize and try to make up, even if she was in the right. On the other hand, April seemed stern.

"She was not changing her mind, which I thought was good if that's how she felt, and that's what she needed to do," Hawke said.

The two young women drove and chatted. April was

excited because the house in Covington had been sold and she would have some extra money. Justin spent money constantly, April said, and she was happy that she would be able to pay off her bills and school loans and have a little extra money.

April dropped Hawke off a few minutes later. Hawke was left with a definite negative impression about the marriage in spite of April thinking of buying her husband a gift at the antique store.

"I mean she was stern in wanting to leave him and she was mad because he wasn't up for having kids, and that hurt her feelings a lot," she said. "And she talked about how he would be mean to her and say awful things to her. Other than that, she didn't go into any depth about fights or anything. But she was stern. She was ready. And I supported her one hundred percent."

Later that week, Hawke, Julie, Aimee and April went to the Bahama Breeze, and Hawke started to boast about her boyfriend's attributes.

"The institution of marriage is outdated," April said. "Don't get married. It isn't worth it."

Williams told her husband about the comment later, and both agreed that April seemed terribly unhappy.

In Thomasville, April told Nair that Justin wanted to discuss an opportunity he had with a British businessman that involved import/export. The business would import spices from the United Kingdom. April was surprised that Justin wanted to include her in a business venture.

April said that while she was in Oklahoma, Barber did their 2001 federal income taxes and they would each get a refund of $600. Barber didn't tell her how much he had earned or mention anything about the mortgage or appraised value on the Jacksonville condominium.

"I can honestly say that she did not know anything," Nair said. "She trusted her husband and always thought he would provide for her and her siblings if anything happened."

The trust seemed misplaced to Detective Cole because Nair also told him that April told him about a woman Barber had started playing tennis with. Cole wrote in a report of the meeting: *She was very upset about this relationship but was scared to confront him.*

"In all the time I have known April, she has always either referred to him as my husband or Justin, even when they spoke," Nair said. "Only once have I heard her say, 'I love you.'"

Nair said that Barber had phoned April late at night once and called her "honey," "sweetheart" and other endearing names. April wasn't flattered. "It made me sick," April told Nair.

There always seemed to be great emotional and financial stress in the marriage. Before the Covington house sale, the Barbers were so strapped for money that April offered a suggestion. "Why don't you talk to Rayonier and see if they could loan us the money?" she asked Justin.

"No," he snapped back. "I'm not about to tell my bosses I don't have the money."

The financial pressure on April and Justin began to ease when, in what turned out to be a stroke of good luck, the Audi was stolen. April told Julie she felt bad about it because she had just complained about the car the day before. The Audi's theft relieved Barber of his hefty car payments and netted him a gain of about $600 in insurance.

"Maybe my griping came true," April told her sister, Julie. "Justin was just devastated."

"How did the car get broken into?" Julie asked.

"He kept his valet key in the glove box and they broke into the car and got it."

Whatever issues there had been regarding payments on April's Rodeo were resolved the same month. More important, the house in Covington was sold and April no longer had to make the backbreaking mortgage payments.

Barber bought a Toyota 4Runner SUV on July 4. Nair said Barber was upset at having to buy a used one and tried to keep the amount he paid secret. April kept peeking over his shoulders to see how much it cost. It was $15,000 and Barber paid for it with a credit card. Barber was angry about taking a step down because he thought his friends would think he had to "downsize."

Nair remembered that the 4Runner was bought on the Fourth of July weekend because Nair held a cookout near his house. Justin was in New Zealand and April drove the 4Runner to attend. She was alone. Around 2:00 P.M., April received a call from Barber, who told her he was tying up a few things at his office in New Zealand before flying home. Nair thought that was strange.

"It's probably four A.M. in New Zealand," he observed. "Why would he be going in at this time? Maybe he's rushing to finish some work."

April didn't seem to be upset. At least she didn't show it.

In the early afternoon of July 30, 2002, less than three weeks before her murder, April finally mustered the courage to challenge her husband about other women. She did it by e-mail. April asked him to please let her know when he was doing things with other women outside of his working environment. She acknowledged that her question would make him angry but that she had been upset about it for three days.

"There is probably not a single woman that wouldn't agree with me on this one," April wrote.

Barber fired back with a caustic e-mail of his own, less than half an hour later. He criticized April for sending a personal e-mail to him at work because it could easily be seen by other people. If April had personal things to ask him and didn't want to do it in person, Barber told her to call him on the phone or write a letter and mail it "the old fashioned way."

Barber wrote a list of his activities for the day and the times they occurred. He said he had gone jogging with Amy Evans and had nodded and waved to other runners, some of whom were women. A woman at the Laura Street Café had flirted with him when he purchased orange juice. April didn't have to be concerned about that, he said, because the woman was older than him and April combined.

Barber told April that Amy wanted him to run at 5:15 A.M. the following morning and he hoped she would back out because it was too early. A bank teller told him he looked like a middle-aged Justin Timberlake; April didn't need to be concerned about that, Barber said, because the woman looked nothing like Brittany Spears.

Just after noon, Barber said he bought a nasty hot dog from a vendor near the Modis Building and The Landing because Chick-Filet and Dan the Hot Dog Man weren't open. "She asked me what I wanted on my wiener," Barber said. "I'm sure she meant my hot dog."

Barber said he was scheduled to get a rental car from Enterprise and that he would speak with Shannon Kennedy, a woman with whom he sometimes played tennis. Should Kennedy not be at Enterprise, Barber said, he would speak with a man who had "effeminate mannerisms" but probably wouldn't make a move on him.

Barber acknowledged that it must concern April that he made new friends on a frequent basis. That wasn't his fault, he said, and implied that she had no one to blame but herself. His friends gave up on asking him to socialize because April was always too tired to go out on weekends.

April sent back an e-mail asking if Barber thought he was funny.

Barber e-mailed back that he thought he was hilarious.

Incredible as it seems, Justin Barber telephoned and asked April to come to Jacksonville because he needed her signature on some financial papers. In spite of the argument and turmoil, and the threat of divorce, April drove to Jacksonville on Thursday, August 15, 2002. Once there, April discovered that Barber wanted to convert their Jacksonville condo mortgage from thirty years to fifteen years. The monthly payments would increase by $300 a month.

April didn't like it. She asked Barber why they would want to do that, when he expected to be transferred in a year. Barber convinced her that even though the monthly payment was higher, they would save a total of $10,000. Giving in to her "financial genius" once again, April signed the papers.

Julie telephoned April from her dormitory room every day from Wednesday through Saturday morning. They didn't talk about anything important. April liked to make

to leave Oklahoma the day after the funeral to get back to Jacksonville so he could meet with detectives, offer his assistance in any way, and to see how things were coming in the investigation.

[Detective] Shaw asked me about Justin and April's relationship. As far as I knew everything was happy between them. Because of their jobs they were apart during the week and I know they made the most of their weekends and time together. Detective Shaw asked me to write about the .22 caliber pistol I have. It was passed on to me after our father died in June. When I transferred to Japan, I put the .22 caliber pistol in an upstairs closet at my mother's house in Edmond, Oklahoma. I do not recall mentioning to Justin about my storing the gun there. I do not believe that he knew the gun was there. The .22 pistol is an old nine-shot revolver that can only shoot one bullet at a time. It has a fixed cylinder with a spring-loaded action rod underneath it.

The SJSO, where Barber arrived that morning, is located at the St. Johns County Government Administrative Complex, on the north side of the city. It's an imposing complex with large buildings housing governmental offices on several acres. Barber seemed to be surprised at how big it was.

"I think it opened his eyes," Cole said. "I believe he thought we were some little Podunk police department with a bunch of rubes. He found out that he was wrong."

Detectives Fagan and Shaw met the group at the sheriff's office. Cole asked Barber if he would do a "walk-through" of the crime with him, while it was videotaped by Fagan and Scott. Barber said that would be fine.

The crime scene was about eight or nine miles from the government complex. Barber was unusually inquisitive; it was as if he were the one who needed to discover information. He quizzed Cole on his experience with the SJSO and the type of crimes he had investigated. Barber wanted to know how long Cole had been a detective in the Violent Crimes Unit and how many detectives were in the unit.

"How many open cases do you have?" Barber asked. "What's the clearance rate on the cases?"

Barber told him there weren't many open cases and the number of cases solved was almost 100 percent.

"The Jacksonville homicide detectives probably have more experience but less time to work their cases," Barber said condescendingly. "I'm encouraged to know St. Johns County Sheriff's Office would have more time to work on the case. St. Johns County doesn't have as much violent crime as Jacksonville."

Cole said that was true.

"When I entered the complex, I was surprised to see how large the department actually is," Barber said.

Cole was only half-thinking about the conversation. The content of Barber's inquisition was what had his attention. "After he saw the complex, he started to interview me," Cole said. "The questions he asked were meant to find out how capable we were at solving homicides. It is very unusual for something like that to happen. I thought, man, this son of a bitch is sizing me up."

The detectives and Barber arrived at the crime scene, just after 9:00 A.M., and the weather was sunny and pleasant. Among the group were two deputies to play the parts of April and Justin Barber as he described what had happened at the beach. Barber had written an affidavit in Shands Hospital about the assault and had stuck to it. They had doubts that they hoped the reenactment would clear up, one way or the other. Cole was also interested in seeing Barber's demeanor as the incident was re-created.

"I don't claim to be the world's greatest detective," Cole said. "But the one thing the good Lord blessed me with is common sense. If something doesn't make sense to me, I say, 'Hey, wait a minute. Let's look at this again.'

Barber thought he was smarter than anybody. He was very arrogant."

Barber said that he and April took off their shoes when they reached the end of the boardwalk and walked south near the waterline for about fifteen minutes. They stopped a few times and sat down in the sand once. They walked another one hundred yards, Barber said, then started back. The two deputies acting as April and Justin performed according to Barber's narrative.

"Could you see the boardwalk from where you were?" Cole asked.

Barber looked surprised at the question. He hesitated. "We could see a little bit. It was dark."

Cole had been to this spot before at night and had not been able to see the boardwalk. There were no lights for miles in either direction and beyond the reflection of moonlight on the sea foam, it was pitch back.

Barber described how they started back south, hand in hand, when April tightened her grip. He looked away from the water, he said, and saw the assailant coming toward them. The assailant was about ten feet from him, Barber said, and had his arm extended with a gun pointed at him. "[He] got right in my face. He was yelling and seemed angry." Although he couldn't understand what the man said, Barber said, he heard the word "cash."

Barber told the man his wallet was in the car and started to get the car keys out of his pocket. At that point, April said something and the man turned the gun on her. Barber said he jumped between them, and thought he had grabbed the gun, and he heard a "very loud" gunshot. He said the gun was small.

"That's unusual," Cole said. "Even a small gun usually looks like a cannon when it's stuck in your face."

"I guess it did look bigger," Barber said, adding that the assailant was much stronger than Barber and was "whipping" him around. Barber fell to his knees and the next thing he remembered he was wet and in the sand, but not in the water. He didn't remember if he was bleeding. He said he didn't even know what had happened.

Barber told how he had dragged April, tried to stop traffic, then finally drove for help when he couldn't find either one of their cell phones.

"I asked him why the drag marks we photographed the night of the murder didn't match his description of what had happened," Cole said.

Barber's eyes widened in surprise. "I don't know."

"Can you explain why there are only two sets of footprints where you said the struggle took place?" Cole asked. "We found your prints and April's prints, but none from a third party."

Barber looked blank for a moment. "I don't know. Maybe the tide washed them away."

"Why would the tide just wash away one set of footprints and not the other two sets?"

"I can't explain it."

They left the beach just after 10:00 A.M. Cole asked Barber to sign a consent form so the deputies could take blood and saliva samples from him. Barber agreed and Cole escorted him to the county jail, where Karen Buller, a registered nurse, collected the samples. Cole submitted them into evidence.

At noon, Deputy Vincent Russo, a composite sketch artist, arrived. Russo and Barber went into an interview room, where they toiled for an hour and a half. When the composite was finished, Cole looked at it. The sketch looked like David Alan Shuey, a violent serial rapist who was on trial in St. Johns County. One of Shuey's victims was raped at Guana Beach while he held a gun on her. The detectives knew Barber kept up with news via the Internet, and Shuey's story and photograph were on hundreds of sites. They started an immediate investigation that proved Shuey was in North Carolina at the time of the attack on the Barbers.

Barber didn't want to go home. He had wanted to stay on the beach longer than the detectives thought necessary. Barber didn't even want to take time for lunch, and he ate only crackers and drank bottled water.

"Most suspects would have been telling us to stop wasting time and get on and look for the person who murdered my wife," Cole said.

Cole started a formal interview with Barber at about 3:15 P.M. Barber recited the background information on how he and April married and had arrived at Jacksonville Beach on August 7, 1999. Barber maintained they had a strong marriage; April had been "tested," Barber said, and was "solid."

Barber said that because April was tired from work and commuting to Jacksonville on weekends, they "pulled out socially" in the past year. Instead of going out, he said, they remodeled the condo. Living apart was difficult, he said, and they sometimes argued.

Cole asked Barber about the theft of his Audi TT in June. Barber said a Jacksonville deputy sheriff notified him of the theft before he even knew the car was stolen. Barber said the keys were found in the Audi, which had been dumped in the river. A 9mm Ruger handgun Barber kept in the car was missing and never recovered. Barber said the expensive Audi was his "turning-thirty" car and that "April was really cool" with the purchase.

Cole asked about the life insurance policy on April. Barber said the policy on April had lapsed because he didn't make the premium payment in July. Since money was tight, he said, he asked April not to pay the premium on her policy. Barber said that he wanted his policy to stay in force so that April and his mother would be protected. Cole asked Barber why he didn't stop at one of the open business establishments or houses along A1A when he drove from the beach to get help for April.

"I don't know," he said, "and I just want to stop talking about that drive."

"If you dragged April all the way up the beach after you were shot four times," Cole asked, "why wasn't any of your blood visible on her clothing?"

"I don't know," Barber said. "If my blood isn't on her, none of this happened."

Cole changed the focus. He told Barber that April knew he was having an affair and planned to leave him when she completed her internship. Barber looked startled.

"I don't know. Things were getting better," he said. "That's a shock. I don't know what to say about it. April never mentioned a divorce. If she was planning on leaving me, I would have been heartbroken. If she was planning on leaving me, why did she initiate sex with me?" Barber said they even had "bonus sex" on the Saturday afternoon before her death. "Bonus sex" was what he called unexpected sexual intercourse.

Detective Cole knew Barber was not telling the truth. Cole came directly to the point. "Have you ever had any extramarital affairs?" he asked. "Specifically with Shannon Kennedy, while you were married to April?"

"No," Barber said adamantly. He said he had some women friends, but there was nothing sexual going on. Barber told Cole he met Kennedy at Enterprise Rent-A-Car Company when his Audi was stolen. They found they had common interests and started playing tennis and going to happy hour together with various friends.

He and Kennedy became "very good friends," Barber said. Kennedy wasn't happy with her boyfriend, Barber told Cole. Barber said he took Kennedy to the Duval County Jail a few weeks ago to bail her boyfriend out. Cole asked Barber whether or not Kennedy's boyfriend was angry because Barber was with her. No, Barber said, he was just too happy to be out of jail.

Barber didn't know that as he denied having an affair with Kennedy, she was in an adjoining room telling Detective Shaw that they were having a sexual relationship.

Kennedy worked for Enterprise car rental, which was located in the Omni Hotel in downtown Jacksonville. Rayonier's corporate headquarters was a short walk from the Omni and Barber often went to a bar in the hotel called Juliette's. Kennedy met Barber when he rented a car from Enterprise after the Audi, which April despised, was stolen and driven into the Intracoastal Waterway. This was less than a month before the disastrous vacation where April had entertained three generations of family, while Barber spent little time with them.

Kennedy said that Barber didn't return the car and she telephoned to tell him that the rental had terminated. They talked and discovered that they got along well. Kennedy was an attractive young woman with long, dark hair, and Barber was blond, handsome and athletic.

Kennedy saw Barber again when he returned to rent a car to use at work. This was before the Audi was replaced in July. It was also during this time that Barber told Julie that he had been at the lounge in the Omni, hoping that she would tell April. Kennedy was unaware of all these machinations, but she knew that Barber was married.

Renting the car took about an hour. David Esposito, manager of the Enterprise office, invited Barber and Kennedy to have a drink at Juliette's afterward. They stayed for about an hour. When they left, Kennedy and Barber decided to go play pool at Sherwood's in San Marco.

"We talked about playing tennis," Kennedy, a ranked

collegiate player, said. "He knew I was here on scholar-ship. He said he wanted to play against me. A couple of days later, he called me at work to go play. One night I went back to his house to have a few beers. We ended up sleeping together. We would play tennis and basketball at least twice a week. We would also go to lunch quite often, because he works across the street from Enter-prise. We ended up becoming very close and we would both talk about pretty much everything. About our family and life in general. Over at his house, he down-loaded Google on the Internet to check [on things].

"We would have a few glasses of wine," Kennedy contin-ued. "Things would generally get physical. I would ask him about his wife. He told me that he did love her and that she was his best friend. He said that they just could not live together. But he also told me that they were sepa-rated because of their jobs. Justin was just a really friendly person. We had a lot of fun together."

Kennedy had a boyfriend that she lived with, at least part of the time. She said he and Barber met a few times and got along well.

"I met a couple of his friends at the pool hall and he met a few of mine at lunch in the Irish Pub," she said. "The last time I saw Justin was two Saturdays ago when he came to the Enterprise to sign his rental-car contract. Sunday [August eighteenth], of course, I never heard from him."

Kennedy later amended her affidavit because she had mentioned inaccurate dates. In the affidavit, she wrote, *On about the fifteenth of August I was at his apartment and he asked me to go running with him on Monday the nineteenth. I answered no because of work.*

August 15 was the day April ended her "vacation" from Barber and, at his urging, cosigned a note to remortgage the condo in Jacksonville, where Barber had slept in her bed with Kennedy. The date Barber asked Kennedy to run with him was the day after April was murdered.

Kennedy said that Barber asked if she would take a trip to Georgia with him and she told him no. Later, he "jokingly" asked Shannon if she would move to California with him.

"I said no and it was never discussed again," she said. "On August tenth, we were together. We went to a bar in Avondale and then to Square One. I was also with him around August first when [my boyfriend] and myself met Justin. It was a Thursday night. I know that I was with him on August fifteenth in the evening. I was also with him on Sunday night, from eight to eleven P.M. on August eleventh."

Kennedy said she and Barber played tennis about two hours a week, but it was never scheduled. "[About] the last two weeks before the incident occurred, we were together quite often, approximately four days a week."

Just before Barber's mother and grandparents were to visit April and three young members of her family in Jacksonville for a late July-August vacation, Kennedy was at Barber's condominium. He was busy putting family pictures on the walls and shelves. Kennedy asked what he was doing. He told her that family members were coming to visit and he didn't want them to think there was anything wrong with his marriage.

Detectives Cole and Shaw took a short break from their respective interviews, where Barber was busy denying a sexual relationship with Kennedy. Shaw informed Cole that Kennedy admitted it without reservation.

Cole returned to the interview room, where Barber was waiting, and said, "Shannon Kennedy told Detective Shaw you were having a sexual affair." Barber denied it. Cole told him again what Kennedy was telling Shaw. Barber stubbornly denied it a third time.

"Shannon is in an interview room," Cole said. He started toward the door. "I'm going to bring her in so we can find out the truth."

"Wait," Barber said. He admitted to having a sexual affair with Kennedy and said that he had lied because he didn't want to get Kennedy involved. Barber admitted that they had sex several times, sometimes even in the bed he shared with April at their condominium.

Cole asked when he and Kennedy had sex last and Barber said it was two weeks before "the incident." At the moment, Barber said, he wasn't sure he intended to keep the relationship with Kennedy.

Barber wanted it to be clear that he had not lied in an affidavit he had written earlier. He wrote: *Detective Cole and I discussed my relationship with Shannon Kennedy. I told Detective Cole that we were friends and not engaged in a sexual relationship.* Barber maintained that what he wrote was true because that was what he had actually told the detective. Even though what he had said was a lie, it confirmed the lie on his affidavit. Barber seemed to be concerned about committing perjury.

Cole wondered how many more affairs Barber had experienced. "The affair was very suspicious," he said. "In the context of a murder investigation, we're not specifically interested in affairs per se. We kind of had a feeling that there were other women. It was the strangest thing. As the investigation progressed, we learned from different sources that he had had at least five affairs. When we confronted him, he admitted it. He was very busy for having been married only three years."

When the interview was over, Barber asked if Kennedy was still with Shaw. He wanted to ask her for a ride to Jacksonville. Shaw asked Kennedy about this and Barber got his answer.

Kennedy drove off alone.

Chapter 18

Justin Barber finally showed some emotion. He became angry. He had told Patti Parrish at April's funeral that he had been in shock and the anger was starting to set in. He vowed to follow her lead in doing whatever was necessary to apprehend April's killer. On September 13, when he talked with Detective Sergeant Mary Fagan, he was mad, but not at the murderer: he was mad at April's family, the police and the news media.

Barber told Fagan that he wanted her to know that April's friends and family believed he was a suspect. What made him think that? Fagan asked. Barber said that Lisa Woods, a reporter from the *Florida Times-Union* in Jacksonville, telephoned him three times and asked him to comment.

"She told him she wanted to get his side of the story," Fagan reported.

According to Fagan, Barber told the reporter, "There was only one story and that's what happened. I don't have any comment." A persistent reporter, Woods didn't give up. Fagan said Barber told her the reporter wanted to speak to his attorney. Barber said he didn't have an attorney.

"He said he [was] very upset over an article he read in

the *Beaches Shoreline,* and about comments made by the sheriff. I told him I wasn't aware of the article, but I would check into it."

Barber told Fagan that Amber Mitchell, who had a degree in public relations, was behind the tide turning against him. He said that none of April's friends or family had called since he returned to Jacksonville.

"Have you called any of them?" Fagan asked.

"I'm too paranoid to talk to anybody," Barber replied.

Barber told Fagan that Patti Parrish and her husband were in town, but didn't bother to call him. He complained again that they had cleaned out all of April's things from the house in Thomasville and had even taken his chair. Fagan asked if he had called Parrish, because perhaps she didn't realize the chair belonged to him. She knew it was his, Barber said.

"I wouldn't have even known they were here, but Charlie (Justin's brother) bumped into them at the sheriff's office," Barber said.

Barber complained that a newspaper in Oklahoma had published an article about the murder based on information provided by "a source close to April." Barber had two other complaints.

"Half of your team is wasting their time out in Oklahoma trying to get background on April and me," he said, "and no one is paying attention or concentrating on the real suspect."

Barber said he believed "April's relatives are mounting a campaign against me."

On a previous occasion, Barber had said that the family had been kind to him during the funeral and preparations. "If it was me, I would say, 'Hey, motherfucker, why did you leave my daughter on the beach?'"

He told Fagan that he was blocking everything out. She suggested that he should see a counselor. Barber argued that a counselor would "just bring everything out" and "set him back." He told the detective, "I don't trust anybody. I don't know who I can believe."

"We're trying to eliminate you as a suspect," Fagan told him.

"When will that be done?" he asked.

"When the detectives are back and we review all of the information, we'll get back with you."

Barber asked Fagan what was going on with his computer.

"I don't know how long it is going to take," she said. "Do you need it back right away?"

"No, I was just wondering what was going on with it."

Fagan told him that she would have Detective Shaw check on it in a day or two.

"Fine."

After returning from Oklahoma, Detectives Cole and Shaw continued the detailed and tedious process of gathering evidence. Much of it required pounding the pavement during old-fashioned police work. Shaw went to several gun stores to check sales records and didn't find anything suspicious. Shaw also bought samples of .22-caliber-short and .22-caliber-long bullets so they could be compared to the bullet that killed April.

Shaw asked David Warniment, an FDLE agent, if he knew of anyone who could perform a lead composition analysis on the bullet removed from April. The detective explained that he had ammunition from two gun ranges Barber was known to visit and he wanted to see if the bullets came from the same lot. Warniment said the only place he knew with that capability was the Federal Bureau of Investigation (FBI) laboratory in Virginia.

Pursuing this lead, Shaw called the FBI and struck out.

Charlie Peters, the FBI lab's lead metallurgical analyst, said he couldn't help. The reason, he said, was because the relationship between the bullets was too abstract and it wouldn't be worth the effort it took to complete the comparison. Peters said if they had found several bullets in Barber's possession, it might be worthwhile. Under the circumstances, there was nothing Peters could do.

The SJSO was looking hard for physical evidence. They had nothing to make a physical connection to the murder and a suspect. Everything they had was circumstantial, not the stuff of a strong case to put before a jury. Sergeant Robbie Gober told Shaw that Dr. Bruce Goldberger, of the Forensic Toxicology Laboratory of Florida, might be able to help. Goldberger couldn't help and referred Shaw to the medical examiner in Fort Walton Beach, who couldn't do the analysis and referred Shaw to someone else. This went on for months and no one did the test. A chance for some solid physical evidence went down the tubes.

The detectives tried several different ways to locate the K-car that Wesley Pryor and Kimberly Gamble, now his wife, Kimberly Pryor, reported seeing parked on A1A, near Barber's 4Runner, on the night of April's murder. The newspaper request for information concerning the car had not borne fruit. Shaw issued another "Be On the Lookout" (BOLO) for a Dodge Aries–type K-car last seen at Guana State Park. At the same time, he requested a BOLO for a white male transient with blond hair and beard seen near the South Ponte Vedra area. A detective stopped a man fitting that description. His name was Jose Bellido, and his hair was gray rather than blond. Bellido was riding his bicycle from his home in Waycross, Georgia, to Miami. He was not the suspect reported, nor was he the dreaded turtle egg poacher who had also been called to the SJSO's attention.

The K-car could be a crucial piece of evidence. If a car had been parked by Barber's, that would mean a third party had been there the night of the murder. Some people speculated that it could have been an accomplice's car, someone who disposed of the gun that killed April and riddled Barber with bullets.

An off-line search by the Department of Highway Safety and Motor Vehicles (DHSMV) reported there were 1,656 K-cars registered in Duval and St. Johns counties. Shaw eliminated the K-cars registered in Duval County, leaving 312 listed for the Jacksonville Beaches and St. Johns County. In spite of the odds against locating the car this way, Shaw and Theresa Mathis, an investigative secretary, tried to locate telephone numbers for the 312 owners. All efforts were in vain, as the K-car never was found.

The SJSO subpoenaed Barber's telephone, bank, insurance, credit card and credit rating papers; they painstakingly sorted through them. They followed leads on suspects and checked two states to see if Barber had purchased a .22-caliber gun. The FDLE's laboratory couldn't tie Barber to the murder because technicians couldn't isolate his blood on April's clothing. In fact, they were unable to show that any of the blood DNA on April's clothing came from anyone but her.

Finding proof of Barber's—or anyone else's—involvement was like trying to gather steam in a bucket. His debt was unusually high, but that didn't mean Barber killed his wife. The same was true of the life insurance policy for $2 million on April's life. Both were possible motives, but there was no direct link to the murder. The downloading and deleting of the song "Used to Love Her" by Guns N' Roses was significant because of the dates. The FDLE was able to show that the song was downloaded to Barber's home computer at 5:16 P.M. on August 17, just five and a half hours before April was killed. The song was deleted from Barber's computer on September 3, the day before deputies told Barber they wanted to examine it.

Barber told SJSO deputies that Eric Maxwell, a fellow employee at Rayonier and owner of the Porsche that Barber envied, became concerned about being portrayed in the media as one of Barber's close friends. During an interview at the SJSO's CID, Maxwell told Detective Shaw he had met Barber in Connecticut when they were both in Rayonier's MBA program. They both earned master's degrees at OU, but Maxwell was one year ahead in the curriculum. He said he had heard about Barber in college, but never met him.

They didn't stay in contact after they were transferred from Connecticut, with Barber going to Georgia and Maxwell to Jacksonville. Maxwell said he didn't see Barber again until the latter was transferred to the Jacksonville corporate headquarters. Maxwell said they began to socialize together, but that they were never close.

"How do you mean you weren't very close, when you were the point of contact for April's family when the incident occurred?" Shaw asked.

Maxwell said he didn't know how he arrived at that position, but he was trying to back out. Shaw said, "He said he didn't feel comfortable being the middleman. He said . . . it wasn't his place to be dealing with her family members when he didn't know Justin all that well."

The relationship Maxwell related was far different from what the deputies had heard from Justin and April's family and friends. According to April's friends, Maxwell was with Justin when April was left with people she didn't know at the company Christmas party while the two men wandered around socializing. According to several members of April's family, Maxwell was with Justin when they brought two girls to spend the night at

Barber's condominium. Barber denied that any hanky-panky occurred and told April she was "making too big of a deal out of it."

During the interview with Shaw, Maxwell explained they often joined others at work for happy hour on Thursdays after work. Since Maxwell became engaged in February, he told Shaw, he had not socialized with anyone but his fiancée. Maxwell told the detective that he didn't know of the affairs Barber had with other women.

"Eric seemed bothered by that question, because he asked me three separate times during the remainder of the interview if Justin really had an affair," Shaw said. "Each time when I answered 'Yes, more than once,' Eric would just shake his head in disbelief."

The deputies interviewed several people that Justin Barber knew. Amy Evans was the woman with whom Barber sometimes went jogging. They met at a happy hour she attended with a male friend and found that she and Barber both liked to run in the morning. Evans said she lacked motivation because she didn't feel comfortable running alone. Barber told her that he wanted to start running and offered to accompany her in the mornings. They ran together less than a dozen times, Evans said, before both lost their motivation.

"That was the extent of our relationship," Evans said.

"What did you know about Justin's marriage?"

"Not much." Evans said she knew that April lived in Georgia because of her job and came to Jacksonville on the weekends.

"Were you ever romantically involved with Justin?" Shaw asked.

"Absolutely not!" Evans said.

Cole asked if she knew Barber was having an affair.

"I didn't know him well enough for that type of personal conversation," she said.

Shaw asked what they did talk about.

She said she and Justin did not talk much since most of the time they spent together they were running and too out of breath to converse, Shaw wrote.

Testing for DNA evidence was not going well, as late as November, and several additional searches of Guana Beach were conducted with metal detectors, people and dogs especially trained to detect gunpowder—the results were negative. Marcie Scott, of the FDLE, conducted a second DNA test on April's shirt. Unfortunately, she said, the samples didn't contain enough DNA to compare, just as it had been with the first samples.

The shirt had tested positive for blood both times. The detectives wondered how there could be blood, but not DNA. Scott explained that the test for blood keyed off when red blood cells were detected. DNA, however, is found in the white blood cells. The blood was simply too diluted for the available technology to find DNA evidence.

Chapter 19

Detective Cole hounded the state attorney each time something new turned up. Every time, though, the prosecutors shot it down because they didn't believe they could prove beyond a reasonable doubt that Justin Barber murdered his wife. Cole was a new detective and didn't yet understand the complexities of building a homicide case. And building this particular case was a Herculean task.

"We knew what he (Barber) did," Cole said, "but the SA didn't always like what we turned up. They kept saying no. They wanted finances to be definitive. They wanted the computer searches to be definitive. I was a pain in the ass and I think they hated to see me coming. But you know what? They were absolutely right."

Cole continued to follow leads and check with the FDLE on DNA and developments in dating the Google searches Barber had made on his home and office computers. The song "Used to Love Her" was downloaded on Barber's home computer, while the Google searches regarding gunshot wounds were performed on his computer at work. Cole couldn't understand how Justin got any work done, because Barber sometimes spent whole days on the computer searching, downloading and deleting.

Cole put in so many hours on his narcotics duties and his attention to the Barber case that he lost thirty pounds. He became a rare sight at home, but his wife supported him. Cole promised to take a week off to spend with the family when the case was closed—if ever.

In spite of having evidence rejected by the SA, Cole continued to dig up information that he thought might complete the case. Time and again, Cole took new findings, or a new take on evidence, to the SA. He was a rookie detective, but he knew the police didn't decide whether a subject was guilty or not. The court did that, and Cole wanted April Barber to have her case heard in court. Cole continued to press on, even though he was the least experienced person involved.

"I learned so much," Cole said. "Every time I thought I had it, the first assistant SA shot me down. He was the voice of reason and I hated him for it. We were both trying to do the right thing. He was probably thinking that I was young and eager. I thought he was smug and didn't know his ass from a hole in the ground. We ended up learning a lot from each other."

Cole's new assignment to narcotics kept him busy. He worked as an undercover agent to help discover and arrest drug rings. The hours were long and often unpredictable, but he put in as much time on the Barber case as he could. The biggest problems in putting a case together were a lack of relevant DNA and nothing to tie Barber's computer searches to April's murder.

At the FDLE computer lab, Chris Hendry continued to probe into the information hiding deep inside Barber's computers. Small gains were made over several months, but nothing that helped the case. Since the FDLE's DNA laboratory wasn't equipped to locate traces of Barber's

DNA on April's clothing, a lab with newer technology was retained to continue the search.

The investigation continued for months. It was the longest, most extensive and complicated case in which the SJSO had been involved. Cole was so immersed in the investigation that he felt as if he knew April and experienced a personal sadness that she had been lost. Everyone Cole had talked with about April described her as being close to saintly, although those same people said April would be the first to deny it.

"Every homicide victim is important," Cole said. "But when you have someone like this, who comes from such a nice family, who had a rough time and still tried to help others, it's just tragic in so many ways."

The interviews the detectives conducted, especially in Georgia and Oklahoma, were shot full of holes by the state attorney, and most of the information crashed and burned. Cole thought the whole situation was "kind of weird." Especially concerning what April told friends and family on her last visit to Oklahoma.

"She was telling everybody that he was cheating," Cole said. "She told everybody she was leaving him. But the SA couldn't get that into the trial because it was hearsay."

"Anything the victim says to another person, unless you can prove he or she said it, is hearsay," said Chris France, the assistant state attorney (ASA) in charge of developing the case. "It's weird—because who knows what's going on better than the victim? You have to be able to prove that the victim said or did something. For example, April told her supervisor at the lab that if anything happened to her, look at Justin."

France felt that the detectives all had a gut feeling that Justin Barber was the killer. Some of them had thought so just a few hours after the murder. It was like seeing a sunset, France thought. They couldn't describe it, but they knew it when they saw it, and they realized that bringing a case to trial requires a lot more than instinct.

Several things bothered the team that tried to put a case together. France was surprised how easily Barber gave up his home computer without questioning why the police wanted it. France believed that most people surrendering their computer to the police would have a lot more curiosity. They would wonder if a possible assailant had been sending threatening e-mails. Was a friend sending e-mails from the computer that he didn't know about? Did April have a jealous lover who killed her, or had *he* been the target? If it was the latter case, was he still in danger? Was he still the target? There were dozens of questions most people would have asked that didn't arouse Justin Barber's curiosity.

The Google searches weren't evidence that Barber had murder on his mind or that he was planning to flee to Mexico or Brazil. France thought the searches could be interpreted as the reactions of an innocent man who panicked under the stress of the murder and subsequent investigation. It could be argued that Barber thought the police were out to indict him—whether he was guilty or not. The searches regarding the wounds could be considered the actions of a victim who just wanted to know more about why he survived and April didn't. All of the seemingly damning Google searches might be the actions of a man overcome by losing his wife and wanting to know more about the events.

Without knowing the dates these were made and deleted, the searches were next to useless as evidence. But if it could be determined that the searches were made during a time frame that coincided with the murder, these would be powerful evidence. The FDLE worked on this thorny problem for months and couldn't find the search or deletion dates. The investigation was grinding its gears and going nowhere.

The only eyewitness to the murder was Justin Barber. As a defendant in a murder trial, Barber wouldn't be required to testify, and there would be no opportunity for the state to cross-examine him. A jury wouldn't get to witness the defendant's body language and vocal inflections, or hear answers to tough questions asked by a cross-examiner. Hell would freeze over before a defense attorney would call on Barber to testify and expose him to cross-examination.

The state attorney knew that Barber would eventually have to give a civil deposition if he wanted to collect on April's life insurance policies. Barber would undergo cross-examination that could peel him like an onion and expose layers of evidence that might not otherwise see the light of day.

Thinking about this, the prosecutors had a brainstorm. They could give a cross-examiner all of the information they had from the investigation and *he* could cross-examine Barber. Although the deposition would be a civil proceeding, Barber would be under oath and subject to perjury. The deposition could be videotaped and maybe, just maybe, the state could introduce the tape into evidence at a criminal trial. France believed the deposition would give the prosecution a more detailed story about what they wanted to present to a jury. At the moment, they had only financial records, statements to the police and computer and DNA forensics that weren't panning out.

Detective Cole thought that presenting Barber's civil deposition to the jury had another advantage. "He thought he was smarter than anyone," he said. "He was arrogant and this comes through on the screen. I may not be the smartest detective in the world, but the good Lord blessed me with a lot of common sense. We're hoping the jury will use common sense to see through the smoke and mirrors of the forensics."

Cole thought a jury would dislike Barber because some of his answers might make them believe that he was "cold, calculating," and not above shooting himself in nonvital areas to provide an alibi.

"He was a risk taker," Cole said. "He had a history of that with the affairs and the stock market. He was willing to take calculated risks for personal gain."

More time passed and the investigation was going nowhere fast. The forensic work moved at a snail's pace. The media interest died and there were only occasional one-paragraph updates by the local press. Would a suspect ever be brought to trial, or would April's murder remain unsolved—or at least unproved?

Unfortunately for April's killer, Detective Cole was passionate about the case. "I just wouldn't let it die," he said. "I'm sure the state attorney's office felt that if I came up there one more time, they would tell me to leave. At the end of the day, I forged some of the best relationships I have in law enforcement. There was a mutual respect between the police and the state attorney."

The passion Cole felt prompted him to do all he could to get the case to court. He was new to homicide and he wanted to rush forward without enough evidence. In his eagerness, Cole sometimes made the more seasoned law enforcement officials tell him to slow down.

"Sometimes you just have to be stopped," he said. "I got so frustrated. Just so many things had to happen to build a case. I was reeled in several times by my bosses and the sheriff. I'm absolutely sure it needed to be that way. They said I was just going to have to wait. My frustration was from knowing that he was out there living big, while his wife was in the ground. It didn't sit well with me."

In October 2003, State Farm Life Insurance Company filed suit against Barber and April's siblings, Julie Lott and Kendon Lott, to withhold payment of a $150,000 life insurance policy. Before paying the insurance, State Farm wanted to know whether or not Barber murdered his wife. This was a break the prosecution had been waiting for.

The SJSO and state attorney's office provided Henry M. Coxe III, who represented State Farm, with copies of their evidence, including the interviews. Coxe was well prepared to grill Barber over a hot fire when his deposition began on October 28, 2003.

Robert Willis, a criminal trial lawyer from Jacksonville, had been hired to represent Barber. Willis believed his client was innocent and considered Barber's demeanor with the police and as a witness almost perfect. Until the deposition, Barber had made few mistakes. Now, on the witness stand, Barber twisted and fidgeted. He used some version of "I don't know" scores of times on even mundane questions. Willis called for a break at the earliest possible time. He was so upset with Barber's testimony that he briefly considered withdrawing as counsel.

Once they had privacy, he turned to Barber and said sharply, "Did you kill your wife?"

Barber stiffened. "Of course I didn't."

"Then why are you making them believe that you did?" Willis asked. "You can't keep saying you don't remember." During his secret grand jury testimony, which was leaked to the press, Justin Barber had already admitted that he had had five sexual affairs during his short marriage to April. "There was absolutely no way they could have proved that," Willis told Barber.

Barber assured Willis that he would do better when the deposition resumed. But he didn't. Barber continued to dig himself into a deeper hole. The state, waiting for its chance to try him for murder, could not have asked for more.

* * *

It's often been said that the mills of justice grind slowly, but they grind exceedingly fine. Chris Hendry relentlessly probed the innards of Barber's computer. The work was tedious and painstaking, but necessary, to find the dates of deleted searches. No times or dates showed up for the searches. The searches could be presented to a grand jury, but would never be relevant if the case went to trial. The dates for the searches *had* to be known—and to coincide with—the framework of the murder.

The state attorney's office gathered all of the key words they thought were relevant and had Hendry look for them on Barber's hard drive. Hendry joined them in Jacksonville on another occasion to help put together another list of key words. Skip Cole helped create a scenario for April's murder. On July 9, 2004, Maureen Christine (pronounced *Christeen-ee*), the assistant state attorney heading the case at that time, had enough evidence to ask a grand jury to indict Justin Barber on charges of first-degree murder.

It was interesting to note that the state didn't know that Barber had left Jacksonville and moved to Portland, Oregon. This knowledge came about when First Coast News pursued a story to update readers on the status of the case. The state attorney's office didn't know Barber had left the state until he was contacted by First Coast News Southern Bureau reporter Maria Tsataros. State Attorney John Tanner told Tsataros there wasn't enough evidence to charge Barber with murder, but when police did, Barber would be returned to Florida.

Before the indictment was issued, Robert Willis, Barber's attorney, told First Coast News that Barber was shot four times and the wounds weren't "superficial," as claimed by the state. "One hit a shrug muscle and another bounced off his ribs," he said. Willis said there was no significance to Barber's moving to Oregon. "Everybody knows where he is, including me. If they've got a case, then bring it on. But, the fact is, they don't."

Barber did not have to be subpoenaed: he flew voluntarily to St. Augustine from Oregon at his own expense to face one of the most intimidating panels in the American legal system. He had changed considerably. Barber had gained several pounds and had shaved his head so that he was bald as a billiard ball. Accompanying him to Florida was a girlfriend from Oregon. Police never released her name, because she had no involvement in the case, but Barber had apparently told her his version of that terrible night of August 17, 2002. Now he was being formally called to answer for it.

A grand jury in Florida is a prosecutor's version of heaven and a defendant's vision of hell. In a capital-murder trial, where the death penalty is applicable, a grand jury must make the recommendation. Otherwise, a prosecutor would have far too much power. Only witnesses for the state are allowed to testify. Members of the grand jury may ask questions of the defendant. There is no greater hot seat in the United States legal system than a witness chair at a grand jury hearing.

A booklet prepared for grand jurors by the Florida Supreme Court Committee on "Standard Jury Instructions in Criminal Cases" tells jurors: *The grand jury has been called both a sword and shield of justice—a sword because it is a terror to criminals, a shield because it is protection of the innocent against unjust prosecution.* The booklet tells the jurors they have "tremendous power" that creates "grave and solemn responsibilities."

Wearing a stylish dark suit and tie, Barber entered the grand jury room on July 9, 2004. The testimony lasted for more than two hours. Since grand jury proceedings are held in secret, we can only guess at what was said. But the grand jurors found the evidence worth issuing an indictment against Barber for murder in the first degree. It took the jury only fifteen minutes of deliberation to reach its decision.

Immediately after the indictment, Detectives Howard Cole and Robert Shaw arrested Barber and took him to the St. Johns County Jail. At the jail, Barber exchanged his stylish business suit for an ill-fitting bright orange jumpsuit, which is the garb for inmates in Florida jails. He was fingerprinted, photographed and taken to a cell after he was processed.

The prosecutors could only celebrate the fact that Barber was in jail and couldn't hurt anyone else. The case still leaked like a sieve, though. A conviction with the current evidence would be next to impossible. The state was counting on new DNA evidence and cracking the computer search puzzle to make its case provable beyond a reasonable doubt. It would take them another two years. Meanwhile, Barber remained locked up in solitary confinement, awaiting his day in court.

Chapter 20

Robert S. Willis is a man people want to believe when he says something. His voice is a mellow baritone that washes over you like a soothing balm. Willis possesses a recognizable, but difficult to define, quality called "likability." Willis makes people feel that they are important and that he cares what happens to them.

These attributes are one of the reasons that Willis is a top criminal lawyer in Jacksonville, and the man Justin Barber hired to defend him. Willis is held in high esteem by his peers. Chris France, who was the lead prosecutor in the case against Barber, acknowledged Willis's formidable presence in a courtroom.

"The way he says things makes you want to believe him," France said. "I've even wanted to believe him, and I'm the prosecutor."

Willis keeps an office in an older section of Jacksonville. It is located in a renovated two-story house that looks cheerful in an otherwise humdrum setting. The office is unpretentious, like Willis. There is no advertisement in the Yellow Pages promoting Willis; he has limited his advertising to a business listing in the regular telephone pages.

Search the Internet for information on Robert S. Willis and almost nothing turns up. Unlike most lawyers, Willis likes to keep a low profile, and doesn't particularly care for publicity, although he is unfailingly courteous to the media even when he could not be blamed for harboring the urge to break a reporter's neck. Willis is so good at what he does that he can afford to fly under the radar.

"We like to keep a low profile," Willis said.

This unassuming criminal lawyer was the man Barber hired to defend him against the murder charge brought against him. If found guilty of the charge by a jury, Barber would be executed by lethal injection or sent to prison for the rest of his life with no possibility of parole.

Not only was Willis absolutely capable, but he believed with passion that Justin Barber was an innocent man. Willis did not think that Barber should ever have been charged. He blamed this mistake on overzealous and sloppy police work.

"They made up their mind early and went after him," Willis said. "They took every sinister reference they could find and applied it to the defendant. They never had a suspect except for Justin Barber."

Willis did not believe that financial gain, or the amount of Barber's debt, were credible motives.

"He was on the fast track to top management at a Fortune 500 company," Willis said. "He was only thirty years old and making one hundred fifty thousand a year. His wife was making seventy-five thousand dollars. A two-million-dollar insurance policy was not a motive for a young man with such an unlimited future."

Willis and his associate, Lee Hutton, believed Barber's version of how he and April were shot. How could it make sense, Willis wondered, for a man to shoot himself four times to cover up shooting his wife? To him, an assailant shooting both Barber and April was the only scenario that made sense. The police blundered when they didn't look more intensely for a K-car, possibly a Dodge Aries, that had been reported parked at Guana Park at the time of the shootings.

Willis believed the police botched that part of their investigation. The police ran notices in newspapers asking owners of K-cars to contact the SJSO if they were near Guana Park the night of April 17, 2002. This was a joke to Willis and later became a joke to Nancy Grace, then of Court TV. Willis thought it was absurd to expect anyone who might be involved in the shootings to turn himself in. Nancy Grace would later say on national television that if you were an accomplice who might have disposed of a murder weapon, please call her in confidence. *Wink, wink.* Willis thought the state had not fumbled the ball regarding this evidence, it had not even picked it up.

The computer searches that the state found incriminating were challenged by the defense attorney. The state had run more than a thousand key word searches and selected the ones they found suspicious, according to Willis. He thought he could take a computer belonging to *anyone* and search it the way the state searched Barber's hard drive and come up with several things that could be seen as sinister. If they used their common sense, Willis believed, jurors would understand that.

Medical examiners, who are state employees, and expert witnesses for the prosecution are sometimes seen as slanting evidence in the state's favor. At least that is how a good defense attorney tries to present their testimony. Willis took it a step further: he hired a well-known forensic crime scene analyst to study all of the evidence where the shootings occurred and present his own evidence. In short, Willis would defend Barber, but he intended to introduce evidence pointing to a third party as the assailant in April Barber's murder.

A year after being indicted by the grand jury, the prosecution had not been able to put a case together. As Barber languished in jail, Oklahoma governor Brad Henry appointed Patti Parrish to a judgeship in Oklahoma's Seventh Judicial District, on October 4, 2004. She was now district court judge Patricia Parrish. Parrish had guided the detectives involved in the investigative stages of the case. She had provided office space in Oklahoma for the SJSO to conduct interviews with April's friends and family and had steered them toward subjects she believed should be interviewed.

Parrish had promised Barber that she would not give up searching for April's murderer until the killer was brought to Justice. The building of a case continued to move slowly. The long arms of Patti Parrish reached John Tanner, a veteran Florida state attorney. Tanner was the top law enforcement officer in Florida's Seventh Judicial Circuit, which includes St. Johns County, where April was murdered. All that the state attorney's office said about Parrish's talk with Tanner was that she wanted to make certain "that the case was receiving the attention it deserved." Tanner, who was interviewed on CBS's *48 Hours:* "Mystery in the Sand," said, "Judge Patti can be very persuasive."

Chris France was an experienced prosecutor who had tried more than 160 felonies as an assistant state attorney in Florida's Seventh Judicial Circuit. Just before he was put in charge of the Barber case, France was trying David Alan Shuey for armed sexual battery and armed kidnapping in an assault on a woman in her home at Ponte Vedra Beach. The composite drawing of the man Barber described who attacked him and April was made shortly after Shuey's photo had appeared in the newspaper after a rape in St. Augustine.

France is a boyish-looking man in his thirties, with a ready smile and an uninhibited laugh. Friendly and easygoing in his personal life, France is all-business when it comes to preparing and prosecuting a case. He is meticulous and can make dramatic moves in a courtroom. During Shuey's trial, France wanted to make a strong statement that the defendant was unmistakably the man who raped and assaulted the victim. France asked the woman to take a close look at Shuey. She stepped down from the witness stand, walked to within three feet of Shuey, leaned over and looked long and hard into his eyes.

"His eyes were the thing that stood out most to me," she had testified. "Drooping. Pulled down at the outer edges. They were set back in his face."

After staring Shuey down, the woman positively identified him as the man who attacked her.

"It took an extraordinarily huge amount of courage for her to do that," France observed. But France knew the woman could do it. Shuey had no chance to win acquittal after that. He was found guilty of all charges and sentenced to life in prison.

France was aided by Matt Foxman, who is also an ASA. Foxman's father is a circuit court judge in Daytona Beach who has tried high-profile murder cases, including the infamous multiple murders and attempted murder by convicted killers Kosta Fotopoulos and Deidre Hunt.

In this notorious murder case, Kosta Fotopoulos, a Greek student at Embry-Riddle Aeronautical University in Daytona Beach, Florida, married Lisa Paspalakis, the daughter of a wealthy local businessman. While Lisa helped manage the family's multimillion dollar empire, Kosta took a beautiful, homeless young woman named Deidre Hunt, as his mistress. With Deidre as his second in command, Kosta tried to establish numerous criminal enterprises, including a group of young thugs to become paid assassins called the Hunter-Killer Club (HKC).

HKC members, Kosta said, would have to kill someone while the murder was videotaped. The tape would be used against anyone who tried to rat them out. Kosta's main plan to quick wealth was to have Lisa killed. He and Deidre made several plans to have Lisa murdered, at least five of which were aborted. But Deidra proved her mettle to Kosta by firing three rounds from a handgun into the chest of a young man named Kevin Ramsey while Kosta captured it on videotape. Then she walked to the victim and shot him point-blank in the head. To make sure the Ramsey was dead, Kosta shot him in the head again with an AK-47 assault rifle, blowing off part of the victim's skull.

The final attempt to kill Lisa involved Kosta leaving a window unlocked at the family's expensive waterfront home. Bryan Chase, age eighteen, was the designated killer. Chase entered the home and shot Lisa in the head as she lay sleeping. Lisa survived, but Kosta killed Chase by shooting him several times with a 9-millimeter handgun, turning Chase into what Kosta described as "hamburger." Both Kosta and Deidre received two death sentences in 1990 from Judge S. James Foxman. Deidre won a new trial on appeal and, in 1998, received two life sentences without the possibility of parole. Kosta is one of several condemned prisoners awaiting a court decision on whether or not Florida's method of execution constitutes cruel and unusual punishment.

The case received international publicity, including a book I wrote, titled *Sex, Money and Murder in Daytona Beach*, which was published in 1991 by Pinnacle Books.

Foxman and France grew up in the same neighborhood and had known one another for years. They worked well together and their strengths complemented one another. France was known for his ability to select sympathetic juries and Foxman for his crisp, clear arguments. The Barber case was far more complicated than any they had seen. They were working day and night, along with Detective Cole, to put together a case that would prove Barber's guilt beyond a reasonable doubt.

"It was a nightmare," France said. "It was frustrating to really know, as a person, from all the stuff you had, that he was guilty and not be able to present it. My obligation as a prosecutor is not just to look for someone to take into court. You have to assess all the evidence, see that it was gathered within constitutional law and see all the elements of proof, or you can't go forward in good faith. Finally it is the right thing to do."

Parrish's talk with Tanner was no doubt in her capacity as April's aunt who understandably was impatient for justice. As a judge in Oklahoma, Parrish had no official influence in the state of Florida. The prosecution was working as hard as it could before she contacted Tanner. Putting a case together with nothing more than circumstantial evidence was drudgery, especially when dealing with complicated forensic information and waiting for additional forensic evidence to become available.

"The forensic evidence was complex and extremely hard for a jury to understand," France said. "You have to respect your jury. They're not stupid, you're not talking in terms of whether or not the jury can grasp this. You're really talking in terms of limitations of trial law, how much time you have and whether or not you have witnesses that can show things in an organized fashion in a way the jury can understand it."

Often lawyers can be muddled in complexities, too. "The lawyers and jurors sit in the same position," France said. "If we don't understand it, we won't present it. How do you show how you went through a computer and say: 'this is what the defendant looked at'? Chris Hendry (the FDLE computer scientist) was amazing."

The prosecution worked at a feverish pace to prepare for trial. Detective Cole stayed with the attorneys to add his thoughts and perspective on the case. The two ASAs got together to tear into all aspects of the case. France said they "worried" each and every piece of evidence.

"It worked out well," he said. "We worked on two or three issues at a time. We were very methodical. Skip Cole stayed with us throughout trial preparation. It's one thing to be a good cop on the streets, but quite another to get a guy in here as smart as he is who also understood what we needed for trial. He frequently had the best ideas of all of us."

When France and Foxman put together their thoughts on what they were "worrying" about, they took it to Cole. The detective had been on the case since the beginning and often could add details or tell the attorneys how he would present the evidence. After that, the entire St. Augustine state attorney staff considered the matters as a group: they pondered evidence they should *not* present, in addition to evidence to be brought before the jury.

"We did this with every element," France said. "It was a nightmare. This was not a case where you turned and burned and hoped for the best. We had to be satisfied with every detail. At the first meeting with defense counsel in January or February (2006), there was some talk about a second-degree murder plea, but they never picked a plea option. They scoffed at our offer. Once we hit trial, we never had a doubt about winning. If they had come out and asked to plea-bargain during the trial, we would not have accepted."

The pretrial work was completed, and Judge Edward Hedstrom, a circuit court judge from Palatka, Florida,

anemic—the jailhouse pallor look. He looked every inch the capable, intelligent and benign businessman.

The media's interest was resurrected with a fury, and in the parking lot outside, satellite television dishes probed into the sky. All of the major area television news divisions were there, and the ABC, CBS and NBC networks were represented. *Dateline* set up microphones and television cameras in the courtroom, as did Court TV, which would broadcast the trial from beginning through interviews following the verdict and sentencing.

Not much spectator interest usually happens at voir dire—to "speak the truth"—which is the process of picking a jury. At this point, most of the preliminary trial work has been done. Nevertheless, the courtroom was packed with spectators. To get a seat in court, one had to arrive before dawn, wait in a long line, which ringed a city block, and hope a seat was available when one's turn came. Although voir dire may not interest the gallery, selecting the jury is one of the most crucial parts of a trial. Defendants who can afford it sometimes spend tens of thousands of dollars to have a specialist advise the defense team during the jury selection process.

Judge Edward Hedstrom took the bench, and after noting that the defendant and officers of the court were present, he called the court to order. The judge noted that the venire (a panel from which a jury is drawn) was present and had been qualified. Before starting jury selection, he asked if there were preliminary matters that first needed attention. The first was a minor formality, but the second was a complicated issue to determine if Barber's past sexual affairs could be entered into evidence. Various points of law were argued. One was that the affairs were remote and not relevant.

The judge told Willis that he would allow the introduction of Barber's past sexual conduct as evidence of motive for murder. Hedstrom said the defendant had denied an affair with Shannon Kennedy and told police he had a normal, happy marriage.

"Evidence of his extramarital conduct . . . becomes relative to refute that assertion," Hedstrom said. "That's the basis—I thought it was relevant. I'm going to stick with my prior ruling."

The judge asked for the first twenty-two potential jurors, and after they were seated, the judge explained voir dire. There were no right or wrong answers, but the potential jurors were obligated to tell the truth about their opinions. An opponent of the death penalty, for example, would probably be excused by the state. Someone who had been a crime victim might be challenged by the defense because he might have a preconceived opinion that the defendant was guilty. Were any of the veniremen related to counsel or the victim or defendant? The judge told anyone who found a question too personal that he would hear their answer in private.

After a break in voir dire, court was back in session. Willis pointed out that one or more of the microphones in the courtroom were picking up discussions at the counsel table. Willis said he didn't know which microphone was transmitting confidential information.

"I just want to put the court on notice of that," Willis said. "I thought we had a clear understanding that that would not happen. And if it is, I'm concerned with it."

After some quick checking, it was determined that the offending microphone was one being used by *Dateline*. The information being unintentionally transmitted by the microphone was from the defense table only. After thoroughly checking all the microphones to insure privacy of counsel, voir dire resumed, this time with Willis questioning.

After introducing himself, Lee Hutton and Margo Stella, an intern working with the defense, Willis emphasized how serious the case was. "A man's life is literally on the line," he said. "And I hope and trust that you will bear with us as we inquire a little further of you."

One prospective juror, who was twenty-five years old, said he had been trying to think of any excuse not to be on jury duty. He explained that his life was stressful, but he believed he could do the job. This led Willis to tell the jurors the case was complicated and they would have to be alert at all times. They could not be distracted by any other issues.

"This man's life is depending on people paying very strict attention to the evidence in this case," he said. "This is, in some respects, a massive case . . . a case with a lot to it. If you lose track of it and you don't pay attention, you're not going to get it. You're not going to get it unless you pay attention every minute. It's going to demand a lot of anybody that's going to be a juror on this case . . . to live up to their responsibilities to this court and to the parties in this case. So I'm real concerned about . . . anybody that would be thinking about other things that they either had to do or wanted to do that might distract them from their ability to be jurors in this case."

Willis asked other questions of the veniremen to determine whether or not he wanted to challenge them. Then he switched his attention to what seemed more like oratory than questioning.

"Probably the tone is going to get a little more somber, maybe a little more controversial," he said. "But let me just set the stage for a series of questions by telling you that Justin Barber has entered his plea of not guilty and has sat here and told anybody that would listen that he was not guilty. And the question before you is whether he's telling the truth or not, or better said, whether the government can prove beyond a reasonable doubt that he's *not* telling the truth.

"We're going to be real concerned with people paying attention to the evidence relating to the facts and circumstances of the shooting of April Barber," Willis continued. "April Barber was his wife. She was shot on the beach in Guana Park, South Ponte Vedra, the evening of August 17, 2002. That same evening, Mr. Barber was shot. Our medical experts think it was three shots with four bullet holes, but regardless, he wound up with four bullet holes in him."

Finally Chris France had to object. He argued that Willis was "going a little bit too far into the facts of the case rather than jury voir dire."

Willis said he intended to go no further. Judge Hedstrom sustained the objection and told Willis to move on.

Willis indicated that the defense would focus on scientific evidence and evidence relating to the circumstances of the evidence. He jumped into the question of infidelity without preamble.

"Unfortunately, there's going to be evidence of infidelity on the part of Mr. Barber," he said. "There is. And 'infidelity' is a nice word. You want to call it adultery, whatever term you want to put on it."

Willis said the judge had ruled that the jury could hear this evidence and that's the way it should be. On the other hand, Willis said he was concerned about whether the infidelity would dominate the jurors' thoughts so they wouldn't give attention that other evidence deserved.

"Everybody understand?" he asked.

The veniremen nodded their heads.

Just to be sure, Willis asked each venireman on whether adultery would influence their decision on the crime with which the defendant was charged. Each said it wouldn't make a difference. Next, Willis turned attention toward the most dreaded result of all—the death penalty.

"It's a very awkward position for a lawyer to be put in a case where the government is seeking the death penalty, because you get a lot of questions about [it]," Willis said. "It almost makes it sound like somebody's guilt is a foregone conclusion, that's why we talk about that. Well, lawyers have got to talk about it . . . because there's always that possibility. Here we're not going to talk about it. We're really not focused on that at all. We're focused on the guilt or innocence of this man, period. And so we appreciate your comments on the death penalty, we're respecting them, but we're not going to spend any time dealing with that at all."

Knowing that both sides would rely heavily on forensic evidence, Willis mentioned that he had made a note to himself about *CSI.*

"Anybody here watch this television program?" he asked. "I think there's more than one *CSI.* Anybody do that?"

Every hand shot up as Willis probably knew ahead of time. Shows featuring crime scenes are among the most popular on television, but the canny lawyer seemed surprised.

"I thought I was going to be the only one that has never seen it," Willis said. "Apparently, it focuses a great deal on scientific evidence in criminal cases and what can be read into it and how you can interpret it, and so on. Everybody here feel comfortable, at least in a general sense, with their ability to evaluate such evidence, listen to experts and try to determine whether that expert makes sense or not, whether it matches up to what you see?"

The prospective jurors nodded their heads.

Willis mentioned that both the state and defense

would introduce photos of April Barber after she was killed. He warned that there would be blood and the photos were disturbing. He asked if this would cause the veniremen to lose their objectivity. Once again, they shook their heads no.

In fact, many of the crime scene investigation television shows depict full-fledged autopsies and blood and gore that would be hard to match in a real courtroom. A jury of twelve and two alternates was impaneled after almost two days of voir dire, and the trial was ready to begin, four years after April was murdered.

Chapter 22

Chris France rose to outline the state's case in his opening statement. He looked relaxed and showed no sign that he and the staff had been working frantically until the small hours of the morning. The boyish-looking prosecutor was warm and friendly, and there was a good-natured twinkle in his eyes.

The first thing France did was to thank them ahead of time for the attention they would give to each witness. "Remember, use all of your senses here," he said. "And listen closely and look closely, however disturbing these pieces of evidence may be to us. That attention throughout this trial will serve you well."

Willis had described the case as being massive, but France didn't think the jurors would have difficulty understanding the evidence. He admitted there was a great deal of information, but said the majority of it was easy to understand. Some things would be more difficult.

"You'll find some new things that you've never heard about, hearing some medical testimony, some crime scene testimony, which you've probably never been exposed to," France said. "I ask that you put any preconceptions from TV, or whatever, aside and listen to their words and their testimony."

With all of the information they would hear during the case, France said they would understand what happened to April Barber and who killed her. The jury would be aware of two things at the end of the evidence presented by the state, France said: number one, a murderer, one who kills, and number two, a phantom, one who was never there.

France told the jury about some of April's personal background and described that Barber was in Rayonier's management-training program. The evidence would show that April was finishing her training in January 2001 at Archbold Medical Center. April moved from Covington, Georgia, to Thomasville, while Barber moved to Jacksonville to pursue his career, France said, and they never again lived together as a married couple.

France talked about April driving to Jacksonville "religiously" on weekends to visit her husband. Barber opened an E-Trade account with an initial investment of $2,000 that became a $58,000 debt because of losses. France said Barber paid for the margin calls on his losses with credit cards.

"This was in addition to paying for his condominium in Jacksonville, student loans and all the other bills our lives seem to place on us," France said. "While [they lived] apart, the evidence will show that it's this E-Trade and the actions of the defendant that he's successfully and almost single-handedly raising the couple's debt, their marital debt, to this level."

The jury had heard about Barber's infidelity during voir dire, but they would hear more. "While he's living in Jacksonville, the defendant has no less than four affairs," France said. "The evidence shows he's living the life of a single man. And I reminded you . . . it's but a three-year marriage."

France spoke about Barber approaching Jay Jervey a year before April was killed to buy two-million-dollar life insurance policies for April and himself. "The defendant walked into that office with a figure of two million dollars in his head," France said. "He didn't have to get sold on it." The jury had heard nothing about the insurance until now and was unaware that Barber had given a different version of how the premiums were paid than the one France was to describe.

"The defendant paid for both policies, as all the billing and everything went to Jacksonville, the Jacksonville address . . . until the final premium . . . which somehow came to April's attention, somehow out of Georgia with the bill going to Jacksonville. April paid that final premium and a few months later would be murdered."

France talked about Barber dating Shannon Kennedy almost openly in the month and a half before April was killed. Barber never volunteered that he was married, but Kennedy found out. France said Kennedy was trying to get out of the relationship, but Barber wanted to keep seeing her.

Around August 14, 2002, France said, "April goes in, again religiously, for another visit to her husband in Jacksonville. . . . The defendant and the victim both signed paperwork to refinance their condo and received a credit line to take out more money at that time."

France told the jury how the state's evidence would show that they went out to dinner, played pool and went to Guana State Park around 10:00 or 10:30 P.M. They parked and walked down to the beach together. Barber never left her.

"You'll hear from evidence concerning crime scene

analysis, see blood evidence," France said. "That evidence will show that at some point the victim ended up in the water, arguing, frightened. The evidence will show clearly and definitively that at that point she was nearly drowned, nearly drowned, unconscious to be sure, but still breathing, her heart still beating. You'll see evidence of abrasions and bruising about her body from the struggle as she's drowned."

France said the evidence would show that April's body was dragged about three hundred feet back to where they entered from the boardwalk. Photographs would show that the body was dragged by "a single manner," meaning that she was dragged only one way, with her heels dragging into the sand. He said April's body was never dropped and that no other part of her body hit the sand.

"The evidence will show you that the defendant then shot her in the face, shot one whom he thinks is dead from drowning," France said, "and then shoots himself, all this with the same .22-caliber pistol, once in the meat of his collarbone muscle, shoulder area, another right here in his upper left shoulder, a wound in his chest area, right chest area, and a through-and-through to the hand, placed the gun up to his hand, fired."

He asked the jury to consider each wound carefully when they heard testimony about the location of the wounds and the bleeding that should have occurred. France said that whether it was part of the plan or not, the defendant left her lying on the boardwalk where she was shot.

"You'll see how she was left there, bleeding out of her face, nose and mouth, down to the sand as she fell after being shot, dropped," he said, "just as she would have fallen, had he merely dropped her after dragging her because of that near drowning."

The prosecutor told the jury that April would have died from the near drowning without resuscitation. "And then the defendant left her," he said. "A murderer."

France told how Barber drove eight miles, past houses, businesses and gas stations before stopping at an intersection. It was at this point, France said, that Barber told of a robbery attempt, that a man walked up, shot April and Barber at the waterline, not at the boardwalk. He asked the jury to listen carefully to that portion of the testimony and give it strong consideration.

"You'll hear interesting testimony again from Detective Cole that the defendant indicated early on he passed out," France said, "didn't really know what happened. The phantom, this robber, one who was never there."

The defendant was airlifted to a hospital and his wounds were treated with antibiotic cream and bandaged. Three bullets remaining in Barber were left in place, France said, all of his vital signs were normal, he had full range of motion of both arms, and he was released the next day. The police looked for a gun and a fleeing robber, but found nothing, France told the jury.

Rayonier, the company the defendant worked for, rented a room at the Omni Hotel for Barber after his release from the hospital, France said, where Shannon Kennedy works. France said Barber tried to see Kennedy, even though she wanted to be away from him.

France told the jury that Barber became a "person of interest" during the investigation. He mentioned the computer searches: medical trauma, gunshot—six months before the shooting. Gunshot, right chest trauma—within six months of the shooting. Right where he was shot. France recalled the purchase of the insurance policy a year before April was killed, computer searches within five months of her death, and in August, soon after their third wedding anniversary.

"At the end of hearing this evidence, when you take the common sense with you and your experiences that you sit there with today, that you have with you right now and apply the evidence," France said, "you'll be convinced that the defendant planned to murder April Barber, shot April Barber on that beach, and murdered his wife."

France took his seat and Willis rose to make his opening statement. After greeting them, he emphasized a point he made during voir dire that the prosecution had just attempted to discredit.

"I used the word 'massive,'" he said, "and I'd use it again. There's been an enormous amount of work that's been put into this case, as you might imagine."

Because there was so much involved in the case, Willis apologized to the jury because his opening statement would be longer than usual. He told them he liked to "slim down" the opening statement as much as he could, but that he wanted to go into detail about the evidence instead of making broad remarks. The key to a just verdict, he said, was going to be the jury's careful attention to everything they heard in the courtroom.

Willis said he wished he didn't have to deal with Barber's adultery, but counsel had spent a great deal of time on it the day before. The state mentioned four affairs, but Willis thought there might have been five.

"There were two that he disclosed in the course of a civil deposition that nobody would have ever known about, because they were what you call 'one-night stands,'" Willis said. Although nobody knew the names of the women, Willis said, Barber revealed the affairs because he was under oath.

"He's not proud of that, he can't do anything about it now," Willis said. "He disrespected his marriage and disrespected his wife by his infidelity . . . but we're hoping . . .

that y'all follow the court's direction, that you consider that for the purpose for which it's offered, and that is the question of whether . . . it provides motive." Willis said the evidence would not show this as motive.

The defense attorney said Barber was "a young man, clearly full of himself, he's twenty-nine years of age, he's making a great deal of money, he's in a very plush job, he's with a Fortune 500 company, he's traveling internationally, and he is not totally unattractive, and there were temptations that present themselves and he gets involved in that."

One affair was in New Zealand, Willis said, a coworker in Georgia, and two other women, Willis said, and Shannon Kennedy, the one the state wanted to talk about the most. There wasn't any contradiction between the state and defense version of the affair with Shannon Kennedy. "It was very common for Enterprise to put on little social functions, little 'happy hour' things for their good customers and they met through that," Willis said. "There was no question there was an attraction. They began playing tennis and eventually that became a physical relationship."

It was important to know that Shannon Kennedy was living with another man in a committed relationship, and that Barber was obviously committed by marriage, Willis stressed.

"Each will tell you that there was never the first suggestion that either envisioned anything greater, deeper, longer lasting," Willis said. "There was none of this, 'We're going to go away together,' or anything even remotely of that sort. . . . There is not a motive borne of that testimony."

So far as Barber checking into the Omni after being released from the hospital, Willis pointed out that it was Rayonier that chose the room. Rayonier, the attorney said, wanted to help Barber avoid the reporters and other intrusions in his life, and he wanted to see Shannon Kennedy so he could apologize for having her involved.

"And, in fact, when he finally did see her, the evidence will be that he broke down sobbing, uncontrollable, because of what he had been through and the fact that he lost his wife," Willis told the jury.

The defense attorney said Barber had shopped carefully for life insurance to find the best deal he could. He said he would present the testimony of an expert to verify that Barber's insurance policies were not excessive. So far as losing money in the stock market, Barber was no different than "a lot of people back in that . . . hotshot era of the stock market, tried to be a player and wound up losing about thirty thousand dollars," Willis said.

"This man was not in any kind of financial trouble at all, as suggested by counsel," Willis said. "Justin Barber was making one hundred–plus thousand a year, his wife was already making seventy thousand dollars, and she hadn't finished her course of study. She was two months away from graduating."

Willis talked about Barber's degrees from the University of Oklahoma and how Rayonier had chosen him to be the presidential MBA. "They select one person each year to be sort of their chosen one, sort of their one that they say has got the right stuff that's going to be on the fast track for senior management in Rayonier," Willis said. "When they're brought in, they're exposed to upper-level management to see how that team operates and then they're specifically placed around the company to give them the experience that will be necessary . . . because they . . . have the right stuff to wind up at the very top of Rayonier. Justin Barber was the presidential MBA."

Insurance companies don't issue $2 million without

doing a lot of checking on finances, credit, health and family history of illness that might make a person a bad risk. The insurance companies want to make money, and a potential policy holder must demonstrate "an insurable interest." First Colony investigated all these areas and were happy to write the policies, Willis said.

"It made particular sense to Justin Barber and to April Barber at the time, partially for the reason that counsel has already indicated," Willis said. "This lady, unfortunately, her mom had passed away in her early thirties from cancer. There was a history of cancer in the family. It is also the case that she had a health problem potentially in the form of cholesterol level of three hundred, though she was only the age of twenty-six at the time the policy is issued. It made a lot of sense to lock your rate in early on, which they did, and purchased two million dollars' worth of insurance for the sum of one thousand thirty a year. It was an excellent deal. And, again, there was no financial motive to Justin Barber. The future—his financial future was unbelievably bright."

Willis said that Barber had made the premium payments for the life insurance policies until he and April decided jointly to drop them. Yet, the last premium payment before her death was made by April from her personal checking account. The facts in the case would lead them to what Willis called the "proper" verdict.

"If you're interested in finding out whether Justin Barber killed his wife, April," he said, "then let's go to the facts. Facts are powerful things. They will lead you in the right direction . . . if you'll listen and follow them."

Willis claimed that on the night April was killed, they focused their attention exclusively on Barber, and "ignored a clue that, if it were a potted plant and fell on you, it would break your head." He said the clue they "almost totally" ignored was a K-car the witnesses reported seeing at Guana Beach the same time April was murdered.

"Yet, within two weeks of the time this death occurred, they (the police) have launched subpoenas for telephone records, for credit card company records, records of First USA Bank, JP Morgan, Chase Bank, Bank of America, American Express, SunTrust Bank, all of Justin Barber's financial records, in an effort," Willis said, "a failed effort, to show that he had some financial problems going on."

In addition to that, Willis said, the state had paid an expert $25,000—and would pay him another $25,000—"trying to prove that Justin Barber had a financial motive. . . . They can't prove it because he didn't. But they launched all of that."

While pursuing Barber, Willis said, the police ignored an obvious lead that "the most rank amateur would have recognized"—the K-car reported on the beach. Instead, after Barber drove from the scene, looking for help, and then was airlifted to Shands Hospital, Detective Cole went to the hospital and interviewed him. Willis said Barber's initial statement was "the same statement" he had given on several occasions in the past several years.

Willis told the jury Barber's version of how he and April ate at a restaurant, went for a moonlight walk at Guana Beach with the intention of having sex on the beach and were attacked by a gunman, who seemed intent on robbery. Willis recounted the heroic, but ultimately failed, efforts to get his wife's body from the surf to find help, even though he had been shot four times.

"He tried to pick her up. . . . He tried to get her over his shoulder, but he couldn't do it," Willis said. "He didn't know, at that time, realize he was shot. He knew his body wasn't working right. He tried to get her over his shoulder, couldn't do that. He wound up dragging her . . .

hooking his arms underneath her arms and dragging her all the way up, with the intention of getting her up to his automobile so he could go get her help. He believed she was probably dead, but he was still making that effort, and it was a Herculean effort, I might add."

Willis told the jury there was no doubt that Barber dragged April because the marks are clearly shown in the police reenactment of the crime. It was only later that they got down to the beach, he said, and the incoming tide had washed all footprints away, including those of Barber and April.

"No one's going to be able to say there were no footprints of this person," he said. "There're no footprints of anyone because the tide has come in and washed it all away. So what we have is the undisputed fact that he did drag this lady along the beach."

Because of his wounds and the effort, Willis said, Barber couldn't carry her. "It finally just overwhelmed him and she slid down the railing and crumpled into the position that she was ultimately found in," Willis said.

The defense attorney emphasized Barber's cooperation with the police. He told how Barber returned from his wife's funeral in Oklahoma and was willing to go to the police station at 8:15 A.M. and be interrogated in one form or another until midnight. Barber never turned down a request from the police to help.

"They asked for permission that very first night at the hospital," Willis said. "He is the victim of a shooting, his wife has been shot, and when they leave this hospital room, before they leave, what do they do? They ask for permission to search his apartment. He gives it without hesitation or limitation. It was in the apartment that they found these insurance policies. They were right in the file cabinet, where you'd expect them to be."

Barber was always cooperative, Willis said. He gave

police permission to search his car; he gave them his computer; he brought home his work computer and handed that over to the police.

"He has never refused a request for [an] interview or to cooperate with the police, up to and including today," Willis said. "That's never happened. Never happened."

Willis said the police would use the drag marks on the beach to prove that Barber was wrong. The prosecution would try to show that April and Barber were walking on the beach and everyone agreed that they somehow ended up in the water, Willis said, but the police don't say why.

"As we all know and everybody believes . . . it's not explained how or why . . . they wind up in the water in a struggle, during which he holds her underwater so long that she loses consciousness," Willis said. "This [is a] partial drowning, or near-drowning experience. After she is unconscious, then he picks her up, in one form or another, and drags her—because you can't dispute that—drags her up toward the boardwalk, closer to the highway, closer to civilization, and when he gets her up there, still unconscious, for whatever reason, he shoots her one time in the cheek."

You don't intentionally shoot someone in the cheek to kill them, Willis said. You shoot them in the brain. He said the shot that killed April was not a well-placed shot, but a fluke. "Unfortunately, what it did was hit her top cervical vertebra and that causes pretty much instant paralysis, you stop breathing," Willis said. "Your heart may continue for a while, but you stop breathing, and that's how she died."

Willis asked that if Barber held April under the water until she was nearly drowned and unconscious, why wouldn't he just continue to hold her in that position if he wanted to kill her. "Why pull her out of the water, take her all the way up by the boardwalk, where you increase your chances of being found, and there shoot

her?" Willis asked. "And then, oh, by the way, shoot yourself four separate times, according to their theory."

The prosecution suggested that scrapes on April indicated a struggle, but he said that wasn't the case. The
scrapes on her arm were consistent with falling down a railing. He said the "punctate abrasions" the medical examiner would discuss were "like an eighth of an inch across. I
mean they're tiny, you can't even hardly see them."

Willis pointed out that none of April's fingernails were
damaged and there was nothing beneath the nails. There
were no bruises to her at all, Willis said, and none on
Barber except for the gunshot wounds.

"So there was no struggle," Willis said. "If she were fighting for her life . . . somebody would have been injured . . .
and there was no such evidence." He said the medical examiner might agree with him about how the abrasions on
April's body got there.

Willis told how Barber, no longer able to carry April,
tried to flag down a car on the highway. Three passed by
before he decided to drive for help. When Willis had
an investigator drive the same route Barber had taken,
the attorney said there was only one business that might
have been open at 11:15 P.M. on Saturday.

"The overriding impression you will get from that is that
it's extremely dark," Willis said. "It's an estate section . . .
with big high gates and mansions and that sort of thing.
Bear in mind that he's intoxicated, he's been shot, he's
watched the horrible scene of his wife being killed in front
of him and he's exhausted himself from trying to carry her
off the beach. So maybe it's not surprising that he wouldn't
do things in a totally logical manner."

Willis told the jury they would hear evidence on blood
transfer—or lack of it—which would conflict with the
facts. Barber was not bleeding much, Willis said, and
April's body was placed in a body bag and the autopsy

wasn't performed until 9:00 A.M., Monday. During the time the remains were in the body bag, he said, blood continued to leak from her body and contaminated the wet clothing that had not been removed from the body.

"That did two things," Willis said. "It impaired the DNA, because the sworn enemy of DNA is moisture, wetness. If you're going to preserve anything for DNA analysis, you have to dry it as quickly as you can. But, importantly, it allowed this blood to accumulate where she was laying and artificially taint the scene and change it from what it was."

The evidence would show substantial blood on April's blouse, particularly around the left sleeve, he said, but he claimed, "This is where it soaked into as she lay for eighteen to twenty-four hours before she was autopsied and these clothes taken off of her." That area is where Barber's wounded hand would have been, but it wasn't there: Willis said it could have been masked by the blood that leaked during the time the remains were in the body bag.

"We don't know one way or the other," Willis said. "We just don't know."

Of course, if the defense didn't know, the inference was neither did the prosecution.

Willis got into more specifics that let the jury know just how complex the forensics in this case would be. There were forty-six different bloodstains on April's pants, and testing showed thirty-six were from female blood. The state, using more sophisticated technology, retested and determined that the thirty-six female stains were from April Barber's blood. He spoke of different ways to measure the XY chromosome to tell if it's male or female. However, the state couldn't say that the stains in the thirty-six areas identified as coming from April's blood, that this blood didn't make blood transfer from the defendant.

"There are ten areas of staining that they can tell you are human blood, but they cannot tell you whether they're even male or female because they've been so degraded by the way that the officers and the medical personnel handled the clothing in this case," Willis said. "They allowed the evidence to degrade to the point where they can't even tell you whether it's male or female. So all ten of those could be Justin Barber [or], for that matter, none. But you can't tell. You don't know."

The state's theory was that April was shot at the boardwalk and was never carried, so there couldn't be any blood transfer, one to the other, Willis said. "That's their linchpin and that's the idea of how they show that what happened isn't true. It's all—"

France interrupted to tell the judge that Willis was arguing rather than outlining the case. France complained that Willis was stating what the prosecution's theory may or may not be, then commenting on how the evidence affected it.

The judge said he thought Willis was trying to explain both the state and defense theories to the jury. He overruled the objection, but warned Willis that he was close to crossing the line.

Willis continued to emphasize what he thought was careless handling of the DNA evidence. Barber was charged in July 2004, he said, "the charge that's bringing you here today, but not until late last year did they finally, somebody did, at least get the idea, we've looked at her clothing to see if his blood is on it, shouldn't we look at maybe his clothing to see if her blood's on it? Because transfer can work both ways."

Finally the state did look late last year, Willis said, and found April's blood on the back and front of Barber's shirt. "Just where it would have been when he tried to put her over his shoulder and if her head had moved around when he's dragging her like this," he said.

Willis said he would try to prove that April was shot

where she was found, but he said the position she was in was more as if she had fallen, the way Barber described. The photograph shows blood flowing the way the head was tilted, obeying the law of gravity. The state inferred from this, Willis said, that April had to have been shot where she lay and not dragged, which would have caused blood to flow in all directions.

"The problem is this," Willis said, "the photographs that demonstrates that . . . the best we can figure out . . . was taken three hours after her death. So the photograph that you will see will not be the scene and the situation at the time of her death initially."

The state and defense experts would disagree on blood flow, he said. But the first ones there, including a police officer, said he did not see any blood when he found April's body. "In fact, he didn't even know how she was injured," Willis said, "couldn't even figure it out."

The jury would hear from EMTs who saw no blood and no bleeding. "So the suggestion that this is scientific evidence, this gravity thing flowing straight down, that this is the scientific evidence upon which you should base a verdict, is simply not going to fly," Willis said.

Having touched on the complexities of blood smear and DNA, Willis gave his version of how the key word search worked: certain words such as blood, murder, gun, homicide and other sinister-appearing words were looked at in Barber's computers. Willis wasn't a computer guy, but he said the FDLE fed the key words into a computer, which spit out singly or in combination whether or not those words were searched.

The FDLE didn't evaluate what the computer provided, but sent a list to the police and prosecutors to peruse and decide which words were significant.

"It's important that you understand, that nobody, even with all this advanced technology, can tell you what occurred before or, for that matter, even right after these particular queries occurred," Willis said. "So out of these hundreds and perhaps thousands of queries that were found on these machines, out of all of those they searched, they found two, 6 months away from this woman's death, that are odd, and they clearly are odd."

Barber never denied making the searches, Willis said, he just didn't remember whether or not he did. Perhaps Barber saw something interesting on one of the *CSI* television shows, an article in the newspaper, or something that triggered his interest in making a search. Willis said no one knew.

"What we know is that, out of thousands and thousands and thousands, those are the ones that they have selected so they can try to draw that awful inference that somehow six months before, for whatever weird reason, he's asking questions about shooting himself in the chest," Willis said.

The defense attorney explained that Barber's four bullet wounds were defined as "superficial" in medical terms, meaning these didn't hit internal organs. Within an inch or so of each body wound, Willis said, there were vital organs that could have killed Barber if these were damaged.

"You can picture, as they would suggest, [Barber] shooting himself on a dark beach," Willis said. "If he's off by an inch, he's a dead man. Does that really make sense?"

The defense hired an expert criminologist to go over the evidence, Willis said, and the expert concluded that the gunshots had to be fired by an assailant. The wound in Barber's hand was a "defensive wound," Willis said. "[He] grabbed the firearm and the gun shoots, comes through here (indicating the left hand). Once the bullet goes through the hand, it loses its spiral, sort of like a football, and begins to tumble just like a badly thrown football."

Willis said the expert had examined the FDLE's findings and determined that the evidence showed that the state never considered the shot in the hand to be a defensive wound. Yet the wound on his right chest didn't show markings that would be left if it was the primary wound. Instead, Willis said, the evidence indicated that the bullet that hit Barber in the right chest was the same one that penetrated his left hand.

Witnesses for the defense would also tell the jury that they saw a K-car parked near Barber's vehicle at Guana Beach on the night of the murder. Barber consistently told police there were no other vehicles parked there when he arrived at the beach or after he and April had been shot. Anyone who had parked there, Willis said, did so after Barber and his wife went down to the beach, and left before Barber came back to go for help. One witness who saw the K-car also was at the intersection when "here comes Justin Barber screaming by them at seventy miles an hour with his emergency flashers on," Willis said.

The police didn't follow up properly on the K-car lead, Willis said. Several days later, he said, the police issued a press release asking for information on the car, then conducted an off-line search to identify K-cars registered in Duval and St. Johns County. They received about three hundred names.

"And then they sent them a form letter saying, 'If you own a K-car, please call us and tell us if you were down on Guana Beach, Saturday night, at about eleven o'clock,'" Willis said. "And to this day . . . the person or persons that occupied that car have never called [to] say. . . . 'I heard four or five shots fired down on the beach that night' . . . suggesting that the only person who would not make that call is the person that fired those shots."

Willis ended by pleading with the jury to follow the evidence and to follow it closely.

The television reporters hurried from the courtroom to give their viewers an update on the trial. They had heard about the forensic evidence for the first time and realized it was going to be a complex trial. Blood spatter. Entry versus nonentry wounds. Financial records. Near drowning. Drag marks. Blood flow. Computer technology. This was the type of stuff that usually made jurors' eyes glaze.

One national television reporter wondered on the air if any jury in Florida would be intelligent enough to understand the evidence. He referred to "hanging chads" and "butterfly ballots," which had stupefied Florida poll workers during the 2000 presidential election. The reporter failed to mention that most people in America had never heard of chads and butterfly ballots, either.

The comment was one of many that would cause controversy during the trial. One commentator would eventually present evidence on the air that the jury would never see and cause the defense to move for a mistrial.

Chapter 23

France's first witness was Lieutenant Ben Tanner, a sixteen-year veteran with the SJSO. Tanner had worked through the ranks as a road deputy to watch commander. During his time with the SJSO, Tanner had worked in various capacities from special weapons and tactics (SWAT) to the bomb squad.

Tanner testified that on the night of April's murder, he was a road sergeant in charge of the northeast quadrant of St. Johns County, an area that includes Guana State Park. The police officer was familiar with Guana Park, its wild, rugged nature, high dunes and three wooden boardwalks that led from A1A to the beach.

On the night of August 17, 2002, Tanner was on duty as road sergeant. He left for the Ponte Vedra area immediately after hearing that there was a shooting there. Tanner's wife, a division director secretary for the SJSO, rode with him that night as a volunteer spotter. Other than that, Tanner had no backup. While en route, deputies on the scene in Ponte Vedra advised Tanner that there might be a second "incident" on the beach by one of the boardwalks. Tanner asked Jacksonville Beach police to check their beach accesses and directed SJSO deputies in the Ponte Vedra area that were not already involved at the crime scene to check all beach accesses throughout the county. A dozen walkways were involved.

Tanner didn't know at which walkway the incident had occurred. All had to be searched. At that time, the police didn't know what the "incident" was. Tanner was near Highway 210 and U.S. 1 when information came over the radio that the incident was a robbery and shooting on the beach. The deputy headed toward Guana Beach while looking for any cars driving too fast, or drivers trying to hide when they saw his police car. Tanner stopped at the dark, empty north access. It was pitch black and there were no cars in the parking lot. The dune was so high the ocean couldn't be seen from the highway.

Tanner got out of his car, flashlight in one hand, and pistol in the other. Not wanting to leave his wife alone, Tanner took her along, and moved tactically, through the parking lot to see if there were any vehicles or anything suspicious. Nothing. Tanner and his wife moved tactically down the curved boardwalk toward the ocean. He described "tactical" as moving in a way that was like slicing a pie, a maneuver that gave him maximum visibility and safety.

The deputy and his wife moved down the curved walkway through the rugged, heavily vegetated dunes. It was so dark that they could see little. Tanner placed a special flashlight on his handgun that illuminated areas where he pointed the weapon. He was concerned about walking into an ambush, going into the dark unknown where a shooting had occurred.

As they neared the beach, Tanner saw a body lying at the end of the boardwalk. He informed dispatch by radio to send rescue and backup. Tanner continued his slow, tactical movements toward the body, while his wife stood by, sweeping the dunes with her flashlight. Tanner felt for a pulse and breathing. He had checked numerous bodies in his career. There was no doubt that the person was dead.

Tanner was a witness who had initially reported that he had seen no blood on April's face. France wanted to create doubt as to whether the deputy had checked carefully enough to know for sure that he had seen no blood.

France asked Tanner if he had determined that April was dead before he actually checked for a pulse and breathing.

"Things were happening pretty quickly," Tanner said. "It would be hard for me to tell you one way or the other. . . . It was a quick glance at best. . . . I was still in a very defensive tactical situation, not knowing what I had out in front of me. I wanted to check her as best I could and keep an eye on the situation at hand."

With that single question and answer, France had cast doubt on how carefully Tanner had scrutinized the body. Perhaps there was blood on April's face and he didn't look closely enough to see it. That was the impression he hoped it would make on the jury.

Tanner said that after he called rescue, there wasn't much he could do except check her pulse and breathing. "In fact, when I bent down to check her for a pulse, I was actually scanning the beach area at the same time. I do recall visibly looking down at her stomach and checking to see if it was moving or if she was moving at all, but it was a quick glance."

Tanner's answer to France's question drove the point home: the deputy had been busy scanning the area for a gunman, while checking April's pulse. France managed to cast doubt on the deputy's earlier statement that he not seen blood on April's face. And he had done it without impeaching the deputy's initial report.

France showed photographs of April's body to Tanner, who acknowledged that these showed the position she was in when he saw her. Tanner verified that he had not moved the body. After he called for backup, Tanner jumped over the boardwalk railing and took up a defensive position about twenty feet into the dunes.

A deputy and an EMT arrived. The EMT checked April's vital signs, but found none. Tanner warned the deputy and EMT to stay on the west side of the body. Shortly after that, a rescue squad arrived and connected April's body to EKG machines and tried to find a heartbeat. Tanner tried to preserve the crime scene, but the EMTs had to move east of the body to attach EKG tabs. Tanner said he told them not to go any farther than necessary to do their job.

"And why were you concerned with that?" France asked.

"Number one, it was pretty soon into it. I didn't know what we had still down on the beach. I didn't know what suspects may be down on the beach. I didn't know what evidence I may have down on the beach. I had a K-9 en route to do a track. If there was anything to be tracked, I didn't want that to be disturbed."

Tanner described how the Jacksonville Sheriff's Office (JSO) helicopter, which was already in the air, arrived to search the area until the SJSO helicopter arrived and continued the search. Tanner said that no one, including EMTs, moved any of April's clothing or the body. France introduced photos showing the body and darkness beyond.

Tanner said the only light available when he found the body was the flashlight his wife carried and the one he had attached to his handgun. There was no natural lighting that he could recall, not even moonlight. The deputy acknowledged that he maintained control of the crime scene and evidence until other deputies came. At that point, he reverted to a supervisory role to secure the crime scene, control traffic on A1A, established a media relation center and made certain everyone had the resources they needed.

"Could you see visible injuries upon the body?" France asked.

"No, sir. When I initially got to her and checked her, I did not see any initial injuries to her."

"Did you roll her face over?"

"No, sir."

"Did you see either blood or foam?"

"I seen a white frothy substance that was down along the side of her cheek in her hair," Tanner said. "It appeared to have some type of red residue to it that I assumed was blood."

Tanner said he didn't use his flashlight to bend down and examine more closely because he had already taken April's pulse and knew she was dead. France took his seat at the prosecution table and Willis began his cross-examination.

Tanner said that he arrived at the Guana Beach parking lot around 11:32 P.M., checked the lot, then went directly to the beach. The deputy said he didn't check to see if the parking-lot gate was locked or not. The gate was usually locked after dark, he said, and he had no reason to think it would not be that night. He testified again as to how he made a tactical approach and found April's body.

"You've already told us there wasn't a whole lot of light," Willis said. "But did you say that you had a flashlight on your firearm?"

"Yes, sir."

"And your wife that was with you had her flashlight as well?"

Tanner said yes.

"May we assume that you used one or both of those

flashlights to illuminate this lady's body when you found her?"

Tanner agreed.

Tanner acknowledged that he had knelt over the body when he checked for a pulse, and acknowledged that he recognized two photographs entered into evidence. One was taken several feet from the body, the second at a more severe angle. Willis asked Tanner if he could see April's face better from the photograph taken from the beach side of the body. Willis said there was little difference between the two photographs.

"You said you saw some froth, some white foamy material?" Willis asked.

"I did see some type of white foamy substance down around her hair." He pointed to the photograph. "It's sort of a reddish color there."

Tanner said that he bent over the body to check the pulse in the carotid artery. That was when he saw the froth. The deputy quickly added, "Remember, I did testify that I glanced down at her stomach area, I glanced down at her face, and then I went back to scanning the beach."

"The fact of the matter is that you didn't see any blood at all, did you?" Willis asked sharply.

"No, sir, not other than . . . what I pointed out on this photograph."

"The question is, did you see any blood at all, Lieutenant?"

"Yes, sir."

Willis was surprised. "You did?"

". . . what I pointed out on this photograph right here."

"Do you recall that . . . a deposition that was taken of you, in fact, very recently, April 12, 2006?"

"Yes, sir."

"Page sixteen. Talking in this same area. You say, 'Well,

as you can see in this photograph here, it's quite extensive around her hairline here. I do recall seeing something there, sort of a white, and, you know, I don't know . . . what it is, to be honest with you. I didn't know then and I don't know now."

Willis read again from the deposition: "Question: 'Okay, but did you also see any blood there in the hair?'

"Answer: 'I did not see any blood at all.'

"Question: 'You didn't see any blood?'

"'I did not see any blood at all. I had no idea where she was wounded at all because I distinctively remember when I checked her for a pulse, I distinctively remember going, 'Where is she hurt at, you know, and I couldn't tell. I couldn't see anything.'"

Willis said, "That would seem to be in contradiction to what you just said?"

Tanner said he understood that, but he was pointing at the redness of April's hair in the photograph and the white froth substance. "I do not recall seeing any blood, what is on the photograph there. Does that make sense or does that confuse the issue more?"

France spoke up and objected to "improper impeachment" of the witness. "He was shown a different photograph there [at] the deposition," France said. "They're from an angle where you could clearly see blood down low to the ground that just—"

"Let me rule," Judge Hedstrom said. "Are you objecting to the form of the impeachment?"

France said he was, and the court sustained his objection. Willis wasn't satisfied. He referred to page seventeen of Tanner's deposition. "I don't know that I asked a question, Your Honor. Can we have a sidebar? I don't want to do what you don't want me to do, but I'm honestly unclear of where we are right now. . . . I just indicated I was going to a page and then there was an objection and that's where we stopped. If I can have a clarification?"

France said, "Your Honor, I object to continued impeachment in this matter. You sustained that objection."

"I didn't sustain continued impeachment," the judge said. "I sustained the form of the impeachment."

France agreed and the judge said, "Okay."

Willis continued his cross-examination. "Officer, it is the case, is it not, that you had no idea how this woman was injured, correct?"

"That's correct, yes, sir."

"And you're saying now that in addition to the froth, you saw some blood in her hair."

Tanner said, "There was a red substance there. Now, whether that was blood, it wasn't thick, it wasn't bright red. . . . It was just a red twinge to her hair, right there around where the white frothy substance was."

Willis listened with impatience as Tanner said that it "wasn't that of a normal blood. . . . I mean, it wasn't visibly blood. Does that make sense?"

"No," Willis answered.

Tanner explained that the red color on April's hair didn't make him think she was injured there. The color, he said, could have been from highlights. What struck him most was the white frothy substance.

"But you're now saying that, in addition to a white frothy substance, you saw something red in her hair?"

"Right around the white frothy substance, yes, sir."

Tanner said he had no idea what had happened to April. Willis jumped on the answer.

"You're a police officer with all these years' experience. You've got a lady laying there on the beach with her face down. You're telling us you got froth. You're now saying that you see some red tinge in it. And you're swearing now and saying, 'Well, I had no idea where she was hurt?'"

Tanner said that was correct. He said he knew she was hurt, but he had no idea how she had been hurt.

Willis asked Tanner whether there was a car parked by a NO PARKING sign when he first arrived at the beach. Tanner said that he didn't see a car. Tanner also acknowledged that the EMTs and rescue personnel had to step over April's body to perform their tasks.

On a brief redirect, France established there were several places to park on the shoulder of A1A as it ran along the beach.

After two witnesses testified, there were clearly stark differences in how the state and prosecution viewed the evidence. Willis tried hard to impeach Tanner, who had testified in a deposition that he had seen blood on April's face, but now said he wasn't sure, that he was too distracted by other things to notice if he saw blood or color highlights in April's hair.

The next witness for the state was John Holmquist, who had been a crime scene analyst with the FDLE for thirteen years. He was stationed at the FDLE's Jacksonville office. France established Holmquist's credentials as an expert who attended continual training yearly to stay up to date. The FDLE analyst had formal training in a number of areas and had been the primary analyst for more than eight hundred crime scenes.

Holmquist told how he headed toward the beach after receiving a request from Sergeant Mary Fagan on August 18, stopping once, briefly, when he saw the police vehicles at A1A and Ponte Vedra Drive. The FDLE analyst looked briefly into Barber's SUV at the intersection before going to the beach to meet Fagan. The state entered photographs of the SUV into evidence after Holmquist identified them as being prints of the SUV.

Holmquist stayed at Guana State Park from 1:30 until 6:05 A.M., attended the autopsy on Monday and checked Barber's SUV at the SJSO impound that same afternoon. France asked Holmquist to check his notes to be sure what day the autopsy was performed. It was on Monday morning, following the murder. France began to question Holmquist in more detail as to what he had done at each place where he helped the police.

Holmquist spent only a short time at the A1A-Ponte Vedra intersection before going to the dark beach. The FDLE analyst started a generator mounted on his crime scene truck and set up two lights. Before mounting the lights, Holmquist held one in his hand while he made a videotape, then mounted the lights so they illuminated April's body and slightly beyond.

With the lights up, Holmquist and Sergeant Raye Tanner followed the drag marks from the boardwalk to the beach. They were the first officials to go onto the beach since the discovery of April's body. The men walked slowly along the drag marks in the hope of finding where the murder occurred. And then they got closer to the waterline.

"We discovered that the drag marks had been washed away," Holmquist said. "We got to the waterline in the sand, and the surf had been coming up and washing away what was there."

The FDLE agent said he checked the drag marks before examining the body because he had feared that the tide would wash evidence away. Turning his attention to April, Holmquist took photographs and collected blood from the back of her right wrist and on the inside of her upper left arm. The blood was blotted with sterile swabs, sealed and marked as evidence. Holmquist also measured the body, bagged her hands and rolled her slightly to check injuries on her back. He also collected froth on April's face to turn over to the evidence lab.

Holmquist explained some of the procedures to the jury. The hands were secured in small brown paper bags to preserve evidence that might be on them. Holmquist measured the length of the drag marks from the board-walk to the waterline. He examined tire tracks on A1A and made casts so tire treads could be examined. There were few tire tracks to preserve because the ground was packed too hard to show tread design.

While following the drag marks, Holmquist saw no blood in the sand. When the analyst examined Barber's SUV at the SJSO impound, he found bloodstains on the driver's door panel and steering wheel. These were pre-served for examination. Barber's shirt and four loose buttons, cut by the EMTs, were found and bagged for transport to the forensic laboratory.

Court was recessed for lunch. One of the jurors caught what she called "a stomach bug" and thought she might need to step down. The judge, attorneys and the juror met in his chamber. Hedstrom said he would ac-commodate the juror any way he could, but if she could try to go on, it would be helpful. Hedstrom didn't want to "burn" an alternate juror so early in the trial. The juror said she would try.

The courtroom was filled to bursting when the after-noon session was to start. Various audio and visual aids were scattered about as the prosecution scrambled to put exhibits together. France asked for, and received, a ten-minute delay to finish marking exhibits and then the jury was called in.

France continued his direct of Holmquist, who left the witness stand to look at the three photos of April's body the state had entered into evidence. The witness identi-fied them.

"Specifically, as to the defendant's [*sic*] hair," France said. "Was it fanned out in that fashion when you first saw her?"

"Her hair was just like you see it and that's exactly how I found her."

"As to blood flow, is that also, when you first saw the victim, what that blood flow looked like?"

"Just like that."

"Could you clearly see the difference between the blood and the foam?"

Holmquist said he could. He repeated how he had made swabs of two blood smears on April and the foam, sealed and marked them as evidence. France noted that April's arms were spread out. He asked if Holmquist moved them to collect the blood samples. The FDLE analyst said he did not, and that her arms were in the same position as shown in the photograph.

Holmquist said the blood on April's arms was visible to the naked eye once he started the generator and turned on the lights.

"And it was after those lights were up, did you then look for evidence, blood evidence, upon her?"

"Yes, after I set everything up and did the work down on the beach. Then I focused on the body."

France asked Holmquist to identify a bag containing the swabs. Holmquist said he had sealed and marked the bag on August 18 for laboratory examination. He explained how he absorbed the blood on the swabs before placing it in containers. France asked him to look at how April's legs were cross-positioned and asked if they were like that when he first saw the body. Holmquist said yes.

France asked whether April's shirt was wet or dry, but Holmquist didn't know. He had not felt her clothing. An FDLE director named Porter told Holmquist that April's clothing was damp. Finished with the photos of April at the crime scene, France turned to photographs of Barber's SUV. Holmquist explained that he had gathered blood samples in a manner that duplicated taking swabs of blood on April.

The prosecutor displayed photographs of April's wounds that were taken at her autopsy. France asked if the wounds depicted in the photograph were the same as those he saw on the beach. Holmquist said he saw blood on the left hand, but not of the scratches on the left arm and shoulder.

This type of minutia is often what causes a juror's mind to start growing mildew because it seems so dull. That wasn't the case with this jury. They had been told that details would be important and they should pay attention. And so they did. They leaned forward and concentrated on the testimony.

Holmquist told the jury that April wore a diamond ring, watch and an earring. The state would use this later in an attempt to discredit Barber's story that he thought the assailant wanted to rob them. If so, why would he leave these items behind?

The FDLE agent described several more trips to the crime scene to look for evidence. He used a metal detector once because he was trying to find the casings for the bullets that had been fired. Holmquist searched for a gun and anything else that might be of evidentiary value, but found nothing.

France guided Holmquist back to the autopsy and asked him to describe the protocol for removing a victim's clothing and saving it for evidence. An autopsy technician removes the clothing under the ME's supervision and they were given to Holmquist, who bagged and marked them, as he did other evidence. All of the items were then listed on forms that were filed with the FDLE's evidence intake session. France knew the defense intended to persuade the jury that the state's handling of blood evidence had been careless. Holmquist talked the jury through the process.

He removed evidence from the operations center and prepared forms for the evidence intake section. Holmquist hand-carried the evidence to intake and it was entered into a computer database. The evidence was kept in a vault. This was the protocol he had used to process April Barber's clothing.

France asked Holmquist to open the evidence bags. One contained a shirt, with areas cut out, that had been marked with a pen called a Sharpie. Holmquist identified the shirt on a photograph of April's body. The agent pointed to an area of the collar.

"Over here, we have the blood that was dripped down from her mouth and the nose and the wounds that have come down the side of her face, down to her back onto her hair," he said. "I believe there may have been a little bit of blood on the shirt collar from that."

"Is it your testimony that this is the only area that had visible blood on it?" France asked.

"Yes, I believe it was just this area here, the front of the shirt. The rest of the shirt, I didn't observe any blood."

Holmquist told the jury that the shirt he just showed them was "very bloodstained" in areas that were not stained with blood in the photographs they had seen of the body at the crime scene. The agent noted that the shirt was sandy and the cuttings from it were consistent with how the FDLE's DNA section would cut samples for further study. France entered the shirt into evidence with no objection by the defense. The state also entered April's capri pants into evidence.

The state offered into evidence blood swabs from Barber's wounds, blood smears from the SUV, Barber's bloodstained shirt, fingernail clippings from April, strands of hair and buttons cut from Barber's shirt by the EMTs.

France showed the videotape Holmquist shot at the crime scene, while the FDLE witness told the jury what they were seeing. He described the diamond ring as the videotape showed it with the stone turned toward her sandy palm. Using a handheld light to illuminate what he was shooting, Holmquist showed the sand near the boardwalk, which is composed of soft sand and crushed coquina shells. The soft sand showed drag marks as the agent worked his way to hard-packed sand at the edge of the water. The videotape then turned and followed the drag marks back to the boardwalk.

Following the short video's conclusion, it was time for Willis to cross-examine. He had at least one huge point that he wanted to make with the jury: the video showed footprints coming back from the beach, but none coming from the boardwalk. Had April and Barber entered the beach area from a different walk-over? If so, why were their sandals parked neatly in the sand at the boardwalk where the body was found?

Holmquist had no answer. As he continued to answer questions about the videotape, Holmquist reiterated that it was dark. There was a scene where he stopped to take a "cursory" look at the body before continuing to follow drag marks.

"But you were clearly able to see blood on her face at that point, even with a cursory look, correct?" Willis asked.

"Yes."

Holmquist said he saw footprints in the soft coquina shell sand, and drag marks to the hard-packed sand at the waterline, where they ended.

"At some point in there, it looks like you go from very soft and to more or less firm, packed sand. Is that true?" Willis asked.

"Yes."

"Did you examine that sand, both the soft and the more firm sand, for any signs of blood, any spillage of blood?"

"As I walked down the beach, I was looking for any blood. I was looking for anything of evidentiary value."

"And you didn't find any?"

Holmquist said he had not.

"You didn't find any when you came over the board-walk, either. There was none on the boardwalk?"

"I did not find any blood, no."

"And you did not find any in the roadway between the boardwalk and [where] Mr. Barber's car was parked, correct?"

"No, I didn't."

"Carrying it one step further, there wasn't even any blood on the door handle to Mr. Barber's car. Isn't that correct?"

Holmquist said that was true.

Willis referred to the firmly packed sand and said it looked as if he had turned around and headed back the way he had come. The FDLE agent said he had come to the end of the drag marks, where the waterline was in the sand, and he had turned to follow the marks back to the boardwalk.

"In other words, the marks actually went down to where the water had come up and washed it out?"

"Yes."

"Did you at any time find tracks either in the soft sand or the hard sand, or the more firm sand, that would show you the tracks that were made by April and Justin Barber going down to the water?"

"I didn't see any tracks that were leading down to the water."

"So, in other words, we didn't see any tracks at all in that—even the firm, packed sand?"

"Down by the water, I didn't see any."

"My question was, did you see any that you could associate with April and Justin Barber?"

"No."

"Well, we know they got down there, obviously, because they were coming back, correct?" Willis asked pointedly.

"Yes."

Willis asked if Holmquist had an explanation, but all he could say was that he searched for tracks and there were none in the area.

"You searched, but the tracks weren't in that area?" Willis asked.

"In the area I searched, the tracks were not in that area."

Even though there was no evidence to prove it, Holmquist said he believed April and Barber came down the boardwalk, where they took off their sandals. Holmquist answered several questions about how and when he took videotapes and still photographs at the crime scene. Willis showed an enlarged photograph of April's face that the state had entered into evidence. Holmquist said he had taken several swabs from April's body. Willis asked about a dark substance at April's right nostril, the one facing upward.

"Did you take any swabs from this area at all around her face?" Willis asked.

"No."

Willis asked him to examine the area. "You can see here, can you not, that there is a distinct darker area of what looks to have been blood flow from her nostril, her upward nostril. Do you recognize that?"

Holmquist said he saw it when he took the photograph, but said he didn't test to see if it was still wet or had dried.

"You don't know any reason why this would have been

dry and this not?" Willis asked, indicating the blood on the left side of April's face.

"I don't know. I don't know if that was dry."

Willis questioned the witness about the blood swabs he had taken and established that Holmquist was at the crime scene until about 6:05 A.M. The FDLE agent said he didn't know when April's body was removed and said there were no discussions about taking April's clothes separately.

"So, her clothing was not taken, she was effectively wrapped and put in a body bag and transported, correct?" Willis asked. Even though the murder occurred late Friday night, Willis established that the autopsy wasn't conducted until 9:00 A.M., the following Monday.

"Do you know of any reason why the autopsy was delayed until Monday?" Willis asked. Holmquist said that was up to the ME. He confirmed that he had taken photographs of April's clothing and kept the clothing. Holmquist made two trips to deliver the clothing to the lab; one on August 22, and another on August 26.

Since forensic evidence was all that either side really had, Willis wanted to cast doubt on the state's handling of April's clothing. Holmquist explained that all of April's clothing was accepted at the FDLE's laboratory on August 26, seven or eight days after the autopsy. During the interim, the evidence had been held in evidence lockers. April's clothing was stored in a "putrid" locker, where wet clothes are held until they dry. Then they are packaged and submitted to the laboratory.

"If . . . the clothing was still wet, in this case it most likely would have been," Holmquist said, "the shirt may have been—"

Willis interrupted him. "I was curious about that. Because you testified on direct examination . . . that you didn't . . . handle this material, on the shirt at least, and

Portrait of April as a bride.
(Photo by AP Images)

April's Florida driver's license photo. *(Photo courtesy of SJSO)*

Justin was a handsome executive at a Fortune 500 company. *(Photo courtesy of SJSO)*

Guana River State Park is dark and lonely at night.
(Photo courtesy of SJSO)

A boardwalk crosses a rugged section of the park to an untamed
beach on the Atlantic Ocean. *(Photo courtesy of SJSO)*

Highway A1A showing the park's wild western preserve and parking lot. *(Photo courtesy of SJSO)*

The boardwalk leads through dense, primitive vegetation to reach the beach. *(Photo courtesy of SJSO)*

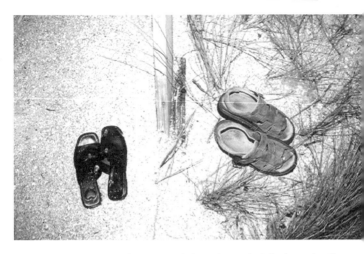

April and Justin left their sandals at the end of the boardwalk.
(Photo courtesy of SJSO)

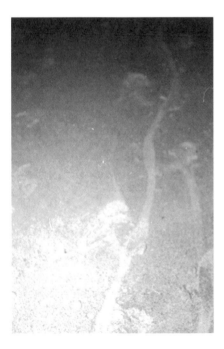

Drag marks show
where April was
dragged on the beach.
(Photo courtesy of SJSO)

The boardwalk traverses thorns, thistles, and other plants.
(Photo courtesy of SJSO)

The boardwalk descends into a jungle-like setting.
(Photo courtesy of SJSO)

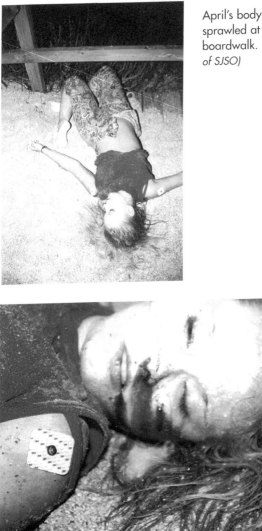

April's body was found sprawled at the end of the boardwalk. (Photo courtesy of SJSO)

Photo shows blood flow only to the left side of April's face.
(Photo courtesy of SJSO)

April's watch and diamond ring were not taken by the assailant.
(Photo courtesy of SJSO)

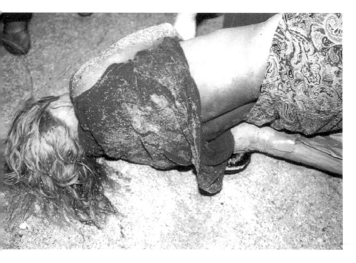

Abrasions and bruising were visible on April's neck and shoulder.
(Photo courtesy of SJSO)

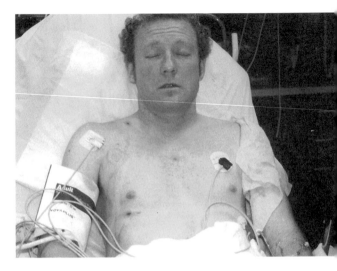

Justin in Shands Hospital after being shot four times.
(Photo courtesy of SJSO)

Wound to Justin's right shoulder. (Photo courtesy of SJSO)

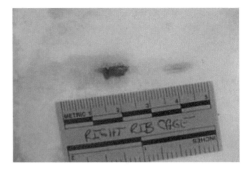

Wound to Justin's right rib cage.
(Photo courtesy of SJSO)

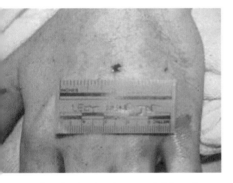

Wound to the back of Justin's left hand.
(Photo courtesy of SJSO)

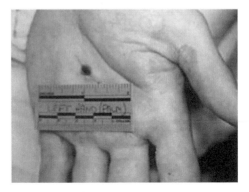

Wound to the palm of Justin's left hand. *(Photo courtesy of SJSO)*

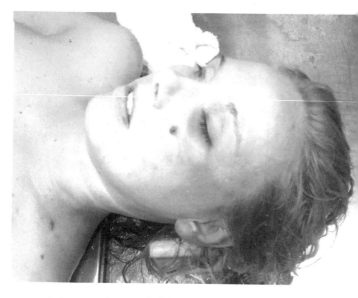

Bullet wound to April's left cheek. *(Photo courtesy of SJSO)*

The bullet that killed April. *(Photo courtesy of SJSO)*

Justin's bloody shirt in the 4Runner. *(Photo courtesy of SJSO)*

April's cell phone in the 4Runner. *(Photo courtesy of SJSO)*

Searchers line up to search quadrants marked by Global Positioning Satellite. *(Photo courtesy of SJSO)*

An investigator digs to find something located by a metal detector. *(Photo courtesy of SJSO)*

Detective Skip Cole examines a shell casing. *(Photo courtesy of SJSO)*

The artist's sketch of the assailant as described by Justin. *(Photo courtesy of SJSO)*

The bedroom in the Jacksonville condo with Justin's computer. *(Photo courtesy of SJSO)*

Justin Barber immediately after his arrest for murder. *(Photo courtesy of SJSO)*

Sergeant Mary Fagan was the first lead detective on the Barber case. *(Photo courtesy of SJSO)*

Detective Skip Cole was lead detective when the arrest was made. *(Photo courtesy of SJSO)*

Circuit Court Judge Edward E. Hedstrom presided over the trial. *(Photo courtesy of SJSO)*

Defense Attorney Robert S. Willis was stunned when Justin was found guilty. *(Author's photo)*

Defense attorney Lee Hutton. *(Author's photo)*

Assistant State Attorney Chris France led the prosecution team.
(Courtesy of the State Attorney)

Assistant State Attorney Matt Foxman made a masterful closing argument.
(Courtesy of the State Attorney)

your only source of information was asking Director Porter, and the word you used was 'damp,' not 'wet.' You specifically said 'damp.'" The defense attorney asked if Holmquist thought something that was damp on August 17 would still be wet on August 19."

"I'm sorry," Holmquist said. "Wet with blood."

Willis asked for an explanation as to why Holmquist waited until August 26 to submit the clothing to the laboratory. The FDLE agent said he was on call that week and worked a great deal of time making notes on the evidence, and he may have been called on other cases. There were any number of reasons why it took him so long to transport the evidence to the lab.

Willis said he was almost finished with his cross-examination, but he asked if the police tried to keep the public from using the beach where April was killed from the time of her death until after the autopsy. Holmquist said he didn't know.

After his lengthy testimony, Holmquist stepped down from the witness chair. The state called for Detective Howard Cole, the tenacious investigator who had been instrumental in keeping the case alive for four years. Before Cole took the stand, the lawyers held a sidebar conference with the judge after the jury left the room.

The jury was called back after a few minutes and the judge addressed the members. Ordinarily, the state would present its case fully before the defense started to call its witnesses. Holmquist was also a witness for the defense, the judge said, and had a commitment the following day. Because of this, the state agreed that the defense could begin its direct questioning of the FDLE agent.

Before Detective Cole made it to the witness stand, Holmquist was required to testify some more. The jury had heard Holmquist give long testimony about evidential details, but they never seemed to lose interest. Members of the audience were equally fascinated by the intricacies involving evidential processing. They were about to get more of the same.

Willis began his direct examination by asking Holmquist to identify photographs of tire and drag marks, the crime scene and interior of Barber's SUV before he entered them as evidence. Holmquist identified a photograph of tire tracks by a NO PARKING sign along A1A, near the board-walk at Guana Beach.

He used black-and-white film because it was the best for capturing detail in tire tracks, but Holmquist didn't remember if the police had directed him to the tracks or if he had found them during his own search of the area. The police, however, told him what area to investigate.

"And you believed them to be of value as evidence— did you not?" Willis asked.

"I did."

Besides photographing the tracks, Holmquist explained how he made plaster casts. He mixed a prepackaged bag of a substance called Denstone with twelve ounces of water to make a thick slurry, then carefully poured it into the tire marks. After it dried, the Denstone preserved the tire markings and could be taken out and used later. Holmquist returned to the scene after the autopsy to take photographs in the daylight. The state wanted to show where the tread marks were in relation to where Barber's SUV had been parked the night of the murder.

Willis received permission for Holmquist to approach the photographs so he could explain specific features to the jury. Willis was trying to establish that the police had practically dismissed testimony from two witnesses who said they saw a green K-car parked by a NO PARKING sign at Guana Beach about the time of the shootings. The de-fense attorney was convinced that Barber's story was true: he and April had been attacked on the beach. Willis believed the K-car was what the assailant drove.

One of the photographs Willis introduced was taken from the middle of A1A. It showed a pedestrian entry sign near a walkway and, not far from that, a mark at the side of the highway. Willis asked what the mark on the highway meant.

"That's just showing me where the casts were," Holmquist said. "The tire impressions where I poured the casts."

"So the . . . area that you were directed to where you took the casts is just about on the highway, and the entrance to the Guana walk-over is right up in front of the crime scene truck, correct?"

Holmquist said that was true and said he had measured the distance of 144 feet from the walk-over entrance to the tracks. The witness returned to the stand and Willis started to focus on April's body, blood, clothing and how evidence was gathered. The defense had made a large composite of various photographs. One photograph showed how April's body had been rolled slightly to her right so investigators could see her back.

"And did we understand that's as far as you rolled her over . . . ?"

"Yes, sir."

"Counsel asked you, 'Did you see any blood?' and you said, 'Not that I observed'?"

"I thought I said that on the rest of the shirt."

"All right. The question is, did you see any blood?"

"I believe there was a little bit of blood on the back-collar area."

"The rest of the shirt—your answer was you didn't see or observe any blood, correct?"

"That's right."

"Are you saying that there was not blood or just that you didn't see any?"

"I didn't observe any blood," Holmquist said. "I didn't do a very close exam to see if there were any minute areas of blood on there, so that's all I can tell you."

Willis ended his direct examination and France began to cross-examine a witness he questioned in direct examination about an hour earlier. France was anxious to repair any damage Willis's examination had done to points the state had emphasized in regard to parking tracks and how evidence was handled. First he took aim at the tire tracks.

"Sir, isn't it true there were other cars parked in the area from which you took these casts?" he asked.

"Yes."

"How many cars were parked there?"

Holmquist wasn't sure, but said there were at least two.

"And isn't it true you picked the particular tracks that you photographed and took casts of because they were the most suitable to be photographed and cast, correct?"

"Yes."

"And you had no other evaluation for their evidentiary value? You didn't have any reason to believe they were connected to the crime at all. Is that correct?"

"I was given information that there may have been a vehicle parked there, so I thought it was prudent to check that area for tracks. . . ."

"But there was nothing unique about the specific tracks that you photographed?"

"Not to me."

"Would it be fair to say that you had no information from anybody at the scene to pick one track over the other?"

"Nobody directed me to one track or the other."

France finished his cross-examination; then, getting to

normal procedure, he called Detective Cole back to the stand as a witness for the prosecution. There was a buzz of excitement among the press corps, which realized that Cole was largely responsible for this case having come to trial. The gallery knew as well. They saw a man of medium height, with a buzz cut and a good-natured expression, take the stand. Would this be the witness who held the key to Barber's guilt or innocence?

Chapter 24

The expression on Justin Barber's face didn't change when Cole took the witness stand. Throughout the trial, his brow was slightly furrowed, the mouth tilted down at the corners. Barber appeared to be stunned and bereft at the same time. During descriptions of the crime scene and autopsy, Barber looked down, and a single tear leaked from his left eye. Newspaper and television reports described him as being unemotional.

Charles Barber, the navy lieutenant brother, said that was typical of how Justin reacted to emotional distress. He closed himself off from the world. Charles said his brother had withdrawn almost as much when their father had died a few years back.

Matt Foxman, another prosecutor on the case, questioned Cole. Foxman was a serious man in his thirties who wore dark-rimmed eyeglasses and seemed to be all-business.

Cole gave his name and gave a synopsis of his seven years with the SJSO. Cole started as a patrol deputy, moved to violent crime, then to the narcotics unit, before becoming a homicide detective.

Cole told how he had been telephoned at home the

night of August 17, 2002, and told about the crime. Before going to Shands Hospital, where Barber had been taken by helicopter, he stopped briefly at A1A and Ponte Vedra Lakes Boulevard to take a quick look at Barber's SUV. Barber was sitting in bed in the trauma unit, where Cole interviewed him and collected evidence, including Barber's pants, belt and underwear. The detective took photographs of Barber's gunshot wounds.

Foxman gave Cole a bag and asked him to open it and identify the items. Cole found a pair of pants and boxer shorts, but didn't see a belt. These were items the detective bagged in the trauma unit. Foxman asked him if they were in the same condition as they had been when he took them into evidence.

"They were damp and there was some processing done to them with some cuttings and whatnot," Cole said. Other than that, they were in the same condition. Foxman entered the items into evidence and then showed Cole photographs that he identified as being those he took of Barber's wounds.

Cole told the jury what Barber had told him about what happened the night of the shooting: it was the same story he had told several times over the four-year investigation. Barber and his wife drove from Jacksonville, had dinner and then drove to Guana Beach. The gate to the parking lot was closed and Barber parked along the west side of the road and they walked down the boardwalk to the beach.

After walking fifteen or twenty minutes south at the waterline, they turned and started back toward the boardwalk.

"What did he say happened next?" Foxman asked.

"He said the subject approached him rather rapidly," Cole said. "He said the subject seemed agitated. By the time he had realized somebody was even there, the guy was kind of right up on them, he was pointing a gun at him.

"He said he thought he heard the word 'cash,'" Cole said. "He said at which point his wife, April, said something, he didn't recall specifically what it was, and the assailant focused his attention on April, at which point he tried to get in between April and the assailant, and the subject started shooting and he basically passed out."

Barber had been unable to give anything more than a cursory description of the attacker's physique and couldn't tell Cole about his face because it was too dark. Foxman asked if Barber told him anything about what happened next.

Cole said Barber told him that he awakened lying in the sand and everybody was gone. He didn't know where his wife and the assailant were. Barber got up and started to look for his wife and found her facedown in the surf.

"And what happened next?"

"He said he pulled her out of the surf and drug her up to the walk-over," Cole said. "And once he got to the walk-over, he said that he believed she was dead, didn't want her to be dead, but definitely believed she was dead, and then he left her there and proceeded out to the roadway."

Barber related to Cole how he had tried to flag down at least three vehicles without success. He got into his car and started driving, ultimately ending at the intersection of Ponte Vedra Lakes Boulevard and A1A.

Cole said that he obtained Permission to Search forms for Barber's Jacksonville condominium and SUV. Foxman asked Cole why the police wanted to search the condominium and the detective said it was to look for anything that could be of evidentiary value. Cole took photographs of documents, including life insurance policies, personal items and financial records.

Later that night, Cole said, Barber telephoned to tell him he was being moved into another hospital room. He gave Cole the new room number and the detective asked if he remembered anything more about the assailant. Barber could not.

"He said it was very dark, he could not see the suspect's face," Cole testified. "And he stated that he was very drunk during the time of the incident."

"Did he relay how he was feeling?" Foxman asked.

"He actually said that he felt fine and he would probably be released tomorrow."

Cole said he met Barber at the Omni Hotel the next day to have him sign a consent form to search April's house in Thomasville, Georgia.

"He asked me, 'Don't you want to ask me anything additional about the incident?'" Cole testified. "And then he volunteered the fact about the gun. It just struck me kind of funny. He said—out of the blue—he said, 'I may have grabbed that gun when I was struggling with the suspect.' It just came totally out of context and I was kind of taken aback from it."

Foxman stopped at this point and reminded the judge that he had wanted to discuss evidence without the jury being present. Following the jury's departure, Foxman said he thought it was time to proffer an exhibit the court had requested at a motion in limine. This meant that the judge would hear evidence and decide if it should be presented to the jury. The defense had objected to the jury hearing evidence about real estate magazines Cole had found during the search at April's house.

"Okay," Hedstrom said. "Go ahead and make your proffer. This is regarding the magazine issue?"

Foxman said that it was and started his proffered examination, which the jury might or might not hear later.

It would depend on how the judge ruled after hearing arguments from both sides.

"Detective Cole," Foxman said, "during the course of your investigation, did it come to your attention that shortly before her death that April Barber had visited Oklahoma?"

Cole said yes.

"Do you know roughly how close in time to her murder?"

"Within a week."

The prosecutor approached the witness stand and gave Cole an envelope and told Foxman there were real estate magazines from the Oklahoma area inside. The magazines were found in a travel bag in the master bedroom at April's Thomasville house. Foxman moved to enter the magazines into evidence, and then turned the witness over to Willis.

"Do you have a single witness . . . who was with Mrs. Barber at the time that she acquired these magazines?"

"Yes."

Willis was surprised by the answer. "You do?" He asked who the witness was.

"Her aunt and her brother."

"We haven't heard that before," Willis said. "You're saying that you have witnesses that were with Mrs. Barber, physically present, when she got these magazines?"

"That's my understanding, correct."

"We didn't hear about that." Foxman rose to his feet. "Go ahead, we need to hear about that," Willis told him. "Go ahead, I'll yield the floor."

"Well, I mean, basically if the court's entertaining argument at this point," Foxman said, "what I think is significant here is these items are found in April Barber's house amongst her belongings, specifically in a travel bag, and she was just in Oklahoma the week prior to her murder, and they're Oklahoma real estate magazines dated contemporaneously with her trip there."

Willis wasn't pleased. "Your Honor, may it please the court. Just for the record, we have deposed everybody we know to depose from Oklahoma and nobody was with this lady that we know anything about. He was specifically asked that question, so if counsel knows something, hopefully, he would share it with the court and with us.

"At this point, at least, it's argumentative, purely," Willis continued, "and only the fact that she's got a couple of real estate magazines in her apartment, period, that is it. There's no relevance to that unless there's some further showing made that evidences her intentions or anything else. I mean, that's just too remote to be coming in at this stage without some further predicate."

The judge looked at the prosecutor. "Mr. Foxman, what point do you think that magazine proves or what point were you going to claim that the magazine proves?"

Foxman replied that if the trial stayed on schedule, he would present a witness in the form of a proffer that would prove that April's cousin was with her on April's visit to Oklahoma. He said she stopped and looked at a house that was for sale, showing that April was interested in buying real estate in Oklahoma.

Hedstrom asked: "Is this the witness that Mr. Willis says he wasn't aware of?"

"No, we're aware of it, sir," Willis replied, "but she doesn't know anything at all about the real estate magazines, if it's the one I'm thinking about, but she says they talked briefly about the possibility of buying a rental house out there, a rental house as an investment."

The judge denied the evidence at that time, but said he would not rule on it until they heard additional testimony.

Foxman wasn't finished arguing. "Just by way of clarification, is the issue troubling the court that they were actually in her possession?" he asked. "I mean, because that seems to be what Mr. Willis's argument, given where they were found. It seems to me that that's pretty clear, that they were in Mrs. Barber's possession. I just want some clarification as to what I need to shore up."

"At this point I don't see any relevancy to them," the judge said. "There's nothing to tie in anything, she just happened to have a real estate magazine in her possession. If there's some witnesses that say she went on a shopping spree and was intending on buying a house in Oklahoma, that might make the magazine relevant, but at this point, I don't see any relevancy. It's just not tied up to anything, in my opinion."

The jury returned to the courtroom and Foxman resumed Detective Cole's direct examination. Cole told the jury that he had returned to the scene of April's death several times after returning from Oklahoma. He and dozens of others from the SJSO searched a wide area, including the parking lot, and along A1A, pushing far into the brush on the west side of the Atlantic shoreline.

"It was done literally by people on their hands and knees cutting through the brush with machetes to K-9 searches," he said. "We utilized helicopters. Any way possible, we utilized."

Foxman asked him if the vegetation at Guana was a good or bad situation when it came to recovering evidence. Cole said it was the worst.

"It's just very thick, it's the middle of August," Cole said. "There's a lot of wildlife up there, rattlesnakes, spiders, a lot of thorns, the dogs were getting injured and the dogs were bleeding. In my opinion, it was very adverse search conditions."

Cole said the search found no evidence, but that the searches continued the following day and for weeks afterward. The prosecutor asked if he searched the area on August 22, 2002. Cole said that he and Shaw had searched the area with metal detectors.

"It's kind of difficult to use metal detectors where there's brush, so we concentrated primarily on the beach and the dunes," he said. "There's the sand, the beach, and then there's . . . high grass before you get to the dunes."

Cole described how he and other detectives did a "walk-through" of the crime, or a reenactment, as Barber described it. The walk-through was recorded on videotape. Barber described the time he left the boardwalk, Cole said, and tried to stop traffic on A1A. He said Barber was very specific.

"He said when he had left April and he had gone out to the roadway, he almost immediately saw headlights coming from the south," Cole said. "That car went by rather quickly. He wasn't even sure whether or not that car even saw him. . . . Right after that, another vehicle was coming from the south, he kind of went out into the road, waved his hand, that vehicle went around him and proceeded north." Cole said that Barber told him he saw another car coming as he headed toward his SUV. "The defendant said he placed himself smack in the middle of the road, so much so that the vehicle had to go around him and, of course, nobody stopped."

There were no 911 calls, Cole said, from anyone reporting someone trying to stop traffic on A1A. Cole told the jury that they used his vehicle so that Barber could demonstrate how he looked in his own vehicle for a cell phone and April's purse. Barber said he had found neither the night of the murder. Barber looked in the backseat when he was asked to show how he looked for his wife's purse and did not find it.

The state then presented an elaborate photographic composite made from GPS imagery to show the area along

A1A where Barber drove, looking for help. The composite showed oceanfront residences along the highway, beginning less than a mile from where Barber started driving, and continued past residential and business areas, until he stopped at A1A and Ponte Vedra Lakes Boulevard. There was a McDonald's less than six miles from Guana Beach, a Walgreens and a Shell station.

Cole told the jury that some of the businesses were open that night and that the area was lit well. Eight miles into the drive, there was a large commercial complex, which contained a Winn-Dixie grocery store; most of this, Cole said, would have been closed.

The prosecutor returned to the walk-through and asked Cole what he did immediately afterward. The detective said they went to the sheriff's office, talked and filled out affidavits. Barber filled out an affidavit that was sworn and witnessed.

"During his time at the sheriff's department on that day, was he (Barber) free to leave?" Foxman asked. Cole said he was. "Was he told that he was free to leave?" Again, Cole answered yes.

"Was he provided with food and drinks by your agency?"

"Yes."

"And offered to take breaks from any conversation?"

"He stepped outside alone numerous times."

After receiving permission from the judge, Foxman approached the witness and showed him a composite letter. Cole identified it containing three separate affidavits Barber wrote and signed, two that night, the third on another occasion. The affidavits were entered into evidence without objection. Cole was asked to read them, one by one.

The first told how Barber and his wife drove from San Marco to Jacksonville Beach to eat at Carrabba's. They sat on the patio outside and each had a drink with dinner. Barber said he finished April's piña colada. Afterward, they went to the Atlantic Restaurant for a drink, but there was a different name on the door, so they didn't go in. They shot pool. Barber drank rum and Coke and April had a vodka collins. The drinks came in tall glasses.

Barber's affidavit noted that he and April played a few games of pool and chatted with other players. They each ordered another drink, he wrote, but neither of them finished it.

After playing pool, Barber wrote that he asked April what she would like to do next and said that she wanted to go for a car ride and a walk on the beach. They had discussed going to Guana Park earlier, he wrote, because they had been there on or near April's last birthday and their second anniversary. It was a place where they liked to stroll on the beach. He wrote that they had sex on the boardwalk at the beach on both of the previous visits.

The affidavit said that Barber drove the 4Runner south on A1A in fairly heavy traffic that thinned as they drove farther from town. He started to pull into the parking lot at Guana but the gate was locked so Barber parked on the west side of the road, south of the parking lot gate.

They walked down the highway a few feet to the walkway down the dunes. The traffic was still fairly heavy, he said, but there were no other cars parked on the road. Barber said they walked down the walkway to the steps that led to the lookout deck. Barber said he thought they would go directly to the boardwalk and make love but that April wanted to walk on the beach.

The affidavit said they walked to the water's edge and turned south. They walked hand in hand with the water flowing back and forth across their feet. Several times they sat at the water's edge and held hands, he said, then headed back. April, Barber wrote, walked on his right, closer to the shoreline.

Suddenly, Barber said, he felt April clench his hand. Barber had been walking with his head down, watching the water. He looked up when they stopped. He saw a man wearing a baggy T-shirt and a dark baseball cap with a lighter logo on it. The man was coming toward them quickly and had his arm extended toward them. Barber said he thought the man held a small gun.

The man alternately pointed the gun at Barber's face and chest, the affidavit said. The barrel of the gun looked like a round tube, according to Barber. The man was white, Barber said, but deeply tanned on his arm and neck. Barber noticed that the skin on the gun hand was pale. The intruder stopped and shifted his weight from one foot to another.

The gunman yelled something at him but Barber said he couldn't understand what was said but he knew the man was angry and yelling. Barber said he thought he could distinguish the word "cash." Barber wrote that he told the man his wallet was in the 4Runner.

The man yelled at Barber again, the affidavit said, and jabbed the gun closer to his face. Barber said the gunman was right in front of him, less than a foot away. The intruder shouted something else Barber didn't understand, but he thought he heard the word "keys."

As Barber reached in his pocket for the truck keys, he said, April said something. She didn't sound angry or confrontational so Barber thought she was speaking to him. Barber said he didn't understand April's words but the man pointed the gun at her. At that point, Barber said, he tried to step between his wife and the gunman.

The gun fired. Barber said it seemed loud and he was shocked. He didn't know whether the bullet hit him or

April. Barber said he froze for a second and then tried to grab the gun. He was able to grab the gunman's hands, he said, but the man was strong and kept jerking Barber's arms around. Barber said he had trouble keeping his balance and lost his grip on the gun.

"I grabbed the gun again and tried to keep him from pointing it at me," Cole read from the affidavit. "I was dizzy and having difficulty standing up and holding on. I fell to my knees and remember trying to get up. I think I blacked out. I was lying on my side on the sand. The sand was wet and I was wet."

Barber said that he stood up and was dizzy and nauseated. No one was around, not even April. He started yelling her name, he said, as he ran up and down the beach looking for her. Barber said that he ran south for a while and then ran back north. Then he saw April face-down in the water not far from shore.

Barber said that he ran through the water and turned her face up and saw a hole in her cheek. There wasn't much blood but he said his wife didn't respond when he yelled at her. Barber wrote that he tried to pick her up and could only carry her short distance before he stumbled and fell. Then he dragged her on the sand and tried to pick her up and carry her over his shoulder. Barber said he couldn't lift her high enough.

It was a nightmare scenario. Barber said he tried to carry April in his arms but he dropped her. After that he tried to carry her with his right hand under her head. He carried her toward the boardwalk, he said, but fell down again. Unable to pick her up, Barber said he tried to drag April by her hands. He couldn't do it, he said, so he tried pulling her by the forearms. Barber said he couldn't keep a grip with his left hand and then he noticed blood on his shirt and didn't know if it was his or April's.

"I grabbed April from behind under her arms and pulled her backwards as far as I could," Barber wrote. "I was tired and dizzy and I was out of breath. And then—I then sat April up and reached under her arms and grabbed the waistband of her pants."

Barber was able to pull April in this manner for a while as he tried to find the walkway that led to the parking lot. The beach sloped upward at a sharp angle and he said he had to stop and rest. At last he got April to the walkway, Barber said, and tried to pick her up and lean her against the rail. If he could get support from the rail, Barber said, he might be able to get her over his shoulder.

Instead, he said he dropped her. He said he was dizzy. He realized that he must have been shot. Barber said he left April on the beach and went to the highway to try and flag down a car for help. Barber said he saw a car coming from the south and he stood in the middle of the road and watched the headlights come toward him. The car slowed, he said, but kept on going.

Barber said he crossed the highway and started to look for his truck. Headlights approached him, he said, this time coming from the north. Barber said the car swerved to another lane and he tried to run in front of it but the car swerved again and drove away.

Barber said he kept heading toward the truck and opened the door. He said he looked for his cell phone in the driver's door pocket but it wasn't there. Neither was it in the center console. Barber said he opened the rear door on the driver's side and tried to find April's purse. That was where she usually kept it, he said, and he thought her cell phone would be inside. This time, he said, the purse wasn't there.

Barber said he got behind the wheel and started to drive north. He said he was afraid that he was dying. If he passed out, he thought, he probably would die.

Barber's affidavit said that he couldn't remember much about the drive. He remembered driving as fast as he could and believing that he would find a policeman in Jacksonville Beach. When he saw a red traffic light with several cars stopped, Barber said he started yelling for someone to call the police. Barber said he tried to tell people where April was but couldn't get anyone to understand him. There seemed to be a lot of people yelling at him and getting into his truck.

"Someone found April's purse and dumped it on the seat next to me, the passenger seat," Barber wrote. "He pulled out April's driver's license, asked me if that was April, I told him yes, and he left. I don't remember what happened next. I might have passed out."

Barber said the next thing he remembered was being in an ambulance and then in a helicopter.

Cole looked up from the sheaf of papers in his hand. "That concludes that affidavit," he said. Cole asked if he should continue reading the next two and Foxman told him to proceed. The second affidavit was dated August 26, 2002, at 9:00 P.M. It included new information and clarifications to what Barber had said in the previous affidavit.

The first thing Barber wrote about concerned an aerial photograph of the beach crime scene that showed only two sets of footprints. He said he didn't understand why there wasn't a third set of footprints. The next affidavit commented on another photograph.

Detective Cole showed me pictures of April with no visible blood," Barber wrote. "I don't understand why my blood was not present in the picture. I carried her and dragged her up the beach. I don't remember much about the drive."

That concluded the second affidavit. A third affidavit

was written by Barber during this fifteen-hour session with the SJSO:

> *Detective Cole and I discussed a life insurance policy with First Colony of two million dollars. I believe the policy expired in July when April and I decided not to pay the premium on her policy. Until then I had made all premium payments. In July I paid the premium for my policy.*
>
> *I have no recollecting of contacting anyone at First Colony in recent weeks since the incident. J. Jervey left two voice mail messages and sent a card. I did not return his calls.*
>
> *Detective Cole and I also discussed my relationship with Shannon Kennedy. I told Detective Cole that we were friends and not engaged in a sexual relationship.*

Cole asked the prosecutor if he should read the next affidavit. Foxman told him to do so. The affidavit was dated September 4, 2002, at 6:45 P.M.:

> *April and I were not having financial problems and did not have at any time during our marriage. My monthly net income is approximately four-thousand five-hundred dollars. The bills I was responsible for include condo mortgage, nine-hundred fifty dollars; condo association fee, two-hundred dollars; utilities, two-hundred fifty dollars; student loans, two-hundred dollars; credit cards, one-thousand two-hundred dollars; groceries, gas, et cetera, five-hundred dollars up to a thousand.*
>
> *April's monthly income at Archbold and her contract work totaled net three-thousand seven-hundred dollars. . . . Her bills include rent on Thomasville house, four-hundred dollars; car payment on GMC Jimmy, four-hundred twenty-five dollars; utilities, two-hundred dollars; student loans, three-*

hundred dollars, groceries, gas, et cetera, five-hundred dollars; credit cards, approximately five-hundred dollars. April was also making the one-thousand two-hundred dollar mortgage on our Covington, Georgia house, which sold in June 2002.

Credit card debt, as I understand it, included Discover, eleven-thousand dollars; three first USA cards, eighteen-thousand dollars; MBNA, fourteen-thousand dollars, and remodeling the condo, fifteen-thousand to twenty-thousand. The equity in the condo is approximately thirty-five thousand dollars, which we were planning to use to pay off the credit cards used in the remodeling.

Other than Shannon Kennedy mentioned in the earlier statement, I was not having any affairs. April and I were not having any unusual marital problems. I was never abusive to her, mentally or physically.

Our recent conversation had included discussions of April finishing her training in January and taking a job in Jacksonville. We are planning the remodeling of the second floor of our condo.

I purchased a Ruger .9 millimeter handgun in a sporting goods store in Folkston, Georgia in the fall of 1999 or perhaps in the spring of 2000. I reported the gun stolen in the summer of 2002. It was in the trunk of the 2001 Audi, which was stolen from my condo parking lot. I do not own and have not owned any other firearms since leaving my parents' household in 1990.

Cole finished reading the affidavits and Foxman asked whether Barber had said anything about his living situation before April's death. They lived apart because of their professions, Cole related, and April traveled to Jacksonville from Thomasville, Georgia, on the weekends. Barber said he went to Thomasville only on rare occasions because there was nothing to do there. Cole said that Barber acknowledged the difficulty of living apart and that it sometimes caused arguments.

Cole told the jury that Barber mentioned the stolen handgun and that he had joined a gun club. Cole said Barber told him he had gone to the gun club just once.

During the investigation, people who knew Barber well had told the police that he always had his cell phone. It annoyed some of them because he would answer it, even if it meant interrupting a conversation he was having with someone else. Foxman asked Cole what Barber had told him about forgetting his cell phone the night of the murder.

"He said that April was rushing him out of the door and he believed he left it on his computer desk on the charger," Cole said.

Foxman asked why Barber didn't stop for help at any of the houses he drove past after April was shot.

"He said he didn't want to get some old man out of bed."

"Did you ask the defendant why pictures you had showed none of his blood was visible on the victim's clothing?"

"He reviewed the pictures very carefully and said . . . something to the effect that if my blood isn't there, then none of this happened."

Cole told Foxman that Barber told him that he did not have any sexual affairs. Cole said Barber specifically denied having a sexual relationship with Shannon Kennedy.

"During the same time frame that you were having this conversation with the defendant," Foxman asked, "did Shannon Kennedy also happen to be at the sheriff's department?"

The detective said Kennedy was there and that he told Barber that she was. Foxman asked Cole to describe the situation.

"I asked him very specifically if he was having a sexual

relationship with Shannon Kennedy. He said no. He adamantly denied it," Cole said. "I advised him that another detective was interviewing Shannon Kennedy and she had stated that they *were* having a sexual affair. I said, 'If I need to, I can just bring her into this room and then we can all get it straight.' At that point, he said, 'No, no. It's true.'"

The prosecutor asked if Barber had made any requests regarding transportation following the interview, which took place August 26. Barber needed to get back to Jacksonville from the SJSO in St. Augustine.

"He asked me if I would ask Shannon Kennedy to give him a ride home," Cole said.

Kennedy refused and Cole ended up driving Barber half the distance to Jacksonville to meet his brother. Cole testified that he had traveled to Oklahoma because "we basically just wanted to meet with the victim's and defendant's families to compile biographical information."

The prosecutor called Cole's attention to August 20 and asked if it had seemed strange that Barber told him he thought he had grabbed the gun. Cole said the comment had seemed odd. Foxman wanted to know if Barber had mentioned a physical struggle with the assailant during the interview at Shands Hospital on August 18.

"When he initially described the incident to me, he never mentioned the struggle at all," Cole said.

Willis objected, claiming that the answer wasn't responsive to the question. He said the question was whether or not Barber had said anything about a struggle with the assailant. Judge Hedstrom asked Foxman to rephrase the question.

The prosecutor tried again. "During your first conversation with the defendant at Shands Hospital, did he ever mention to you that he had a physical struggle with this assailant?"

"No, initially, no," Cole said.

Willis objected again. He said the question was whether Cole, during his initial interview with Barber at the hospital, had heard the defendant say he might have been involved in a struggle.

"Now he's twice said, not initially, no. Does that mean that night?"

"Yes or no, Detective Cole," the judge said. "Did he mention it or not?"

"You said initial conversation, correct?" Cole asked.

"At Shands Hospital," Foxman said.

"No—"

Willis interrupted a third time. "The interview at Shands Hospital, are you saying at no time during that interview he said anything about being involved in a struggle?"

"Your Honor—"

"That's not what I'm saying," Cole said.

Judge Hedstrom intervened before the situation got even more out of order than it already was. "Go ahead and answer the question," he ordered.

Foxman asked the question another way. "And referring to the early-morning hours of the eighteenth, when you interviewed the defendant at Shands Hospital, did he mention that he had been in a physical struggle?"

"Yes," Cole admitted.

Foxman asked him to tell what Barber described. Cole said that Barber initially said that when the assailant focused his attention on April, Barber grabbed for the subject's arms.

"Did that change in the conversation that you had with the defendant on the twentieth?"

"Notably . . . it stuck out in my head for a couple different reasons. Yes, it did."

Cole said that when he was called out that night, he

thought he was responding to a robbery. That was strange to him because, during the time he had served the St. Johns County Sheriff's Office, he had never heard of a robbery occurring at Guana Park. Foxman asked what the SJSO had done to solve this "potential robbery."

Cole talked about the extensive searches in the area and noted a car that had been mentioned at the trial by Willis.

"It was very vague information," he said. "We didn't have a year, make or model in reference to the car. However, we did take that information the best we could and tried to research that information, which never netted any results."

Cole said the police followed up on the vague information that Barber gave them. Foxman brought Cole's attention back to the car and asked him to tell the jury what the description of the car had been.

"An older model, dark, box-style sedan," he said. "One of the witnesses described it as being like a K-car, an Aries K, or something to that effect."

"To your knowledge, was it described as a K-car or like a K-car?"

"Like a K-car."

Cole said the police didn't know the license plate number, the year the car was made, the color or what kind of car it was other than the "inference" that it was a K-car. The police, he said, took that information "for what it was worth" and found the names of three hundred people in the area who owned K-cars.

"We made efforts to call these folks. It's a very old car so the reality of the situation is a lot of these cars probably don't even run anymore," Cole said. When that effort proved fruitless, Cole said the police sent a form letter to the K-car owners that asked if any of them knew anything about the incident.

Foxman asked what resulted from that.

"Nothing."

Foxman tried to cast doubt on the reliability of witnesses who reported seeing the K-car the night of the murder. "As to the witnesses who allegedly saw this K-car–like vehicle somewhere in the vicinity of Guana Park, was the information ever helpful to you?"

Cole said it wasn't and Foxman asked why not.

"Guana is very vast and at night—you know, I worked the midnight shift there many times—and if you don't know where you are at any given time in the park, it can play tricks on your mind. If you drive by and you see something significant and maybe drive ten miles, you may see something else, but you don't really have a point of reference. So, it can play tricks on your mind. So, it's very hard to say where you are at any given time in the park. We believed, based on that and some other reasons, that it was more than likely probably not in that location."

The state knew that Willis was going to claim that the police never had a suspect other than Barber, and that they paid little attention to other leads. The K-car's presence at Guana Beach the time of April's murder would bolster that claim. Foxman's questions and Cole's testimony were casting doubt on the defense's witnesses before they even testified.

Cole reinforced the testimony by noting that Barber had not seen a car when he arrived at and left the beach. So far as Barber's description of the assailant, it was vague, Cole said. Barber had not been able to see the assailant's face because it was too dark.

"Without any information or description about the alleged assailant's face, were you able to do anything with that information in the early part of this investigation?" Foxman asked.

"I don't see what you could do with it."

Cole said that no other suspects emerged during the investigation, but if one had, he would "absolutely" have investigated. With that, the state concluded direct examination. It was 4:15 P.M. and some of the jurors were nervous: not because of the trial, but because Tropical Storm Alberto, just downgraded from Hurricane Alberto, was in the Gulf of Mexico and headed toward Florida's northwest coast. Tropical storms are fickle and don't always go where meteorologists predict. The storm was huge, and Alabama, Louisiana, North Carolina, South Carolina and Florida were on alert. The storm had dumped several inches of rain in the Caribbean and still had sustained winds of up to forty-six miles per hour.

Judge Hedstrom addressed the jurors and told them he was aware that storm conditions could postpone the trial the next morning. He said he would meet with the court staff in chambers, watch the weather reports and notify them if the 9:00 A.M. session would be postponed because it got "too nasty." The jury was excused for the day and they joined the crowds of Floridians purchasing candles, flashlight batteries, nonperishable food and water, in case they were locked in by Alberto.

Barber went back to jail, which was one of the safest places to be during a storm, because of all the steel and concrete.

Chapter 25

Tropical Storm Alberto came ashore near Cedar Key on the north Gulf Coast. It was a huge storm. The wind blew down trees, limbs and smashed windows across the state and on up into North Carolina. The Atlantic Ocean at St. Augustine was the color of lead with high waves and whitecaps. Wisps of ocean spray swirled like dervishes across the surface.

As tropical storms go, Alberto caused minor damage, and the jury returned to the courtroom in St. Augustine at 9:00 A.M. Detective Howard Cole was about to be examined by Robert Willis and the expectation was that Willis would try to skin him and hang the pelt out to dry.

Willis came out swinging and tried to show that Cole was too green in 2002 to have been an effective detective on a complicated homicide case. Cole testified that he had been with the sheriff's office for three years at the time, with service that included two years in patrol, almost a year in narcotics, and several months as a detective in the homicide investigative unit at the state attorney's office. Besides the Barber case, which took up most of his time during those months, Cole testified that he worked on two other homicides.

Willis asked, "At the beginning of this investigation, back in August of 2002, you were not the lead agent or the case agent, were you, sir?"

"Not by title, no sir."

"Well, by conduct or any other way, were you the case agent at this point?"

Cole testified that Detective Robert Shaw was the case agent and Detective Sergeant Mary Fagan was in charge of the investigation. Because of promotions and transfers that moved Fagan and Shaw into different positions, Cole testified that he had been the de facto case agent almost from the beginning.

Willis questioned Cole's involvement in every aspect of the case, beginning with the interview with Justin Barber at Shands Hospital the night April Barber was killed. Cole testified that Justin Barber was in the trauma unit with the usual monitors attached to his body when the detective identified himself and explained why he was there. Willis noted that, on direct examination, Cole testified that in one version of the interview, Barber said he struggled with the assailant, but said in another version that there was no struggle.

"You made reference at some point to the idea that he had made a statement giving you some description of the events of that night," Willis said. "But on the second time around, he had made some reference to the fact that a struggle occurred."

Willis apparently wanted to create reasonable doubt as to whether or not Barber had been too rattled by the events of the night to give consistent testimony. The defense attorney asked if Barber's initial statement was substantially inconsistent with the statement he made later. Cole agreed that it was. Willis also brought out the difficulty Barber had describing the assailant because the night was so dark. The detective testified that Barber remembered the attacker as being strong.

Cole had recorded the interview on audiotape, but there was so much static that it was almost unintelligible. Transcriptions of the recording were passed out to the jury, but Judge Hedstrom told the panel to consider only what they actually heard on the tape recording as being evidence.

The tape was mostly unintelligible as Barber described having dinner in Jacksonville Beach with his wife and going for a walk on the beach. When Barber described the attack by the gunman, the recording was slightly easier to understand but still didn't make much sense.

". . . fired the gun (inaudible)," Barber's voice said. "We started fighting and I felt like he was hitting me and I don't—I don't know what happened after that."

Barber recounted how he woke up on the beach, couldn't find April, and started to look for her. He described finding her facedown in the surf and his attempts to get his wife to safety, but could carry her no farther than the boardwalk. Willis directed Cole to the transcript of the tape just played for the jury.

"Mr. Barber's describing what happened," Willis said, "and you asked the question, 'Were you able to get any hits in on him? I mean, if we find him, will he have any injuries on him or anything like that?' And he answered, 'I didn't get to hit him. I was grabbing for the gun. I wasn't swinging at him.' And then you followed up and said, 'Did you ever get a hold of the gun?' And he said, 'I had a hold of his arms.' Is that accurate?"

"Yes, sir."

"So you had raised the question before of whether he had grabbed the firearm, and he had really answered a different question. He answered by saying he grabbed the arms, correct?"

"I understood it as he grabbed ahold of the subject's arm."

Willis noted that when he was speaking with Barber at the Omni, the defendant asked if Cole wanted to speak to him further about the incident. Cole said that was correct.

"And he volunteered that, right?"

"Yes."

"Do we understand you to say that you were surprised or you found it strange . . . this business about Mr. Barber saying that he believed he had grabbed ahold of the gun?"

"It wasn't in the context of the situation, so it struck me as odd," Cole said.

"Was the context of the situation that Mr. Barber asked if you had found the gun? And continued to say he believed he grabbed ahold of it during the struggle with the suspect?"

"I don't know that he conceded that we found it," Cole replied, "but if we had found it, yes, that was the case."

Willis asked Cole to read the first full paragraph of his report.

"It says, J. Barber asked me if we found that gun—if we found the gun . . . and continued to say he believed he grabbed ahold of it during the struggle with the suspect. I asked J. Barber to contact me when he gets back from Oklahoma . . ." Cole said. "He stated he would come back earlier to assist in the investigation."

"So . . . we could read it to say he's continuing to say he believed he grabbed the gun," Willis said, "or you could read it he continued on and said he grabbed the gun. Do you understand what I'm—"

"Yeah, I think your first analysis would be correct."

"Well, had he said that before?"

"That he grabbed the gun?"

"Yeah."

"No," Cole said. "Not the way I understood it. That's why it caught me by surprise in the context of this conversation."

Willis seemed exasperated. "And you considered that to be a significant discrepancy or something that aroused your suspicions?"

"I could elaborate further on why I thought that if you like."

Willis established that Barber was in Oklahoma to bury his wife while Cole and Detective Shaw searched April's house in Thomasville. Cole agreed that he saw Barber next on August 26 and asked him to come to the sheriff's office at 8:15 A.M. the next day.

On that morning, Cole testified, they went through the "walk-through" of the incident as Barber had described it. Afterward, Barber met with a sketch artist to assist in drawing a likeness of the assailant's face, and voluntarily gave blood and saliva samples to the police. Another interview began around 1:00 P.M. in the afternoon.

"You told counsel that he was given food and drink during the course of that interview," Willis said. "What time did the interview start, one o'clock?"

Cole said that was correct.

"And what time did he leave that evening?"

"Very late as I recall."

"Almost midnight?" Willis asked.

"Sure."

"So from one o'clock in the afternoon until almost midnight, he was there answering your questions?"

"Yes, sir, he was."

"Isn't it the case that at 1:25 P.M. you gave him soda and crackers?" Willis asked.

"Yes."

"Did you give him any other food or drink that you recall other than that?"

"Without referring to my notes, I couldn't say," Cole replied.

"You couldn't say," Willis sneered. "The setup for the interview, this was at the police station, your sheriff's office station?" He asked the detective to describe the interview room.

"It's not a very large room," Cole said. "It's a small room, like half of a small bedroom. It has a table, a few chairs."

"And were you alone in there or with someone else."

Cole said he was alone most of the time with Barber and said that the room had equipment for recording interviews on video- or audiotape.

"Can this be done secretly?" Willis asked. "Just by pushing a button?"

"It could be if you chose to do so."

"So the person that you're interviewing wouldn't even know that he's being recorded?"

"Not necessarily."

Cole testified that the interview was not recorded. Willis asked if there was a directive from the sheriff to tape record interviews with suspects, particularly in serious cases such as homicide or robbery.

"That may have been the case then," Cole said. "That was not our actual verbal policy per our chain of command. I think the sheriff cleared that up with you."

Willis seemed incredulous. "So in other words, you had a written policy that said you're supposed to tape record an interview with a suspect in a serious case," he said, "but it was the practice and the informal policy that you did not do that?"

"We did not," Cole agreed.

Willis asked what the reasoning was behind the policy

and the practice. Cole said there were logistical reasons.
It was a long interview, he said, and all of the videotapes
were too short. These would have to be changed frequently, Cole said, resulting in the loss of information
while the tapes were reloaded. Cole said the SJSO con-
ducts an interview to "get the meat of the matter" and
then offers the interviewee an opportunity to make a
videotaped statement. He said that had been the policy
since he had worked with the SJSO.

Willis was exasperated. "So instead of having a thirty
second or a minute break after six hours, you don't have
anything at all for the whole six hours?"

Cole said that was the policy and that it had never
been an issue in the past.

Next, Willis wanted to know more about the affidavits
Barber wrote that had been entered as evidence. Willis
noted that the interview Cole conducted with Barber at
the jail didn't begin until 1:00 P.M. and didn't end until
about midnight. Before that, Barber had been with the
police to talk through the crime scene. Willis painted a
portrait of a man who was devastated by the trauma of
seeing his wife murdered, been shot himself, and who
had just returned from his wife's funeral. Following all of
that, Willis brought out, Barber had been with police for
hours answering questions, interviewed in a small room
by police, given only a short break, and fed just a bottle
of water and a package of crackers during a sixteen-hour
ordeal. Willis tried to show that the police were too
aggressive.

"When you get to a certain point, where you say, 'Let's
stop, and I'll have you write what we just went over?' Is
that the idea?" Willis asked.

Cole said it depended on the context of the situation
"Do you have some collaboration here?" Willis asked.
"Isn't there somebody that sits, supposedly outside of the

interview room, and monitors this conversation? Although they don't record it, they monitor it?"

The detective said that would have been the case. Willis referred to one of Barber's affidavits containing the sentence, *I observed the overhead video on the beach, I don't know why there did not appear to be other footprints.* Cole explained that he had shown Barber an aerial video of the crime scene taken from a helicopter at night using forward-looking infrared radar (FLIR). FLIR is the same technology used by heat-seeking missiles and the U.S. Army's night-vision devices.

"Are you saying that you don't see any other footprints (besides those of April and Justin Barber) on the tape?" Willis asked.

"We were talking more about the waterline in question."

"Did you point out to him that they also didn't find April Barber's or Justin Barber's prints close to the waterline?"

"The tide did take away some of the evidence. . . . This was very early on in the investigation."

"So it would not be accurate to say that there were no footprints on the sand," Willis said, "suggesting that the footprints belonging to a third person, assailant, somehow were not there?"

"We couldn't say one way or the other."

Willis continued to read from Barber's affidavit: *Detective Cole showed me pictures of April with no blood visible. I don't understand why my blood is not present in the picture. I carried her and dragged her up the beach.* "What about that? Which picture did you show him?"

"Her lying on the boardwalk. There were numerous. I didn't mark the particular one I showed him."

Willis asked if the photograph showed April lying on her back. Cole said, yes, just as she had been found. The detective told the jury that, at the time, he did not know that blood on the inside of April's left arm was from Justin Barber.

"You know it now, though, don't you?"

"Yes."

"So what you told him was, there's none of your blood on her, Mr. Barber, how do you explain that? Isn't that basically what you said to him?"

Cole said, "I told him by looking at the picture there didn't appear to be."

"We now know there was (blood), don't we?" Willis asked.

"In two very isolated places, yes."

"And one of them under her left armpit."

"Yes."

"And, of course, then you did not know about any of April's blood on Justin Barber's clothing, did you?" Willis asked.

"Of course not."

Willis showed Cole an aerial photograph showing the types of homes along the beach, starting about a mile from the Guana Beach walk-over. The houses continue along the waterfront from that area to where the road curves and goes into Ponte Vedra. Willis asked Cole to characterize the homes.

"They're very nice homes," Cole said.

"Five million dollars and ten million dollars worth of home?" Willis asked.

"I would imagine."

"Do you recall a single one of them that does not have a wall and a gate in front of it, or some sort of security system?" Willis asked.

"I'd say maybe half, seventy-five percent. And they're certainly lit at night."

Cole testified that the total distance Barber drove after

leaving the beach was about nine miles at speeds varying from forty-five to sixty miles per hour. Willis asked why this was significant to Cole.

"It's hard for me to believe that, if someone is trying to obtain help, they would drive nine point six miles if that truly was their goal," Cole answered.

"What do you think the goal was? Why does it make a difference here?"

"I think it shows a little bit of panic, sir."

Willis asked him to explain what he meant.

"Something went terrible wrong," Cole said.

"Right. And so he had to, what, have a few minutes to regroup and think his way through this, a 'what do I do next' kind of thing?" Willis asked.

"You can characterize it any way you want. It's very odd."

"[It] may be odd, but you made a point of showing all this. What's the significance? What would you have us infer from that, that he panicked and was trying to figure out what to do next?"

"He may have driven for that reason and maybe to dispose of evidence."

"Like what? The gun?" Willis asked.

"Perhaps."

Willis reminded him that the police believed that Barber had been planning to murder April for about seven months before she was killed. Willis asked Cole if the police thought they had evidence or "—at least you believed (it was) evidence—of his premeditation going back to February when he made a query on a computer about a gunshot trauma to the chest?"

"That is true," Cole said.

"So from your theory, he's been working on this murder since February. You don't think he could have had some plan for getting rid of the gun if that's what this was all about?"

"And it may have involved driving away from the scene," Cole countered.

"Again, why is it significant . . . that he traveled . . . whatever it is?"

"I just don't see how anybody could accept the fact that he left his wife on the beach and was looking for help and would drive that far away to get it."

"It's odd?" Willis asked incredulously. "It's odd?"

"It's inconceivable," Cole snapped.

"Inconceivable." Willis shrugged his shoulders. "Does it change anything that there's evidence, and you know of that evidence, that he's driving seventy miles an hour down that highway with his flashers blinking?"

"I don't know what it would change."

An important part of the defense case was how the police had handled the report by two witnesses who testified that they saw a K-car at the murder scene. During his direct examination, Foxman had been careful to establish how little information the police had about the alleged car: no year, no model, no make, no color and no license tag. Cole also testified to the vast monotony of Guana Park in the dark and how easily it was to become disoriented. How could the witnesses remember where the car was within the unchanging landscape? Foxman had tried hard to show that the police did everything possible, considering how little information they had.

On the other hand, Willis wanted to show that the police had botched a key lead with all the bumbling ineptitude of slapstick comedians. *Court TV* anchorwoman Nancy Grace wondered if, among other possibilities, the K-car might have been driven by an accomplice who disposed of the murder weapon.

"You thought it (the K-car) was a false—not a false

lead, but there was nothing there, correct?" Willis asked Cole.

"I said that, based on the vagueness of the description of the vehicle, it was difficult to follow up on," Cole said. "Based on the witness testimony involved, it was unlikely that it was parked in the place that they believed it was parked."

"I'm concerned," Willis said. "You say that you believe there was no credible evidence that there was a K-car or any car there in that little parking area immediately adjacent to the walk-over on the east side of the road."

"I can explain why I believe that it was unlikely it was there."

Willis asked him to do so.

"We had two witnesses, Ms. Barbour—no relation—and her son drove by there. They put Justin and April walking, hand in hand, down the beach. They also placed the car there," Cole said.

There was some confusing testimony about who did or didn't see two cars. Justin Barber claimed that he didn't see a car when he first stopped at the beach and that he didn't see a car when he left to seek help. Carol Barbour said there was a car near the crime scene, but her son Jordan said there was not. Both said they saw April and Jason Barber walking, hand in hand, on the beach.

Had there been a car parked there, Cole testified, Justin Barber would have seen it because it would have been present when Jordan and Carol Barbour saw Justin Barber and April Barber walking. Willis agreed that was true.

"Right," Cole said. "Justin Barber either didn't see a car or he's lying."

"You have one of two people who think they saw a car," Willis said. "Why would that not be of interest to you if they place a car there?"

"Justin said there wasn't," Cole replied. "They're (the

Barbours) placing a car in Guana. I'm not disputing that." The detective went on to explain that being able to pinpoint the exact location where the car was parked would be almost impossible; the wilderness landscape is just too much the same. "If something is not significant to you at the time, you are not going to be able to put in place and time where you saw something versus something else. It's just too vast."

Willis established that Wesley Pryor and the former Kimberly Gamble, who was now Pryor's wife, had reported seeing a K-car parked at Guana Park. "The Pryors are the people who followed Justin Barber's vehicle, tended to him at the line of St. Johns County and Duval, and immediately drove back down to the area on their own," Willis said.

So as far as Carol Barbour and her son, Jordan Barbour, were concerned, Willis said, there was no doubt as to where they saw a car parked. Those witnesses had showed the police where the car was, Willis noted, so that investigators could make casts of tire tracks.

"With all due respect to the witness, I believe they were mistaken, too."

"You just made that decision?"

"No, I did deductive reasoning," Cole said.

"Let's leave Justin Barber out of this for a moment," Willis said. "You've got three separate witnesses. You've got at least one of the Barbours who says that there was a car there. You've got these other two people who drive by and comment on it to each other and then drive back within thirty minutes because they're interested enough, and they both say, 'Now this is where it was, we saw it.'"

"There's no question that they saw a car," Cole said. "I just don't believe they saw it where they thought they did, sir."

"And so you just excluded any further investigation of that?"

"Certainly not." Cole reiterated the vagueness of the information received about the car and that, in his opinion, it wasn't viable. Regardless, the police followed the lead to the best of their ability.

There were so many confusing questions about who saw what, when, where, if it was Barber or Barbour, both pronounced the same, that the courtroom turned into a Tower of Babble. No one knew who was talking about what. Even the names *Justin* and *Jordan* became part of the confusing mix. Witnesses had not been able to agree whether they saw a K-car or an SUV. The Pryors, one of whom had been named Gamble at the time of the murder, still called Justin Barber's Toyota 4Runner a Blazer.

The questions and testimony ran in a confusing circle.

The detective said the best description was that the vehicle reported being spotted resembled a K-car, such as a Dodge Aries. Some Aries owners in St. Johns and Duval counties were contacted by telephone but none resulted in information of evidentiary value.

"Did we understand that you then sent out a form letter . . . that said . . . 'If your car was down on the beach Saturday night, August 17, at about eleven o'clock, please call'?"

"More or less," Cole replied.

Willis asked if that was the extent of the investigation of the K-car sighting.

"I really don't know what else you can do with that vague information."

Under questioning, Cole noted that the videotape made of Barber's "walk through" of the murder was almost unintelligible, even after the police paid a specialist to "clean it up."

Cole said that was true and it had not been played for

the jury because it was too hard to understand even after the cleanup. There was nothing wrong with the video portion of the tape, but only fragments of what was said could be heard over the roar of the wind and crashing surf. The audio made little sense. Words and disjointed sentences could be understood: "Angry yelling. I heard him . . . grab the gun. I don't know if the first shot hit me . . . Got down on my knees and I tried to get her over my shoulder. I couldn't hold her. She was heavy."

Barber's story of the attack, shooting, and the events immediately after were brought out again. When Foxman began his redirect cross-examination, he was careful to establish that Barber said he heard only one shot before passing out. Cole testified that Barber "went into the details of the struggle a little bit more. That he was trying to hold on and the guy was kind of whipping him around . . . and then he remembered waking up on the beach."

Under redirect examination, Cole said Barber told him the assailant was bigger and heavier than the defendant. Foxman asked Cole to identify photographs of Barber's wounds. "When you saw the defendant that evening, were you also able to observe his head, arms, torso, hands, legs?" he asked.

"Maybe not his legs, but certainly everything else you described."

"Did you observe any bruises, scrapes, scratches, anything that would indicate a significant struggle?"

Cole said he had not. Foxman asked him if he saw anything unusual about the gunshot wound to the right chest, below the nipple. Cole started to answer but Willis objected, claiming that the detective should be qualified first as an expert on gunshot wounds.

"If he wants to describe the wound as he sees it, fine," Judge Hedstrom said, "but I'm not going to allow him to offer any opinion as to anything about the wound."

Foxman acknowledged the limitation and asked again if there was anything unusual about the gunshot below the nipple on Barber's right chest. Cole said the shape was unusual as compared to the shot on Barber's left shoulder. Cole said that the shot to the right chest appeared to have been fired at more of an angle.

Willis spoke up. "Excuse me for objecting, but that's just doing what we objected to earlier."

"That's somewhat of an opinion, but I'll overrule the objection," Hedstrom said.

Cole said Barber told him he fainted after the first shot. Even so, there were gunshot wounds to each shoulder, the hand and right chest.

"If he fainted after the first gunshot, did he explain any scenario that would explain the other wounds?" Foxman asked.

Cole said he wasn't aware of any.

"Did the defendant say that he saw April get shot?"

"No, he did not."

"Mr. Barber says he hears one gunshot and passes out," Foxman said. "Did he say at any point when he came to that he saw the gunman?"

"He did not see the gunman."

"Did the defendant . . . offer any explanation or reason for why, as he lay so vulnerable on the beach, that this assailant let him live?"

The answer was no.

"Did he (explain to you) while he was passed out, this assailant took nothing of value from himself or April?'

Cole answered, no. The detective described what Barber told him: that he found April in the water and tried various ways of carrying her. Foxman asked him to describe it in more detail.

"He basically said that he fished her out of the water," Cole said. "He attempted by carrying her in a cradle position. That didn't work. He attempted to carry her by just pulling her hands with her on the ground. That obviously didn't work. He attempted to get her over his shoulder to attempt a fireman's carry. He was ultimately unsuccessful with that. And then I think he drug [her] most of the way, as he describes in his statement. Basically he got her up with her back to his chest, his arms underneath her arms, and kind of either held his hands out or grabbed hold of her pants and pulled her up the beach. He described doing those various things numerous times."

Foxman showed Cole some of the photographs of April's body that had been taken by John Holmquist of the FDLE. Cole stepped down from the witness stand to look at the enlarged photographs.

"Do you see any evidence on Mrs. Barber's pants of the defendant's attempts to carry her by holding onto the top of the pants?"

"No, other than the fact that they're undone."

"Looking on the top line of her pants and her stomach, do you see evidence of anyone's blood?"

"No, sir, I don't."

Cole testified that Barber told him he had dragged or carried his wife about 300 feet from the water to the boardwalk up a sloped area. Foxman referred Cole to enlarged photographs of April's body and asked him what he knew about blood flow.

"It follows gravity," Cole said.

"The defendant says that to get to the boardwalk, he tried to carry her at least three different ways, correct? . . . And that included dropping her, correct?"

Cole said it was.

Foxman asked if the blood flow depicted in the picture was consistent with Barber's story. Willis immediately objected.

"Your Honor, we're going to have experts on this issue. He is not an expert."

Judge Hedstrom sustained the objection. Foxman continued his redirect examination by asking if Cole found any evidence of a third-party assailant on either Barber's or April's body. The answer was no.

The prosecutor asked what a case agent does and Cole told him that the homicide division is small, and in a case of this magnitude, everyone would get involved. A case agent keeps track of what's happened and coordinates the investigation. Foxman mentioned the unrecorded interview Cole had with Barber and asked if that was the same day that Barber wrote three affidavits. Cole said it was. The detective said he gave Barber all the time he needed to include everything he wanted to say in the affidavits.

Foxman next wanted to clarify why Cole had discounted the Pryors' report on the location of the K-car. He asked the detective to explain "deductive" reasoning. As fans of Arthur Conan Doyle's fictional sleuth Sherlock Holmes know, this is the method Holmes used to confound friend and foe with his keen, accurate thoughts. It was Holmes who said something to the effect that after all logical conclusions are excluded, the only one left is the answer, regardless of how absurd it might seem.

Cole geared up for what was to be a rather long explanation of his version of deductive reasoning.

"Basically, I took a look at the situation as a whole. And if I'm correct, the Pryors recalled seeing a car along A1A, and then also recall being passed by Mr. Barber, who drove by some four or five miles up the road. Based on that time frame, I don't see how it's possible that that could have been there based on the fact that Justin got to his car and was able to pass them.

"If you were to believe that that car was still there," he

continued, "you would have to believe . . . what the defendant is saying is true, that this robber would have done what he was going to do to them, the attempted robbery and all that business, and then leave. And then Justin . . . passed out, couldn't find his wife, dragged her the many different ways that we described, left her on the boardwalk and left.

"The robber would have almost had to have waited to the very point that Justin came to the roadway to have left and that doesn't make logical sense," Cole said. "Because Justin . . . went out to the car, no car was there, he flags down three cars, gets in his car and passes the Pryors not four or five miles up the road. You're talking about a very narrow window. So, with all due respect to the Pryors, I do believe they saw a car, I just think they saw it down the road."

Cole's answer showed the common sense that the prosecuting attorneys said was invaluable to them in building the case against Barber. Foxman asked the detective to elaborate on why he thought the defendant drove so far from the scene of the crime. Cole said he believed that Barber had scripted the murder, but something happened that threw him off the script. Cole said he believed that Barber drove off in a fit of panic because his careful plan had gone wrong.

The prosecutor asked Cole to elaborate some more on why he had been surprised on August 20 at the Omni Hotel when Barber volunteered that he might have touched the assailant's gun.

"I was there for a specific purpose," Cole said. "I wasn't interested in speaking with him about the incident at that time and he initiated the conversation. I wasn't expecting it." The detective said he was taken aback by the question because there had been footage on television news programs the night before that showed a K-9 dog searching the dunes. Foxman asked how that associated with his surprise at Barber's question.

"That maybe we'll find the gun," Cole said. "And, if we did, that would be an explanation as to why we would find any evidence on the gun."

Foxman asked Cole why, during the interview of August 20, he asked Barber about his extramarital conduct. Willis objected, saying that the question was irrelevant. The judge overruled him.

"In the context of this situation, we just wanted to see basically if there were any other people that we might need to be looking at," Cole said. "You've certainly got to look at a spouse's behavior in the context of this situation."

Cole testified further that during the investigation, the police had found no physical evidence that anyone besides Barber and his wife had been on the beach the night of the murder. Foxman ended his redirect examination, and Willis had some questions to ask on recross-examination. The defense lawyer asked Cole if he remembered Barber mentioning the gun at the initial interview at Shands Hospital. Cole said he remembered, but that it seemed out of context when Barber asked it at the Omni.

"And this is eight-twenty in the morning," Willis said. "He specifically asked you, 'Don't you want to ask me about the incident? Don't you want to question me further?'"

"And my answer was no, not unless you can tell me something about the suspect."

"And he volunteered at that point to . . . get with a sketch artist and try to do better with his description of this individual," Willis said. "He stated he was drunk that night and it was dark, but he might be able to recognize the suspect if he saw him again."

"I don't know what to say, other than that comment just struck me."

"I understood that it struck you," Willis said. "But you're saying that the reason it struck you is because you saw a news report the night before on the evening news, apparently, saying that there was some search going on for this firearm."

Cole said that was true, and Willis added that the search for the firearm had been unsuccessful. Cole verified that.

"What are you suggesting . . . that he was covering it in the event that if they found the prints, that he was able to say that I reached out so you could find my prints on the barrel of the gun? Is that the idea?"

"The thought crossed my mind."

"And that's why it so shocked you and surprised you?"

"Yes."

"I thought this individual was supposed to be this premeditated guy that's been planning since February. You wouldn't think that he would worry about prints on a firearm, would you?"

Cole said he didn't know what Barber would think about.

"Don't you agree that your mind seems to go—if there's a sinister connotation and just a regular, logical one—your mind goes to the ultimate sinister one on every single thing that you encountered about this man? Is that true? . . . If you've got a choice, you know, the thing about half empty and half full, the cup's half empty or half full. . . . You pretty much regularly find that his cup is not just half empty, it's dry, don't you?"

"I follow the facts, sir."

After further questioning, Willis wondered what kind of third-party physical evidence Cole would expect to find if there had been an assailant and physical violence. Cole answered, "DNA."

"DNA? Why would we have DNA?"

"I think the way DNA is today, if you were in some kind of close proximity struggle with another individual, it's possible that there could be some kind of transfer there."

"And you find it significant that there's no evidence of a third-party DNA, right?"

"There's no evidence of any third person period."

"Except perhaps the K-car?"

"Perhaps Justin's statement, and as you all say, the K-car."

"And the K-car again," Willis said. "You're already given some of the reasons you discounted. We've gone through the Barbours and that did not support your view. The current one is that you've done a reconstruction and you therefore think that that disallows it."

Cole said he thought the Barbours' report was "highly unlikely."

"And so you didn't pursue it at all?"

"We pursued it as best we could. It wasn't a viable lead."

Cole testified that Barber had said he dropped April the first time he tried to pick her up. Willis asked if there was sand on the front of her blouse. Cole replied that she had sand all over her. Willis turned to the gunshot and established that Barber said he heard only one shot.

"He has consistently said that he heard only one shot immediately prior to this struggle, or as this struggle is commencing. Is that it?"

Cole said that was true and said it was during the interview at Barber's hospital bed where he first heard that.

"He was keenly aware at that point, was he not, that at least he had been shot—had had four holes in him—so he knew that he had a number of shots, and he also knew that his wife had been shot because you were there, right?"

"Yes."

"So the time that he told you what had happened down there on the beach that night, Justin Barber was keenly aware of how many shots, at least, had been fired?"

Cole said that seemed likely.

"Can you give any explanation why a logical person who is trying to come up with [a] scheme or scam to cover his involvement in a crime would say that he heard only one shot if he knew there had been four or five fired?"

Cole answered that he had no comment as to what Barber was thinking or why he said he heard only one shot.

"You don't think—" Willis started to ask a question but Cole interrupted.

"The simple fact is that's what was said."

"You don't think he would do better lying if he were lying?" Willis asked. "Is there any reason you can come up with why he would say only one shot, unless it happened to be the truth?"

"I can't imagine."

Willis turned away. "Nothing further."

Foxman had one further question on redirect examination concerning the police focus on Barber following the murder.

"Is it unusual for law enforcement to investigate a person who's actually on the scene when a murder takes place?"

"It's Homicide 101," Cole said.

Foxman thought that was enough. He completed his redirect and Hedstrom called a recess for lunch. The gallery had been glued to Cole's testimony for eight hours, as had the jury. Willis believed that his case was stronger than the state's. The prosecutors had the opposite opinion. Cole, the detective who had kept the case alive for four years, had just finished eight hours of tough questioning. He had been tenacious and convincing. Now the gallery was waiting for the juicy part.

Shannon Kennedy, Barber's mistress, was the first witness scheduled to testify in the afternoon session. Anticipation charged the courtroom like static electricity.

Chapter 26

Foxman said, "State would call Shannon Kennedy."

The heads of the people in the gallery swiveled to look back at the entrance to the courtroom. An attractive young woman, simply dressed, with long, straight brunette hair parted down the middle, and wearing eyeglasses, walked nervously down the aisle as a hundred pairs of eyes watched. Kennedy was pretty, but had done little to advertise it. She appeared to be nervous as she took the witness stand. Barber did not look at her, but kept his eyes downcast, with his stonelike stoicism in place.

Kennedy was sworn in and told the jury that she was in management training at Enterprise Rent-A-Car in the Omni Hotel during the summer of 2002. She said she met Barber when he rented a car and that they became friends when he asked her and David Esposito, Enterprise manager, to have a drink with him at a happy hour sponsored by Enterprise. For the record, Foxman asked Kennedy to identify Barber in the courtroom.

"At some point, beyond just renting cars and business interaction, did you begin a social relationship with Mr. Barber?" Foxman asked.

Kennedy answered that she did, a week or two after he

rented a car. It was in the summer, she testified, perhaps as late as July 2002.

"Would you two start hanging out, doing things together?"

"Eventually, yes."

Foxman asked her what they did.

"We would go for happy hour after work, maybe go to lunch, played tennis a couple of times."

"At some point, would this become a sexual relationship?"

"Yes." Kennedy bit her lower lip. She testified again that the sexual relationship began in July 2002.

"How long did this remain a sexual relationship?" Foxman asked.

"Probably for about three weeks."

Kennedy testified that at first she didn't know Barber was married, but discovered later that he was.

"What sort of things did the defendant say about his wife or his marriage?" Foxman asked.

"He said that he loved her, he just couldn't live with her . . . at one point. He didn't say a lot, to be honest."

"The crime charged here happened on August 17, 2002. About the week prior to that, do you remember getting together with the defendant? Do you recall him asking to go away to Georgia with you?"

"Yes."

"Do you believe, based on your recollection, that at least one of your sexual encounters happened within one week of August 17, 2002?"

"It's a good possibility, yes."

"During the same general time frame, do you remember the defendant asking you to go with him away to California?"

Kennedy testified that he did, and that she did not

accept the requests to go either to Georgia or California with Barber.

"Ms. Kennedy, during some of the times that you would see the defendant socially, would you have occasion to go to his apartment there in Jacksonville?"

Kennedy said she did, and Foxman asked if it looked as if anyone lived there besides Barber. She said that it didn't originally, but she noticed photographs going up on the walls and shelves.

"Did you have a conversation with the defendant about that?" Foxman asked.

"He actually brought it up to me."

"And what did he tell you?"

"That there was either her family or his family coming into town and he needed the pictures to go up." Foxman asked if Barber explained why. "Just to make it look like they remained happy," Kennedy answered.

"Did you try or attempt to stop seeing him?"

Kennedy said that she did, but that he would telephone her and drop by Enterprise. Foxman asked if Kennedy saw Barber shortly after the murder on August 17. She testified that she saw him at the Omni Hotel when he stayed there after April's murder. Kennedy said she didn't see him for a week or two after the murder. At about that time, she testified, Barber telephoned.

"Several months after the murder, did he come by and give you a gift?" Foxman asked.

"Yes, he did."

"What did he give you?"

"A jar of maple syrup."

Foxman concluded his direct examination without exploring the significance of the maple syrup, if there was any. The gallery was left wondering. Willis stood to begin his cross-examination. He asked her about the two telephone conversations she had mentioned.

"And one of those calls, maybe the first one, did he tell you that he tried to save his wife and was unable to do so, or words to that effect?" Willis asked.

"The initial one (conversation) at the Omni Hotel, he actually came in, didn't call."

"And when he came into the Omni, what did he look like?"

"Did not look good."

"Was he crying?"

"He was crying, yes."

"Did he look like a wreck?"

"Yes . . . he said he tried to save her."

Kennedy testified that Barber never tried to start their relationship again after the death of his wife. She said the relationship before April's death had only lasted two or three weeks. Willis asked if Barber had asked her to go away to Georgia with him.

"Yes . . . kind of came out of nowhere."

Willis asked if Barber had told her he would be on a business trip in Georgia for a couple of days and asked her to accompany him. Kennedy said she knew he was talking about going on business. The defense attorney wondered if the suggestion that Kennedy go to California with Barber was a joke.

"I think that one was probably jokingly, yes." Kennedy said she took it as a joke, and Barber never brought it up again.

"I don't mean to embarrass you, but . . . you were involved with another gentleman at the time, were you not?"

Kennedy said she was and that they lived together when she had the affair with Barber. There was never any discussion between Kennedy and Barber that they should leave their partners and start a life together, Kennedy testified. It wasn't even remotely alluded to.

"Any statement about 'we're in love' or 'we have this deep relationship' or expressing a desire for such a relationship?" Willis asked. Kennedy said they did not. "It was essentially you enjoyed his company and he was having things that he enjoyed with you?"

"Yes."

Willis finished his cross-examination and there was no redirect by the prosecution. Looking relieved, Kennedy left the witness stand and the courtroom. Again, the heads in the gallery swiveled and a hundred pairs of eyes watched. There was never a reason to think that Kennedy had been involved or knew anything about April's murder. She was simply a young woman who unwittingly became involved with a man who would be charged with murder. The prosecution and the defense both excused Kennedy from further testimony.

David Esposito was the corporate sales manager at Enterprise Rent-A-Car, where Shannon Kennedy worked. Esposito said Kennedy had been a friend and employee for five to six years. His company sponsored a happy hour on occasion for its corporate customers, and he met Barber at one of them. They became somewhat friendly and socialized on occasion. Esposito said that he visited Barber when he was in the hospital with gunshot wounds. He visited, he said, because he thought it was appropriate, as a business associate, to pay his respects and offer condolence and any assistance he could.

Within a day or two after Barber was released from the hospital, Esposito said, he saw Barber at the Omni, exchanged pleasantries, and Barber asked to speak with Kennedy. Esposito didn't think it was a good idea.

"What did you do in response to that?" Foxman asked.

"I was pretty adamant, no, he probably should not do that, not a good idea. He was pretty insistent, so I offered him my cell phone to call my office, which is adjacent to the Omni Hotel lobby."

Esposito said he let Barber use the cell phone because he thought face-to-face contact between Barber and Kennedy was inappropriate at that time. Esposito testified that he went back to his office after Barber finished the call, and five minutes later, Barber came in. The manager left his personal office and went to the front where Barber was and once again offered condolences. Kennedy had done the same. Barber continued to talk and Esposito asked him to leave.

"I personally escorted him out of the office," he said.

That wrapped up the prosecution's direct examination. Since Willis had no questions, Esposito was released. The state was told to call its next witness, but Foxman said the trial had reached a point where the judge previously said a matter should be discussed without the jury present.

Foxman told the judge that the state wanted to proffer the testimony of Randas Honeman, who was known as Randas Hawke when SJSO deputies interviewed her in 2002. Honeman was a relative April had spoken with concerning her troubled marriage when she visited Oklahoma before she was killed.

Honeman was sworn in and identified herself as being April's first cousin, and the last time she had seen April was just a few days before her death. April was there for her sister Julie's sorority rush. Honeman had taken a week off from work so she could spend time with April. She said the two shopped, went to lunch, ran errands and talked.

"While April was out in Oklahoma for that visit, did the two of you . . . see a house that was for sale?" Honeman said yes, and Foxman asked what April said about it.

"While we were driving through this neighborhood, we

saw a house and so we pulled over," Honeman said. "April pulled over and jumped out and scoped the property out, just walk toward the back and just tried to see . . . get as much information about the property as she could."

Foxman asked if April seemed interested in the house. Honeman said they both were, that the house was nice, cute and in a great area. Honeman said that she and April had a conversation about purchasing the house, but that Honeman had been in no position to buy.

Foxman told the court that he had a few other questions for the witness, but that he was finished with the proffer. The judge asked Willis if he wanted to voir dire on the proffer.

"I don't want to question on the proffer," Willis said. "We do want to object to the proffer. It's hearsay."

Foxman argued that hearsay applied to statements. He said he didn't want to admit a single statement from anyone other than the witness testifying. The prosecutor argued that the testimony provided the context to admit testimony on the real estate magazines that were found by police in April's Thomasville home.

"Mr. Willis's counterargument to this is always, 'Well, you're inviting the jury to speculate,'" Foxman said. "We're not. . . . We're inviting them to take the proper inference, and that is the fact that if the court were to hear all of the hearsay evidence, that April Barber was very much planning to move back to Oklahoma, and move back alone, more to the point." Foxman argued that the information was "highly relevant.

"Your Honor, quite simply, it speaks to motive," Foxman said. "You have in theory here the marriage breaking, Mrs. Barber leaving her husband."

The judge asked if this occurred in mid-August.

"This happened the week before the murder," Foxman said.

"Is there any evidence that Mr. Barber knew that she was looking for a house or knew that she had the magazines?" the judge asked. "Otherwise, that's an inference on an inference."

"At some point in this trial, we're going to be asking this court to allow hearsay evidence from, as it turns out, one of the closest friends of April Barber. . . . It's not a decision . . . that the court needs to make today, but just so you understand it. The case law is very specific in Florida as it relates to victim state-of-mind hearsay."

April's close friend that the prosecutor referred to was Amber Mitchell, the woman who told police April was dissatisfied with her marriage and wanted a divorce. It was strong evidence if the judge allowed it to be admitted.

"Traditionally, it (hearsay) is not allowed in a homicide case," Foxman argued. "Even under what I would argue absurd circumstances when it's clearly relevant, it is not allowed. That's the general rule. However, the appellate courts are clear that under certain circumstances that victim state-of-mind hearsay can become relevant and thus admissible—"

"Do you have any case law?" Hedstrom asked.

Foxman said that he would, but asked if he could present a thumbnail sketch of what he would cite. He said hearsay could become relevant if the court decided it was a way to rebut a defense. Foxman said that if everything in the trial went as expected, Barber would present an affirmative defense, claiming that somebody besides the defendant killed April Barber.

To rebut that defense, the prosecutor said, the state would need specific testimony from Amber Mitchell, who would tell the jury that April's mind-set was not just to think about leaving, but that she had already confronted him, and if things didn't improve, she would leave him. The prosecutor claimed that confrontation, coupled with the fact that there would be no two-million-dollar insurance payoff if April divorced him, was the motive for the murder.

"It rebuts the defense that someone else killed her," Foxman argued. "The fact that she confronted her husband with the fact that she wasn't happy with the way he was acting and that she was leaving." He said the state would ask to submit that rebuttal evidence at the appropriate time.

"But this goes hand in hand with that," Foxman said. "And there's really no inference to be gathered. I would argue to the court it's absolutely the truth."

Willis said he wasn't clear on the argument. He asked if the testimony Foxman wanted was intended to lay a foundation for the real estate magazines they had previously mentioned. Willis started to say something else, but Foxman interrupted. It was his understanding, Foxman said, that the court wanted to see some evidence that would allow the admission of testimony concerning the magazines.

"It's affirmative evidence, eyewitness evidence," Foxman said, "that Mrs. Barber, while up in Oklahoma the week before the murder, is, in fact, looking at property that's for sale."

"Can this witness testify that she saw her acquire these magazines while she was in Oklahoma?" the judge asked.

Willis answered that the witness couldn't, but he wanted to question Mitchell about that subject. Hedstrom told him to voir dire on that point. The defense attorney asked Honeman if April gathered any information on the house they looked at in Oklahoma. Honeman said none that she knew about. April took a telephone number from the sign, Honeman testified, but there were no brochures available. Honeman said that, to her knowledge, April was not getting information on other real estate in Oklahoma before her death.

Willis concluded his voir dire. "That's all we have, sir. Your Honor, if the court is considering this state-of-mind idea, we have some case authority on that."

Hedstrom said they were not talking about that now, but about the issue of admitting the magazines. Willis argued that Honeman's testimony was hearsay, even though she was trying to communicate April's intentions. It didn't matter whether the intent communicated was verbal or nonverbal, it was still hearsay. The judge asked Foxman to address that. "I think the nonverbal conduct is hearsay," Hedstrom said. "What exception to the hearsay rule are you offering this testimony as the basis for admitting the magazines?"

The argument about the admissibility of hearsay evidence continued. Judge Hedstrom was concerned about what case law supported the witness testifying about non-verbal conduct. The prosecution said nonverbal conduct wasn't governed by the hearsay rule. Foxman said if someone sees a person writing down the number of a house that is for sale, it isn't a statement, it is behavior.

The judge asked for case law to support the inference from two people looking at a house they liked and the witness saying she wasn't interested. The argument then centered on whether April's actions, as reported by the witness, was state of mind rather than something April said.

Both Willis and Foxman argued case law to support their arguments. It was an important piece of evidence for both the defense and prosecution. If someone saw April pick up the real estate magazines, it would bolster the state's case that April planned to leave Barber: this supported their claim that Justin Barber would not have received a two-million-dollar life insurance payoff if they were divorced. If the magazines weren't admitted into evidence, the defense gained because it weakened the

state's motive for murder. The lawyers and the judge ran
in circles on the issue, like dogs chasing their tails.

After all the arguing, Judge Hedstrom said that they
were back to the relevancy argument. He cited case law
and said, "In order for evidence to be relevant, it must
have a logical tendency to prove or disprove a fact which
is of consequence to the outcome of action. . . . My question to you . . . as I asked you today: what, in fact, . . . are
you claiming that proves or tends to disprove?"

"That she's leaving her husband, sir," Foxman said.

"That's not what this witness says," Hedstrom replied.
"She just said they stopped to look at a house. . . . If you
want to proffer the testimony, that's fine. We'll deal with
the magazine issue again later."

"What was the legal objection to the magazines?"
Foxman asked.

"Relevancy," the judge said. Willis nodded his head.

After a few more arguments, the judge said that he
wasn't satisfied to the relevancy of the magazines other
than with Honeman's testimony. "Because she really
doesn't know anything about it."

With that, Foxman was told he could continue his
proffer. He asked Honeman if April had talked with her
about buying the house they saw, and Honeman replied
that they did. "She was the one looking to purchase and
move," she said. "I was just going to be her roommate."

Foxman established that plans were for only April and
Honeman to live in the house. He asked why April wanted
to buy the house and move in with Honeman.

"Because she was going to leave her husband and
move to Oklahoma," Honeman said.

Foxman concluded and the judge asked if Willis had
any questions. "I don't have any questions," he said.
"Every single bit of that's hearsay. There's not a thing in

there that's not." Hedstrom asked Willis to repeat what he said because the judge didn't hear it well enough.

"Every bit of it is hearsay," Willis said. "This is getting strange, that we're relying upon hearsay to form an evidentiary foundation for other hearsay. We're using inadmissible hearsay to form some evidentiary bridge for other hearsay, when there can be no connection shown by nonhearsay testimony. . . . It doesn't make any—I'm having trouble . . . following all of that, to be honest with you."

They renewed the argument concerning hearsay evidence relating to what April said and her state of mind. Foxman said it was premature for him to take testimony on April's state of mind because the law required that he do that in rebuttal. He would not question the witness for testimony about April's comments at that time. The prosecutor added that the testimony he would seek was from the witness's observations.

Before the jury could return, Willis asked, "Is the court going to permit this testimony?"

"He's not going to ask her anything about the victim's statement," Hedstrom said. "She's only going to testify to what she just testified to."

"Judge, it's not relevant. It doesn't—"

"I think that's going to tie it up, hopefully, in rebuttal."

"Well, Judge, if he's going to do it on rebuttal," Willis argued. "Let's wait until rebuttal, because we've got some arguments against that." The argument about state of mind continued and Willis said the defense had case law to back its position.

"Your objection to this testimony is relevancy?" Hedstrom asked.

"Yes. The nonhearsay testimony that she could offer right now, there is no relevance to at all. Absent April Barber's communication, there is no relevance. We stopped and looked at the house. I was not interested in the house."

The judge sustained Willis's objection. Foxman told the court he wanted to have the witness establish April's existence and to admit a photo of April when she was alive. This brought another objection from Willis and a brief argument that started that ended when the judge ruled in Foxman's favor. The jury was returned to the courtroom.

"It is—perhaps a silly question, but the law requires it," Foxman said. "Is this somebody (April Barber) somebody that you knew as a live human being that you would talk with and have a relationship with?"

Foxman received permission to approach Honeman and showed her a photograph of April. The witness identified it as a photograph of April Barber. April's eyes were shining with good humor and mischief, her blond hair shimmered and a bright smile was visible, which made people feel that she was easily approachable and friendly, even though she was stunningly beautiful.

Foxman had no more questions after publishing the photograph to the jury. Willis had no cross-examination. There was nothing he could say or do to diminish the powerful effect of the likeness of the living April Barber.

The arguments between the lawyers had taken far longer than Honeman's testimony. The battle was a foreshadowing of what was to come.

Chapter 27

Expert witnesses in homicide trials aren't a dime a dozen—they are more like several hundred thousand dollars a dozen—but they are necessary in today's sophisticated world of criminal investigation. The state's first expert witness was David Siegel, who was a certified public accountant who specialized in litigation support services, forensic accounting, fraud investigation, solvency and bankruptcy services.

Ordinarily, the side that calls an expert witness will have them testify to their credentials. Many times, the other side will stipulate that the witness is an expert so the jury doesn't have to listen to a recitation of jobs, degrees, honors and other boring minutia. That would not be the case in Barber's trial: each expert witness would be thoroughly questioned about his or her background. Each side seemed to be trying to "outexpert" the other side.

Siegel testified to a long list of impressive credentials to establish himself as an expert, and then said that he had examined Barber's bank accounts, bank statements, credit card statements, savings, retirement accounts and any and all financial documents related to Justin and April Barber.

"I would call it a forensic financial analysis of the financial documents," Siegel explained.

Siegel said the records he examined were from January 2001 through September 1, 2002. Barber had seven credit cards during that period, Siegel said, and his credit card debt jumped from $9,725.48 in January 2001 to $58,487.94 on September 1, 2002.

Siegel testified that the debt accrued because Barber took cash advances from his credit cards to pay for losses in the stock market. The prosecution produced a large visual aid showing Barber's credit card information. Willis interrupted and asked to voir dire an aspect of the exhibit. Willis wanted to make certain the jury realized that Barber's American Express company credit card was included in Siegel's examples.

On the company card, Barber sometimes paid the balance and was reimbursed by Rayonier, and sometimes the amount was paid directly by the corporation. Siegel told the jury that the company credit card showed no cash advances and that the balance remained stable.

"You think that, nonetheless, should be on this chart as far as his credit card activity, to do an assessment of his personal activity?" Willis asked.

"Well, to the extent that it was a credit card that was his credit card, it's included in the analysis."

Willis concluded his voir dire and Siegel stepped to the financial exhibit and outlined Barber's financial activities. The exhibit was put into evidence without objection. Siegel told the jury that he had analyzed credit card rates for the period in question and ound that Barber's interest on that debt was 16⅞ percent. In January 2001, Barber's minimum total credit card payment was $430, Siegel said, and $1,357 in September 2002.

Under cross-examination, Siegel said that most of the fifty-thousand-dollar debt was to pay cash advances for losses in the stock market. Barber had not done well in the market, Willis said, just as many other investors had lost money.

"He did poorly, yes," Siegel said. "He lost over thirty-four thousand dollars."

Willis established that Siegel's firm had been paid $25,000 to examine Barber's financial records and that another $25,000 was due. Willis noted that Barber's debt increase totaled $50,000—the same amount Siegel's company was being paid. What relevancy that had to the case was not made clear at this point.

During the time frame that he examined Barber's financial records, Siegel admitted, Barber was sometimes late on a payment, but there were no problems. "His debt was managed," Siegel testified. Siegel also testified that Barber reported $105,000 a year in income and that April reported $73,600 annual income.

Siegel said he knew they lived apart and maintained two separate households. "So the nut of your testimony is he was not delinquent, he was not behind," Willis asked, "and his debt on his credit cards went up fifty thousand dollars?"

Siegel said that was true. Willis completed cross-examination, and Foxman's redirect examination reiterated that most of the cash advances on the credit cards were to cover losses on margin calls.

Jay Jervey wore a loose tropical shirt, which wasn't tucked into his trousers. His white hair and full beard, coupled with his deep tan, spoke of a man who spent a lot of time outside rather than a businessman who sold millions of dollars in life insurance. Jervey was a man with a sense of whimsy: he kept an old-fashioned telephone booth in his office. But when he came to life insurance, Jervey was all-business.

Foxman elicited testimony that Barber had come to his office in the middle of July 2001, after looking at First Colony Insurance Company's Web site, to see about buying term life insurance policies for himself and his wife. After discussing it, they settled on a two-million-dollar life insurance policy for each of them. Jervey said he believed Barber had those figures in mind, but he couldn't remember for certain five years after the fact.

Jervey explained how a person qualifies for an insurance policy, based on numerous factors that include a physical examination, and that both Barber and April were qualified. The insurance agent said he learned of April's murder when he read about it in the April 19, 2002, issue of a local newspaper.

Following procedure, Jervey notified First Colony that there was a death claim, and he "probably" called Barber within five days to express condolences and to start the claim process. Willis cross-examined Jervey, who said that he telephoned Barber and left messages on his voice mail after reading about April's death. Barber, he said, did not call back for two weeks.

He telephoned and left a message, Jervey testified, but he didn't remember the time frame. Willis asked if Barber waited until September 5 to go to Jervey's office to start the claim. Jervey didn't remember, but said he would take Willis at his word.

"So much of our business is done through computers," Jervey testified. "We have a mainframe in our office and a lot of our notes are in the system, as we say, and are not handwritten in the file."

Willis received permission to approach the witness and showed him a copy of his earlier deposition to see if it refreshed Jervey's memory. Jervey said it looked familiar, and that his office had called and left a message because Barber wasn't at home. He also said they contacted First Colony.

"Do you recall what you told us about how he appeared when you met with him for the first time in the process of initiating a claim?"

"He didn't look the same as he did when we took out the application papers."

"Specifically, didn't he look like 'death warmed over'?"

"Yeah. He looked bad," Jervey said.

The smallest detail can be of great importance in a murder trial. This was shown when Willis asked for a discussion without the jury present during the direct examination of Deirdre Maddox, a claims leader with Genworth Financial, which was associated with First Colony. Maddox, who was in charge of April's claim file, received a subpoena to produce the documents.

Both sides had agreed that certain parts of the documents could be blanked out before being presented to the jury. After the jury left the room, Willis explained that the information had been "blacked out" and it was too apparent. Willis wanted the parts that were blacked out to be covered with Wite-Out. He didn't object to the omissions, just to using black as opposed to white.

Foxman said, "One of the things is, you know, when you have to redact something, you're onto the copies—"

"There's different ways of redacting things," Hedstrom said. "I think you're complaining that it's too obvious that it's redacted."

"That's exactly—" Willis said.

"Would that be as to art?" Chris France chimed in for the prosecution.

"That's what I'm saying," Willis said. "I don't think it's a big deal."

"Well, can you white it out and recopy the page to make it less obvious?" Hedstrom asked. "Is that what you want to do?"

Willis said yes, and the judged asked the clerk if she had any Wite-Out. The clerk had Wite-Out. The judge said, "Take this Wite-Out, and if you don't know how to use it, the clerk will show you."

Willis said, "I've seen it done before, but I don't know."

"Let the clerk do it," the judge said.

"We're just going to redact it in white rather than black. Redact the section on other insurance period, and just be done with it."

"Could you place a piece of paper over that entire section and copy that page?" the judge asked.

"Sure," France said.

The court went into recess for a few minutes while the prosecutors hotfooted it downstairs to take care of the paperwork. Court was back in session shortly afterward, with the Wite-Out done to everyone's satisfaction. Maddox was still on the witness stand and Foxman resumed his direct examination.

He said, "One thing I noticed about [April's policy] is in the application section of the document. There's a section that requests if someone other than the owner, in this case April Barber, is to be notified or receive correspondence as it relates to the policy. That area was checked. Did you notice that?"

"Yes, I did." When asked whose name was there, Maddox replied, "It was Justin Barber."

Foxman asked if that was unusual.

"Normally, they only send out the premium notices,

unless it's requested, to either an irrevocable beneficiary or the owner or the insured."

In other words, it was unusual for Barber to be receiving information concerning April's insurance policy. Foxman had no more questions and there was no cross-examination. The prosecutor called Mitchell Walters as his next witness. Walters was director of information technology at Rayonier, Barber's employer.

Walters testified that he was asked to take the hard drive from Barber's laptop computer. Walters said Barber brought the computer to his office and he removed the hard drive and gave it to Ed Frazier, who was Rayonier's general counsel at the time. Nothing else was done to "tamper" with the computer, Walters said.

Foxman approached the witness with a large envelope, borrowed scissors from the clerk and had Walters clip a corner and peek inside. Walters identified what he saw in the envelope as being the hard drive from a laptop computer. He said there was no way he could tell if it was from Barber's computer.

Walters said the protocol for computer use at Rayonier was for employees to have their own account and a personal password, which they could never share. Each individual picked his password and even the information technology division didn't have it. Company policy, he said, prohibited the sharing of passwords. There was no policy about sharing computers.

Foxman concluded and Willis had no questions. Ed Frazier, a senior vice president at Rayonier, was the company's associate general counsel at the time Barber handed over his computer. Frazier explained the details of getting Barber's hard drive to ensure that there had been no mix-up or confusion. Delray Lopez, chief of security at the time for Rayonier, hand-delivered the hard drive to the state attorney in St. Augustine.

Frazier looked inside the envelope that Walters had opened. Frazier identified a laptop computer drive and a letter he had placed inside the envelope in 2002 designating it as the hard drive to Barber's laptop.

Willis had no questions when Foxman completed his direct and Detective Howard Cole, still under oath, was called to testify. He identified the laptop hard drive and described how it was taken into evidence. Foxman entered the laptop hard drive into evidence for the state. Neither counsel wanted to examine Cole further, and Robert Shaw, who had been a detective on the case in 2002, was called to testify. Shaw was currently studying aviation and was no longer with the SJSO.

Shaw identified a desktop computer that Barber turned over to him in 2002 at the defendant's Jacksonville condominium. In response to a question by Willis, Shaw said Barber had agreed to give the computer to the police, and that he had it packaged and ready for them when they arrived to get it. Shaw stepped down from the witness stand, but was not dismissed because Willis said he was subject to recall.

The trial was moving faster than anyone thought it would, and Foxman asked for a fifteen-minute break. Even though things might have been going well in the courtroom, the state attorney's office was trying to crack an imminent problem. Part of the prosecution's evidence was a song Barber had recorded and deleted on his home computer. The song was easily played with special software from a copy of the original hard drive. Unfortunately for the state, it had to be played from the original hard drive. So far, the FDLE had not been able to crack the nut that would get the song to play from the original drive. Time was running out, and all involved had knots in their bellies.

* * *

Patti Parrish, April's aunt, now a district court judge in Oklahoma, took the witness stand and testified that April was more like a daughter than a niece, and that April lived with her for a year and a half before marrying Barber. April's mother, Nancy, was Parrish's sister and she had died when April was a senior in high school.

Parrish said she learned of April's murder when Barber's mother, Linda, told her on August 18, 2002, early in the morning. Parrish said she had several conversations with Justin Barber before April's funeral, one of which was lengthy.

Foxman asked what Justin Barber told her about the shooting. Barber, she said, told her he had been shot five times [actually, he had been shot four times], but didn't know whether or not April had been shot. The prosecutor asked questions about a telephone conversation Parrish had with Justin Barber on April 19, 2002.

"Did you ask him if he tried to find a pulse on April Barber?"

"Yes. I asked him—he told me he thought that April was dead because she wasn't talking. And so I asked if he tried to find a pulse, he said no. So I asked him did you . . . try mouth-to-mouth resuscitation. And he said no."

Under Foxman's direct examination, Parrish testified to a conversation she had with Barber the day before April's funeral in Oklahoma. Parrish said Barber told her that he and April had been drinking and that he was drunk. Barber told her that April was not.

"Did he describe for you whether or not when he arrived and left at Guana Park he observed any vehicles?" Foxman asked.

"Yes. I asked him if he had seen this car that was mentioned in one of the newspapers. And he said the car was not there when they got to the beach and that it was not there when they left the beach. He didn't see the car at any time."

Foxman asked if Barber had said anything about seeing blood on April's face.

"He told me that April was bleeding and that there was blood on her face."

"Did the defendant . . . discuss the fact that he had driven away from Guana approximately ten miles to Ponte Vedra Lakes Boulevard?"

"Yes. He told me that the reason he drove so far without stopping to get help was because there weren't any lights on, on any of the houses that he passed."

Foxman finished his questions and Willis had none. It was a break for a jury that had been concentrating hard on the evidence. The state's next witness would be on the stand for quite a while and it was too late in the day to begin his testimony. Judge Hedstrom adjourned until the next morning. The jury had no idea just how difficult to follow the testimony to come would be. And the state was still worrying whether or not it would be technically possible to play a deleted song from Barber's home computer.

Chapter 28

Chris Hendry, the computer whiz at the FDLE, was scheduled to be the first witness when court convened. Hendry was the technician who had labored over Barber's computer hard drives for more than two years to retrieve search information that had been deleted.

Before the jury was called in, Willis renewed his objection to the admission of the computer evidence. It had been heard before the court in limine and he wanted to make it a continuing objection. The judge noted the objection. Willis's second objection was admission of evidence the day before regarding evidence concerning Barber's computer at Rayonier.

Willis said a state witness from Rayonier made it clear that there were no prohibitions against people using the computers of other employees. Willis argued that it assumed information on the computer could have been from someone other than Barber using it. The judge said there was no evidence that anyone but Barber used the computer. After a short discussion, the judge noted Willis's objection.

Hendry was called to the stand to testify without the jury being present. Hendry identified himself and answered questions to qualify himself as an expert in retrieving information from computers. The FDLE expert testified at length to his experience, education and other qualifications.

For the computer illiterate on the jury, Hendry explained that the hard drive on a computer is like having information stored in a notebook, except it is stored on magnetic platters. Photographs, Web pages, text, documents and anything that can be digitalized can be stored on the hard drive.

Hendry mentioned the specialized software the FDLE used to search the hard drives. The software was developed for use by police. Hendry showed the jury a computer processing unit (CPU) and explained that he could use the specialized software to find information through unique codes assigned to different kinds of files. When he looked for text, Hendry said, he looked for key words, which he described as being in a certain sequence. If he looked for key words on a hypertext markup language (HTML), the unique coding identifying it would be at the front of the text.

Hendry explained how search engines, such as Google and Yahoo, list an "index" of sources that contain key words that the user enters. The witness walked to a large exhibit the state had prepared. Hendry told Foxman it looked like a Google search that looked for information on the key words "trauma, cases, gunshot, right and chest" that were entered. Hendry said the exhibit depicted the first ten pages of 2,090 pages that the search found containing key word information. The search took less than a second.

The exhibit was entered into evidence over Willis's continuing objection.

"The search [for] 'trauma, cases, gunshot, right, chest,'

were you able to date when that search was done?"
Foxman asked.

"Yeah, the date of that one was created on February
14, 2002." He gave the technical directory of the file designated to it on the Internet.

Hendry looked at another Google search made February 20, 2002. He testified that it was another search
that used the key words "medical, trauma, gunshot and
chest." The search turned up 4,280 items, called "hits,"
which was completed in less than half a second. The
search, he said, was made between 2:58 and 2:59 P.M.

Foxman showed Hendry another exhibit that the witness said was another Internet search that used the key
words "Florida" and "divorce." This search, Hendry said,
was performed July 19, 2002, and that the search had
been deleted. It could only be found by using specialized
software, such as Hendry employed.

The searches that Hendry had testified to so far had
been made on Barber's laptop computer, which was provided by Rayonier. Foxman asked him to explain what
the word "Kazaa" meant. Hendry replied that it was the
name of a peer-to-peer program that allowed people to
exchange files on the Internet. Then he identified an exhibit as being a song that Barber downloaded called
"Used to Love Her" by the band Guns N' Roses.

The song was downloaded on August 17, 2002, at 5:16
P.M. That was just hours before April was murdered, and
probably about the time she was getting ready to go to
dinner in Jacksonville Beach with her husband. The
song was deleted on September 3, 2002, the day before
Barber turned it over to the police for examination.

This was also the song the state worried about being
able to reproduce. Hendry had difficulty with it up until
the last minute. Nevertheless, Foxman asked Hendry to

play the song. There was an eerie silence in the court-room and then the song played.

The lyrics were crystal clear. As implied in the title, the lyrics talked about someone loving a woman, but he had to kill her. Even though she was buried in the backyard, the lyrics said, he could still hear her complain. The jury could see the lyrics printed on a board the state had prepared.

Foxman asked Hendry to repeat the date that the song was deleted and had no further questions. Willis cordially asked Hendry how he was, then said he was going to ask a question that would test his memory. He had deposed Hendry in May and the FDLE computer expert told him that Barber had deleted another song on September 3. Hendry said a Guns N' Roses song "November Rain" was deleted from Barber's hard drive.

"Can we tell who logged on?" Willis asked. "Was it Mr. Barber or April Barber? Can you tell?"

"No, sir. I do not have that information."

Hendry acknowledged that Barber's home computer contained 1,695 songs, including "Used to Love Her."

"Can you tell whether or not that music was even played that afternoon as opposed to being downloaded?" Willis asked.

"No, I don't believe I can find out whether it was actually played."

"So we don't even know whether it was played on the August seventeenth afternoon?"

"Correct."

"What was your technical capacity when you played that song just now?" Willis asked. "I asked if you had the technical ability to play this song [at the deposition]. What was your technical ability? Did you have it recorded? Did you play it on the computer or what?"

Hendry explained the complicated way he had played that song and "I'm Moving On" by Rascal Flatts for

Willis, Detective Cole, Foxman and Lee Hutton in January. Willis asked, "But you're able to play them on the computer?" Hendry acknowledged that he could.

"Focusing on the afternoon of August the seventeenth, beginning at five o'clock, there was kind of a recording or downloading session—was there not—on that computer?" Willis asked.

Hendry said there was. "So, in addition to the song by Guns N' Roses "Used to Love Her," didn't the recording session begin more or less with a song called 'Rascal Flatts'?" Willis asked.

"'I'm Moving On' was by Rascal Flatts," Hendry said.

"Was there another song that was downloaded called 'Fire Woman'?"

"Yes, sir, by the Cult."

"Rascal Flatts and 'I'm Moving On' was the first of the songs recorded at five o'clock, was it not?"

"Rascal Flatts was first. 'Fire Woman' was second."

"How about the next one after 'Fire Woman'? Was that 'Rise'? And was that recorded at five-oh-three P.M.?" Willis asked.

The computer expert said that was correct.

"And after that, there was another Guns N' Roses song called 'You're Crazy,' and that was recorded that afternoon?"

"Correct."

"And then you've got 'Knockin' on Heaven's Door' at five-seventeen P.M."

Hendry answered yes.

"We've got 'Used to Love Her' at five-sixteen P.M. . . . You've got 'November Rain' at five twenty-five P.M. The next one is 'You Could Be Mine, another Guns N' Roses song at five twenty-eight P.M. There was a song called 'She Loves Me Not' by Papa Roach. A song 'So Excited' that was downloaded at five-twenty P.M.?" Willis asked.

Hendry said that was correct.

"I think we have something like sixteen songs recorded or downloaded that afternoon?" Willis asked.

"That's what I remember."

"And we can't tell whether any or all of those were played that afternoon?"

"Correct."

Willis asked if there was any way Hendry could tell if any of the songs had been played between the time they were downloaded and deleted. Hendry said he couldn't.

"So we have a total of one thousand six hundred ninety-five songs on his computer, sixteen of which were downloaded the very afternoon of her death?"

"Correct."

"And out of those, we brought this one into the courtroom?" Willis asked.

"Correct."

Willis was showing the jury that the state used "selected" facts and cast them in a light that made them seem "sinister." The state mentioned the download of "Used to Love Her," but made no reference to the fact that sixteen other songs had been downloaded during the approximate time frame. Neither did it mention the 1,600-plus songs downloaded to Barber's computer.

Willis mentioned that Barber was in the hospital for "a couple of days" following the shooting on August 17. Yet, Hendry's analysis showed activity on August 18 at 3:08 A.M. when Microsoft Outlook started. Hendry said Outlook could have been set to start automatically or the program could have been opened by a user. There was no way he could tell. Willis asked if there was another program started the same day at 7:44 A.M.

"Correct, there was. That was one where the Outlook was started, Outlook Express or Outlook was started for the first time."

"And that one does require manual operation?" Willis asked.

"That one does require one because—if you don't have a profile or you haven't opened it before, once you've opened Outlook for the first time, it will create the directors, the file structure, and Microsoft likes everybody to feel warm and welcomed, so they send you automatically a Welcome to Microsoft Outlook, so there's automatically one message generated with a date and time stamp of when it's created."

Willis asked if there was activity on Monday, August 19, at 7:51 A.M., and Hendry said it looked like there was work done on the Internet. The activity could have been done automatically, but normally it would have been done by an operator.

Hendry told the jury one of the specialized programs he used while investigating Barber's hard drives was EnCase. Willis asked if that was the program that searched for key words on the hard drives after these were entered on EnCase.

"And if we understand it correctly, the way it works is that you plug into the machine and it searches out to see if those words have ever been part of a query—is that it?"

Hendry said that was one of the tools he used.

"Do you know or can you tell us how many queries total were on Mr. Barber's Rayonier machine, his work machine?" Willis asked.

Hendry replied that he used a special program called Access Data because it was easier than EnCase when looking for key words. "Access Data does it real nice for us and I can run those searches," Hendry said. "And what I have for a Google search using the term Google search, there are one thousand nine hundred fifty-four hits totaling seven hundred fourteen files on the hard drive."

"I hate to say it. . . . What does that mean in English?"

"That means that the words actually spelled out Google Search together appear one thousand nine hundred fifty-four times. That can mean they appear multiple times in a document." He said there could be four hits recorded in the same file.

Hendry said he also used the MSN search engine in addition to Google. On the MSN Search, he said, he found ninety-two hits in thirty-two files. When he looked at Yahoo's search engine, Hendry said he found 120 key word hits on thirty-one files.

Willis asked if Hendry could give a "reasonable" number of searches made on the Rayonier hard drive. The FDLE agent said he used a "stress term estimate" and that there were "easily" more than 2,200 hits on the drive.

"So, out of two thousand two hundred, we have three or four that are here in the courtroom this morning?" Hendry said that was correct. Willis wanted to know how many key words the state gave him to search on Barber's computers.

Hendry said the original list was about thirty-five key words, with another thirty added on the second search, to total about sixty key words.

"So about sixty key word searches that ultimately led you to this right here?"

Hendry said that was true. "When you get that raw result, that is to say those queries that would incorporate the key words, do you make any kind of evaluation yourself as to what, if any, of these searches have value in the context of the case?" Willis asked. "In other words, whether they mean anything or not?"

Hendry testified that when there were so many key words involved, and he got thousands of hits, he couldn't judge whether it was of value or not. He said they would basically eliminate the data except the few words around the key word. Hendry said that pared-down list went back to the investigators and was explained to them. If the investigators wanted something, the FDLE pulled it from the hard drive. He said the FDLE doesn't determine what is or isn't of value to the investigation.

"What you're telling is, you get that raw material, you give it to the police, the prosecutors, [then] the police and prosecutors go through the various queries and they decide which ones may have some significance to the case?" Willis asked.

"Correct."

"That was the process that was employed in this case that deal with these three or four, whatever they are here?"

"Yes."

Willis asked Hendry if there was any way he could tell whether or not any of the hits were opened and read. The expert said he could not, nor could he say how much time a user spent reading a search. For example, he said, he might have a search page open but using the computer for something else. A search page could be open for three hours, he said, but a user may have spent only a minute or two looking at it. Hendry's analysis would show it open the whole time.

"So . . . you really can't tell us . . . whether he was reading an article out of the *New York Times* or *Time* magazine or something that might have prompted this. You can't tell us what happened before these searches?"

"No, sir, I cannot."

"You can't tell us essentially what happened after these searches, either?"

"That's correct."

"So they're just there and we don't have a context to put them in?"

"Correct. I can only provide you the data as it resides on the computer."

Willis completed his cross-examination, and Foxman, on redirect examination, asked if Hendry could tell how many of the songs downloaded on August 17, 2002, were deleted and marked for deletion. Foxman answered that he found "Used to Love Her" in the delete bin. That was all Foxman asked.

"You also said that there was one other that may have been deleted," Willis said on recross-examination. "A Guns N' Roses song at the same time?"

Hendry said it may have been deleted, but he had not been able to locate it in the delete bin on Barber's computer. "The [song] does not exist on the machine," he said.

When Willis finished, the state played Hendry's deposition for the jury. It took about three hours with two 15-minute breaks. Listening to this complex evidence did not seem to lull the jurors into a stupor. Throughout Hendry's testimony, both live and on the televised deposition, their attention was riveted on the proceedings. It seemed clear they were working hard to understand.

Willis was optimistic about how the trial was going. Under the law, Barber was considered innocent until the state proved him guilty beyond a reasonable doubt. The defense attorney believed the state's case was shredded by reasonable doubt. He thought it was possible that the state would ask that the charges be dismissed and that his client would walk away a free man. The state, however, had no intention of throwing in the towel.

"When we were ready to go to trial, we went to trial," France said. "We never once thought of dropping charges or considering a lesser offense. The defense made no offers for a deal and neither did we."

It was a fight to the finish.

* * *

It was showtime in the courtroom. The show was one that Robert Willis did not like when he saw it live. The show the jury would see was the three-hour videotape of Barber's deposition in a civil trial over a life insurance policy April had with State Farm Life Insurance Company. Barber had done everything superbly until the SJSO and state attorney's office armed Henry M. Coxe, attorney for State Farm, with all the information that had been gathered on Barber and his marriage.

For whatever reason, Barber became one of the worst witnesses against himself that Willis had ever seen. Barber's testimony during the live deposition had prompted Willis to call for a break. Privately, Willis asked Barber, "Did you kill your wife?" Barber was shocked. "No," he said. "Then stop acting like you did," Willis told him. Barber had promised to do better, but when his deposition resumed, he continued testifying in the same way.

During the deposition, Barber used some form of "I don't recall"—which is like saying no—118 times. A witness who uses that form of "answer dodging" is often seen by others as trying to hide something.

The same video- and audiotape would be heard by a jury that would decide whether Barber lived or died. The bustle of setting up the paraphernalia necessary for the jury to see the tape had been set up and court was convened. The video began and focused exclusively on Barber, who was dressed in a suit and tie, bearing an expression that hid what he might feel.

Coxe asked the usual questions about where Barber had lived, where he grew up, his education, and where he went to school. Barber wed Dana Montgomery in 1992, and the marriage lasted five years. They had no children.

Barber talked about his current hobby of mountain biking, lifting weights on rare occasions, and that he sometimes played pickup games of softball or flag football. His activities kept him in what he called "fairly good shape."

Coxe asked if he played tennis and Barber said he played tennis with Shannon Kennedy in 2002, and no one else. The attorney asked if Barber had told anyone since 2002 that he had played tennis with several other people. Barber said he didn't recall.

Barber's weight-lifting habits were described as Coxe seemed to be building a foundation to show how Barber was strong enough to overpower April and commit murder. During the summer of 2002, Barber said, he couldn't remember whether or not he had lifted weights. Barber said his other hobbies, aside from the ones he had already mentioned, included watching sports on television and listening to music. Rayonier had issued a computer to him for company use when he was hired, Barber said, but he was "functionally literate" with computers before that.

Primarily, Barber said, he used the Internet for business, games and news. Coxe asked if he had researched the Internet for the phrase "wound ballistics" in 2002 before April's murder. Barber didn't recall. Neither did he recall researching the terms "medical trauma" and "gunshot wounds to the chest" during the same time frame.

"You say no, or you don't recall?" Coxe asked.

"I don't recall."

"Did you, with your Rayonier computer, enter the key words: 'Prime/suspect/notcharged/murder/case/Florida'?"

"No."

Willis interrupted: "Do you have a time frame for that? Just at some point?"

"Did you?" Coxe asked.

"I don't recall."

"Did you do a search and research on the Internet the subject of homicide cases and gunshot wounds to the chest?"

"I don't recall."

"Did you, prior to April Barber's death, do an Internet search on the subject of death from acute blood loss?"

"I don't recall."

"Did you do an Internet search on the subject of transfusions for massive blood loss?"

"I don't recall."

"Did you do an Internet search on the subject of bloodstain pattern analysis?"

"I don't recall."

"Did you do an Internet search on different criminal cases in the state of Florida?"

"I don't recall."

Barber said he didn't recall doing an Internet search on the St. Johns County Sheriff's Office, but he said he did search the names of different assistant state attorneys in the St. Johns State Attorney's Office.

The witness said he sometimes shopped on the Internet and had bought some clothing, toys and a stuffed armadillo. Coxe asked if, before April's death, he had researched any form of body armor. Barber said he bought a bulletproof vest two or three years ago on eBay. He said he still had the body armor and kept it in his closet when he lived in Jacksonville.

"Did this bulletproof vest have a plate in it of any kind?"

"I don't recall."

"Did it have anything that would be inserted on the chest area of the vest?"

"I don't—I don't recall."

"Did you, prior to your wife's death, do a search on

the Internet on the subject of the amount of blood loss necessary to be declared dead?"

"I don't recall."

The prosecutors knew that Barber had purchased the bulletproof vest, but did not think it was of much significance. Rayonier had companies in South America where Barber often visited. Kidnapping of businessmen is rampant in some of these countries, and many Americans traveling there wear bulletproof vests and carry handguns.

Barber answered questions about some of his friends in Jacksonville and then turned to his marriage with April. The witness told Coxe they had no children because they weren't ready.

"Did you tell anybody during the course of your marriage that you refused to have children with April Barber under any circumstances?"

"I don't recall."

"Did you ever tell any person in the course of your marriage that you would not have children because you did not believe she was capable of raising children?"

"I don't recall saying that, no."

Coxe asked about the houses he and April owned and asked when he sold the house in Covington, Georgia. It was in the summer of 2002, Barber said, but he didn't recall the exact date. Pressed further, he said the house was sold in late June or July.

"At the time the house was sold or immediately prior to, were you experiencing financial difficulties?"

"No."

Barber testified that they owned a 1994 Rodeo, a 1997 GMC Jimmy, a 2001 Audi and a 1997 Toyota 4Runner when the Audi was stolen and dunked in the St. Johns River. Their finances were "largely" handled separately, Barber said. When asked to explain, Barber said they had separate bank accounts and paid their own expenses.

Barber testified that he was a day trader in the stock market in 2001 and 2002. Coxe asked if he was successful. Barber said he was not.

"Assuming the description, then, would be unsuccessful, how unsuccessful were you?"

"I don't recall exactly how much money I lost."

The defendant testified that in 2002, before April's death, he had approximately $40,000 in credit card debt. He also had a mortgage in Jacksonville, student loans and a loan on the GMC SUV. Barber said he owed about $10,000 in student loans and paid $14,000 from borrowing against a credit card to buy the Toyota 4Runner.

April had a degree in radiation therapy and worked in Tifton, Georgia, early in their marriage, he said, but they lived in Douglas. They both commuted to their jobs and back. Barber rented an apartment in Milledgeville for several months. Coxe asked if April commuted to visit him in Milledgeville.

"We saw each other on the weekends, but there was no furniture in the apartment," Barber said, "so I was sleeping on an air mattress. So I would usually travel to Douglas or she would come to Milledgeville, especially when we started our house hunt. When we were going to permanently relocate to the area, we started looking for a house."

They bought a house in Covington, Barber said, and April started a new job in Conyers and he was transferred to Eatonton, Georgia. They lived in the house together about six or seven months, he wasn't sure. After that, Barber was transferred to Jacksonville and bought a condominium in January 2001.

Coxe asked Barber if he had a good marriage during the time April worked in Thomasville and he lived and worked in Jacksonville. Barber said it was a normal marriage with its ups and downs.

"What would be an example of the ups?"

"An example of—we were in love."

"Any other ups?"

"I don't recall specifically."

Barber said they argued like normal married people on occasion. He said that living apart was stressful and they didn't see each other as much as they needed. Coxe asked what their arguments were about. Barber said that he didn't recall specifics, but the arguments were caused by living apart.

"That's your best recollection?"

"While we lived in Jacksonville, that was it. Prior to that, we argued about April's siblings occasionally that lived with us for a time. But that time had passed."

Barber testified that April's brother and sister, Kendon and Julie, lived with them in Douglas for about a year. It was a stressful time, he said, and it took a lot of work and energy for a newlywed couple to care for them. Julie, he said, was a strong-willed teenager who would not follow the household rules, and April had made the decision to have Julie return to Oklahoma. Barber said it was April's idea to try and keep Kendon, but he was returned just months later to live with relatives in Oklahoma.

April went to Oklahoma "a week, maybe two" before her death, because Julie was involved in a sorority rush, Barber told the jury. Barber said he didn't remember if April flew out of Jacksonville or a Georgia airport.

"Had she told you prior to leaving for Oklahoma on that weekend that she wanted out of this marriage with you?"

"No."

He admitted that April had questioned him about seeing other women. He said he didn't remember when the conversations took place. Barber said he received one or two e-mails from April asking about other women, but he didn't recall when. He said he might have answered them, but he didn't remember.

"Do you remember getting an e-mail on July 30, 2002, asking you to explain what was going on with respect to other women?"

"I don't recall that."

"Did you send her an e-mail on July 30, 2002, and recount in detail an entire day of your life as to who you were with and what you had been doing?"

"I don't recall that."

"Did you send her an e-mail and say that that included playing tennis with some other people, including Shannon Kennedy, and that her boyfriend was there?"

"I don't recall that."

Barber said that April asked in July and August of 2002 who Shannon Kennedy was, but he didn't remember the whole question. He told April that Shannon was a friend.

"Did you tell her anything else besides she's a friend?"

"I told her that we played tennis together occasionally and would go have a drink occasionally."

Barber testified about meeting Kennedy through Enterprise in the spring or summer of 2002. Coxe asked him to explain their relationship.

"We were friends," Barber said. "I think that—I don't know why—we became sexually involved very quickly."

"Where?"

"In the condo."

"In your home?"

"Yes."

Coxe asked him how frequently they were sexually involved. Barber said he didn't recall, but thought it was five or six times.

Barber didn't remember what type of birth control

they used, if any. He said he probably used a condom, but didn't remember. Barber said he didn't remember telling Kennedy that he and April couldn't live together.

"Do you remember the date your wife died again?"

"Excuse me?"

"The date your wife died." Barber said he believed it was August 17. Coxe continued: "Were you planning on August fifteenth to go to Georgia on August nineteenth?"

Barber didn't remember. Neither did he remember asking Kennedy to go to Georgia with him.

"Did you ask Shannon Kennedy, in the days immediately—or did you tell Shannon Kennedy in the days immediately prior to your wife's death that you very well might be moving to California?"

Barber said he had been approached about a company talking to him about a job in California, but he did not remember mentioning it to Kennedy. Coxe asked if Barber had inquired whether or not Kennedy would go with him to California. The witness said he did not.

"Did you meet with Shannon Kennedy and engage in sexual relations approximately four times a week in each of the two weeks immediately prior to April Barber's death?"

"I don't recall," Barber said. "That sounds like too many times."

"How many times do you recall?"

"I don't—like I said, six times, maybe. I just don't recall the time frame. We didn't have sex every time that we saw each other outside of work. I just don't remember."

"Did you have a sexual relationship with another woman in Georgia while you were married to April Barber?"

"Yes."

Barber could not remember the woman's name, but said he met her at a bar in Milledgeville.

"And did you have sexual relations with a woman in New Zealand?"

"Yes." Barber said he was married to April at the time. He said the woman's name was Carolyn, and they stayed in touch occasionally by e-mail.

"How many times did you have sex with Carolyn?" Barber said he thought it was two times. The woman was an employee of Rayonier at the time, Barber said, but had changed jobs. He had no idea how to contact her.

"Did you tell April Barber that you ever had sexual relations with Shannon Kennedy?" Barber said no. "Did you tell April Barber that you had sexual relations with this woman in Georgia whose name you don't recall?" Barber said he did not. "Did you tell April Barber that you had sexual relationships with Carolyn McKay in New Zealand?" Barber said no.

Coxe referred to Barber's previous testimony that he and April had a good marriage with no unusual problems. He asked if April had expressed concerns in 2002 about their marriage. Barber admitted that she did, but he said he didn't recall what she had said.

"Did you ever tell anybody during the course of your marriage that your first divorce was an embarrassment, and you would never let that happen again, no matter how this marriage went?" Coxe asked.

"No, I never said anything like that."

The plaintiff's attorney asked about Barber's religious affiliations and he answered that he was a nonpracticing Christian. He said, "I would describe most of my relatives as being Pentecostal. Baptist, some of them."

Coxe wanted to know if Barber had ever told anybody he would never get divorced again, no mater how his marriage went, because of his family's faith. Barber said

he did not recall saying that. The defendant said he had
not told anyone that he wouldn't get divorced because it
would be a personal embarrassment to have been divorced twice.

"When is the last time you spoke with Shannon Kennedy?" Coxe asked.

"I don't know exactly. It would have been in the
months following April's death, on business, renting a
car through Enterprise." Barber said he talked to Kennedy just several days after April was killed, but didn't see
her. He said he did not have sex with Kennedy following
his wife's death.

Coxe established that Barber had some familiarity
with guns, growing up around them, going to Reserve
Officer Training Corps (ROTC) and shooting at a target
range. The attorney switched the focus back to April.

"After April Barber returned from Oklahoma the week
before she died," he asked, "other than the weekend that
she died, had you seen her, or had she returned to Georgia and then come to Jacksonville the following week?"

Barber said he didn't recall. Coxe continued to press the
issue. "When, on the weekend of her death, do you remember her getting to Jacksonville?" Barber said it was
probably on a Friday evening, because that was when she
usually arrived. April drove to Jacksonville from her job in
Georgia. Coxe asked what time had she arrived the weekend that she died, and Barber didn't remember. He didn't
remember whether or not he was home when she arrived.

"Had she not been there for two weeks, though?"
Coxe asked.

"I don't recall her being there prior to her trip to Oklahoma."

"You don't remember if you were home when she
came to Jacksonville the weekend she died?"

"I don't remember."

"What did you do Friday night?"

"I really don't remember at all. I remember that—I think April and I spent Friday evening together at home, maybe at a restaurant, but—I—I don't remember."

"I'm asking you about the Friday night immediately before the Saturday night she died."

"Yeah, I . . ."

"You just don't remember?"

"I don't remember."

Coxe said: "Let me ask you about the day she died. . . . Do you remember that day?"

"Vaguely. . . . We had sex that day. I remember that."

Having sex during the day was not something they usually did, he said, but April was on the bed, putting on her makeup. They kissed, and one thing led to another.

"Mr. Barber, did she tell you that she was flying the week before to Oklahoma out of Georgia because she didn't want to see you?"

Barber said no. It was his belief, he testified, that April didn't want to spend the extra money on airline fare.

"Do you remember anything you did during that day *before* you say you had sex with your wife?"

"No, I don't." Barber said he didn't remember anything he and April talked about that day.

"Did she tell you she was leaving you?" Coxe asked.

"No, she did not."

"Did she tell you she wanted out of the marriage?"

Barber said no. Neither did she tell him that the marriage wasn't working, he said, nor did they discuss any other issues.

"Was it . . . 'I'm so happy you're back after two weeks'?"

"It was a nice weekend. It was. We had a nice dinner Friday and we were preparing to go out Saturday in celebration of our anniversary."

Coxe called attention to the two-million-dollar life insurance policies that were purchased on each of them from First Colony Life Insurance Company approximately ten months previously. He thought both insurance policies had been canceled, he said, but added that he didn't express surprise to anyone when he found out that April's policy was still in force.

The fact that he didn't express surprise that the policy was still in effect, Coxe said, was the point he was trying to make. Especially since Barber said he thought the policy had been canceled.

Coxe asked if on the night before April was killed, April had asked about Shannon Kennedy: *Who is that woman you're playing tennis with? She didn't say she wanted out of the marriage; she wanted a divorce; she was going to leave you; she couldn't put up with you anymore?*

Impatiently, Barber said he had answered no to those questions several times. The answer was still no.

"And when you were at the Ritz or Carrabba's or in between, did she bring up the question of, in whatever words, who's the tennis player? Who is this Shannon Kennedy? How come I've never met her, or anything like that?" Coxe asked.

"I don't recall that conversation. I recall having a very good time. And I don't think that would have been part of that conversation. I just don't remember it."

Coxe asked Barber about the drive to the beach and going for a walk at Guana Park along the Atlantic shoreline. He didn't remember what they talked about. Certainly, he said, he didn't remember saying anything about leaving. He said it was just normal conversation.

Under Coxe's questioning, Barber told his version of the attack on the beach by an unknown assailant. The scenario he painted for Coxe was the same one he had related in various police interviews. The details didn't change, including a struggle with the assailant, dragging

April up the beach, trying in vain to stop a car for help and his mad drive to look for help.

Coxe asked if Barber was having financial difficulties when his Audi was stolen a few weeks before April's death. Records show that his insurance paid him more than he owed on the stolen car. Barber didn't remember, but did say they were not having money problems.

The plaintiff's lawyer wanted to know why Barber lied to Detective Cole when asked if he had had a sexual relationship with Shannon Kennedy.

"I was embarrassed."

"Did you tell him about the woman from New Zealand?"

"I don't recall."

Coxe asked why he had not told the truth about his sexual affairs.

"I was ashamed and embarrassed, and I didn't want to talk about it."

Barber said he recognized the named Brian Stedman and said he had been a friend in graduate school. He said he talked with Brian frequently after he and April were married, but he had never mentioned his affairs. Barber conceded that it was possible that he mentioned affairs to Stedman, but he didn't remember. Barber said he would not have been embarrassed to discuss his affairs with Stedman.

Barber admitted that he had advertised himself on an Internet dating service with the intent of meeting other women. The witness said he had a sexual encounter with another woman he had met at the bar in Milledgeville where he had previously met another woman. Barber said he also had a sexual relationship with a woman named Karen in Baxley, Georgia. The witness said he did not recall if there were others.

Counting Kennedy, Barber had testified to having

affairs with five different women during his three-year marriage to April. A correspondent on CBS Television's show *48 Hours* told Barber's attorney that Barber had "hot pants." Willis replied that didn't make him a killer.

Barber denied that he had joined a singles' club or any other private club. The lawyer asked if Barber had told any of his friends that his private life was none of April's business. Barber didn't remember. Coxe asked if Barber had ever told Brian Stedman that he would never have children with April.

"It would have been out of character. I don't recall saying anything like that."

"Why would it be out of character? I understood you to say earlier it would not have been surprising for you to tell Brian Stedman about affairs that you had, correct?"

"Yes."

"So if you would tell Brian Stedman about affairs you were having or had had during your marriage," Coxe asked, "why would it be out of character to tell Brian Stedman that you would not have children with April Barber?"

"I would never say anything disrespectful like that about April to Brian."

Coxe asked what had happened to the Great Dane he owned in Covington. Barber said he thought he gave the dog to a coworker.

"Is that what you told other people happened to the dog?"

"No. I believe we told people that the dog died at the vet, but I don't remember exactly."

Barber insisted that he believed the two-million-dollar life insurance for April had lapsed, even when the agent who telephoned and left a message on his voice mail told him the claim was being processed. The defendant said he thought the insurance company had made a mistake. Barber said he didn't remember whether he received the message before or after April's funeral.

The long videotape ended. Barber didn't seem to change his expression. It was clear why Willis had been concerned about the deposition. Barber appeared to be evasive in his answers and seemed nervous at times. Only once, when talking about his wife's murder, did his eyes tear. In court, Barber was handsome, composed and compelling; on video, he appeared cold.

Chapter 29

Jason Hitt was a crime laboratory analyst in the biology and DNA section at the FDLE in the Jacksonville Operations Office. After long testimony to qualify himself as an expert, Hitt began the formidable task of explaining DNA, how it was found, treated, and what "matching fingerprints" meant.

Hitt had started with April's shirt, underwear, capri pants and scrapings in marked containers. The SJSO had asked him to look at certain parts of the items to tell them what he could determine about the DNA. He explained that DNA is an acronym that stands for deoxyribonucleic acid, often called the building block of life.

"Our science is kind of littered with acronyms," Hitt said. "Deoxyribonucleic acid is a very long name for a very long molecule and it's found in every cell in your body except for red blood cells."

Hitt explained that DNA contains a coded sequence of information that makes us who we are: babies get half from their mothers and half from their fathers. Everyone's DNA is different except in the case of identical twins.

The type of DNA testing he did at the lab in Jacksonville is called STR DNA testing, with STR standing for short tandem repeats. Hitt explained that throughout the DNA molecule there are specifically identified areas called loci. At each loci, there are two pieces of information— one from the mother, the second from the father. In STR DNA testing, the investigator looks for repeating sequences of information.

This repeating loci information is found in every individual, but the amount of information in each loci varies with each person. This is what makes us different. The information in the STRs is so specific that positive blood matches can be easily made in circumstances where the DNA hasn't been somehow degraded or polluted.

First the stains had to be tested to see if they were composed of blood. Hitt used a procedure called a phenolphthalein test, which uses a chemical that turns bright pink in the presence of blood. There is no change in color if a stain isn't blood. The phenolphthalein test turned pink on all the samples Hitt tested.

On September 19, 2002, the DNA technician identified blood on April's pants. Small cuttings, to be used as samples, were taken from the bloodstained areas. Hitt said the FDLE lab doesn't randomly test articles, but studies the areas to which the investigating agencies direct it.

"That's one of the misnomers about forensics," Hitt said. "It's personally my opinion that we do not solve crimes. We aid investigations. We help to lend scientific evidence to what has already been proposed as to what occurred during the alleged offense."

The FDLE was told to look at the front of the shirt in two different areas, and two from the back of the shirt identified as D and E. On September 18, 2002, the areas tested positive for blood. He said the heavy saturation of blood on the back of the shirt exhibited a great deal of blood loss. The stain was so thick Hitt could see localized stains, so he sampled two areas of the stain.

The shirt was sent back for a second investigation to see if there were other bloodstains on the shirt. Hitt took further samples and found additional blood. Cuttings were taken from those areas. The blood expert said the sample size needed for an analysis is only about three millimeters squared.

France asked, "You wouldn't get a positive for blood out of other fluid, semen, vomit, dirt and water mix, correct?"

Hitt explained that the test is "pretty good." He said it used the presence of hemoglobin, the oxygen-carrying portion of blood. Sometimes false positives are reported, but he said that it is so difficult to get a false positive that he has failed when he tried intentionally to create one in his laboratory on numerous occasions.

Hitt said that there was difficulty getting a DNA profile off the samples taken from the shirt. He explained that too much blood being present can be a problem. He elucidated: "Inside a blood sample, we get DNA from a portion of your blood. Blood is not a very simple substance. It's a mixture of a whole bunch of different components. The DNA profile we get from a blood sample is actually from the white blood cells.

Inside blood, you have your oxygen-carrying hemoglobin housed in your red blood cells . . . extremely prevalent in a bloodstain. The red cells are actually what causes blood to look red. Unfortunately, sometimes the hem of the hemoglobin molecule can actually inhibit our DNA testing."

Should that happen, Hitt continued, the FDLE has methods to help obtain DNA that was found on the first try. A process called DNA extraction is used that will lift a bloodstain off a shirt so that DNA can be obtained. When too much DNA causes problems, it can be diluted.

The inherent danger with diluting DNA, Hitt said, is that you can dilute the DNA concentration so much that it is impossible to find a result.

Hitt testified that there were several bloodstains on April's pants. Cuttings were taken from those areas for possible DNA testing. There were also stains on Barber's shirt that were blood. One stain at the right front shoulder was described as "massive." The FDLE took cuttings from bloodstains on the shirt for possible DNA testing.

After Hitt performed these tests, he testified, he transferred the evidence to another laboratory blood analyst. Bloodstains were also found on Barber's underwear, Hitt said, but he did not identify the stain around Barber's belt.

With that, France had no further questions on his direct examination, but Robert Willis had plenty. Handling of April's remains and her DNA were two areas where he thought the police made grave errors in execution and procedure.

The first thing Willis wanted clarified was that the state admitted the same evidence on two separate occasions. And then he asked why the SJSO advised the FDLE to limit its examination to certain areas of the clothing. Hitt said that was true.

"And what were those areas again? So far as to Mrs. Barber's pants, what were those areas again?"

"The understanding was to examine the pants for the presence of blood, to concentrate the search in the front and the back waist area of the left-hand side," Hitt said.

"Does that mean that if you see other areas of bloodstaining . . . you're just not supposed to pay attention to it?"

"No. At that point, I was just following directions. We were looking with the understanding of 'let's start with these areas,' and then we can always go back and rework this evidence if that information obtained doesn't show us anything."

Willis asked if Hitt saw any other areas of interest, other than those pointed out by the SJSO during the first examination. Hitt said there were other stained areas.

"What did you do with respect to those?" Willis asked.

"They were not tested at the time."

Hitt said he thought they probably were bloodstains, but he didn't do any testing. He told Willis that an area in the back left side of April's pants tested positive for human blood during the first examination. He testified that the pants were retested for the second time on September 28, 2004, more than two years later.

At that time, Hitt said, the SJSO had widened the scope of the FDLE's investigation to take other samples from the front and back of April's pants.

"But at this time, it was strictly to test on the front of her pants, but not test on the back?"

"I tested both areas on the front and on the back."

"Maybe I misunderstood. I thought you said you were instructed to test on the front but not the back. Is that true or not true?"

Hitt said he didn't remember, which is as good as saying no in a trial.

Willis wasn't satisfied with the answer. "I thought I asked that. Were you given any limitations or specific directions other than to find what bloodstains you could at the time of this second submission?"

Once again, Hitt said he couldn't recall.

Willis turned Hitt's attention to April's blouse and asked him to repeat the instructions for the first test. These directions were to take five samples from the shirt, concentrating on the front and back of the left shoulder area.

"Did you make a determination you needed to take

five samples, or were your directions to take five samples?" Willis asked.

"My supervisor agreed with the investigator of the case to take five samples total."

"So, in other words, they identified the areas for you to sample. Is that correct?"

Hitt said that was true. Willis called his attention to April's blouse. "This blouse [is] obviously saturated with blood, right?"

"I would think so."

Willis referred Hitt to an area around the left armhole where two patches were cut out. Hitt said he made the cutouts for further investigation. Hitt also made the other cutouts—five in all—to which Willis called his attention. Hitt said he made no samples from the middle of the blouse.

"Why would that not be?"

"I said that I would take five cuttings," Hitt said. "I took three from the front. This stain to me (the center of the blouse) is very difficult to identify whether or not there could be more than one person present. I took two samples, in the understanding that the shirt isn't going anywhere. We can go back and take additional samples, if necessary, at a later time."

Willis jumped on that. "You said this would be very difficult to see whether or not there is more than one person's blood represented in something like this, correct?"

"For me it is, yes."

"So you took those samples that we can see the holes from. Have you gone back since that time and taken more samples out of that same area?"

"From the same area, no."

"Okay. What did you understand your testing was designed to do here? Did you understand the question was whether or not there had been blood transfer from one individual to Mrs. Barber's shirt?"

"That was my understanding."

"And you had already told us that you have found blood in the upper left inside of her arm, of Mrs. Barber, the swab that had been taken there?"

"Yes, sir."

"So at no time have you ever gone back and tested the rest of that area of her shirt?"

"No."

"And no one's requested you to do that?"

"No."

Willis turned his attention to April's capri pants and established that Barber was arrested and charged with April's murder on July 9, 2004. Hitt said he didn't receive April's pants for testing until August 10, 2004.

"One month after the indictment in this case," Willis said. "The shirt that Mr. Barber was wearing, when did you receive [that] shirt?"

Hitt said he received Barber's shirt the same date and tested it on May 12, 2005. Willis asked Hitt to step down to an exhibit of Barber's clothing and asked him to identify a stain on the front of Barber's pants. Hitt had written the number 6 on it. Willis was also interested in two other stains, one on the pant leg. Small cutouts had been taken from both stains.

Willis had Hitt identify a stain on the bottom right side of Barber's shirt and another in the middle back of the shirt. Willis completed his cross-examination and France stood for redirect.

"What DNA result does a mixed sample give you, Jason Hitt?" France asked.

"A mixed sample is one that you would identify the presence of more than one person in the same cutting."

"And in all of these articles in evidence, you have no such result?"

"I can't say that off the top of my head. . . . I did review some of the work of the DNA analyst, but I don't have those results in front of me to remember if there were any mixtures."

"Absolutely. Now, as far as resources of the laboratory or how you expend these resources, if you would have received these pieces of evidence without instruction, do you have the ability . . . or the resources to test every section of it?"

"Usually not."

Hitt testified that agencies often request pared-down examinations of various articles. "And if you make such requests, is it often with an invitation to come back and see if this helps you?"

Hitt said it was true and that the FDLE lab often goes back to look at evidence for additional information. Willis had a few questions on recross. He asked Hitt about the examination of April's blouse.

"Had you been left alone to find out if somebody else had swiped blood on this shirt," Willis asked, "would you not have taken samples all throughout this, random samples, to see if that might have been concealed beneath this larger, saturated bunch of blood? Wouldn't you have done that?"

"It's rather always something that I have to contend with that there is something present on an exhibit that I didn't identify, yes."

"But . . . that much blood . . . that saturated blood could easily conceal a smaller quantity of blood beneath it, and if you don't hit the spot with one of your cutouts, you're never going to know that, correct?"

"That's correct. But in analyzing this exhibit, it's very difficult to make a determination as to what area to sample from in order to demonstrate whether or not this that you're presenting is even possible."

"Shouldn't have to be your call, should it? That ought to be the investigator's call?"

"We work under the understanding that we are assisting investigations, yes."

Sometimes it seemed that witnesses were practicing strategic obfuscation, answering the questions without making things any clearer. The jury was straining to make sense out of it all.

France had further redirect. "As to that blouse just referenced . . . no DNA identifying anybody could be typed off of what you cut off there, correct?"

"I don't recall," Hitt said.

France asked if he had reviewed another analyst's DNA tests, and he said he had.

"Is that not when we got in the discussion about diluting the sample in the attempts to derive DNA off that shirt?"

Hitt said yes, and added that if he had the results in front of him, he could testify to it.

There was no recross-examination and Hitt was asked to step down. He wasn't released, however, because the state said it might call him to testify further. Another FDLE laboratory analyst took the stand for the state. Her name was Nicole Lee. France led Lee through her impressive background to establish her as an expert. Lee explained how she took custody of the evidence and how it was tracked and stored at the FDLE laboratory.

Lee explained that after receiving cuttings from Hitt that were suitable for DNA testing, she made even smaller cuttings to put through the DNA process. The first step was to extract the DNA from the substrate and then from the nucleolus of the cell. After extraction, she determined how much DNA was present in the extraction, and then made copies of the thirteen areas that were studied for forensic DNA analysis.

Following that, Lee ran it through a genetic analyzer, which gave her a graphical visual representation of the DNA, which she compared to evidence samples within the case and known samples collected from individuals involved in the case.

"And here you have both knowns from the defendant as well as the victim, April Barber, correct?" France asked.

Lee said that was correct. France asked her to start with Barber's shirt and describe her findings through DNA analysis. He corrected himself and asked if she did a presumptive test before the DNA analysis to discern whether it was male or female blood. Lee said she "ultimately" determined a male DNA profile from the shirt that matched Justin Barber.

"What do you mean by 'ultimately'?" France asked.

Lee said she tested all nine cuttings, but she found results on only four of those. She stepped to the large exhibit before the jury and identified those four sections of the shirt as the upper right corner, inside the bottom near the buttons, on the opposite side of the buttons on the bottom, and the upper opposite shoulder.

"And what were those areas and those results again, please?"

"In those areas, I got a male profile that was consistent with Justin Barber."

Lee testified that there were no other DNA profiles obtained from other areas of the shirt. However, she located two samples of human female blood, but no DNA profile. The same tests that were performed on the shirt were also utilized on April's pants. Lee did DNA testing on eight locations on the pants and found April's DNA profile on five of these.

"So it's her blood?" France asked.

"Yes."

France asked her to describe the areas where she found the DNA profiles. These were on the outside waistband in back, another directly below that, two areas on the inside near the zipper, and along the bottom, near the start of the legs. Lee explained the steps she took to reach her conclusions about the DNA and said she performed the same tests on Barber's pants.

The blood analyst was not able to develop a DNA profile from any of the stains she tested, but was only able to determine that two were for human female blood. Those bloodstains were on the upper button area on the outside of the pants and around the cargo pocket on the left leg. She said those were the only results showing female blood.

France finished his direct examination, and Willis began his cross-examination by asking about Barber's pants, which were on a hanger in front of the jury. Lee verified that when she tested the pants, she found nothing to indicate male DNA.

"So anything you found, either you couldn't identify what it was, or it was female? Is that true?"

"That's correct. None of my quantitation results indicated a male DNA present."

"Was that because this material, by the time you got it, was so degraded that you just couldn't do it?"

"Not likely, because I was able to show that there was some DNA present on the pants."

"Why wouldn't your testing tell us at least whether this was male or female material?"

"There was material presented that showed to be female, but not to be male."

Willis asked Lee to explain what she meant. She said there was blood on the pants that indicated there was female DNA present, but when she tested a second sample from the same stains, no male DNA was present. Lee clarified that two stains at the top of the pants front, just to the right of the button, showed female blood. The other bloodstain was beside the left-side cargo pocket front leg, and it was also female.

Lee noted that most of the blood on Barber's shirt was his own, but there were two stains identified as being female blood. One stain was close to the shirt bottom and the other near the middle of the back.

Willis asked her about staining on the left-hand side of the back of April's pants near the waistline. The defense attorney asked if she could compare the stains to anything that would allow her to say what these were. Lee said her diagrams didn't identify the stains and that she had not marked them.

"Do you know that these pants were submitted to another laboratory down in the Cocoa Beach area?"

"I was not."

"But again, you can't tell us anything about this one, whether it's male, female or whatever."

"I didn't do the testing on those." Lee said she could only testify that it was clearly female blood.

Willis showed her the back of April's blouse, stained heavily with blood. "Would you agree that this is pretty much saturated with blood?" Lee answered yes.

"If you're looking to see if there's other blood that had been left on this, a blood transfer," Willis asked, "would it not have been prudent to take multiple samples of that to test the entire area in effect?"

Lee said she had taken several samples from the shirt.

Willis pointed out that her samples seemed to have been from only two sections on the back. Lee said that was true.

"So the rest of that whole area of bloodstaining, you don't really know what that is?"

"That's correct. I did not test it."

Willis asked if the main interest was to determine if there was blood transfer near the left-hand arm opening. Hitt and their supervisor, Marcie Scott, were in on those discussions, Lee said, and she was not. She said she did not know why they didn't cut other sections for testing, particularly in that area of the blouse.

Willis had nothing further and France asked on redirect examination what the results were when she tried to derive a DNA sample for the part of the blouse in question. Lee said she took multiple samples, and after making tests on fifteen of them, she could only determine the sex of the bleeder.

"Why couldn't you get any DNA out of there?"

"I believe that there is something in the fabric of the shirt that was inhibiting or making my testing not go as well as it should," Lee said.

It was Willis's turn again. He reminded Lee that she tested blood on the left inside of April's arm, and a swab from the right wrist. "And the right wrist tested positive of Justin Barber. In other words, it was Mr. Barber's DNA?"

Lee said it was. He asked about the blood on the left underside of April's arm. Lee said it also produced a positive profile for being Barber's blood. Lee was excused and the state called in another expert, Dale Gilmore, forensic DNA supervisor for Wuesthoff Reference Laboratories. It was odd for someone from Wuesthoff to be called as a witness for the state.

France asked Gilmore if he frequently worked with law enforcement agencies "in criminal cases, such as this?"

"Yes, sir, we have," Gilmore replied. "Not quite such as this. . . . Our primary function is to help defense attorneys, which is a little bit different because we have been used here by the prosecution."

"My mistake," France said, noting that he had always seen Gilmore on cases he tried.

Gilmore said the state had received a pair of woman's pants with bloodstains and some sections removed. The pants came to him from the FDLE. The cuttings were normal procedure in evidence received from both prosecutors and defenders. Gilmore said the evidence had been properly preserved. The FDLE was specific in what it told Gilmore it wanted him to investigate.

"The item had a number of bloodstains on it, and they wanted to know if the bloodstains were from a male or female."

Gilmore explained how he conducted the test. He used a genetic marker referred to as amelogenin, which is used to determine if a DNA sample comes from a male or female. France asked him how a blood sample, where the blood was mixed, would appear on the test.

The witness said he looked for "peaks" in a mixed sample. There are two peaks in a mixed sample, Gilmore said, with one peak significantly higher than the other. France asked if he found any such peaks. No variance in the peaks was found, Gilmore said. He analyzed forty-six samples, and of the thirty-six that were successfully typed, all were from a female.

Gilmore noted that the evidence was returned to the state attorney's office and that he received a second request to analyze the pants after January 2005. The second test was not simply to determine male or female DNA, but to complete a DNA profile where possible. France asked what the results were.

The bloodstains weren't in very good shape for DNA extraction and typing, Gilmore testified. "I found out that the stains had been left wet, which rapidly causes the breakdown of DNA. So only partial DNA profiles were available to most of the stains. All of the stains were at least consistent with being from the same person."

"When you indicate the pants were left wet, are you referring to the actual date of this incident?" France asked.

"Yes, sir."

"Is salt water one of the worst things to run into?"

Gilmore said it was not and that moisture of any kind causes a rapid breakdown in DNA cells. France wanted to know if the areas where he did get results matched April's DNA profile. The witness said he matched the profiles for April Barber that he received from the FDLE.

"Were you given any limitations in the areas where you were to look when you analyzed these pants?" France asked. Gilmore answered that he was not.

The handling of the evidence was an important part of the case Willis built in Barber's defense. April's remains were placed, fully clothed, into a body bag just hours after she was murdered. The body remained in the bag over the weekend before the ME performed an autopsy. All of April's blood flowed out of the body and into the bag.

"I want to hopefully take away any confusion, not add to it," Willis said. He mentioned that Gilmore had said he circled stains in green where he could not get the material he needed. Gilmore said that was correct.

"So everything circled in green, that means you can't tell us whether it's male or female?" Willis asked.

"That is correct."

"You just can't tell one way or the other?"

"That is correct."

"So all ten could be male, all ten could be female or they could be something else?"

Gilmore said that was true. The thirty-six areas where he could make a determination, he testified, were all female, with some of them matching April's DNA profile.

"We've only got male or we've got female," Willis said. "So if we've got female's, it'd be pretty clear that it's April Barber, correct?"

Gilmore agreed.

"Is it theoretically at least possible that some of these other thirty-six could also be masking smaller amounts of male blood underneath there?"

"Yes, sir, that's correct. Just to thoroughly answer your question, PCR (polymerase chain reaction, a method used in molecular biology) uses a very small portion of a large stain," Gilmore said. "They say the best thing about PCR is it requires a small sample. . . . The worst thing about PCR is it requires a small sample.

"A large stain and only the marking on the small section, which may be as small as three millimeter by three millimeter, is removed from that particular stain," Gilmore continued. "And so, yes, sir, it's possible that there could be other sources of DNA in the large stains. I did nothing that would rule that out."

Willis said, "Somebody commented to me it's almost like drilling for oil. You just might miss it if you don't hit the right spot. Is that true?"

"Theoretically, yes."

"You mentioned that you had some information about the way this material was handled at the outset," Willis said. "That would include that this material, the pants themselves, were left on this woman's body while it was still wet. While the pants were still wet and stored for a couple days before being removed and not treated specially thereafter, they were wet with salt water. What is your reaction to that?"

"That's a very poor way to handle your evidence," the state's witness said.

The defense ended its cross-examination and the state had no redirect. Court recessed until the following morning. It had been a big day for the defense. Willis had clearly shown flaws in how the investigators handled evidence at the crime scene.

Chapter 30

The dead talk to Dr. Terrence Steiner. He learns more about them in death than he would if they were alive. Steiner is the medical examiner for District 23 in Florida, and has been for seventeen years. District 23 includes St. Johns County, where April was murdered and where he performed the autopsy on her body on August 19, 2002.

After establishing Steiner's credentials as an expert forensic pathologist, France explained how Steiner conducted an autopsy. He would begin with an external examination of the body to find external injuries, take X-rays and collect clippings and scrapings. He would look at the clothing, jewelry present, blood spatter, blood smearing and obvious injuries. He would next collect trace evidence, such as fingernail clippings, hair strands, trace fibers, and check for sexual assault.

As part of April's autopsy, Steiner x-rayed the head because of the apparent gunshot injury to the left cheek. Internal organs, skin, muscle and flesh were examined.

Steiner said April wore a sleeveless pink shirt, slacks, underwear and no shoes. He bagged that evidence along with clippings, hair strands, blood samples and fingerprints. He signed them to the custody of John Holmquist, of the FDLE. April wore earrings, a wristwatch and a diamond ring with the stone turned toward her palm.

"Did it come off easily?" France asked.

"Yes, that's why I removed it. It's an alleged robbery, and . . . some women, you can't get the rings off and I wanted to take that off. This ring was evidently not sized correctly and was one reason it was spinning around."

Steiner said he couldn't tell the jury anything about the blood on April's clothing, because he didn't want to contaminate it. He said the hands had been bagged at the crime scene and the body rolled into a large sheet of thick plastic and delivered to the morgue. There, it was transferred to a sliding metal tray.

"While the body had to sit there," Steiner said, "blood continued to postmortem drain from her face, and soaking her scalp hair and also pooling behind her head, and this had also, I believe, had worked down and did some blood soaking of the back of her clothing."

The drainage pattern for the blood flow was caused by gravity. April looked her age, which was twenty-seven, and she was five feet three inches tall, and weighed 112 pounds. Steiner said he saw multiple abrasions and the gunshot injury.

France handed Steiner photographs of the autopsy and asked him to identify them; then he asked if they were medically necessary for his testimony. Steiner said he could talk all day about the appearance of abrasions, but he didn't think he could verbally describe them.

Nine composite photographs of the autopsy were placed into evidence, and Steiner described them. The first picture revealed an abrasion over the left clavicle that was three-eights of an inch long. He described an abrasion as rubbing off of skin, such as skinning your knee. The abrasion he referred to on April's left clavicle was made while she was alive.

Steiner looked at two additional photographs showing April's left arm, a portion of the left side of her body and her slacks. He said no blood was visible on the slacks, but he saw blood on the left side of her hand. Abrasions up and down the left arm were made while April lived. The abrasions were still oozing blood, caused by gravity.

"What does this oozing blood tell you?" France asked.

"Well, you're down to dermal tissues, which are little tiny blood vessels, which have been damaged and post-mortemly will drain by gravity."

Steiner noted that the beach where April was killed was laden with crushed coquina shells and that the abrasions were consistent with skin being rubbed by the shells. The ME noted other small cuts and abrasions and then looked at a photograph of April's wound.

On the photograph, the bullet wound looked round, but he said it was actually more of an elongated injury. The gunshot was not a straight-in shot. There was no gunshot residue on April's face and no stippling or fouling.

"Was that gunshot wound also made while April was alive?" France asked.

"Yes."

Steiner said the bullet was still in April's head when he performed the autopsy. The bullet passed slightly from her left to right at about a ten-degree angle, blew a hole in her left cheekbone, and passed through both sinuses, punched a hole through the back of the nose and struck and embedded itself on the first cervical vertebra. The bullet didn't go into the bone, but flattened out and buried itself in the membrane, or periosteum, covering the bone. That was where the ME recovered the spent slug.

Steiner looked at a tube and case number and identified the contents inside as the spent bullet that he had removed from April. The bullet was distorted and measured about ten millimeters long and five millimeters in diameter. The spent slug and all of the scrapings, samples and other evidence gathered at the autopsy were turned over to Holmquist for study by the FDLE.

The ME identified another photograph taken at the crime scene. It showed the left side of April's face and shoulders as it lay at the end of the Guana boardwalk. Steiner described it: "It shows liquid and dried blood coming from both nostrils onto her left face. It shows the bullet injury on her cheek with blood coming and blood coming from the angle of her mouth, goes around her cheek. Right beside it, her hair's laying flat, is a teaspoon and a half of white foam."

France asked if Steiner could specifically discern from where the blood was coming.

"Well, this is foam one would expect to see if someone that had died in salt water," Steiner said. "It's usually around the nose, but if there's any significant breathing and their mouth is open, can be both nose and mouth, or if they breathe only through the mouth.

"This foam is of bodies that have recently died, drowned. I'm talking within a day, not ones you get a week or two later. It's due to actual water intrusion into the lungs during the drowning experience."

There was a gasp in the courtroom as the gallery envisioned the horror. Tears flowed and grief twisted the faces of both April's and Justin Barber's families. Barber bit his lower lip and looked down at the table. A tear streamed from his left eye. It was the first time during the trial that he had cracked under the emotional stress.

Steiner continued to explain about drowning and the foam. The water destroys the surfactant lining of the lungs, which is a complex lipoprotein. The lungs are made of millions of air sacs, each with a small hole in it where air passes when we breathe out. The holes don't collapse and keep us from inhaling our next breath because surfactant stability keeps it open. If not, Steiner said, we would be gasping in vain to get our next breath because all of the lungs' air sacs would be closed.

The ME said the water damages the protein that mixes with it. "Don't forget, all the mucous glands lining your trachea and bronchi that have mucus," he said, "and has this white quality and is not specific for drowning, but we're seeing two out of three (drowning victims) with it (the foam). It's more common in seawater than freshwater. And here, it's evidently been around the nose and, with the bleeding, has flowed out."

Steiner said the foam is sticky and will eventually wash off, but it didn't in April's incident. It moved aside when the bleeding forced it. He said the foam came from April's nose. Lifeguards would see it on victims who had almost drowned, but were revived.

"What other types of death do you see this foam produced?" France asked.

"Rarely, I've seen it in drug overdoses . . . but again, very rare. Cocaine and methadone, heroin."

Steiner said the composition of the foam from drug overdoses is different because these don't cause pulmonary edema, but come from damage that causes blood to leak inside the lungs and mix with blood. "You still have air in that lung that wants to bubble out, so that's a frothy pulmonary edema, but it's not foam, and they're very different. When you have a body with evidence of submersion or immersion of water, I think it speaks for itself."

Steiner explained that the blood in the photograph of April's face didn't flow to the right side of her face. He said that meant her head was in that position when she was shot and stayed in that position. If one went anywhere else, the blood was going to change direction.

It seemed that the evidence was becoming more confused. April showed froth from drowning, but blood flow said she died where she was shot. And that was more than one hundred yards from the water. What was going on?

Steiner had a photograph to illustrate his point about the blood flow. The body was carefully lifted from the gurney and carried up and down the steps to the morgue. Because of gravity, he said, there was still some blood flow from the wound in the back of her sinuses into her nose, and came from the left nostril, with just a drop at the edge of the right nostril.

The medical examiner compared the photographs of April's body at the beach and then at the morgue. He said the picture at the morgue showed significantly more blood.

"What does that tell you?" France asked.

"We know she was dead, the paramedics have called it. And this wasn't active bleeding. This is just postmortem draining, which we would expect to see."

Steiner used an illustration from an actual cross section of a cadaver from a European anatomy book that had been prepared for the jury. He used it to show why the blood on April's face came from the gunshot wound. Using a pencil as a pointer, the ME traced the bullet's path through the inside of April's head until it lodged in her vertebrae. The force of the bullet, as it tore through tissue and bone, caused interior damage and bleeding. He said the bullet struck close to the brain and the concussion caused bleeding in an area of the meninx, the membrane that covers the left temporal lobe. Steiner said the injury was similar to breaking one's neck.

The spinal fluid below the C3 vertebra was clear and there was no bleeding evident. "With the blunt of the impact, not only the brain, the tip of the brain and the brain was injured—which you can see was swollen moderately— edema of the brain, and it impacted on the . . . spinal cord at that point." The portion of the brain that was damaged controls the sympathetic nervous system, which regulates breathing, heartbeat and other involuntary bodily functions.

"All of your centers for respiration are above that, so breathing should stop," Steiner said. "Your heart can continue to beat for seconds or minutes by different mechanisms." France asked him for the "bottom line" of the physical effects when the bullet hit April's vertebrae.

Steiner said that, among other things, it would have affected her spinal cord. France asked if he believed April was shot where she lay.

"This photo shows . . . how much blood flow can occur. And if there's this much blood, she would have had to have been carried in that position for how many feet to get there without movement. I can't explain that."

In other words, the medical examiner didn't believe April was shot in the water. He believed she was almost drowned to the point of death, dragged to the boardwalk and killed there with a bullet fired into the thin bone of her cheek.

"In addition to April's breathing being cut off when she sustained this wound, could she walk?" France asked.

"No, she would have lost consciousness immediately."

France backed up to talk about the foam on April's face. "Is it our testimony that April Barber was drowned and deceased when she was drowned?"

"No. She suffered a near-drowning episode."

France asked the ME to explain that for the jury.

"She had the gunshot injury, which is going to cause loss of consciousness and probably loss of respiration," Steiner said. "If it occurred at the time that she fell in the water, her heart still continued to beat, she would still show these findings submerged in salt water."

The medical examiner continued his forensic medicine lesson to a jury that appeared to be fascinated. Each drop of blood has a million or so tiny red blood cells, he said, and if it is put in water or any liquid not as dense as the red cells, these will try to equalize the pressure by absorbing the liquid. The cells will absorb too much and then pop. Anyone who has cut himself sees this process, he said, which is called hemolysis: one doesn't see the blood cells, but the water will turn red.

The effect is just the opposite in salt water, which is denser than freshwater because of the sodium chloride it contains. In salt water, the red cells try to concentrate by shrinking. Because of this, there is no hemolysis with salt water. That was the reason the foam on April's face was white and not tinted with red.

The state was going to ask for the death penalty if Barber was found guilty. To do that, the prosecution had to prove that the murder was especially atrocious or heinous. France asked the ME to explain how April's breathing was affected by the near drowning. Steiner said it would be similar to how a person felt if he swallowed a soft drink or coffee the wrong way.

"I think you know how violent that is to your body, and that's not even into your lungs," he said. "That's just getting near the top of your voice box. If it keeps getting in our lungs, we'd all be in the hospital with aspiration phenomena a couple of times a year . . . because it's very insultive to the lung.

"But in drowning, the water actually does enter the lung and you get a violent constriction of your vocal cord to prevent any more," Steiner said. "You become hypoxic and acidodic—and you lose consciousness. And during this time, your heart will beat until—with lack of oxygen, minutes." Steiner said the throat would eventually relax and water would go into the lungs. On rare occasions, he said, people who were drowned in cold water have been resuscitated after being unconscious for more than an hour.

"So in her state, there on the beach after she was placed in this near-drowning state, she was breathing?" France asked.

"I don't know if she was breathing, but . . . if the gunshot injury didn't occur there, then she still had a heart rate."

Steiner said that scenario was consistent with the amount and location of the foam on April's face.

"And her heart's still beating?" France asked.

"No, you don't have to have the heart beating for the foam after the initial insult."

France recalled that Willis had asked Holmquist if he had received an article of clothing from the funeral home rather than the ME. Steiner replied that a clerical assistant made a clerical error in filling in a form regarding custody of evidence. Steiner said he was the person who handled April's clothing and that he transferred all of it directly to Holmquist. He said there was a "chain of custody" sheet on all of the evidence with his signature on it.

France completed his direct examination and turned the witness over to the defense. Willis started where France had ended, regarding the custody of April's clothing. He showed the ME an inventory sheet and asked if it was an accurate copy of the original. Steiner said it was made by a secretary, but he assumed that's what it was. Willis entered it as a defense exhibit and approached the witness and continued the same line of questioning. He asked what the sheet of paper was.

Steiner said it was an inventory sheet for body release from the morgue, but that it was completed by a part-time morgue assistant. The person who picked up the body also wrote on the custody sheet. Willis said he was not suggesting that Steiner filled the sheet out personally.

"But it does say at the bottom of this that the body, valuables—"

"I know, it's a clerical error."

"That's the point," Willis said. "It says the body, valuables and clothing were released to the funeral home, doesn't it?"

"Yes, that's what it says."

"So somebody, a human being somewhere, actually made a mistake?"

Steiner said yes.

"Is there anything sinister, or can we draw any inference from a mistake of that sort?" Willis asked. "Or are we both just going to call it what it is, a mistake?"

"Yeah. It wouldn't surprise me if you get more than one person involved."

The defense attorney noted that April was murdered on Saturday, August 17, and wondered why the autopsy wasn't done until the morning of Monday, August 19. Steiner said it was probably because that's what the investigating officer requested.

"Do the investigative officers tell you when you're going to do your autopsy?"

Steiner said it was a joint effort and he didn't want to do an autopsy when the investigators were not there. He said they were busy collecting and processing evidence from late Saturday until early Sunday morning, trying to process the crime scene before high tide or other erosion. Steiner said the police were busy with blood spatter, searching for a gun and finding evidence on or in Barber's SUV.

"So the bottom line, it was at the request of the police officers this autopsy was not done until Monday morning?" Willis asked.

"It was probably a joint decision. We'd rather do it Monday. It wouldn't make any difference."

During the cross-examination of Dale Gilmore, the state's witness testified that not removing April's clothing from a body still oozing blood was not a good way to handle evidence. Willis asked Steiner about that.

"It was also the case that the autopsy . . . and removal of clothing was not done until Monday morning. Is that true?"

Steiner said it was.

Cross-examination reaffirmed the way Steiner was employed. He was self-employed and had a contract with three counties to provide forensic services. Steiner said the police called when they had a case, and that he worked with police officers and the state attorney regularly.

"So it's not as if you're an independent physician in private practice in the typical sense in that you have outside clients, is it?"

"Yes, I could have outside clients."

"Maybe the better question is, do you have outside clients?"

Steiner said that he occasionally had outside clients. Under further probing by Willis, Steiner said that in the past twelve months only five of the 245 autopsies he performed were private. Steiner testified again that he had been the medical examiner in the district for the past seventeen years and had been an expert witness anywhere from twelve to fifteen times a year.

"Approximately how many of those would you guess were matters where you were being called as a witness for the prosecution?" Willis asked.

"Any that weren't civil?"

"Isn't it the case that you have a very small percentage of your practice that's civil or private or anything other than testifying for the prosecution?"

"On court cases, yes."

Willis would return to this subject later, but for now he began to question the ME on the cause of April's death. The state and defense had widely differing versions of where April was killed at Guana Beach. Steiner reiterated his testimony that he believed that April was killed by a gunshot wound to the cheek and died on the spot from those injuries.

"Was it your opinion that this death was caused right where she lay? In other words, the picture that you were shown, is that where you believe she was shot?" Willis asked.

"What I'm saying, I can't explain the blood drippings from any other reason."

Willis brought in a larger photograph of the one the state had presented of April's wound. Steiner identified it as an enlargement of the photograph he had just testified to for the state.

"Would you identify what you're talking about as far as . . . the features of this photograph as it relates to the nature of the wound?" Willis asked.

"You have blood—liquid and dried blood coming from both nares and from the left angle of her mouth and from the bullet, all going this way. . . . You have the foam inside her hair, the blood soaking of the hair, the sand, clothing, none coming out of the right side, none going on the top of her face."

"Do you know when this photograph was taken?" The ME said he didn't. "Do you have any . . . idea of the time interval between the time that she was killed and the time that this photograph was taken?"

"No."

"Would it surprise you to know that it was somewhere in the neighborhood of three hours or so?" Steiner said no. "Would you expect any changes in her appearance or condition between the time that she was shot and the time that this photograph was taken?"

"Again, not without movement."

"Tell us if these matter: This is obviously blood . . . coming out of the side of her mouth. . . . This is obviously blood coming out of this bullet wound that she had?" Steiner answered yes.

"How about this nose drainage here?"

"That's blood and this is—also looks like oxidized blood."

Willis asked if there was a difference between oxidized blood and hemolyzed blood. The ME said there was a difference.

"There is? But—you also believe this, too, is blood, that is to say this darker stain that's coming across. Is that right?" Steiner said it was. Willis asked him about the blood flow from April's nostril. Steiner said it looked to him that the blood flowed out and then down at "a near right angle."

"Near right angle is not right angle, and gravity requires right angle—does it not?" Willis asked.

"Her head's in that position going that way. Her head was a little, not totally flat."

Willis returned to his original question. "Do you believe that Mrs. Barber was killed exactly where she lay? In other words, that was the position she was in when the fatal shot was fired?"

"What I'm saying is I can only explain this blood pattern and the lack of blood elsewhere with her being shot where she lay."

"Literally where she lay?"

Steiner answered yes.

"Would you care to hazard a guess as to what the angle of the bullet was that went in here (indicating the left cheek) and went into her cervical vertebrae?"

The angle of the bullet was ten o'clock, Steiner said, ten degrees. Steiner said this wasn't a guess, that he had measured it. Willis showed him a photograph showing April at the crime scene. Steiner said he had seen the photograph, but that it had not been taken by his office.

"Are you suggesting that . . . whoever shot this lady laid a gun down at or below the surface of the ground?" Willis asked.

Steiner said that when someone is shot, the head is going to move from the impact. "So all bets are off on what her initial position was," he continued. "It would have been almost straight up."

"You're telling us that the impact is right to left?"

"No. The trajectory."

"Would that not necessarily mean that she'd rotate in the other direction?"

"No."

"The force would be going in that direction?"

"No, it's going from front to back. . . . She's on soft sand, and no . . . I wouldn't dare think that, you know, obviously [it] ought to go this way or that way or head up, no." Steiner testified that the bullet found in April was small and later it was identified as being a .22-caliber projectile. After Steiner identified a photograph showing the slug as measured against a metric ruler, it was entered into evidence.

Steiner answered no when Willis asked him if he knew anything about the ballistics of a .22-caliber weapon. Willis asked if he knew there were three categories of .22-caliber projectiles: a short, a long and a long rifle. Steiner said he knew that and added that he had no opinion what the difference would be in an injury caused by the different categories.

"But if this were a short, if the testimony were to be that this is probably—"

"I think I just answered the question."

Willis said he was more interested in the ME's opinion about the degree the victim's head would have moved if shot by a .22-caliber short. Steiner said, "I think the impact of this injury . . . this is about as close to the midline as you can get. . . . The head could have moved after that as a final—you know, at the time of death."

"Apparently, you're secure in your position that this lady was not moved," Willis said. "I mean, that's the bottom line. You think she was not moved from the time that she was shot right where she lay—is that it?" Steiner said that was correct.

Willis asked the ME if he had become aware of any means that were established in court the day before that April's blood was on both the defendant's shirt and pants. Steiner said he didn't know the specifics, but not to forget that April was bleeding from her abrasions.

"And so how would that explain—" Willis started to ask.

"I mean, it's on her—blood on her hands."

"How would that explain blood on the lower right portion of her shirt or blood on his leg?"

"I can't explain that. I'm not involved in the physics of what happened or alleged how she got from Point A to Point B."

"How exactly would you explain her blood being approximately right here in the middle of the back, based upon your findings?" Willis asked.

"I have no idea. I don't know how she was carried."

"So, in other words, you can't explain it at all?"

"I wouldn't even attempt to explain it. I'm not privy to that information," Steiner said.

"Would you recognize it's squarely inconsistent with your opinion in this case?"

"No. I think if she was manipulated, there ought to be a lot of blood somewhere . . . from this head drainage."

Willis wanted to go back to that. The defense attorney said Steiner had already established that blood follows gravity when someone dies and the heart stopped beating. Steiner said that was true, eventually.

"The testimony or the statement was that this lady was shot and then went into the water. Would it not be the case that whatever blood was initially coming out, wouldn't that blood be washed away by the wave action?"

"It could, but, if so, how come the foam wasn't washed away?" Steiner responded.

"What foam?" Willis asked. "If she were drowned in the water, as you suggest, then carried, wouldn't there be foam on her person if she had come [from] immediate foam?"

"This foam is very sticky. It doesn't just blow away. It stays where it is. Maybe I'm misunderstanding. . . . You say what happened to the foam and I'm not sure—" Steiner continued.

"If water washed the blood away, which was coming out of her nose," Willis said, "which in and of itself could have washed the foam away, why is it still there?"

"Because more comes out when she lays down," Steiner said.

It was getting confusing so far as who was questioning and who was answering.

"Well, once it's gone, it's gone. It's not remade," Steiner said.

"It doesn't continue to travel up your esophagus—"

"No, it wasn't in her esophagus. Her esophagus was full of food that she had vomited at the time of death," Steiner said.

Willis asked where the foam came from and Steiner answered that it was from the initial drowning. The defense attorney couldn't seem to get Steiner to answer his question.

"By what method does it get into the outside, sir? That is my question."

"Compression or some . . . attempt at breathing where she—"

Willis interrupted. "What channel or canal does the foam get out of the lungs into the outside world, sir?"

"Comes out the back of your throat, up into your nose and out," Steiner said.

The defense attorney and the ME, with seventeen years' experience in testifying, continued their verbal sparring.

"Doesn't it come up the esophagus—"

"No."

"Am I just using bad terminology?" Willis asked.

"Yeah," Steiner said. "I think if you looked at the picture of the cadaver, I showed the voice box and right behind it is the esophagus. That's where the esophagus begins—"

"Well—"

"—it's going this way."

"Forgive me, then," Willis said. "I don't want to mislabel something. Let's call it a throat."

"Throat will be fine."

"We can agree that it comes up—huh?"

"Throat is fine."

"That's where it comes from?" Willis asked.

"Well, it originates in the lungs and then—"

"And then comes up the throat?"

"Into the nose."

"Is that not a process that continues, sir?" Willis asked, finally having been able to clearly establish how the foam got on April's face. But the dueling wasn't over.

"No," Steiner answered.

"In other words, it just loops out at the time that you have that problem and then it stops?"

"Yeah. After you express it, it's gone. That's why you don't see it in all the drownings. And how about the ones that the paramedics resuscitate, and I still get the autopsy, the foam is gone. It's not still being made."

Steiner said he didn't think it was necessary to test the foam. "It's foam. It speaks for itself."

"Did I understand you to say that this idea of foam is only consistent with the concept of drowning?" Willis asked.

"No, I didn't say that."

"Well, isn't it the case that foam—the production of foam—is consistent with asphyxia, cutting off the supply of oxygen to the lungs?"

"No," the ME said. "You're thinking of pulmonary edema. I totally disagree. . . . Pulmonary edema is a frothy fluid. This is white foam. . . . And . . . yes, pulmonary edema is associated with asphyxia, not foam."

"So you think this is diagnostic of drowning—" Willis started to ask.

"No, I testified, no. I did not, because I can rarely see it in other instances of death."

"You don't see it in anything other than your cocaine overdoses?"

"I've seen it in cocaine," Steiner said. "I've seen it in opiates, again, very rare. And I've rarely seen it in a small amount in SIDS (sudden infant death syndrome) tests, but . . . it's not a white foam, it's more of reddish foam."

"But the white foam is only found in drownings and—" Willis said.

"And rare other cases."

"And rare other cases?" Willis asked.

"Yes."

"In your opinion?"

"I think it is a scientific fact," Steiner insisted.

Willis asked the ME if he was aware of the testimony two other doctors had given in depositions regarding the case. Steiner said he had heard nothing. Since the ME could not comment on this testimony, Willis moved to another subject.

"You talked about what you characterized as other types of trauma to this lady, and you were shown a series of photographs," Willis said. "I think, as you told us, you examined the fingernails in this case, did you not?"

"Yeah. I visually examined them and they were clipped."

"They were perfect, weren't they?" Willis asked.

"Yes."

"There was no sign of breakage or anything of that sort?" Steiner said there wasn't.

"Did you find any kind of material under them, such as if they had been scratching someone or anything of that sort?"

"I wouldn't have been able to look for it because they're clipped and I wouldn't want to destroy it, no," Steiner said.

"As far as these abrasions that you spoke of, you said that they were caused—with one exception—when she was alive. Is that your opinion?"

Steiner said it was. He answered yes when Willis asked him if he was familiar with the term "perimortem." When the ME said he was, Willis asked if the abrasions could have been made during the period of perimortem.

"Well, perimortem, it depends," Steiner said. "It can be—term can be used for a variety of things. Perimortem is either right at—right before the time of death. Once you're dead, you're postmortem."

"That's right," Willis said.

"So the body is still alive."

"You don't expand perimortem to the time immediately before and immediately after—"

"No, that's postmortem. The body is dead, that's postmortem. That would be incorrect."

"So anybody that used that term to cover that period would just simply be wrong in your testimony?"

Steiner hedged. "I think they're misusing the term . . . and I don't know why."

The witness reiterated that the abrasions on April's body were linear except for one, which was what he called "punctate." Willis held up a composite exhibit showing close-ups of the area by the victim's ear.

"It looked to be two or even three small little somethings there behind the ear," Willis said. "Do you recall that one?" Steiner did.

"Would you hold that up so the jury will please know which one we're talking about?"

"It's awful hard to see," Steiner said.

"They are awful—"

"The ones in the line behind the ear."

Willis said Steiner had not said in previous testimony what the size of the wounds were. He asked him to do so.

"I think, like an eighth of an inch," Steiner said.

"Very, very tiny?"

"Yes."

Steiner said he had already testified that he didn't know how the wound occurred.

Willis asked: "Would there be anything consistent with someone grabbing or trying to carry her, just handling her generally?"

"Yes, but she would have been alive. . . . I think these are premortem pictures."

"You told us previously that in a drowning-type person, the heart would have continued to beat for a period of time," Willis reminded the ME. "How about a person who's been shot in the cervical vertebrae, such as this lady?"

"I think seconds to minutes."

"But her heart would continue to beat, wouldn't it?"

Steiner equivocated. "Could."

"So, even with your definition, it would be during life, it would be prior to death, correct."

Steiner dodged. "You got a heartbeat."

"Okay. Is the answer to that yes?"

"Yes."

Willis pointed out an area on April's left shoulder that Steiner had identified as having been traumatized.

"This is the collarbone," he said.

"And that's the one that's postmortem?"

"No. It was [the] one over the right chest. I don't even have a picture. I said it didn't show any significant vital reaction."

"Okay. This one. How large was that one?"

"The scale's right there (in the picture). I believe three-eights of an inch."

"Three-eights of an inch?"

"Yes."

"Okay. And, again, that's not very large?" Willis asked.

"Three-eights of an inch," Steiner repeated.

"Is there any kind of depth to these at all?" Willis asked.

"No."

"Any kind of bruising at all?"

"No, no bruises. But these don't rub the surface of the skin off versus the ones on her arm."

"We're going to get to those. . . . But this [is] a punctate thing, it's—"

"This is more than punctate," Steiner interrupted. "This is more oval and three-eights of an inch by whatever size."

"Would there be anything inconsistent with sustaining a little abrasion like that if you're carrying somebody, trying to grab somebody, that sort of thing?"

"I couldn't tell what—some type of pressure, in pressure, or movement caused that."

Willis pointed out what Steiner agreed appeared to be an abrasion on the elbow. Steiner said it was caused by the skin being rubbed off on a rough surface. Willis wondered if Steiner knew what probably caused the abrasion.

"From what I saw at the scene, I think it's some type of shell."

Willis asked about the abrasions on the top of the hand and asked if Steiner thought it was part of a linear abrasion that ran down from April's shoulder.

"The blood would have been dripping from that and you can easily see how it could have ended up there with movement, even on the other hand, yes."

"What I'm asking, is there a separate injury on the hand? Is this an injured hand?"

"I think there was. I don't have a clean picture."

Willis asked him to look at his autopsy report. Steiner looked and couldn't find it. Neither could Willis. He said that's why he asked if the blood just ran down or if there was a wound.

Steiner repeated that he didn't have a clean picture, but that he should have it with him somewhere. Willis asked him to find it. "I want to know whether that's an injury or whether that's just some blood that wound up on the back of her hand."

"Oh, there was blood drippings on the back of the hand," Steiner said.

"There may have been, but that doesn't mean there was an injury. Tell us whether there was an injury on her hand."

Steiner found the picture he was looking for and was

finally able to answer the question: "No, I couldn't tell from the picture that this is injury, no." He told Willis that his autopsy report didn't mention an injury to the back of April's hand.

"Why do we got pictures of that here in this courtroom?" Willis asked. "Why do we have pictures in this courtroom showing blood on the hand when there's not an injury associated with it?"

"You'd have to ask the prosecutor," the ME said. "I didn't pick these pictures."

The cross-examination was more like two men arguing than a courtroom procedure. Steiner seemed intent on being vague, while Willis prodded for specifics. Both men interrupted one another. Willis asked if Steiner had seen a picture that showed the scratch that ran along April's shoulder to her hand. Steiner said he didn't know, and then Judge Hedstrom stepped in.

"Let me ask both, don't overtalk each other," he admonished. "I mean, I know there's a tendency to respond, but wait and finish and respond. Try to separate your question and answer, as the court reporter is having a little difficulty."

Willis asked Steiner again if he had seen the photograph and the doctor said he had. The ME described it: "This is the left side of the body and looking at the left— later left arm and she has abrasions to her upper part of her arm and her elbow and the forearm."

The photograph was entered into evidence and Steiner was asked to step down to look at a photograph of April at the morgue after the body had been rinsed. The photograph was from the left side. Steiner pointed out several small abrasions.

"What would you say about these, as far as whether they're postmortem or perimortem?"

"These are perimortem injuries."

Willis pointed out that the abrasions seemed to be in a linear pattern and Steiner agreed.

"They seem to run along the same line, though," Willis said. "Do you find these to be consistent with the idea that she was leaning against the rail like that and slid down it? Would that be consistent with that idea?"

"It would have to be a rough rail. . . . It wouldn't be smooth wood."

"Uh-huh. Like a rail there at the walk-over on Guana Park Beach?"

Steiner said that was a decking-type rail and seemed to be made of smooth wood. He added that if there was a piece of driftwood on the beach that was rough, it should also have blood on it, if the injury was caused by the railing.

"Exactly where do you think these injuries came from?" Willis asked.

"I think this is a coquina injury . . . shell injury, some type."

"From what, from being—"

"From the beach, in the water. I don't know. I don't know. I can't define what caused that abrasion. And the only thing I have at the scene is the coquina shell and the decking," Steiner said.

"Yeah," Willis said. "And you don't like the idea of just sliding down a rail like that and causing one continuous thing as she's sliding down and falling to where she was finally found?"

"I don't think a rail is rough enough to cause that. When I injure myself on my deck or my grandkids, it's always splinters."

"But the coquina shell, you think just being drug across the coquina shell would cause that kind of an injury?"

"Oh, yes."

"Just the weight of the arm dangling?"

"Oh, not the arm—no, not the arm dangling—the weight of the body on the arm."

"Do you have any evidence—has anybody told you at any point—that Mrs. Barber was being drug across on her side, across coquina shells?"

"I don't have any information on the circumstances."

Willis told him to sit down in the witness chair and he would see if he could find some. The defense attorney presented photographs that had been identified as drag marks from the waterline to where April's body was found. Steiner said he could see two distinct furrows and said they could be heel marks from being dragged in the sand.

"Well, obviously, that would not be consistent with your idea that she is being drug in a way that would cause that injury, correct?"

"Oh, no—"

France objected to the form of the question, saying that Willis had made that statement. Judge Hedstrom told the defense attorney to rephrase the question.

"Didn't we understand that . . . your opinion was that this injury was caused because she was drug on her side?" Willis asked. "I thought I understood that from you, maybe I didn't—"

France objected, saying that Steiner had never used the word "drug." The judge overruled the objection.

"You were asking me if just dragging an arm could cause it and I said no," Steiner said. "Not without the pressure of the body. You've got to have pressure, too. I mean, you walk across the dunes, you don't have bloody feet. So, no, I would not expect that just an arm flopping, no. And I think it would be inappropriate to comment on seeing photographs when I'm not privy to anything about them. I think that would be out of my realm."

Willis pressed on: "Well, in fact, if you assume—"

"And I mean, I agree that, yeah, those could be foot marks," Steiner said.

"If you assume—"

"Even heel marks."

They were tangling like cats and dogs with interruptions. Judge Hedstrom stepped in. "One at a time, Mr. Steiner and Counsel."

"Doctor, if you would assume that the lady was pulled under her arms and drug across the beach like that, including the area of the beach where the coquina shell is, and those were the marks that were made, just those furrows, would you agree that that action would not account for the injuries that you have found on her?"

Steiner said he would agree. Willis completed his cross-examination, but France had more questions on redirect. France asked if the abrasions just referred to were consistent "with the weight of one's body or another's body grinding you into that coquina."

"Any coquina," Steiner answered.

"Thank you. As to the stomach contents indicated, what about the contents of the stomach, how far up had—"

"They had gone all the way up to the esophagus." Steiner said there was food in April's stomach that had not been digested at the time of death. France asked if the blood from the left nostril could have gastric materials in it.

Steiner's answer was complicated. "It could have been oxidized by—it's methemoglobin. We all have methemoglobin. Methemoglobin, your body—the iron in the hemoglobin is essentially turned to rust, which is useless. So the body converts it back immediately to normal non-rusted iron. So—or you couldn't carry oxygen except for—and it's brown. And it's just by oxidation or acid, and there's certain drugs that can—in individuals that have severe threatening crisis by converting all of your hemoglobin, or a large part, to methemoglobin. But that's what it, to me, represents."

It was a difficult answer to understand, but France seemed to be satisfied. The prosecutor asked if one of the acids was consistent with acid found in the stomach. Steiner said that it was in the throat, and if it was there, it would eventually come out the nose.

"Did you check the nose and sinus areas for evidence of drowning?"

Steiner said he exposed that area when he had to remove the bullet. But he said there was no additional foam, just hemorrhagic bleeding into the parts damaged by the bullet.

France noted that the ME had mentioned that some foam can be made by a drug overdose. He asked if there was any evidence of drugs or alcohol in "the defendant's" body. Steiner said no drugs or alcohol were detected in the victim's body. Both prosecutor and defender were finished asking questions, Steiner was excused and the jury left the courtroom for a fifteen-minute recess.

France said he would like to make an oral motion to amend the record. He noted that he had said "the defendant" when he meant to say "the victim" when he asked about drugs or alcohol in the system.

"I never heard of a motion like that," Willis said. "The record is what it is. If he wants to call him back or something of that sort, that's a different issue."

"If that's an objection, I'll sustain the objection," Hedstrom said. "You're free to call him back if you wish," he told France.

"Absolutely."

Chapter 31

Except for being shot four times, Justin Barber wasn't in bad shape when he arrived at the Shands Hospital trauma center in Jacksonville.

Dr. Joseph J. Tepas, professor of surgery in pediatrics at the University of Florida College of Medicine, was assigned to the Jacksonville campus. He was on duty in the trauma unit when Barber was airlifted to Shands after the shooting at Guana Beach. After establishing the doctor's credentials as an expert, France asked for his initial assessment for Barber.

Tepas said he was hemodynamically, neurologically and physiologically stable. France asked the doctor to explain each category. "Essentially hemodynamically means that he did not have evidence that he was bleeding to death, that his vital signs were essentially within normal limits.

"Neurologically meant that he was awake, alert, aware of his surroundings, able to communicate with us and had no evidence of neurologic impairment or diminished level of consciousness. And physiologically stable means that essentially the combination of both of those things, he did not appear to be at risk of any imminent demise."

Tepas said Barber answered their questions and didn't seem confused. Barber's vital signs were within normal limits. France asked Tepas about the condition of the defendant's wounds.

"He had five wounds of his torso and left-upper extremity," Tepas said. "And the most significant of them would have been the one that was located about three or four sonometers below his right nipple. There was a second wound that was also of significant potential concern that was at the base of his right neck. There was a tangential type of wound located on his left shoulder and then there were two wounds on either side of the palm of his left hand."

France asked how Barber was treated. Tepas said that in a patient with gunshot wounds, it was important to assess damage to organs and tissue beneath the skin. The hospital made an imaging survey to study Barber's internal organs and tissue, but there was no evidence that posed a threat to his survival. The survey showed pieces of metal in Barber's body.

"The wounds themselves are of a minor nature," he said. "They just required wound care, which is to keep them clean and let them heal."

Tepas said the pieces of metal seen by X-ray appeared to be shards of the bullets that penetrated the skin. None of the bullets were removed, the surgeon said, because the only reason to take them out was if they posed a danger to important organs or became infected.

"By and large, many people are wandering around our planet with lots of metal in them," Tepas said.

The doctor said the only bones broken by the bullets, including the shot to the hand, was a cortical fracture on Barber's left humerus. The bullet under the right nipple wasn't fired straight in but at an angle, and the doctor added that determining a bullet's path once it is under the skin isn't easy.

"It's very difficult to say where a bullet goes, especially a low-velocity weapon . . . primarily because the bullet interacts different planes of soft tissue and hard tissue. It may impact a rib and ricochet, it may go from a tissue, a soft tissue, that's reasonably firm into one that's much more gelatinous, for example, through muscle into the liver. All of these do not yield a perfectly identifiable, predictable straight line from A to B, which is why whenever we encounter a patient who's had a penetrating injury, we have to assume that all organs are potentially at risk until we can confirm otherwise."

In Barber's case, Tepas said, none of his organs were at risk. The fracture on Barber's left shoulder wound, the surgeon said, was "unicortical," which meant that only one side of the bone was injured. France asked about the pain associated with the type of injuries Barber experienced.

Tepas said that pain is a combination of objective neurologic and subjective anxiety-drive process. Because Barber had four soft-tissue injuries, Tepas said, they would have caused significant pain. Because damage from the bullets was limited, Tepas said, it would be unlikely that he suffered "overwhelming" pain.

"Anything consistent with the defendant passing out?" France asked.

"It's not inconsistent, I guess, is the best way to answer that question."

France completed his direct examination and Willis began his cross. He asked Tepas to look at X-rays of Barber's hand and asked if there were any bullet fragments remaining. Tepas said the X-rays showed four views of Barber's wrist. There was a radiologist's report attached to the X-rays.

The report noted multiple bullet fragments located over the midportion of the third and fourth metacarpals, Tepas said, and three different views of the left hand showed metallic fragments behind the metacarpal bones in the soft tissue of the fingers. "More importantly," Tepas said, "the second and third fingers' inclusion of bullet fragments visualized in the hand, no fracture or dislocation." The surgeon said bullet fragments were lodged in the hand, but there were no fractures.

Willis called the doctor's attention to the bullet wound to what he called the right "shrug" muscle. Tepas said the wound was at the bottom of the neck. Willis asked if the bullet's trajectory was downward. That wasn't impossible, Tepas said, but added that neither was it "completely" true.

Tepas explained: "The wound was a somewhat elliptical . . . puncture here. . . . The location of the wound here does not in any way, shape or form guarantee that the bullet went this way, this way, that way. It would seem likely that it could have gone down like that, but there's no way to say for sure."

Willis asked if he had correctly heard Tepas's previous testimony that "if someone is shot in a situation like this, you really can't accurately predict where that bullet is going to go?" Tepas said that was correct.

"And that's just generally true in any shot of the body, of this one at least, with the possible exception of this through-and-through of the hand?" The doctor said that was correct. Willis asked Tepas to approach a chart so he could give the jury a brief anatomy lesson. The witness recognized the illustration as a standard chart that showed the vascular system and related internal organs.

Willis had drawn red circles on the chart to show where Barber's entry wounds were located. Tepas agreed that the chart was accurate except for the chest wound below the right nipple. That wound should be slightly lower, Tepas said.

Willis asked about the hand. "What might be affected by a shot like this—if this had been varied a half inch or just a short little distance?"

Bones would have been shattered in the hand if the bullet was half an inch off from where it struck, Tepas said, and there would be significant nerve damage. The wound to the humerus would have passed through the deltoid muscle, Tepas said, and nicked the bone, but caused no threat to survival. Willis pointed to the chart and asked what it was.

Tepas explained that it was a vein and was forming into the subclavian vein. He said there was an enormous network of veins that wrap around the auxiliary artery as it becomes the brachial artery. Willis said what he wanted to know was if that posed a major risk if the shot had been slightly off.

Tepas said it would not cause death. Next he talked about the wound to what they agreed to call the shrug muscle. There are major nerves there, the doctor said, in addition to the carotid artery and jugular vein. The bullet wound to Barber's shrug muscle did not jeopardize the blood vessels or nerves, Tepas said.

"How about if it varied like an inch one way or the other?" Willis asked.

"The possibility that if it were here," Tepas said, pointing to an entry point half an inch from where Barber was actually shot, "it would cause more trouble to these vessels." He said it would probably result mostly in soft-tissue damage.

"But this is the vena cava, is it not?" Willis asked.

"No, it was the subclavian vein," Tepas said, "that joined with the jugular vein to form the superior vena cava, inferior vena cava here, which enter the right atrium right there."

Willis showed where he had marked the entry wound to Barber's lower right chest. Willis asked about it.

The wound was located right over the lung, Tepas said. Depending on the trajectory of the bullet, it could obviously damage major organs—or it could pass right through. Willis asked the doctor to give examples of what could happen with a shot like that. Fired at the proper angle, the doctor said, the bullet would "make things difficult" for the heart.

"Many times, patients are shot in the chest and the bullet goes right through . . . disrupting some of the lung, causing the lung to collapse and collecting blood in the pleura space," Tepas said. "This is treated with simply a chest tube, which will expand the lung. This all heals. While it's very dramatic . . . it's not that great a threat to life."

"If . . . it hits the heart, is it a threat to life?"

"Most of the time, not always if you're in a trauma center and someone is there to sew it up."

The surgeon explained that the heart and other vital organs are "extraordinarily well protected" by the rib cage, which can deflect a bullet. Willis asked if there's any way to predict what would happen when someone is being shot.

"Not . . . worded like that. There are certain indications to us that give us an idea of what potential organ risk is, Tepas said. "Clearly, one of them is muzzle velocity. Another is distance from the muzzle. The third would be circumstances. The fourth would be what the patient was wearing. All these things are chips in a mosaic that give us a picture that we then build from."

Even doctors have trouble reading another doctor's handwriting. Willis showed Tepas a routine psychiatric evaluation made on patients who have suffered major trauma. Willis indicated the report and said: "There's a section there, and it's handwritten. I don't know that you can read it, but maybe you can—it has the initials 'MSE.' What does that stand for?"

"It's an evaluation. Mental—"

"How about mental status evaluation?"

"Mental status evaluation would be my guess, yeah."

Willis asked Tepas to read it.

"All right. Here we go: 'Patient alert and oriented times three, mood depressed with—'" Tepas seemed to will the word to appear to him.

"Congruent?" Willis offered.

"'—affect. Patient was transferred throughout—'" Tepas strained again—"that's, 'Patient was—'"

"Tearful?" Willis offered.

"'Tearful.'"

France spoke up. "Objection to counsel reading for the witness. If he can read it, fine."

The objection was sustained and Tepas continued reading, getting better at deciphering the writing as he went on: "'Throughout the—this evaluation and distraught by grief his—for his wife, who was killed in the shooting. Patient's voice was soft, to a whisper at times. Patient expressed significant guilt repeatedly questioned whether he made the right decision regarding leaving—leaving his wife on the beach to get help.'

"'Patient also angered that no one would stop and help him. Patient anxious at this time to learn—to leave the hospital and locate his wife's body. Patient reporting having a'—it looks like 'a foggy,' I guess is that word— 'memory of the shooting, stating that everything happened so fast. Overall thought process intact, within normal limits.'"

Willis asked the doctor to look at the physical evaluation

that was written by the team of the *Trauma One* flight service as it airlifted Barber to the trauma center. The report noted that all of Barber's gunshots were cleaned and covered with bandages. None of the wounds were bleeding when Barber was picked up at the crime scene on A1A and Ponte Vedra Lakes Boulevard.

"They reviewed all of the gunshot wounds that he had that they saw and concluded that all of these gunshot wounds had no bleeding noted at the site?" Willis asked for clarification. Tepas said that was correct and the defense ended its cross-examination.

France began his redirect and tried to repair any damage that Willis had done. He asked Tepas if nitrates and parts of material from the bullet were in all the wounds. Tepas said that was true and France asked what that meant about the ammunition and its caliber.

Tepas said the ammunition was "pretty cheap." He said it came from a low-velocity weapon and the bullet broke apart when it hit even soft tissue and left fragments behind. Tepas said that meant it was not a high-quality metal projectile.

"The psychiatric section you just read, it indicated that the defendant felt guilty," France said. "Would that also be consistent of one who just murdered his wife?"

"Well, one would hope."

France ended his redirect and Willis had no more questions.

The state called Detective Robert Shaw to the stand. Shaw had testified earlier. France simply wanted to ask if it was September 4, 2002, at about 8:00 A.M., when he took custody of Barber's computer. Shaw said it was. France asked him how the computer showed activity when it was in police custody. Shaw answered that he had clicked on the Outlook program to find family contacts and phone numbers.

Willis was brief on his cross-examination and verified that Shaw said he turned the computer on that morning. Shaw said he had. Shaw testified that he didn't know anything about activity that showed on the computer on August 19.

David Warniment, an FDLE firearms examiner for more than thirty years, can see volumes of information when he looks at a gunshot hole or a spent slug. The expert witness for the prosecution had stunning information: the bullet wound in Barber's right shoulder was made by a cartridge that somehow misfired.

"That round . . . was defective in some way," Warniment said, "which caused an incomplete combustion or improper burning of the propellant. In other words, the bullet in the right shoulder didn't strike with the velocity and power of a normal bullet." Warniment said he knew this from the clumping of propellant around the wound, instead of it being more uniformly disbursed.

The FDLE expert examined a bullet, a fired bullet, a short-sleeved shirt and pants. France questioned Warniment and found that the bullet that killed April was fired from a .22-caliber short or a .22-caliber long cartridge. There weren't specific enough markings on the projectile for him to tell anything about the gun that fired it. A bullet was fired from the old double-action .22-caliber revolver from the Barber home in Oklahoma and didn't match.

Bullets leave markings that are unique to the guns from which they are fired. Hundreds of thousands of these markings are on file with a database called National Integrated Ballistic Information Network (NIBIN). Twenty-two-caliber bullets are not in the NIBIN because the marks on these are vague and become more distorted even when passing through soft tissue. The reason for this is that the projectile is made of soft lead and not jacketed with a harder metal, such as copper, that is used in higher-velocity weapons. The .22-caliber bullet is one of the lowest-velocity projectiles manufactured.

When any cartridge is fired, Warniment said, it leaves gunshot residue on nearby objects. The residue is found with the naked eye, with a microscope, and chemicals that detect tracings that can't be seen. Residue can be removed by washing or even through the process of being packed, such as the material he examined in this case. Moisture can also cause residue to dislodge and it can be removed by laundering.

Warniment found gunshot residue on Barber's shirt in four areas, but none on his pants. There was nothing unusual about the residue on the shirt except for the clumping on the right shoulder. All of the gunshot wounds were made at close range, maybe as close as twelve inches. Warniment estimated that the shot to the left shoulder was fired about six inches away.

Examination of the bullet taken from April's body was a .22 caliber, but Warniment couldn't tell if it was a long, short or long-rifle type. He explained that the .22-caliber long cartridge is longer and contains more powder so that it has more punch and velocity. France turned the witness over to the defense. Willis had made an enlargement of a clothing diagram Warniment had made. The witness testified that it was an accurate depiction of his charts except for some spotting. The chart was entered into evidence.

Warniment reiterated that he had found no gunshot residue on Barber's pants and testified again as to the residue on the shirt. He explained where the entry wounds were located and why there were six bullet holes in the shirt when Barber was shot three times in the torso. The shirt may have been pushed into folds by the bullet, the witness said.

"Is there a possibility or is it consistent with what you would find here, that this shirt was grabbed by someone and that caused those folds at the time . . . the entry wound occurred?" Willis asked.

Warniment said the fabric was folded over, but he had no opinion on whether or not that was consistent with the shirt being grabbed.

"But with the fabric being folded over, in fact?"

"Yes, if the fabric is such that the bullet can penetrate it three times, then . . ."

The FDLE expert said he didn't know which of Barber's wounds were associated with those three holes. He had not been asked to make that determination. Willis asked Warniment to identify a deposition, notes and photographs he had given to the defense earlier. Willis identified these items as being his.

"So if we have an expert rely upon your notes, he can rely upon those things which are recorded here for his opinion?" Willis asked.

"If he wants to, yes."

The defense had no more questions, but France wanted to redirect. The prosecutor asked if there was propellant on the projectile taken from April's head. Warniment said there was. It wasn't uncommon to find this, he said, because the projectile might have had a bore somewhat larger than usual and that it picked up residue that was already in the gun barrel.

The witness told how he would have conducted an experiment on a human hand that was moving as Willis had indicated in his cross-examination. Warniment said he would determine the cartridge caliber, type of ammunition and firearm involved. He would make a simulated human hand with a 10 percent ordnance gelatin and he might cover that with a latex glove to simulate skin.

France asked Warniment to explain in more detail. The expert told the jury that a 10 percent mixture of ordnance gelatin simulates actual human tissue, as well as animal tissue. A bullet fired into it, he said, would show how much damage it would have caused in human tissue. Depending on the caliber, the bullet would pass through the gelatin and make a temporary cavity that would close into a permanent cavity, which would be smaller in diameter.

France asked how his hypothetical experiment would work if the gelatin didn't close the way skin does. Warniment said he would not make such an experiment with gelatin of that nature, because the experiment would be irrelevant.

The line of questioning didn't seem to make much sense unless one knew that Willis planned to introduce evidence of such an experiment that he had hired an expert to perform. France was making a preemptive strike. It worked: during his presentation of the case for the defense, Willis was unable to introduce the experiment into evidence. Having accomplished his foundation for later use, France completed his redirect examination. Willis had no questions for the defense. Warniment was excused and the state called Jerry Findley, president of Findley Consultants, which deals primarily with blood pattern analysis and death scene reconstruction.

Like the other expert witnesses, Findley's years of experience were presented from a period spanning more than thirty years. Findley seemed as solid as a fortress carved inside granite. France asked if the papers he now showed to Findley contained an accurate copy of his résumé. Findley said that it did and France asked to enter it into evidence.

To some consternation, Willis objected.

"Pardon?" Judge Hedstrom asked in surprise.

"He can testify to his qualifications, but it's not proper for him to put it in. It's hearsay."

"Putting in CVs (curriculum vitae) and résumés have always been admitted," France replied.

There was a short argument about whether or not the jury would give the résumé undue weight. The judge overruled the objection and the résumé was admitted. And then France continued with questions that further established Findley as an expert par excellence.

Findley gave the jury a tutorial relating to bloodstain pattern analysis and crime scene instruction. He explained how the size, shape and distribution of a bloodstain can provide a great deal of information. A swipe stain shows which way a hand is moving when it leaves blood. Wipe stains are made when blood is already on an object and is smeared. A transfer stain is when blood moves from one surface to another.

Blood flow is determined by gravity, and there are bloodstains that are made under high to low velocity called impact stains. If a person cut his finger and blood oozed out and dripped, that would be a low-impact stain. Medium-impact stains are spattered and often caused by someone being hit with a blunt object, like a baseball bat. When an assailant brought the baseball back after impact, Findley said, blood would be cast off, which is another type of staining that can be determined. High-velocity impacts are created by a great deal of energy, usually from a firearm or high-speed equipment.

"So, by being able to determine the types of stains we have and knowing how they're created," Findley said, "it can tell us a lot about a sequence of events that took place, how much blood got to be in certain places and where it could or could not be, based on the total circumstances. We use this in reconstruction and reconstructing the sequence of events that took place."

Findley looked at the volumes of evidence gathered about the shooting of Justin and April Barber, examined photographs and clothing of both. Following his examination, Findley compared his evidence with statements Barber had made. He said he found five major inconsistencies.

The blood flow on April's face, Findley said, was straight down. Barber's written statement said that he moved the body or changed its position nine times, yet the blood flow continued down the right side with variance. He asked the jury to remember what he had said about blood flow being determined by gravity.

"If the body had been moved that many times," he said, "the head would have changed positions, at which time the blood flow would have changed positions." He said there would have been several different blood flow patterns if the body had been moved that often. "The blood flow . . . is consistent with her head going back, hitting the sand and staying in that same position. It didn't change once the blood flow started."

At France's request, Findley stepped to a large photograph already in evidence showing blood flow on April's face. Findley indicated the blood flowing out of the mouth, nose and wound. Findley said the flow was consistent and never changed directions. Had the head been moved in any direction, Findley said, it would have changed the way the blood ran.

Findley referred to Barber's written statement and the defendant's descriptions of how he had carried his wife: *I carried her a short distance before I stumbled in the water. . . . I tried to pick her up. . . . I picked her up in my arms and dropped her. . . . I tried the other side. . . . I pulled her by her hands. . . . I pulled her by her forearms . . . From behind, under her arms . . .*

Reached under her arms and grabbed the waistband . . . and I tried to pick her up and put her on the rail.

"Is it your opinion, sir, that Mrs. Barber was, in fact, shot up by that boardwalk?"

"When she fell and the blood started was right there. She didn't move."

"Do you see any—position in the blood on her face which indicates any other direction?"

"No, sir. I don't see a blood tinge or anything else that would indicate the blood even flowed in another direction."

France asked if there were any indications that April's face had come into contact with the beach sand. Findley said there was probably a transfer on the bottom part of her face. April's head was slightly higher than the beach, he said, and the blood was probably caused by EMTs who probably turned the head slightly when they checked the body. Findley said he believed that created a transfer on her upper cheek.

The courtroom was quiet as the jury and gallery was engrossed in this powerful testimony. It was a real *CSI* show, like the ones on television, except it was real. Someone had been murdered. This was actually happening. There were furrowed brows as the jury concentrated on the evidence.

"The defendant . . . grabbed her . . . the waistband of her pants," France said. "Did you find any evidence that, in fact, he had?"

"No, sir. There was no blood around the front waistband and the fly area. None of his blood was in that area at all."

"And why should you have found blood, according to his story?"

"If he was shot at that time and you got blood on your

left hand, when you reach around and grab, you're going to transfer blood from you to the surface you touch."

Findley said the drag marks were not consistent with the ways that Barber said he dragged his wife. One way Barber described dragging April, Findley said, should have caused her buttocks to leave drag marks in the soft sand. Findley said there was no chance the tide had washed the marks away because these were made in soft sand, above the high-water mark.

The crime scene analyst said there was no evidence to indicate that April had been dragged by the arms, because the waistband of her pants were pulled high in back and friction from being dragged would have pulled them low. There would also have been sand accumulated in the waist, he testified. Findley said there was not enough blood in Barber's SUV to indicate that he had searched for a cell phone. The blood found in the SUV were transfer stains on the inside of the driver's door and on the left side of the steering wheel.

There were no blood transfers to indicate that Barber had reached into the driver's door pouch, the center console and the driver's-side rear door. "There was no other blood left anywhere that was found in that vehicle," Findley testified.

"Would you expect to see blood on the door handle and the steering wheel?" France asked.

"Yes, sir, if he's going through the vehicle."

Findley testified that he found some drops of blood in the lap and pocket areas of Barber's cargo pants. The drops seemed to have dripped straight down, he said, which would be consistent with him driving while bleeding from the left hand. France showed the witness a close-up photograph of April on the beach that showed her upper left arm.

The prosecutor said, "That area of blood has been

identified previously in this courtroom as the defendant's blood. Do you have an opinion as to how that blood smear was made?"

Findley said it was a linear-transfer stain that could have been caused by anything touching April's arm that had blood on it. However, Findley said, it wasn't the type of blood transfer that would have been made by Barber dragging April by the arms. If you pulled somebody and your hand was wet with blood or water, Findley said, there would be some slipping, which would make a swipe rather than a transfer. There would be movement showing, and Findley said there was none.

The analyst said he saw several bloodstains on Barber's shirt, but no high-impact stains. He said the other stains were transfers or flows. A bullet passing through a part of the human body, he said, causes high-velocity spatter. France asked if the stain could be from a shot through a hand.

France completed his direct examination. Findley's last answer had left some people looking confused. Willis was one of them. On cross-examination, he said he didn't understand what Findley's answer was on France's last question. He asked him to explain high-impact velocity splatter again.

Findley explained again and said he saw no evidence of high-velocity impact spatter anywhere on the shirt. He testified that there was substantial bleeding, however, on the front of the shirt. "There's a good bit of blood on there," he said.

The witness agreed that the blood could obscure high-velocity impact spatter, but probably not all of it. The stain on April's upper inside arm, Findley testified, was a transfer stain. His analysis wouldn't have been different if he had known the photograph showing the stain was taken several hours after April's death—unless the body was handled.

"In other words, if you put them in a body bag and if they stay in a body bag for a period of time," he said, "you may get some transfer there. . . . But as I looked at the photograph, it appeared to be at the scene."

Willis called Findley's attention to the drops of blood on Barber's cargo pants and asked if it would interfere with his analysis if the DNA analyst found no male blood on the pants. The witness said he would find it unusual, because the blood dripped straight down. Willis asked if this was inconsistent with the theory he presented to the jury.

"Maybe as it pertains to just these stains," he said. "I'm not sure where the blood sample was taken from. If the blood sample was taken from the center of this, then it would be a question of how it got there."

Willis pressed his advantage. "Doesn't your opinion presuppose that that is male blood? You're saying it's Justin Barber's blood, right?"

Findley said it was consistent with the source of the blood being above the stains. That would be consistent with the blood dripping while Barber drove. But only if his hand was actively bleeding, Willis continued. Findley said that was correct.

"And you base that on what, on the little smudge on the inside of the car?" Willis asked.

Findley held firm and said he based it on the blood drops going straight down. Willis asked him why he thought Barber didn't check the SUV as he said he had when looking for his wife's purse or cell phone. Findley said Barber was bleeding when he made a transfer stain on the inside of the driver's door and steering wheel. Willis asked if there were any other bloodstains in the vehicle.

Willis asked Findley if he knew police checked the

wooden walk-over from where April's body lay to A1A and found no bloodstains on it. Findley said he knew that.

"Does that bother you at all, as far as this would be dripping?"

"I don't know at what point Mr. Barber was shot, so it doesn't bother me."

Willis pointed out that no blood was found on the ground, on the street, next to the car, not on the walk-over and not next to the body in the sand. There was none of Barber's blood found anywhere, he added. "Does that change your mind at all?"

Findley said it did not. Willis turned to the drag marks. He noted that Barber said that he had tried to pull her at one point but couldn't, so he tried sticking his hands underneath her arms. Why did Findley believe that happened in soft sand? Willis asked.

Findley referred to Barber's statement describing how he tried to carry April. Willis asked if Findley was simply making an estimate of where the drag marks should be, based on how long Findley thought it would have taken Barber to get there. Findley said no, it was because the photograph showed drag marks by the waterline, and there were no buttocks drag lines there.

Willis showed Findley a photograph of the drag marks where the sand changed from being hard to soft. Findley agreed that there was no difference in the drag marks in either type of sand.

"And would you agree that that is entirely consistent with someone that is pulling his wife by putting his arms under her armpits and dragging her like that?" Willis asked.

Findley said it would depend on how high Barber lifted his wife. He admitted that dragging by the arms or wrist would leave the marks. Willis asked him where he saw Barber dragging by the wrists.

"Well, I don't," Findley said. "That was the important part, because he stated he did. He said he grabbed her by the wrists and was pulling her by the wrists."

Willis said they were not communicating. The drag marks he referred to in the photograph from hard to soft sand were at a point when Barber dragged April by holding her under her armpits. The witness would only agree that there were only two drag marks in the sand. Then why, Willis wanted to know, did the absence of buttocks imprints in the soft sand mean that Barber was not telling the truth? Findley testified that the photograph didn't show any buttocks drag marks anywhere.

Willis turned to blood transfers again. Findley agreed that none of Barber's blood was found on the waistband or back of April's pants. The witness looked at his notes and concluded that he had not looked for Barber's blood there.

"I did not see any," he said, "but she was in the body bag, and [in] the body bag, of course, blood would continue to flow, so it could create a problem."

Willis indicated a bloody area where a cutout had been made and examined. The examination could not tell if the blood was from April or Barber. That was still the situation, Findley testified. Willis asked if the witness was confident that the blood flow on April's face indicated that she wasn't moved from where she was killed. Findley said that was true. However, he didn't know how much time had passed between the time April was shot and when the photograph was taken. Findley added that it wouldn't matter if the body had not been moved.

"You said something about once the blood starts flowing—that's your phrase . . . it flows in the direction of gravity?" Findley said yes. "Would it be helpful to know when the blood starts flowing?" Willis asked.

"The blood would start flowing as soon as she was injured." Willis asked how long it would continue to flow. Findley said if a person was sitting upright and died immediately, his heart would stop, and any blood in his head would drain and flow from his nose or mouth. If his body wasn't moved, the blood wouldn't go lower because of gravity.

Findley said he knew of the scenario where Barber said he found April shot and facedown in the water. The witness agreed that Barber picked April out of the water.

"Would you agree that as long as her head stayed above the rest of her body, there would not be any additional significant flow?" Willis asked.

"It would be hard to move a body that many times without changing the position of the head."

"Would you expect some immediate gushing out of blood when that occurred?"

"No, just maybe an oozing out. If she's dead already, it would be an oozing out of blood."

Findley said he knew some of April's blood was on Barber, but Willis said he could not have known that in the spring of 2004 when he formulated his report. He didn't know, Findley said.

"Because it wasn't even known to anybody, the prosecution included, right?"

"As far as I know."

Findley said he believed that April was not moved from the time she was shot as she lay on the beach.

"How do you account—and it is a fact—that her blood is on Mr. Barber? He's got it on his belt, right at the front of his pants, he's got it right in the middle of his back. How do you account for that if she wasn't moved after that?"

"She had other injuries."

"She had what?" Willis asked in disbelief.

Findley said that April had abrasions down her side that produced blood. Any contact with it would cause blood transfer, he explained.

"So what are you suggesting? That he turned around, his back to her, and rubbed his back on his wife's side?"

Findley said he thought the transfer was made when he tried to use a fireman's carry to move his wife. He said April would have been limp and the transfers could have been made on anything they touched.

"Mr. Findley, don't you understand the injuries to her occurring down the left-hand side occurred right there where she was found?" Willis asked.

France stepped in to object. "Your Honor, that's ridiculous. That's an improper question. He said it was a fact, that's an improper question."

The judge told Willis to rephrase.

Willis asked where April got those injuries and Findley said they were made when she was in the water. Willis asked if he meant the linear abrasion that ran the length of April's arm. Findley noted that he wasn't a doctor, but that was his opinion.

"And that would also explain how he got the blood here on the front?"

"I can't explain it. I'm just telling you that this blood could have come from anywhere at any time, the blood on him. It didn't necessarily have to happen after she was shot."

Willis completed his cross-examination and there was no redirect by the state. The prosecution had finished earlier than expected and the state rested its case. Judge Hedstrom told the jury it would be sequestered for deliberation when the defense completed its case. They were told to make necessary arrangements and admonished not to talk about the case or to read or watch television news regarding it. The judge noted that the media coverage had been extensive.

The jury was sent from the room and Willis made a motion for a judgment of acquittal. "This is a pure circumstantial evidence case," he argued. "The law in Florida is abundantly clear on circumstantial-evidence matters—if there is a reasonable hypothesis of innocence, it must be indulged, if there are two competing hypothesis, that's not enough.

"The best that can be said of the state's theories is that they are just that, that they offer an alternative to the statements that the client made that fall, in my view, fall short of being that kind of evidence that establishes guilt beyond a reasonable doubt."

Foxman countered that the state was not required to conclusively rebut every possible variation of events. It was required only to introduce competent evidence that was inconsistent with the defendant's theory. Foxman cited expert testimony and photographs that countered the defense claim that April had been shot and killed at the waterline and dragged. "We have rebutted the very specific theory of innocence flooded by the defense," he concluded.

Foxman said he would read case law into the record. Hedstrom said he would reserve a ruling until all evidence was heard. With that, court was recessed.

Chapter 32

Willis began the defense's case by calling Michael Halloran, a financial advisor with Northwestern Mutual Financial Network and also a professor at the University of North Florida. The defense attorney said he wanted Halloran to help the jury understand an insurance situation in the case. Per established procedure, Halloran answered queries to establish him as an expert.

Halloran testified that his company was conservative, but it would issue a policy to a woman twenty-six years old equal to twenty-one times her income. The two-million-dollar policy on April was well within that formula, he said. April also qualified for that amount under other underwriting guidelines, Halloran said.

The witness confirmed that April owned her policy with First Colony Insurance and had full control over it. Halloran also verified that April applied for the policy, because her signature was on the application.

A representative of First Colony interviewed April at the Jacksonville condominium and verified that April had been cooperative and answered all questions regarding her medical history. He testified that April's premium was "a good deal" in the insurance business.

Willis completed his direct examination and Foxman asked Halloran if he knew that April's mailing address was listed as Jacksonville, when she lived five days of the week in Georgia. Halloran said he knew that.

"She is the owner of the policy, you say that she is the decision maker in that regard," Foxman said. "Yet it appears she is not even the one receiving correspondence from First Colony, correct?"

"That's correct, but—"

"Would you agree with me if I said that some people don't need life insurance?" Halloran answered yes, but not in cases where both husband and wife have an income. The analyst testified that if one spouse was totally independent of the other, the amount of insurance needed would be less.

Foxman asked if Halloran made money selling insurance and he said he did, and the more he sold, the more he made. Even so, he testified, he wouldn't sell insurance to anyone who didn't need it.

"And you're certainly not here to comment today on whether two million dollars is motive for murder, are you?"

"No, I'm not, because I didn't know their personal situation."

Foxman was finished and Willis had no further questions. Willis took a breather and his associate, Lee Hutton, called Brian Erb to the stand. Erb was an engineer/paramedic employed by St. Johns County Fire/Rescue. Erb said that he and his partner, Michael Carter, arrived at the crime scene in 2002, two minutes and thirty-seven seconds after being dispatched. They were directed to where April lay on the beach by police. They were at her side with a cardiac box, cardiac monitor and an air bag two minutes later.

Erb said he assessed the patient's airway breathing

and circulation, and he looked for obvious bleeding. Erb said he did not notice any obvious bleeding. April was not breathing and had no pulse. He could see no obvious injuries. Erb attached the cardiac monitor and April was flatline, no heart movement. April's eyes were unresponsive when he shone light in her eyes. He spent three to four minutes examining her.

"And again, you stated that during that time you saw no obvious bleeding at all?"

"No, sir."

Hutton showed a photograph of April's bloody cheek, taken four hours after Erb examined her. "Did you see any blood like this?" Hutton asked. "No, sir," said Erb.

On cross-examination, Erb said he looked for blood, but didn't see any. Neither did he see any foam. Erb said he touched the body as little as possible and did not move her head.

Hutton called Suzi Brown, a paramedic with the Jacksonville Fire/Rescue Division, to testify as to Barber's condition at A1A and Ponte Vedra Lakes Boulevard. Brown said Barber had no radial pulse, and that, plus his gunshot wounds, made her think that he might be going into shock. His pulse was rapid at 126 beats per minute.

Under cross-examination, Brown told France that she feared internal bleeding and ordered the helicopter that took Barber to the trauma center at Shands Hospital. France referred to the symptoms Brown observed with Barber. He asked: "Some of those signs you descried as early features of shock, could that also be consistent with adrenaline associated with one who's just murdered his wife?"

"Objection," Willis said. "That's argumentative and improper questioning."

After the judge sustained the objection, France asked

if Brown would be surprised to find out later that Barber had no internal bleeding. Brown testified that she had the patient's best interest in mind and treated him as if he might have been suffering from penetrating injuries.

"I do treat assuming the worst," the paramedic said. Brown added that Barber was not paralyzed in any way, but he could not have lifted a heavy weight because of the wound in his left hand. She did not smell alcohol on Barber.

Brown's testimony was completed and Hutton called Wesley Pryor to the witness stand. Pryor and his wife, who was his fiancée on August 18, 2002, were in St. Augustine on vacation. Pryor said that as he drove north on A1A he saw a dark-colored K-car on the ocean side of the road near a NO PARKING sign. A short distance later, he saw what he thought was a Blazer parked on the other side of the road near the Guana Beach parking lot.

As Pryor neared the intersection of A1A and Ponte Vedra Lakes Boulevard, the Blazer—or SUV-type vehicle—"flew" by him with its emergency lights flashing. Pryor testified about how he and Kimberly tried to help the driver, who was Justin Barber. Pryor said someone called 911 and he told the dispatcher about it and continued to try and comfort Barber, who was breathing fast. He smelled alcohol that made him think Barber had been drinking a "medium" amount of alcohol.

Pryor said Barber's hand wound wasn't bleeding or oozing. Neither was there much blood on the other wounds, Pryor testified. After telling the police that he had seen Barber's car parked a mile or so down the beach, Pryor changed his mind about going straight to Jacksonville, and drove back to the scene.

The Blazer and the K-car were not there. He followed a police officer down the boardwalk to the beach, where there were several officers with flashlights. He said he could see the victim's body and face.

"Specifically with the face, did you see any blood on the face?" Hutton asked.

"No, sir."

Pryor said he and his wife waited around until after a search of the beach had begun, gave their statements, then left.

Hutton ended his direct, having presented three witnesses who testified that they did not see blood on April's face. Foxman began cross-examination to try and repair whatever damage had been done to the state's case. Pryor said he did not see the K-car well enough to remember anything specific about it, such as the color or the tag number. Neither was he certain how many walk-overs there were to Guana Beach.

The only other question Foxman had for Pryor was whether or not he had moved April's head. The witness said he had not. The defense had no redirect and called Pryor's wife, Kimberly, to the stand. Kimberly was trembling and breathing rapidly.

"I'm going to say the same that I said to your husband," Hutton said. "Take a deep breath. It's all right."

Kimberly's testimony was similar to her husband's, but she added that she had remembered where the SUV and K-car were parked and pointed out those specific locations to the place. When she tried to help the driver when he stopped at Ponte Vedra Lakes Boulevard, Kimberly said, "He was hyperventilating, very nervous and kind of scared."

Although the interior light came on when she opened the door, and the intersection was lit up, Kimberly said, she didn't see a purse inside the SUV. There was blood on Barber's left hand, she said, but it wasn't gushing or dripping. When she and her husband drove back to the beach, Kimberly noted that the K-car and SUV were gone.

When questioned by Foxman on cross-examination, Kimberly remembered having described the K-car as being medium to light in color. Kimberly said that Barber's right hand had been shot, when the wound was actually to his left hand. Foxman finished his cross; he had cast doubt on how well the Pryors remembered what they had seen. A question that couldn't be asked was how many people driving past a parked car at night would remember the license tag number.

Robert Shaw was scheduled as the next witness for the defense, but he had been detained by a family emergency in California. The court decided to use a deposition Shaw had given on December 8, 2004, as his testimony. Willis played the role of prosecutor while Hutton sat in the witness chair and read Shaw's answers.

Judge Hedstrom told the jury they should treat the testimony as if Shaw were testifying live.

Shaw's testimony was that he had issued a BOLO for a dark-colored Dodge Aries, but had no other specifics to offer on its appearance, such as the tag number. Shaw received no responses from the BOLO. Shaw issued the bulletin a day after the shooting and he didn't know why it hadn't been sent sooner.

The off-line search for owners of K-cars, Shaw had said: "Geez, yeah—that was a mess." When no police gave information on the BOLO, he said, the SJSO made an off-line search through the Florida Crime Information Center, the National Crime Information Center and anyone in the area who might own a Dodge Aries. Then the SJSO published advertisements in local newspapers and asked for a search by the DHSMV. The DHSMV told

Shaw it was going to take a while. That search wasn't requested until September 5.

Shaw's deposition noted that searching for the car *was like a last-ditch effort because we knew it was like going to be a needle in a haystack type of situation.* The SJSO received several hundred returns from the DSHSMV search, wrote a form letter asking about the K-car at Guana Beach the night of the murder.

We just started addressing envelopes to everybody on the list, Shaw's deposition noted. He said that a lot were returned because people had moved or the address was bad. Nothing gave the police a lead on the K-car.

"You just sent out a form letter and asked them to come and call you or write you and tell you whether they had been in the area that night, is that it?" Willis asked. Playing the role of Shaw, Hutton said that was basically it. The deposition ended and court broke for lunch.

The jury needed the energy provided by lunch. It was time for the defense to call its expert witnesses. Hutton called William J. Bodziak, a forensic consultant who specialized in falsified documents, footwear and tire impressions. The credentials to qualify him as an expert included his involvement at the tragic Oklahoma City bombing several years ago. Bodziak had written, lectured and testified in places as far away as Guam.

Bodziak testified that he had reviewed depositions, investigative and crime scene reports and photographs involved in this case and had studied two casts. A composite of the two casts, showing the tread marks found at Guana Beach, were entered into evidence. The photographs were taken by John Holmquist, of the FDLE. Two photographs of the same tire tracks taken by Bodziak were also entered.

Bodziak testified that there were other tire tracks that indicated other cars had driven, parked or made turns. By comparing the tread marks and evidential markings, Bodziak testified that none of the tire tracks matched. The expert went into great detail to explain how he would have conducted an investigation of the tire tracks. The bottom line of his testimony was that the tires didn't match: the tires could all have been different makes on the same car or from one tire on four different cars.

The police could easily have compared the tire tracks in the sand to the vehicles of the three hundred or so people the DMV noted owned K-cars. It was a procedure the police didn't do. "If there were some vehicles that had even the same two designs recovered from the crime scene, that would be extraordinarily important because it would be unlikely another vehicle would have the same two designs," he said.

Foxman's cross-examination established that numerous cars had left tracks in the area and there was no way to tell if any of the tracks had been made by a K-car. Foxman delved into the arcane areas of tread, spacings, grooves, markings and dozens of other things that are used to identify tires. The lengthy direct and cross-examinations seemed to establish nothing.

But the previous testimony by Shaw seemed to show that the police had bungled a lead on the K-car, regardless of how remote it may have been.

A legal brouhaha began when an expert witness for the defense had made red marks with a Sharpie pen while examining Barber's shirt. In fact, France argued, the expert bought another shirt with a pattern that exactly matched the one in evidence. The expert was to use that shirt for his examination rather than the actual shirt.

Unfortunately, the original shirt was stained red where touched by the expert's Sharpie, making it seem that the bullet holes were bloodier than they really were. Chris France said the witness was warned that this would happen, but he did it anyway. He said the witness marked four spots in red ink on Barber's shirt that were "evidentiary sensitive. The prejudice to the state is obvious." France wanted the judge to question one of the court clerks who knew of the incident.

Adrean King, the clerk, said she had counted four dots on the shirt on the prior day. Judge Hedstrom asked, "I assume . . . that those four dots overlay blood spatter or blood spots on the shirt, or are they in areas that are not covered by blood?"

"Your Honor, that's the point," France said. "They're in an area which witness after witness has testified that they did not find blood or tissue evidence. This is not a black or green Sharpie. It is, in fact, a red Sharpie and it obscures this evidence. You just don't touch evidence like this. That's why we put it in evidence."

Willis asked the court to look at the shirt. According to his memory, he said, the dots weren't in areas that had been previously identified. "If you look, I think you will see very, very tiny—I think you can cure this problem very easily without making a big dramatic scene out of it."

Judge Hedstrom said he was concerned about whether the dots could be isolated to demonstrate to the jury how and why they got there. Both France and Willis agreed that this could be done.

Willis said that the witness, in his testimony, could apologize to the court for his error. "There was no intention to do anything to quote/unquote tamper with this evidence," he said. "I hope the court accepts that."

"I'm not attributing any ill will," the judge said. "It obviously tampers—"

"Tampering has occurred," France said. He said the marks were particularly important in a case like this. He wanted the court to give an instruction to the defense. "It's not okay to have done this," France continued. "It is a big deal."

"Well, in fairness, I think the state is grossly over-reacting to this and trying to take advantage of it to try to disparage Mr. Jason (the expert witness), because they know he's an essential witness in this case," Willis shot back. Willis said that to issue an instruction in front of the jury would diminish Jason's status. He added, "I think that's what they're doing here."

"My intentions are pure in this matter," France said. "I resent that last comment."

The argument continued and the judge asked the clerk if she was present and foresaw what would occur when Jason was preparing his exhibit.

"Yes, sir," King said. "I asked him to be careful when he was marking, because it may bleed through onto the state's evidence."

"And what was his response?" Hedstrom asked.

"He said he was not marking through, so I took his word for it."

"Was not marking through?"

"Yeah, marking through, like the marker bleeding through to the other shirt, the state's evidence."

"Did you discover the mark-through after the first mark or all four of them?"

"After all four of them, because he assured me that he

wasn't marking through. So I was allowing him to do whatever he needed to do, whatever his job was."

King told Hedstrom that when she noticed the mark-throughs, she told the witness she would notify him and the state. King said Jason apologized to Willis, and the shirt was taken back into evidence before she telephoned the judge and prosecutors.

Willis asked if they could take testimony from the witness to clear things up.

The judge said France's point was well taken and he intended to give an instruction to the jury. The judge said the instruction the state had prepared for him could convey "some sinister intent" to the jury. Hedstrom asked France if he thought the marks were deliberate or accidental.

"I can't speak to what he was doing," France said. "He's had access to the shirt continuously throughout this case."

The judge said his question was whether France had reason to believe the marks were intentional.

"Judge, I wasn't there."

"Give me your best shot. Give me your best—"

"I'm not going to say that. But the fact is, it was done. It's permanent. . . . It affects a piece of evidence that is vital in this trial. I didn't say willfully tampered. . . . That is what he did."

Willis countered that he saw no benefit to anyone from the staining. "There's absolutely no reason in the world to have done this. There's no benefit to us in any sense whatsoever. It's an embarrassment that it happened. So we've got to take that hit, but to suggest that somehow we have impugned the verity of a piece of evidence, that's just simply not true."

"I'm not willing to buy into that portion of what

happened," Hedstrom said. "I don't really think Mr. France is advocating that to the court. I realize the state is concerned about it, and rightfully so." The judge said he thought the best thing to do was to take the shirt, tell the jury what happened, tell them what the dots were and to ignore the red dots.

Willis said he thought that was the way to handle it. The judge told France he didn't know of any other way to do it. It could be done in the form of instruction or in open court with the jury. However it was done, it *had* to be explained to the jury.

France said: "Read a formal instruction by the court, Your Honor."

Hedstrom said he didn't want to do that, for fear of prejudicing the jury against the defense by implying a sinister intent. The judge said the state could not be prejudiced by such an instruction, but it could very well prejudice the defendant.

But the argument continued. "Candidly, sir, we are making a huge mountain out of a little molehill," Willis said. "I'm sorry that this happened, but—"

"I'll settle it real quick," Hedstrom said. "I object to the word 'tampered' and 'impaired veracity.' If you can soften that, take away the implied sinister intent," the judge told France, "then I will give the proposed jury instruction. So if y'all want to take time to work that out now, feel free to do it. Otherwise, let's go."

Argument over wording and intent of the instruction continued for several more minutes. The judge wanted the jury to know what had happened, but he didn't want to prejudice the jurors against the witness. He knew that an instruction by a judge carries great weight with a jury. Hedstrom wanted the jury to know what had happened, but that it wasn't done with the intention of tampering with evidence. Finally the issue was resolved and Willis called the next witness for the defense.

Dr. William Quinton Sturner was a medical doctor specializing in forensic or medical/legal pathology. He retired in 2004 as Arkansas chief medical examiner, Sturner said, and this was the only case in which he was involved. His credentials included a Fulbright scholarship and stints in the ME offices in New York City and Cook County, Illinois. His credentials were so numerous that he couldn't remember the number of books he had written, but he believed it was four or five.

Sturner looked at photographs of Barber's wounds and offered opinions on them as being far more serious than portrayed by the state's witnesses. The shoulder wound that broke the humerus could have caused major damage to blood vessels, including the brachial artery. The wound to the shrug muscle, Sturner said, was near the subclavian artery, which comes from the aorta, and was also close to vital organs.

"What would be the result if that particular organ, that is to say this subclavian artery, was penetrated?" Willis asked.

"Extensive hemorrhage."

"And possible death?"

"Possibly, yes."

The bullets missed the major arteries and organs, Sturner said, and there was no major bleeding. Willis asked him if there was a connection between the injuries to Barber's hand and the lower chest wound below his nipple.

"Very much so," Sturner said. "Because I think this . . . blackening around the wound is a contact wound. In other words, the barrel was very close against the palm when it discharged." Sturner said the bullet passed through

Barber's hand and entered his body below the nipple. It was what he called a reentrance wound. He said the wound was different from the others found on Barber's body.

"I'm suggesting that . . . during a scuffle, which took place, this hand was over the tip of the barrel, contorted, of course." Sturner illustrated by putting his left hand in front of his right side, palm facing out. "Because of the struggle and with discharge, it passes through and then reenters the chest area."

"All of the information you see here is very consistent with that scenario?"

"It is, yes."

Willis asked if he had an opinion as to whether or not Barber's other wounds were made by a third party, instead of by Barber shooting himself. Sturner said they were made by a third party. There were four wounds, he said, or three if you counted the hand wound and reentry wound as one. He said one or two self-inflicted wounds was not that rare, but it was "most unusual" for someone to shoot himself three or four times. In more than forty years, Sturner said, he had not seen such an incident.

Sturner said it was important to remember that all of the body wounds were near major arteries and organs. The witness said any of the body wounds could have caused a vagal reflex, which causes unconsciousness because of trauma in the chest and upper abdomen. In Sturner's opinion, Barber could have been knocked unconscious for a while.

Sturner next looked at photographs of April at the crime scene. Willis showed an enlargement of April's face and asked him to look at dark material coming from her right nostril. Sturner said it appeared to be congealed blood. He said the blood was discolored because of dryness, the water she was in or because of stomach juices.

The witness said he was familiar with Barber's account of events: April was shot and he pulled her from the ocean and tried to carry and drag her in different ways. Willis asked whether the blood flow was consistent with Barber's explanation.

"It's consistent," Sturner said. "First, in my view, she was shot in the location near the water and therefore has excess blood in the sinus and so forth, because it's a head wound, this side (left) to bleed into the nasal cavity and down the lip. So I think that happened. Plus—other blood which had come out was probably washed away by the waves because she was, as I understand, found face-down in approximately one foot of water. . . . So that could have all been washed away except for perhaps some of this that has begun to bleed."

The photograph was taken more than three or four hours later, Willis said. "What can you tell us about the rest of the bleeding there? Is that what you would expect to see?"

Sturner said it was after April lay so long on the sand. The blood might not have been there before that, he said, because the blood represented a rebleed. The witness testified that the blood running down April's left cheek was caused some time after she had been placed where she was found.

The few abrasions and punctate wounds found on April's body, Sturner said, appeared to be superficial. He believed they were perimortem, which meant one can't tell if they were made before or after death. Sturner said they were probably made at the time of death, but they were minor. The witness clarified perimortem as meaning "around the time" of death. It could be a short time before or after death occurred.

The marks on April's body were "scrapes," he said. "There were no cuts or bruises to suggest pressure and that sort of thing."

"Do you see any evidence in this that she was involved in any kind of a violent struggle at all?"

"No, sir, I don't." Sturner said he examined the autopsy report regarding her fingers and nails. "I found no breakage and no damage and no hand or wrist injuries of any kind."

"We had no damage to her fingernails?" Sturner said no. "We had no bruises, we had no cuts and we had no marks around her neck or other places you might expect?" Willis asked. Sturner said there were none.

"There was not an altercation prior to her death," Sturner said.

Willis showed Sturner a photograph of the linear abrasion on the edge of April's arms up to the shoulder. Dr. Steiner, the ME, had testified for the state that the abrasion occurred while April was being dragged to the beach. He had testified that the wood railing on the boardwalk could not have caused it.

Sturner disagreed. "There is a statement that the husband propped the wife up on an area at the steps of the dock going up toward the road and she slid down, slid down with her arm," he testified. "I think that injury is consistent with that scenario."

Willis asked if the abrasion was made when "she was somehow ground into the coquina by the weight of another person's body." This was another state theory of what might have happened.

"I find that a little difficult to accept. You would think if she's ground, there would be other areas which are similar to this. I would also expect some curvature or some arching if there's a struggle, instead of a direct linearity. That would make it unusual, I think."

"In other words, you would expect other parts of her body, like her hips or her legs or something, to experience a similar injury if that were the case?"

"I would think so."

Willis asked the witness to tell the jury about the foam on April's face.

"Foam can often be seen in cases of asphyxia, including drowning, including carbon monoxide poisoning, even in drug overdoses. And froth is also associated with any asphyxial component, such as what probably happened in this case. The decedent, having been shot in the cheek, had a wound near the spinal cord."

Sturner said there was bleeding around that area of the spinal cord. He said that was a vital portion of the body because it was where the trigger zone for respiration was located. If that was damaged, a person could not breathe.

"So this woman had an asphyxial situation in process as soon as she was shot," he said. "My opinion would be that her breathing stopped shortly thereafter. And as long as the heart does keep beating—it probably beats a few seconds, maybe a couple of minutes after that.

"So this is the mechanism that took place after she was shot, and she probably fell in the water at that same point in time."

Questioned further, Sturner said that April's breathing stopped almost immediately after she was shot, but that the heart would continue to beat because it wasn't controlled by the spinal cord. "The myocardium is a beating skeletal muscle, unlike the rest of the muscles in the body," the witness said.

The heart would continue to beat for a minute or two. There was no way for Sturner to know for sure.

The expert witness for the defense had presented strong evidence that supported Barber's version of the assault. It was in conflict with the state's expert witnesses, even though they all viewed the same evidence. Sorting it all out would be a difficult job for the jury.

Willis was finished with his cross-examination and France rose for redirect. His first questions would be intended to discredit Sturner's testimony. "Sir, are you saying . . . that the foam and the froth and all of these events are the same thing?" he asked.

They were at different times, Sturner said, but the froth would occur shortly after April was shot. He said that April was lying facedown in the water and that the wave action might have had an influence on foam. The heart stopped beating, he said, a minute or two afterward.

France asked if it was Sturner's opinion that the froth depended on April being exposed to water after being shot. No, Sturner replied, an asphyxial event took place. It was a "very big" one because she was shot in the cheek and the bullet damaged the area of the spinal cord that controlled her breathing. The control for breathing was shut off.

Then what caused the foam? France wanted to know. Sturner explained: "The froth is an asphyxial type of component that forms. There's damage to the alveolar-capillary membrane in the lungs after an episode like this. If you're unable to breathe, this happens and frothy material can take place. Again, I would emphasize I couldn't exclude the possibility of some water contributing to this at that time."

"Can you—or do you exclude the possibility that she was nearly drowned and then shot?" France asked.

"I don't see a lot of evidence for that. The autopsy shows that she has some frothy material in the trachea and bronchi, but her lungs are not that heavy. They're probably half the weight I would expect to see in a drowning. There was no water in the stomach. . . . She may have swallowed some, she may have aspirated some, but I don't think I would use the term 'drowning.'"

France asked if the witness relied on the defendant's statements as to where April was found to make his determination. He said that he did, and that he relied on the statements to be true. Sturner said the evidence supported that.

"You also stated—you found that she was dead at the waterline, correct?"

Sturner said he thought so, depending on Barber saying that he could get no response from his wife when he pulled her from the water. Not even when he shook her. Sturner said April may have been dead at that point.

France asked April's vital signs at the waterline and Sturner said he didn't think there were any. Barber said he didn't hear any breathing or heartbeat, Sturner said. He added that he only knew what Barber had said. "But it seems as though she may well have been dead," the witness continued, "therefore, no vital signs were present."

France started to predicate a question by saying that Sturner had based his opinion about April's death partly on the fact that her head never moved. The witness interrupted. "I think her head may well have moved," he said. "I think she lost a lot of blood being facedown in the water from the gunshot wound."

Once again, Sturner said he was relying on the accuracy of Barber's statement about where April's body was found. The witness said he had considered the various ways that Barber said he had tried to carry his wife.

France asked Sturner to show how Barber's left hand would be positioned to be wounded the way the witness described it.

Sturner said it would be hard to illustrate, but that in a struggle arms and hands can be distorted. It was awkward for him to show his left hand below his right nipple with the palm facing outward. He said there was nothing other than Barber's word to prove the defendant didn't shoot his own hand.

The witness had a long answer to explain the bleeding from the gunshot wound on April's left cheek. Sturner explained that the bullet passed through various tissues, including the maxillary sinus and posterior nasal cavity. That would rupture blood vessels. Even though the bullet didn't go into the brain, there was some bleeding there and on the right side of the cervical spine, which was caused by the bullet slamming into the vertebrae. Although there were numerous places from which blood would have flowed, Sturner said the area of the maxillary sinus and posterior nasal cavities were the most probable places.

France asked the witness if he thought April bled quite a bit. Sturner said she could have, but he didn't know. The wave action would have washed away blood and caused bleeding, as well as gravity. The prosecutor wanted to know if the water washed away all of the blood.

"No, because we had some coming up on her, as we see in the photograph where she lays," Sturner said. "In other words, a rebleed—positional blood coming out of her nose and mouth."

France stated that part of Sturner's opinion was that it was possible April was shot at the boardwalk. Sturner testified that he didn't say that, but that there was no way he could exclude that with absolute certainty. He said he didn't think it happened that way.

"You don't favor that scenario?"

"Well, that wouldn't be my opinion."

"Is it possible, Doctor?"

"Yes, indeed. Anything is possible, Counselor. I just think it's—as I see the case—it's unlikely."

France asked if Sturner called April's lacerations "perimortem" injuries because he didn't know if they were made before or after her death. Sturner said perimortem means around the time of death, from five to fifteen minutes before or after.

"You don't exclude the possibility that they were made before she died, as much as fifteen minutes before she died?"

"And I don't exclude the possibility that they were made after, either, so—"

France cut him off. "I have no further questions."

Willis had some questions on redirect, particularly where it regarded April's bloody cheek. The defense attorney asked Sturner if he had examined the statements and depositions of the first responders who said April wasn't bleeding when found, and there was no blood on her face.

France objected to the question as leading the witness and Hedstrom sustained it.

Willis asked what the first responders said. Sturner said some reported that there was no bleeding, or they didn't see any bleeding. Noting that Sturner had relied, to some extent, on Barber's description of what had happened, Willis asked if the physical evidence supported that scenario.

"The final analysis—was your job to compare the physical evidence, the forensic medical evidence, with the statements of Justin Barber as to what happened that night." Sturner said yes.

"Did you find the physical evidence, the forensic evidence, the medical evidence that you found, the review of all materials in this file, consistent with or inconsistent with what Justin Barber says happened?" Willis asked.

"Consistent with, Counselor."

"Thank you."

Willis was finished and France had no redirect. Some people in the gallery were puzzled about the conflicting stories. Bloggers on the Internet debated whether or not Barber was innocent or guilty. Several local attorneys, including the state attorney who was the first attorney for the Barber case, made comments on Court TV, which broadcast the trial live from beginning to end.

One statement made on Court TV (regarding Barber's purchase of body armor on eBay) prompted the defense to ask for the charges to be dismissed. It was denied. There was also a leak of transcripts from the grand jury that indicted Barber for murder. Grand jury procedures are confidential, but somehow excerpts were broadcast on a local television station. This leak prompted an investigation into the state attorney's office, which was continuing at the time of this writing.

Chapter 33

Alexander Jason spent much of his present time rebuilding the past. Jason, the next witness for the defense, was a crime scene analyst who specialized in shootings. Jason's job was to analyze evidence and determine how and when a shooting occurred, the angle of the bullet fired, and how many people were involved. He was an expert in ballistics and had no difficulty establishing that fact.

Unfortunately for him, Jason was also the expert who had made red smudge marks on Barber's shirt after it had been entered into evidence. The lawyers had argued at length about the penalty for this and had agreed that the court would issue an instruction to the jury. Lee Hutton completed his direct examination to establish Jason's credentials, and Judge Hedstrom read his instruction to the jury, which amounted to a slight rap on the knuckles.

"Alexander Jason, in the course of examining the shirt, took the shirt and placed four red dots with a Sharpie marker at a place on the shirt of evidentiary value," the judge said. "These marks, which will be identified to you in open court, are not of any evidentiary value and are not to be considered by you as evidence.

"You are further instructed by the court that you are

not to consider this act by Alexander Jason as evidence against the defendant."

The instruction was mild, but Jason seemed to be shaken and embarrassed. Hutton asked the expert to explain how the error occurred. He did so at length and said his procedure was faulty. "It was wrong," Jason said. "I should not have let that happen. It did happen. It was inadvertent. But that's what happened."

Having apologized and explained, Jason began to answer direct examination by Hutton. The shirt was the first item of evidence Jason testified about. He explained that there were more holes in the shirt than bullet wounds and that not all of the holes lined up to the wounds. After testifying to his detailed analysis of the shirt, Hutton concluded that the shirt had been contorted.

"Mr. Barber said in his statements that he was involved in a struggle. Would you find the position of the bullet wound on the body compared to the shirt consistent with that?" Hutton asked.

"Yes, it was consistent with a struggle."

Hutton explained how the shirt could have been pulled and stretched out of position during a struggle. A struggle would also account for three holes being made by one bullet, he said, because the fabric was folded over when struck by the projectile.

The primary evidence for blood flow was from photographs of April's body at the crime scene, which Jason said he had studied for hours. He said he understood the state's theory that April had been shot where she lay or stood on the sand. "It depends on which witness you're listening to." Hutton needled the prosecutors.

After trying to ask about blood flow several different ways and having objections to them sustained, Hutton created a hypothetical scenario: someone is on the beach, his wife is shot there, he tries to carry her up the

beach in different positions, and finally could go no farther after getting to the boardwalk. The body isn't moved
from that position. Hutton said he wanted to talk about
blood flow associated with that scenario.

The defense attorney presented three photographs of
April lying on the beach with blood on her face. Jason
said he understood that the photographs were taken
from three to more than four hours after April was shot.
The witness explained how he examined the gunshot
wound and blood flow.

A visual examination was performed, but Jason said
one had to go deeper than that. "Here we see blood flow
on her face. We see the entry wound here and blood flow
there. We see this froth, which I'm told occurred—"

"Objection as to hearsay," France said. "He's got no expertise at all."

The motion was sustained and Jason started again, referring to "white liquid" instead of "froth." He said he
would get back to that. Jason studied the photographs
and asked himself to think of how many ways there
could have been blood flow if the head had not been
moved. Gravity, he said, was the only answer.

"So you're saying that if the head had not been moved
at all, you're saying that's what you could expect for the
blood flow pattern?" Jason said yes. The witness explained that the blood from April's wound would be expected to flow straight down if the head had stayed in a
fixed position. He said that the white liquid (foam)
flowed over blood that was already there. He said he
studied the white liquid carefully and was unable to find
blood in it.

"If there's blood dripping down on this, I would think
you would see it," he said. "There's no red at all in there."

But Jason said he found areas that seemed to have occurred because of movement. He referred to an area on the

right corner of April's face. He said that would probably not have happened if the body had not been moved. The blood would mostly likely go straight down, unless there was dried blood already there and new bleeding mixed with the older flow.

Jason said there were some bloodstains on April's face "and I don't know how they could get there. If you were just laying in that position and she's bleeding, how the blood could jump up to this position. . . . Something put those blood droplets up there, something caused them to be there, and I don't think it could be the pull of gravity as she's lying there."

Noting that he had reviewed Barber's statements about what happened on the beach, Jason stated that none of the evidence was inconsistent with the defendant's story. Hutton noted that the medical examiner testified that April was shot in the position in which she was found. Jason said he didn't think that it was possible, and Hutton asked him to explain.

The wound was obviously not a contact wound, all of the experts agreed on that, Jason said. They also agreed that the bullet didn't enter straight into April's cheek, but rather at a ten-degree angle. When considering that the shot could have been fired from at least a foot away and the angle, Jason reached a startling conclusion.

The shot that killed April would have to have been fired from beneath the ground if she had not been moved after the shooting. "The way the wound path is, with this angle and her head being down on her left side . . . as I calculate it, puts it into the ground—I don't see how it would be possible," he said.

Hutton asked about the possibility of a .22-caliber bullet having enough power to move the head. Jason said it couldn't do that because a .22-caliber projectile weighs about as much as a dime and the head weighs from nine to eleven pounds. Even higher-caliber bullets wouldn't make the head move, he said.

"Bullets don't move people," he said. "It's only in Hollywood." He described an experiment where he wore a bulletproof vest, stood on one leg, and had a guy shoot him with a rifle. "So it doesn't knock you over. It's all Hollywood stuff. It's all war stories."

Hutton asked if the trajectory would be different if the bullet came from a higher-powered gun. Jason said that any movement would be caused by impact, after the bullet stopped. By then, the bullet's path had already been made. If there was any motion from April's head—and he didn't believe there was—the wound path would still reflect back to the origin of the shot, which would be beneath the ground.

The defense attorney asked his opinion on how the evidence squared with someone dragging an unconscious person up the beach, lifting them to a standing position at the boardwalk, then shooting her. Jason said that would be very difficult.

"Anyone who's ever had the misfortune of handling a dead body, somebody who's totally unconscious, it's a very difficult object to handle," Jason said. "And you're saying that someone held her up and shot her?" he asked.

"It's been proposed."

"That would be very difficult. . . . She was five-three, she weighed one hundred twelve pounds, she was wet. It would be very difficult to hold her up. And you have to have the gun farther than twelve inches from her face, maybe eighteen inches. It's very difficult to do."

Referring once more to Barber's shirt, Jason agreed with Warniment, the state's witness from the FDLE, that there was clumping of gunshot residue on the upper left side. Jason said the clumping could have been caused by bad, very old, contaminated or wet ammunition. Because of the shape of the entry wound below Barber's right nipple, Jason said it was a reentry wound. That was consistent with a bullet passing through Barber's left hand before hitting his body.

Jason said he fired a .22-caliber bullet through ordnance tissue, which simulates human tissue, which was the same thickness as Barber's hand. Jason made the experiment using both .22-caliber short and .22-caliber long-rifle ammunition. There was significant gunshot residue in the ordnance tissue, but none on Barber's shirt at that point. If the wound in the right chest was a reentry wound, Jason said, there would be no high-velocity blood spatter because the bullet would pass straight through the hand, shirt and tissue. There would be no room for spatter to develop, he said.

Jason had overlooked something in his notes: he had performed the test on a one-inch-thick slab of ordnance simulant, as well as the half-inch slab. The witness measured Barber's hand with a ruler and found that it was about one inch thick. Following this, Hutton had no further questions.

France immediately took the offensive on cross-examination. "Sir, would you consider accuracy and precision kind of important in the performance of your job?"

Jason said he did. France questioned the expert witness about the marks he had made on Barber's shirt by accident. France didn't mention the mistake Jason had made, but it wasn't necessary. The jury knew and Jason looked uncomfortable.

As to the shape of the wound on Barber's left hand being consistent with the defendant shooting himself, Jason said that was true.

"I asked you if it [was] consistent with the defendant shooting himself through that hand?"

"It could be, yes."

"Is the right chest gunshot wound not consistent with the defendant [creating] that wound himself?"

"He could have, yes."

France turned to blood flow and mentioned a small, dark substance at the exterior of April's right nostril. The prosecutor mentioned that Jason had mentioned blood flow that looked fresher down the face. This was from the mouth and left nostril.

"My question to you as to that: you, in fact, do not know what was coming out of that other nostril. Is that correct? You assume it's blood."

Jason said that was true, nor did he know if there was gastric material involved in her stomach. He mentioned that this wasn't described in the autopsy. France asked bluntly if the medical examiner's testimony would speak better to that issue. Jason asked what issue he meant.

"Of what the material was."

"I don't know if it would be better, but it's testimony."

"Better than you?"

"It could be."

France asked him the name of the underlying tissue beneath the skin. Jason said there was some muscle there; then he said he wasn't a medical expert.

"And with that said, have you also received any medical training in how the bleeding would have occurred from those internal structures?"

Jason said he had and France asked him to describe it. The witness said he had taken several training seminars in the pathology of gunshot wounds. He also discussed blood flow in a video he produced called *Gunshot Wounds*. But he did not have training in treatment, Jason said, just analysis. France asked why there was none of Barber's blood on April's pants if he was wounded when he dragged her. France said only April's blood was found.

"I think there's more blood that is not identified," Jason said. "It could be anybody's blood."

France pounded away. He noted that in direct testimony Jason had said it was possible that April was shot at the boardwalk. "Yes or no, sir?"

"Answering yes or no would not be fair to the jury in understanding my answer. Please describe how she was—"

"Is it possible?" France asked again.

"Is it possible if she was lying as she's depicted in the picture?"

France wanted to talk about that. He said Jason had indicated that the gun would have had to be under the ground. Could April have been unable to move her head because someone was holding it, she was unconscious or for any other reason? France asked. Jason said he didn't understand the question.

"When you gave that opinion, are you assuming for the sake of that opinion that her head absolutely never moved?" France asked.

"Before she was shot or after—"

"Yes, sir, before she was shot."

"By Mr. Barber's account, she was shot one hundred yards or some distance away and dragged there, so I'm not sure what you're saying."

"So you're depending on that being the truth?"

"No, I'm not. I'm examining his version."

"You said it was possible she was shot up at the boardwalk, correct?"

"It's physically possible. Yes, it's possible."

France asked if Jason believed April's head never moved when she was dragged up the beach. Jason replied that it might or might not have. He said no one could determine that. After hearing testimony on the ordnance simulant the witness used in his ballistic test, France ended his cross-examination. France had practically skinned the witness and hung the pelt to dry.

Hutton rose for redirect and asked why the witness chose the ordnance simulant that he used. Jason said he used it because the cavity made by the bullet remained open on this simulant and could be more easily studied. The other simulant available closes once the bullet passes through because it has an elastic medium.

"I should mention also that I did this experiment again with fresh pork meat to see what real tissue would do."

France immediately objected: "That's a *Richardson* issue." Hutton said that was fine.

"You have no objection to the objection?" the judge asked. "I'll sustain the objection, then."

Hutton asked for a bench conference to discuss the issue. The jury was taken from the courtroom. Willis said: "He asked for a *Richardson* hearing, Judge. We don't object to a *Richardson* hearing. We object to the objection." Counsel approached the bench to argue the point. Simply explained, a *Richardson* hearing can be held when information is used in court that wasn't presented during the discovery process.

France said the state had not heard of the experiment with the pork meat until now and had not been provided with the results of the test. The prosecutor said it was ridiculous for the witness to testify about it.

Hutton took issue and read from Jason's deposition: "Are there any other mediums to shoot through?"

"Well, I'm going to shoot through a piece of pork, I just haven't. Just to see how it works also. I'm pretty confident it will act just like a tissue simulant to filter out the particulates."

After more argument, Judge Hedstrom asked if the test had been performed. Jason said that it had been done and the results were no different than they were with the simulant. Hedstrom asked where the prejudice was to the state.

"Because we can't test it," France said. "He can't just spring this up and then say, 'Well, gee, it was the same, it's all okay.'"

The judge listened to arguments for a while longer and then decided that the rules of discovery had been inadvertently violated by the defense. Hedstrom ruled that the test results with pork could not be entered into evidence and that he would not allow testimony about it.

The jury was called back and Hutton considered his redirect examination, which allowed Jason to give a detailed discussion of how the tissue simulant was developed, why and how it reacted to projectile penetration. After the history lesson, neither the defense nor prosecution had further questions.

The defense rested its case and the jury was sent from the courtroom, while the lawyers argued to the judge regarding rebuttal evidence. The judge disallowed state rebuttal evidence regarding April's state of mind. Willis renewed his motion of Judgment of Acquittal. Hedstrom denied it. After calling the jury back, court was adjourned for the day. Closing arguments would start the following morning.

Chapter 34

An eager crowd surrounded the courthouse building on Wednesday, June 21, 2006, well before daybreak. Excited people, hoping to get a seat in the courtroom when closing arguments began at 9:00 A.M., jostled for position. Reporters and television camera crews from the major networks scurried about setting up equipment. Thick, insulated cables snaked across the ground to trucks bristling with antenna and satellite dishes. The media coverage for the trial had been extensive throughout the nation, and local attorneys had been anxious to be interviewed. The closing argument phase of a trial is like the championship round in heavyweight boxing—but the stakes are infinitely higher.

That was going to cause a problem when Judge Hedstrom brought court to order at the appointed time. Willis had a matter to bring up before the jury was brought in. The defense attorney said that Maureen Christine, the original head prosecutor during the murder investigation, had been interviewed on Court TV, which is broadcast throughout the nation. He said that Christine disclosed evidence that had been ruled inadmissible in trial. He was concerned that some of the jurors may have seen or heard this information.

Saying that Christine had disclosed that Barber had bought body armor and talked about "other bad stuff she heard about Mr. Barber, and this, that and the other things." Apart from ethical considerations, Willis suggested the jurors be asked "in a gentle way" if they had been exposed to any of the numerous news broadcasts about the trial. Hedstrom said he would ask the jurors before they got started.

The jury was seated, and following the judge's explanation of the closing argument procedure, Foxman rose to make the closing argument for the state. Foxman got quickly to the point: the state had presented evidence to convince them that Justin Barber murdered his wife.

"With those hands you see resting on the table, [he] took a .22-caliber pistol, pointed it right at his wife's face and pulled the trigger." Foxman said that Barber planned the crime so thoroughly that "he thought he was going to outsmart the police, the prosecutors, everybody." The prosecutor said that was why the jury needed to rely on its common sense to guide them as they waded through the evidence that had been presented.

Barber sat at the defendant's desk and made nonstop notes on a legal pad.

Foxman said the state had to probe three things beyond a reasonable doubt for the jury to convict Barber of first-degree murder: April Barber was dead; the death was caused by the criminal act of Justin Barber; there was a premeditated killing of April Barber.

"There is only one debate: did Justin Barber kill her?"

The case had been what Foxman called a crash course in forensics and crime scenes. Foxman said that gravity dictates the way blood flows and Barber's story of how he dragged his wife from the surf to the boardwalk didn't make sense. "Bear in mind, under his version of events, she's already shot at this point, he picks her up out of the water, manages to go just a very short distance" before he had to stop. The prosecutor noted that Barber said he tried several ways of carrying her.

"April Barber is not, under his scenario, dead—she's on her way to death," Foxman said. "It's a limp body. Imagine the ways that that head would be moving and bleeding from that gunshot." He said the photographs proved that blood flowed downward and that the head had not been moved after April was shot.

Barber claimed to have dragged her, Foxman said, but there were only two drag marks, for feet. There would have been a third drag mark for her buttocks if that had been true. The state's expert witnesses, he said, testified that April had suffered a near-drowning episode, but that she was still alive when Barber shot her. Foxman reminded the jury that the trauma surgeon who treated Barber described him as being neurologically, hemodynamically, and physiologically stable. The wounds were so minor they were treated with antibacterial ointment and Band-Aids, Foxman said.

"Contrast that for me for a moment. Four gunshot wounds to the defendant, salve and Band-Aids. Again, one gunshot to April Barber, right in the face, killing her."

Foxman asked if Barber passed out after the first shot, as he said he did, how could one possibly explain where the other bullets landed on him? He told the jury to keep in mind that the wounds were consistent with being self-inflicted. Detective Cole, Foxman noted, said the wounds looked "funny" to him, and that Dr. Tepas described them as "tangential"—off to the side.

"Members of the jury, use your common sense, gunshot wound here, gunshot wound here, here and over here compared to the vital areas, all of those wounds are out and away. Out and away."

That the bullet holes in Barber's shirt didn't match up didn't mean there was a struggle. In fact, he called that "quite a leap." Foxman said it was "absolutely fascinating" that Alexander Jason said there was no blood spatter on the chest wound.

"This is the exhibit that he permanently altered . . . by marking it with a red marker," he said. "This is the man who told you how precision and accuracy is critical to his analysis. And . . . he permanently alters it with a red marker, right by the things that's of evidentiary value. There's no blood tissue there. That's an important point, yet red marker is there. For the man who needs to be accurate and precise."

Foxman said the position of Barber's hand was so contorted that Dr. Sturner couldn't get his hand into the position to demonstrate it in the witness chair. "Does that make any sense at all?" he asked. "There may not be blood spatter, but there's going to be blood and tissue on the other side of the hand, and there's not. There's just red marker."

He said the defense experts had to think that, too. "How else could you possibly explain a contact wound to the hand for somebody who is passed out?" Foxman asked. "Did the phantom, once Justin Barber was passed out, supposedly pick up his hand and shoot his hand? No. Based on the defendant's story of hearing one shot and passing out, [he] had to come up with something that would explain that wound to the hand. I argue to you, it does not make common sense."

Foxman explained his reasoning for why witnesses differed on whether or not they saw blood on April's face. The first person on the scene was Lieutenant Ben Tanner, who said he saw foam and red fluid around it. The next two people to see the body were Erb and Pryor. Neither of them said they saw blood.

"A critical point to that for your understanding is that neither of them said they saw the wound, either," Foxman said. "And everybody knows the wound was there at that point. They didn't see the wound—logic would dictate they wouldn't see the blood."

Foxman said the side of April's face that was bloody was facing away from where Erb and Pryor were standing. "Dark as can be, out there on that part of the beach," he said. "I mean, the photographs you have that illuminate this have the benefit of huge portable lights and flash photography."

The prosecutor argued that because these witnesses didn't see blood, it proved that April's head had not been moved after being shot. He said, "They didn't move her head, which preserved our blood flow evidence and also is consistent with their training, preserve the scene. That's good work."

The bullet that killed April caused instant paralysis, Foxman said. That meant she could not have moved her head after the shooting. He said it was critical to realize that there would be no breathing.

"If there's no breathing, there's no foam . . . which flies in the face of the defense theory that April Barber was shot before she was in the water," Foxman argued. "But because the defendant held April Barber down in the water before she was shot, she was still breathing. . . . He held her down until she was unconscious and limp, which allowed that foam to form."

Foxman said an expert witness for the defense was defeated by the evidence. "This is the theory in a nutshell as told by Dr. Sturner," he said. "The victim bleeds out in the water after being shot. The water miraculously washes away the blood, all of it, mind you. The victim doesn't bleed in the nine ways she's carried and dropped—for one hundred yards up the beach. Then somehow, when she's laid onto the sand there at the boardwalk, somehow blood comes out.

"Well, members of the jury, this body does not bleed at the convenience of the defendant. Physics did not cease to exist on August 17, 2002, in North St. Johns County. You know that the victim did not bleed out in the water, because Dr. Steiner testified that from the photographs, her color looked normal. Even though she was deceased, the color looked normal, meaning she had not suffered massive blood loss."

He told the jury of another contradiction in Sturner's theory: April bled out in the body bag.

"I'd like to talk a little bit about the search for the phantom in this case, the alleged robber," he said. Foxman described the searches by hundreds of people, trained police dogs, helicopter and people crawling through thorns and hacking their way into the brush with machetes. They found nothing.

The Pryors are strangers to the area and weren't familiar with the remote stretch on A1A. Pryor said it was a dark-colored K-car, his wife said it was light in color. They still called Barber's car a Blazer, when it was a Toyota. They referred to a ten-mile drive as being only four miles. Mrs. Pryor testified that Barber was wounded in the right hand, not the left.

The Pryors' testimony was unreliable, Foxman said. If they even saw a car, he said, it was nowhere near Barber's Toyota 4Runner.

So far as Barber driving ten miles to find help, he could easily have driven his vehicle and parked it so that it blocked both lanes on A1A, Foxman said. Someone would have had to stop. At least someone would have telephoned 911 to report the incident. Barber drove ten miles, he said, because he wanted the tide to come in and erase some of the evidence on the beach, and he needed to dispose of the gun.

Barber also lied about his marriage and his affairs. Foxman said that just four to six weeks before April's murder, Barber started a sexual relationship with Shannon Kennedy. That continued until two days before the murder. Barber said it was a casual relationship and that's what Kennedy believed it was. The evidence, however, told that Barber took the relationship more seriously, Foxman said.

"The defendant asked Shannon Kennedy to go away with him to California and to Georgia, within one week of the murder," the prosecutor said. "Not one place, but two." Kennedy thought he was joking, but Foxman argued that "in the politics of men and women, the truth is often said in jest."

The first place Barber went "after being released with his ointment and Band-Aids," Foxman said, was to the Omni Hotel, where Kennedy worked. Barber insisted on seeing her even when the manager told him not to. "He went in anyway. . . . David Esposito . . . had to all but kick the defendant out of the Enterprise office."

When Barber finished his interview with the police, he wanted to ride home with Kennedy. A couple of weeks after the murder, Barber called her, and a few months later, he brought her a gift of maple syrup. He asked if that sounded as if Barber considered the relationship casual.

The prosecutor said Barber's credit card debt rose by $50,000 in just a year and a half. Barber bought a two-million-dollar life insurance policy for both himself and April, because he thought it was a good deal. And eleven months later, he decided to let it lapse. "Let it lapse?" Foxman asked. "It was a good idea eleven months ago? Nothing has changed in their lives substantially, yet now they decide to let it lapse. Is that true? It's up to you to decide."

Foxman asked the jury to remember that it was Barber who received the premium notices in Jacksonville, while April was living in Thomasville, Georgia, and "was nothing more than a weekend visitor. Logic dictates that Justin Barber told his wife to pay the last premium payment so that when he was questioned by police, and he knew how suspicious two million would look, he could say, 'I thought we let it lapse, I had no idea my wife paid that.'

"Put nothing past this man. This crime is that diabolical."

Foxman talked about the computer searches, but focused on Valentine's Day, February 14, 2002, when Barber searched "trauma cases, gunshot, right chest." Again, on February 20, 2002, Barber searched "medical trauma, gunshot, chest."

"This is no accident or mistake," the prosecutor said. "This is careful progression of Internet research. The defendant is preparing himself for what happened on August 17, 2002, six months in advance. . . . What are the odds of somebody researching gunshot wound to right chest, getting a gunshot wound to the right chest six months later? Those odds just don't exist."

Foxman talked about the music Barber downloaded on his computer on the day his wife was killed, particularly "Used to Love Her" by Guns N' Roses. "Imagine the visual on this as April Barber's getting ready for dinner and the defendant's having his own little concert," Foxman said. "Psyching himself up for what he's about to do." The prosecutor noted the significance of the song being deleted one day before the computer was surrendered to law enforcement.

Less than a month before the murder, Barber researched "Florida divorce" on the Internet. In mid-

August, Shannon Kennedy testified that she was in Barber's condo and he was putting up pictures of his wife and family. Before she even asked about it, Foxman said, Barber told her that relatives were coming to town and he needed to keep up appearances.

Foxman said he would talk to the jury later. "When I do, I'll be asking you to return a verdict of guilty as charged for first-degree murder."

The closing argument appeared to be flawless. It cut through the complexities from expert witnesses and tied together a case that seemed almost unmanageable. Foxman seemed to have hit a home run, but Willis's closing argument was still to come.

Willis greeted the jury and thanked them for their rapt attention and said he knew they would reach the proper verdict. He said he would ask for a verdict of not guilty. Willis asked the jury to pay close attention to his closing, because the state would have a rebuttal to his closing and he didn't know what the prosecution would talk about.

"There has been no . . . positive or direct evidence in this case of any kind," he said. "This is a pure circumstantial evidence case—that's what it is."

Willis said there was no gun recovered and no evidence that Barber ever owned the type of gun that killed April. There was no evidence, he said, that Barber ever had such a gun in his possession. He said there was no evidence that Barber had fired a gun that evening.

"Perhaps most importantly, there is literally no evidence in this record and no evidence that's come before you to suggest or support the idea that he shot himself," Willis said. "Shot himself four times."

The attorney said he mentioned this, because there

appeared to be so many problems with the state's proof that "I'm concerned sometimes that, in effect, the jury kind of looks for a defendant to prove himself innocent."

Several times expert witnesses were asked if it was possible that Barber shot himself in such a way. "He's got to say, of course that's true. It's not what he believed . . . given all the facts, but it is possible. Possible is not the way our law works. It's not sufficient for the government to prove that it's possible that he did this crime. The government has got to prove beyond a reasonable doubt that he did do it."

Frankly, Willis said, he didn't like the concept of talking about the concept of reasonable doubt because "it sounds like a lawyer trying to do some weasel something or another." He said that we need to remember that when the government charges a citizen with a crime, the government's evidence must be so overwhelming that there is no reasonable doubt.

"I'm not trying to burden you beyond what I'm sure you already feel," he said, "but it is the case that a jury makes that decision. . . . Whatever you decide, that will be the decision, so it's an enormous decision. And that's why I'm hoping and knowing that you will give me your kind attention, as I think you gave to counsel for the state. . . ."

Willis said they all knew or had heard about wives or husbands killing one another in the heat of passion. Barber wasn't accused of that: he was accused of an enormously premeditated crime, which reached back into February of that year.

The state, he said, was suggesting two motives, and that one was adultery. That wasn't really offered as a motive, he said, but it was intended to make the jury feel "less well" about Barber. The real motive the state suggested, he said, was $2 million.

Willis said he might be naïve, but to think that an ordinary person like Barber, with no history of violence of anything, to even contemplate killing his wife or any other person, it was such an enormous departure from his morality that the presumption of innocence should be huge.

Barber was the last person in the world who needed to be concerned about money, Willis said. The defense, he said, paid an expert $50,000 to do a financial assessment of the defendant. He lost money in a two-year period in the stock market, Willis said, but so did many others.

Willis talked about Barber's $75,000-a-year base salary, and the insurance company thoroughly evaluated his finances before issuing the two-million-dollar policies on himself and his wife. An inspection showed that Barber earned a total of $105,000 a year and April earned $73,000, with an increase in sight when she completed an apprenticeship.

"Mr. Barber is thirty years of age and is making one hundred five thousand dollars a year," Willis said. "With all of his future ahead of him with a Fortune 500 company, two million dollars is not the motive for Justin Barber, certainly not the motive to kill your own wife."

Willis said there was no dispute that Barber and April went out to dinner, then to the beach for a walk. Just because Barber couldn't remember every little detail of their conversation, Willis said, the state tried to show that any syllable he uttered was false. The defense had intended to call a mother and son to testify that they saw April and Barber walking, hand in hand, just as they passed the area of Guana Park. This incident was mentioned by Detective Cole in testimony, Willis said, and the defense could not use it because it was hearsay evidence.

The defense attorney mentioned that Barber's version of what happened on the beach was consistent, but the state misrepresented the defendant's words. Barber said he heard one shot before he passed out, Willis said, not that he was shot one time and passed out. Why would Barber lie about that? he asked.

Willis said the experts could agree or disagree as to what killed April. Both doctors agreed that death was caused by a gunshot to the first cervical vertebra. The only real departure, he said, was the near-drowning episode. Dr. Sturner could not rule that out, Willis said, but had not thought it likely, because there was no water in the stomach and the lungs did not weigh what he would expect them to.

"We know that she was killed," Willis said. "There's not really much of a departure in that. In either scenario, the one that they're suggesting to you or the one that we're suggesting to you would probably fit well within those facts."

The defense attorney said there was no dispute about the drag tracks on the beach. Those marks proved that April was unconscious when she came across the beach; there could be no doubt about it, because there was no other way to explain it.

It was also true that April had minor abrasions, but that it was not evidence of being involved in some violent confrontation. There was no bruising, there were no cuts, there were no notable scratches of any kind, Willis argued. He argued that the state had developed its own version of events.

"Somehow when we're down on the beach," Willis said, "that somehow something triggers it, something they don't know, because, again, there's no direct evidence, that they wind up in the water and that Justin Barber basically attempts to drown his wife or does hold her under to the point where she loses consciousness."

The state's argument that Barber started to drown his

wife and somehow decided that he should shoot her instead made no sense. "If murder was his intent, if Justin Barber was the assailant," Willis said, "if his wife was unconscious in the water, why would he not simply continue the drowning? All he would have to do, I mean, if murder was in his heart, just drown her and push her out into the water, and who could say she didn't go for a swim with her clothes on? Who could say that didn't happen? Nobody."

If murder was Barber's intent, Willis asked, why would Barber even take her to the water? He said it didn't make any sense.

"There was nothing that you would see from the evidence that this lady had been in a struggle for her life. All that is consistent with what Justin Barber said happened."

The first people to see April's body saw no blood on her cheek, Willis reminded the jury. In his testimony, Tanner said he thought he saw what might be some blood in the hair, Willis said, but Tanner had said flatly in a deposition that he saw no blood at all.

"I'm not going to make conclusions from that," Willis said. "Those are the facts that are what happened in this courtroom."

In fairness to Tanner, Willis said, he had been around the crime scene for hours and became confused as to when he did or did not see blood. The same could not be said for Wesley Pryor, who checked April's vital signs and saw that she was dead. Willis said Pryor saw no blood and he looked closely while examining her.

Most important to that, he said, was the testimony of Brian Erb. He took issue with the state's opening statement that put Erb on the side of April's body where he could only see the back of her head.

"His testimony was clear, explicit and unambiguous," Willis said. "He assessed this lady, including putting his head down to her mouth so he could test whether there was breathing. He checked her eyes to see what was going on with her eyes and whether there was any response. You can't do that kind of assessment unless you're seeing that person.

"He did the assessment," Willis continued. "He testified consistent with his report. He said he had an independent memory, but he also said it was absolutely consistent with his report, which was 'no obvious bleeding.'"

Willis returned to the minor abrasions on April's body, and to the lack of cuts and bruises. There was no evidence consistent with April being in a struggle. "If this guy were trying to hold her down to kill her, if Justin Barber was doing that, she'd be fighting like a wildcat. She is not going to settle for some little something like this. There are going to be bruises on her body, her perfect fingernails are going to be scarred and torn."

The state, Willis maintained, claimed there were two motives for Barber to kill his wife: "Adultery and two million dollars."

Willis noted that Barber and his wife were financially well-to-do. With bonuses, Barber had earned $105,000 the year before April was killed, and April's salary was $75,000 a year. Together, their annual income was $180,000 per year. Willis described the success Barber had achieved and stressed that he had absolutely no history of violence. "If ever there was a presumption of innocence, it is Justin Barber. The last thing on his mind was money."

On August 17, 2002, Barber and April went to dinner and played pool at the Ritz before deciding to take a moonlight walk on the beach. They drove along a desolate and lonely Highway A1A, which follows the Atlantic Ocean along most of Florida's east coast. After arriving at Guana State Park, Barber parked the car and they walked toward the beach.

"We know they were on the beach because the Barbours (Carol and Jason) saw them walking, hand in hand, down the boardwalk to Guana Beach."

A key part of the state's case, he said, was that April sensed something was wrong somewhere along the walk; Barber had intended to harm her, and she tried to get away from her husband. According to the state, Willis said, that was when Barber held her under the water, kicking and fighting, until she became unconscious from a "near-drowning" experience.

Willis said the state's scenario made no sense, while Barber's version of what happened did: they had been attacked while walking in the surf. "We know she was in the water, because she was wet," he said. "Was there a near drowning? No."

Willis called the jury's attention to drag marks from the surf to the boardwalk. "This is not a theory, it is a fact. There is no doubt that she was unconscious." He said the "state concocted its own version of events" and claimed that Barber held April underwater until she was unconscious, and then dragged her to the edge of the boardwalk to shoot her.

"Why would he do that?" Willis asked. "Why would he drag her and then shoot her? Why not just drown her? Why drag her up where there were lights and were closer to the road where people drove by? It makes no sense at all. If you look at all of the damning evidence," he said, "it really isn't damning at all."

One of the state's arguments against Barber's version of the story was that there was very little of Barber's blood on April or her clothing. Willis pointed out that there was a touch of Barber's blood under April's left arm, which was consistent with trying to drag his wife for help.

Willis noted that the medical examiner did not come to the scene of the crime that night to look for evidence.

Instead, April's remains were put into a body bag fully clothed and taken to the morgue, and she wasn't autopsied until Monday morning. April bled out in the body bag, and smaller stains of Barber's blood would have been obliterated.

"The way they handled the evidence is why they didn't find his blood on her blouse," Willis said.

Willis noted that there were forty-six areas where blood was found on April's pants. Thirty-six were from April. Barber's blood, Willis said, had congealed under April's blood. He said ten of the areas of blood were "degraded," because the way the police handled the evidence made it impossible to categorize.

So far as Barber acting "confused" when asked about all of the details of the shooting, Willis said that was normal. "He had been drinking, shot four times, and seen his wife shot. Is it a stretch of the imagination to think he might be a little confused?"

Willis made a point that the defense had actually had to seek out and present evidence of Barber's innocence that the state "selectively" excluded. The defense attorney noted that the case was largely based on experts for both sides. Willis wanted "a word about dueling experts." Willis said the defense had found the most knowledgeable experts it could. "We make no bones about it."

He cautioned jurors about the possibility of bias toward the state on the part of the medical examiner, even though the bias might be unintentional. "He works with the state attorney and police regularly," Willis said. "They see each other often. Some inferences could be raised from that, that are probably fair." Willis said the medical examiner did the same thing the state had done in building its case: "Selective presentation of the facts, while ignoring others."

Although most of the blood on April's face was on the

left, the way her head was tilted, Willis said, there was a small flow from the right nostril and this made Barber's explanation of the attack being made in the surf credible. He said April was already dead when Barber managed to get her to the boardwalk. "Blood doesn't defy the laws of gravity" and flow upward, Willis said. He added that no water was found in April's stomach, further discrediting the "near-drowning" incident presented by the state.

Willis pointed out again that the first three people to examine April saw no blood on her face or anywhere else. Willis said that the photographs the jury saw that portrayed blood from April's mouth and left nostril, which had streamed down her face, weren't taken until three or more hours after the first people saw the body. The state's contention that Barber lied about the struggle and shooting on the shoreline was false, he said. "It simply won't fly."

Willis said that a prosecution expert had testified that the abrasions on April's arms were "consistent" with having been dragged over rough coquina. The defense attorney argued that there were no shell fragments in the abrasions, but there would have been if Barber had been trying to drown his wife.

"If he was trying to hold her down, she would have been fighting like a wildcat," Willis said. "She would have had more scrapes and injuries, broken nails and so forth."

Willis said the state had made "light work" of Barber's injuries, saying they were minor and were treated only with antibiotic ointment and Band-Aids. He claimed: "The facts are different" and used an anatomical drawing of a human torso to bolster his point. The bullet shot through Barber's hand wouldn't have killed him, he said, but the bullet fired into Barber's left shoulder broke the shoulder bone.

The bullets fired into Barber's shoulders and right chest

could have killed him, Willis said, because "you never know where the bullet is going. This is especially true with a small-caliber weapon." The wounds were too close to major arteries and organs for someone to inflict them on himself, Willis said. "They could have been fatal wounds. Thank God he survived, but he could just have easily died."

Willis used a transparent drawing of Barber's shirt, showing the bullet holes, and transposed it over a photograph of Barber's body—the holes didn't match up with the wounds. Had Barber shot himself, Willis said, they would have. There was one area where the shirt seemed to have been overlaid to get three bullet holes with just one shot. That the holes in the shirt varied so widely from where bullets entered Barber's body indicated that Barber had struggled with the assailant, just as he said. Willis said the shirt would have been jerked out of position during the struggle.

"Nobody is smart enough to pull their shirt out of place while shooting themselves," Willis said. Most especially, he said, when there was considerable pain involved with the bullet wounds.

Willis acknowledged that in most cases where a spouse is murdered, the surviving spouse is considered a suspect. "There is nothing wrong with the client being considered a suspect," he said. "But not to exclude others." He said that Barber's story was "just what happened." Willis said the state never had another suspect and didn't follow up on the lead about the K-car.

Drawing the jury's attention to the key word searches made on Google, Willis said it wasn't conclusive that Barber made them. For the sake of argument, he asked the jury to assume that he did. There were more than 22,000 key word searches made on the computer. "The FDLE used their own key words," Willis said, and picked out the ones that helped them build a case against

Barber. "Obviously, they're going to pick out the worst," Willis said. Only a handful of the successful searches related to what the state could use against Barber, Willis pointed out.

Referring back to Barber's wounds, Willis said the state's theory that Barber shot himself was preposterous. "Nobody in his right mind will shoot himself once, let alone four times," Willis said. Aside from the risk of killing one's self, Willis pointed out that being shot was very painful.

The defense attorney thought the state attached an undeserved sinister motive to the downloading of music on Barber's computer. He noted that Barber had downloaded 1,699 songs, and that sixteen were downloaded on the day of April's murder. Out of the sixteen songs, he said, the state selected Guns N' Roses "Used to Love Her" in its attempt to build a case against Barber. "The character of the case is selective evidence," Willis said. "They selected facts and picked the most sinister things they could."

Willis said the prosecution had made a point of showing that Barber deleted the Guns N' Roses song from his computer the day before the police took it into custody. Willis said that Barber didn't know the police were going to ask for the computer and that he gave it to them voluntarily. "How did he know the police were coming for the computer?"

Barber cooperated with the police every step of the way, Willis noted. The defendant did not have to be subpoenaed to give affidavits, depositions, give police interviews without legal counsel, and he voluntarily came from Washington State to testify before a grand jury. Willis said this was additional proof of how the state used selective evidence.

The state also made too much of the fact that Barber left his wife on the boardwalk and drove nine miles looking for help, Willis said. The prosecution did not think about Barber's state of being, Willis said, when it insisted that he could have stopped at any one of numerous houses to wake somebody up to get help.

"Who cares about the length of the drive?" Willis asked. "It doesn't have anything to do with the case. He panicked. He had been shot four times and seen his wife shot. I would panic, too." He said this was additional "damning evidence that never was damning."

So far as April's two-million-dollar insurance policy was concerned, Willis noted that she went through all of the proper steps. He said that April applied for the policy, took the required medical examination and was interviewed by the insurance company's representatives. Willis said the insurance company found that the two-million-dollar policy was "appropriate" for April's health, age and income. An expert witness for the defense, Willis pointed out, testified that insurance equal to twenty-one times April's income would be appropriate. April earned $75,000 and would have an increase in a few weeks, following completion of a two-year apprenticeship.

Willis called attention to the lack of interest the police had shown in the K-car that the Pryors saw parked near Barber's SUV. The police didn't even put out a bulletin for the car until two days after the murder, he said. Willis was critical of how the police went about searching for a K-car. The police sent a letter to all registered K-car owners in the county and asked them to come forward if they had been at Guana Park on the night April was murdered.

"Come on," Willis said with disbelief.

Willis said that Barber talked willingly to the police anytime they wanted. Barber even took the police to the crime scene and showed them the areas he remembered while the police made an audio/videotape. He stressed again that Barber willingly gave his computer to the police; they didn't have to get a warrant.

The defense attorney said that Barber didn't excuse the sexual affairs he had. "Young men, when they get to be thirty years of age and they're doing well, my memory is that they start feeling pretty good and pretty foxy about themselves sometimes and do things they shouldn't. He did and he can't do anything about it. He was young, he was full of himself. He was too embarrassed to say anything about the affairs."

Willis told the jury that the state had not presented all of the facts. "We brought facts to this case that the state didn't." He also admonished them that they shouldn't consider whether or not any particular scenario was within possibility.

"That's not how it works. The evidence has to be so persuasive that there is no reasonable doubt.

"We believe that if you will follow those facts, you'll come to the conclusion, the correct conclusion, the one that the law will require of you, and that conclusion will be that this man is not guilty of this crime.

"That's all we have this morning. Thank you."

Those were the last words Willis would have to say to the jury before it began to decide whether or not Barber was guilty or not guilty of first-degree murder. The state had a rebuttal argument that Foxman rose to present.

The prosecutor argued that the state's experts tested thirty-six out of forty stains on April's pants for DNA. The other ten were too degraded to be of value. All thirty-six stains that could be tested, he said, were from April. Foxman said Barber never grabbed April's pants where Willis said he did. "Talk about selective use of facts," he said.

Striking out at the charge that the state did not present evidence of people who saw Barber the night of the murder, Foxman said, "My apologies for only presenting the treating physician, a friend who saw him, a social friend, David Esposito and Detective Skip Cole."

Foxman called the jury's attention to the defense medical examiner and the medical examiner for the state. "One who testified for the state, the medical examiner of this district, who has been for seventeen years, Dr. Steiner," he said, "and then Dr. Sturner, who works for the defense. Dr. Steiner is the one who performed the autopsy. He is the one who made the findings, did the examination, was there when these photographs were taken. Dr. Sturner is just looking at photographs. I don't diminish his qualifications. You have the difference here of firsthand knowledge and someone who's looking at it secondhand."

As to Barber's wounds being potentially serious, the prosecutor said everyone knew that. "That's why the defendant researched it meticulously," he said, "so as not to hurt himself on August seventeenth. That's why he prepared himself to stage this robbery."

Foxman told the jurors that his recollection was that testimony showed that Barber knew a day ahead of time when police were coming to pick up his computer. That was why he had time to delete the Guns N' Roses song. But where memory is concerned, Foxman said, the jurors must rely on their own recollection of testimony.

The prosecutor said there was no evidence at all to show that a third party was involved in the crime. "The phantom does not exist," he said. "The defendant tells law enforcement that this is a normal and happy marriage, but for the occasional argument. He denied infidelity. The truth of the matter is there's the July nineteenth search for divorce in Florida, the time where he's telling Shannon Kennedy about putting pictures up, that he's trying to keep up appearances for family. And then the defendant admitted, as you saw in the videotape, to five different affairs in a three-year marriage. Is that a normal or happy marriage under anyone's criteria?"

Foxman noted that Barber specifically denied a sexual involvement with Kennedy until detectives informed him that Kennedy said it was true. "Don't let the defense tell you that Justin Barber is cooperating and helping law enforcement, when he is, in fact, lying to them," Foxman said. "That's not help, that's hindrance. Why did he lie? When asked, 'I was embarrassed,' he said. Embarrassed? Shouldn't his emotion have been grief?"

Foxman shot down the theory of the shooting being the result of a robbery gone wrong. He noted that the big diamond ring on April's finger came off easily. Nothing was taken. Barber, according to his story, was blacked out on the beach and a robber could have taken his time gathering their valuables. Doesn't make logical sense, Foxman said.

Why drag April to the boardwalk after the near drowning? Foxman asked. He said he wanted to get April into the 4Runner and drive away from there. This would have eliminated a crime scene at the beach. Barber was deeply in debt, he said, and he knew he would not get $2 million in insurance if they were divorced.

"Why did he have this plan?" Foxman asked. "The argument's very clear when you start to look at the reasons why he committed it. He wanted it all. He didn't just want to evade a prosecution. He wanted that, for sure, and he wanted the two million dollars and he wanted sympathy for being shot and he wanted to look like a hero who tried to save his wife. He wanted it all."

Foxman said it was "incredible premeditation" when Barber bought the insurance policy on April eleven months before she was killed. Barber had two million motives to kill his wife, he said. He talked about down-

Chapter 35

Waiting for a jury to return with a verdict in a murder trial is a nerve-racking experience. Not only is the defendant stressed while his fate is being decided by twelve strangers, so are the lawyers and the friends and family of the victim. The jury began deliberations on June 21.

Robert Willis was certain that the jury was with him and that Barber would be acquitted. At the worst, Willis expected a hung jury. Chris France tried to relax: he presented the case to the best of his ability and the rest was out of his hands. Detective Howard Cole, the man who had spent five years on the case, may have been jumpier than anybody.

"When it went to the jury," he said. "I thought our chances of winning were slightly better than a heads-or-tails coin toss."

When fretful lawyers are told the jury wants to go back to the courtroom, they rush back, expecting a verdict. The lawyers were called back to court on Thursday, June 22, but the jury had no verdict. Instead, they wanted to hear the testimony of Steiner, Findley and Jason one more time. With two clerks playing witness and questioner, the jury listened to the long testimony for the second time, and retired to continue deliberations.

On Friday, June 23, the lawyers once more rushed to the courtroom, only to find that the jury wanted to see a portion of Barber's video deposition again. It was too late in the day, so the jury was to see the videotape the next day. It was Monday, June 26, and the dawning of a typical Florida summer day. Before the sun rose over the Atlantic Ocean, the eastern sky was painted with streaks of gold, red and purple that melted into the water. The sun appeared first as a red ball floating in a pale blue sky and gradually turned a blazing white. Steam rose from the ocean in wispy tendrils and from lawns still damp from overnight sprinkling.

It was hot and humid at the St. Johns County Circuit Courthouse by 7:00 A.M., where people were lined around the block to get a seat so they could see if Justin Barber would live or die. The jury had worked hard for weeks as it listened to complex testimony and sifted through difficult forensic evidence to reach its verdict. If the arduous work had drained the desire to perform their civic duty at the highest level, the jurors didn't show it.

The jury watched the videotape of Barber's testimony and resumed deliberations at 9:25 A.M. They reached a verdict at 11:19 A.M. and found Barber guilty as charged of premeditated first-degree murder. Barber's family seemed to sag as they heard the verdict and Barber flinched. There may have been relief among April's friends and family, but their faces registered no joy: the verdict didn't bring April back to them.

A capital-murder trial consists of two parts in Florida. The first is the guilt phase, which had just been concluded; second is a penalty phase, where the jury hears aggravating and mitigating factors to help them decide on a sentence. In Barber's case, there were only two choices: death or life in prison with no possibility of parole. The witnesses are usually family members and friends of the defendant or victim. They are allowed to speak without being examined or cross-examined. The defense usually wants to present the defendant in the most favorable light, while the victim's bereaved family wants to show the life, hopes and dreams of the deceased were destroyed, and how their own lives would suffer from the loss.

The judge is not bound by the jury's recommendation, but is required to give it "great weight." Most defense attorneys see this as a last chance to make a favorable impression that could save their client's life. The defense usually has friends and family members tell about the defendant's good points to show that he is not a monster who should be put to death. Sometimes defendants apologize to everyone who has been hurt by the murder. They beg for their lives.

That wouldn't happen today.

The tension shot up as Justin Barber entered the courtroom with two deputies. Instead of a business suit and tie, he wore a blue jailhouse jumpsuit too large for him. He looked small and frail. Steel shackles cuffed his ankles and wrists, which were locked to a steel chain around his waist. Barber's shoulders were hunched and he walked in the slow, dreary shuffle that shackles allow.

Tension escalated the instant the jury entered the courtroom moments later. It is customary in every courtroom in the United States for everyone to stand up to show respect for a jury. A bailiff said in a loud voice that was more of a command than a request: "All rise." Everyone did.

Except for the Barber family.

They remained seated to signal what they thought of the jury, which had found Barber guilty of murder. There was an audible intake of breath in the gallery at this show of contempt for a jury that would recommend whether Barber spent his life in prison or was sentenced to death by lethal injection.

Judge Hedstrom called the court to order and Foxman began to speak for the prosecution. Among the aggravating circumstances, he said, were that April was killed in "a particularly heinous, atrocious and cruel fashion" and that Barber committed the murder in "a cruel, cold, premeditated fashion." The motive was "specific gain: a two-million-dollar life insurance policy with him as the only beneficiary." Foxman asked the jury to remember that the policy didn't go into effect until eleven months before the murder.

"The defendant went to the insurer's office knowing what he wanted," Foxman said. "He told the agent what he wanted." He said that the agent had "never once met April Barber." Foxman said it was also "an unusual application because the owner would be April Barber" and that she was the person who should have received the premium notices for payment to keep the policy in force.

The prosecutor reminded the jury of the debt Barber had accumulated on his credit cards to pay for losses in the stock market. Foxman said Barber needed the money not just to pay the debt, but to live "the high life" as a single man. This was so compelling a motive, that it moved Barber to commit a crime that was "heinous, atrocious and cruel," Foxman said.

"Gunshot wound was the ultimate cause of death," he said. "It is clear that before she was shot, she suffered near drowning. The presence of foam meant April was alive when she went into the water. When someone experiences near drowning, they would be unconscious and incapacitated. April's last breaths were underwater and without air. The abrasions (on her skin) were the result of the rough shells under the water and she struggled for her life because she knew death was waiting for her. She had foreknowledge of death, extreme anxiety and fear. The defendant was utterly indifferent to her suffering."

Foxman spoke in a soft, unemotional voice that made the horror he described seem even more monstrous.

"It was cold and calculated," he said. "The defendant did it after calm, cool reflection. He was not prompted by rage but by a calculated, prearranged plan to commit murder. Premeditated murder is deliberate and ruthless. I can argue that bringing a gun down to the beach satisfies cold calculation. But it doesn't stop. The insurance policy went into effect a year before the murder. He even got April to pay the last premium to give him plausible deniability to the police."

And what about the searches made on the Internet? Six months before the murder, Foxman reminded the jury, the defendant researched "gunshot to right chest." The prosecutor said Justin conducted "generations" of searches that clearly showed careful planning and cold calculation.

"That was heightened premeditated meditation," Foxman said. Barber searched "Florida divorce" and learned that Florida is a community property state, Foxman continued. Not only would the defendant not receive the insurance premium if he divorced April, the prosecutor said, they would split their assets.

"He planned a staged robbery six months in advance," Foxman said. "He learned (by researching Florida divorce law) that there would be no two million dollars in insurance going into his pockets." The prosecutor called attention to the songs that Justin had downloaded on his computer: "Used to Love Her," "I'm Moving On," "Knockin' on Heaven's Door."

"That tells us the defendant definitely had murder on his mind."

Foxman concluded by saying again that the murder was particularly cold, calculating and cruel. He asked the jury to recommend a sentence of death for Justin Barber.

The courtroom was eerily quiet as Robert Willis rose and walked slowly toward the jury, his shoulders slightly bowed, as if carrying a burden. Willis has a manner in court that is confident—without being threatening—and a soothing baritone voice that rarely shows how he feels. The way he walked, the furrowed brow and the deep sigh that heaved from his chest before he spoke signaled the duress he felt.

"I can't say good morning, because it's not a good morning," he told the jury. "We didn't expect to be here. We didn't expect to be in this sentencing phase. The verdict shocked us. But we are where we are and so we need to move on."

Willis took a deep breath. "What we can agree on is that your decision is whether Justin spends the rest of life in prison and dies by whatever means or until executed," he said. "Either way, Justin Barber never leaves the penitentiary until he dies. That's the only decision you're making today."

The defense attorney said that he had listened to all of the state's evidence and felt that the case against his client was not proved beyond a reasonable doubt.

"There's a real temptation to reargue. I was secure in my belief that we would not be here (the presentencing hearing) this morning. You have found against us. You have found against us, and let's recognize that."

Willis scowled briefly at the jury. "I don't know how you got where we are, but you did it, and that's where we are," he said. "Apparently, you have found every sinister inference that could possibly be found. I don't know if you can still do that this morning. But so be it."

Willis explained that the law allows the defendant and others to speak for him before sentencing. "It's basically an open door to present evidence as to the nature on trial, typically family and friends," he said. "This is a man who had never been in trouble with the law a day in his life. He was thirty at the time of this crime. His family, to this day, believes he was wrongfully convicted. The pain and torture they feel is unimaginable. We talked with Mr. Barber about them testifying," Willis said. "He will not put his family through that. He will not plead for mercy for a crime he didn't commit. That's all we have."

Patricia Parrish, April's aunt, walked to the witness stand to address the court on her niece's behalf. In Oklahoma, Parrish is a district court judge who presides over courtrooms similar to where she now testified. Parrish took small steps and her expression reflected deep sadness and anguish. She appeared so vulnerable that it was difficult to envision the strength she must possess to be a presiding judge.

"I'm Patti Parrish, April's aunt," she said in a small voice after she sat. "In the last few weeks, we've talked about the last few hours of April's life. I would like to speak on behalf of her to give a glimpse into the rest of her life."

April was more than a victim, Parrish said. She was a daughter, a sister, a niece, a friend, a radiation therapist and an intern who wanted nothing more than to help others.

April used a phrase spoken by Abraham Lincoln, Parrish said, that she made her own personal mantra: "Everything I am and hope to be I owe to my angel mother." Parrish recalled that physical and emotional hardship her mother's death placed on April's young shoulders as she tried to be sister, friend and mother to her younger brother and sister. April still had a bounce in her step and managed to graduate as salutatorian of her senior class at Hennessey High School.

Parrish noted that the family wasn't wealthy and that April struggled financially to get through college. April made it with a combination of part-time jobs, student loans and family help, Parrish said. April, who had competed in several beauty pageants, won a scholarship in a pageant where, during the talent phase, she gave a hilarious recitation of "Casey at the Bat."

"She was thrilled and surprised," Parrish said.

She remembered April as a pug-nosed little girl, with blonde hair, who grew into a woman who wanted to spend her life helping others. April changed her course of studies at the start of her junior year to study radiology, Parrish said. April wanted to do it so she could help other women with the same disease that had claimed her mother's life. April worked as a radiation therapist in Thomasville, Georgia, after graduation from the University of Oklahoma. She pursued a two-year internship to become a dosimetrist, but was murdered two months before completing it.

While April attended college, Parrish said, she worked

extra jobs so she could have money for regular visits with her brother and sister. She married Justin Barber, Parrish said, and she became her siblings' temporary guardian and had them move with her and her new husband. "She wanted very much to be together with the kids to make up for the hardship they had been through," Parrish said. "She was newly married, young and working full-time. It was terribly hard . . . when the kids returned to be closer to their family. She did what she thought was best for the kids."

Parrish told the jury that April had been a surrogate mother to her brother and sister, and that she never missed being in touch with them on important occasions. April was ecstatic when her sister Julie was crowned high-school homecoming queen. "Julie called to make the announcement," Parrish said. "You could have heard April's cries of joy even without the cell phone."

Just a few days before her murder, April visited Parrish's home in Oklahoma and went with Julie when her sister joined Kappa Delta Sorority. "It was a big day for girls," Parrish said. "April was thrilled. She was determined to be with Julie on that special mother/daughter day."

Parrish fought against tears as she neared the end of her statement. "Our family has lost a thoughtful, compassionate woman who was determined to live a life of usefulness," Parrish said. "[April] once summarized her philosophy: 'I don't think the purpose of life is to be happy. It's to be responsible, to be compassionate, and to matter, count, to stand for something, to have made a difference.'

"She sacrificed her happiness for the happiness of others. She was useful, compassionate, she mattered and she made a difference. Death cut short all her dreams and aspirations. She will always be missed, but we rest in the assurance that someday we will see April again."

The courtroom remained still as Patty Parrish took her seat. Justin's eyes filled with tears and his chin trembled throughout much of what April's aunt said. When she sat, he wiped a tear from his eyes with the knuckles of a manacled hand. The only other person to speak was Amber Mitchell, April's best friend, the woman who had admired Justin Barber to the point of helping them meet, because she thought they would make a good couple. One can only imagine the welter of emotions within her heart.

Mitchell recalled that she and April had been sorority pledge sisters and April had been maid of honor at Mitchell's wedding. A businesswoman who owns her own information technology consulting firm in Oklahoma City, Mitchell had a difficult time keeping a quaver from her voice.

"April [was] one of those people whose goodness radiated from her soul," she said. "She wasn't perfect and she would be the first to tell you that. But she had the most compassionate and well-intended heart of anyone I ever knew."

Mitchell said that April was exactly how one would expect someone to be who had grown up in a small, friendly town where everyone knew one another. April, she said, adopted people, nurtured them and cared for them. "April grew from cute, pug-nosed little girl with big dreams into a beautiful woman achieving those dreams. [She] was one of Hennessey's shining stars."

As Mitchell talked, April's essence seemed to come into the courtroom, like the mythical phoenix bird that rose from its own ashes. During the trial, April had been reduced to an object that was the source of blood spatter patterns, drag marks, blood loss, entry wounds, body bags, autopsy and dozens of other evidentiary *things*.

With each word Patti Parrish and Amber Mitchell spoke, April's essence was resurrected as a charming, happy and good-hearted person.

April kept her good cheer and plowed ahead in high school to graduate second in her class, even though she had endured "immense personal tragedy in her family during her senior year." April's thoughtful and generous nature came to life—turning from studies in biology and premed to help those with cancer. With her drive and motivation, she graduated at the top of her class.

She became the dedicated daughter of her mother, Nancy, and became her home-based nurse when Nancy was diagnosed with terminal lung cancer during April's senior year. April also struggled to be a substitute mother to her sister, Julie, who was in grade school, and Kendon, who was a toddler. Tragedy seemed attracted to the family. "This is a wonderful, hardworking family that has suffered more tragedy than any family deserves," Mitchell said. "Last New Year's Day in college, April told me that she had just survived the first year in her memory when a member of her family had not died. She hoped the jinx was broken."

The cruel irony brought tears to many in the gallery, including Justin's and April's respective families: after hoping that tragedy had taken a detour around the family, it collided head-on with April at a beach more than a thousand miles away.

"During [the] last three years of her life, [April] worked every day . . . to help those battling the disease (cancer). Initially, she was a radiation therapist and her experience helped her talk to others. Her heart longed to do more for them and in her mind she knew she could handle bigger challenges.

"She was classy, but not arrogant, and was as happy at

a rodeo as a five-star resort. She bounced when she walked. She was quick to stand up for those she loved. She was smart and witty and had an endless supply of love. She felt compassion for the underdog and she saw herself that way. April was a survivor who worked hard for everything she had.

"When she was killed, April had almost fulfilled her dream of becoming a dosimetrist," Amber said. "It's hard to know where to begin to [judge] the impact of her loss. April collected people. Her inner group could not be more diverse. She saw and celebrated the best in people. She was never judgmental. She always saw past the inadequacies of others, sometimes to her own detriment. She would still be serving as a blessing to everyone she met."

Mitchell dabbed at her eyes and continued. "We all carry an indescribable pain."

Her family loved her, but April's upbringing was not always rosy, Mitchell said. All her life, April pushed to rise above her circumstances. She worked her way through part-time jobs, scholarships and student loans. In the last year of life, her confidence grew. She was surer of her life, what she wanted and what she deserved. It was wonderful to watch it grow.

"April told me she would never live to be an old woman because of cancer," Amber Mitchell said. April was preparing those around her for the possibility, Mitchell said, but none of her friends and family were. Their grieving, she said, had been mangled and devastated by anger and a slow search for justice.

On September 15, 2006, Judge Hedstrom issued the sentencing order. He did not believe the evidence was conclusive enough to show that April had suffered near drowning and the crime didn't meet the standard for being heinous, atrocious and cruel. Barber's refusal to speak for himself also weighed on the judge's decision. Without Barber or anyone speaking for him, Hedstrom said, the jury was not exposed to mitigating factors that could have influenced its decision.

Barber was sentenced to life in prison without the possibility of parole. He will spend the rest of his life in a Florida prison. For April's friends and family, there will never be enough tears to wash away the grief. Patti Parrish said the family lived in the knowledge that someday they will see April again.

A Note from the Author

This story is heartbreaking on so many levels. April Lott Barber was a spirited young woman with so much to offer the world and who withstood many tragedies in her life without losing her generosity of spirit. The pain felt by her family and friends is beyond my comprehension, even though I know what it's like to lose a daughter.

Justin M. Barber was an "all-American boy" growing up and was a handsome business star riding a rocket to success. How this tragedy came about is difficult to understand. Mr. Barber came from a good, decent family, and they are suffering a loss now. There had been no history of violence in his life.

It was a long, arduous journey to arrive at a verdict of first-degree murder against Mr. Barber. The trial was difficult to follow and I have never felt more grateful for our jury system. The jurors struggled with all their hearts and souls to reach the verdict and recommend the sentence.

When the jury began to deliberate, a straw vote reflected its division: five were in favor of acquittal, five favored a verdict of guilty and two were undecided. The jury was split down the middle. The jurors wept as they struggled to reach a verdict; they trembled and held hands. One male juror believed he was looking at an innocent man and could picture events playing out as Mr. Barber described. A woman was unshakable in her belief that Mr. Barber was guilty.

The jury wrestled with the testimony of experts and the state's claim that Mr. Barber's wounds were self-inflicted to give his story credence. The DNA blood evidence was what finally convinced the jury to reach a unanimous verdict of guilty as charged. Jurors trembled and wept later on when they voted eight to four for a sentence of death by lethal injection.

Mr. Barber maintains his innocence and vows to fight the conviction until he dies. The prosecutors and investigators have no doubt that Mr. Barber murdered his wife. Robert Willis, Mr. Barber's lead defense attorney, fully expected his client to be found not guilty. At the worst, Mr. Willis thought the trial would end in a hung jury. He was truly stunned and disappointed at the verdict.

"We found the only twelve people in Florida who believe that he is guilty beyond a reasonable doubt," he said. "The facts simply do not support it."

April's family found no solace in Mr. Barber's conviction, but it concluded a long and painful episode in their lives. April is still gone. Patti Parrish says the family is assured that they will be with April again. I pray that she is right and believe she is.

Justin Barber regrets being "the world's worst husband" and has no excuses for that. He plans to appeal his conviction of murder.

MORE SHOCKING TRUE CRIME
FROM PINNACLE